RELIGIONS EAST AND WEST
Second Edition

RELIGIONS EAST AND WEST

Second Edition

Ward J. Fellows
College of San Mateo

Harcourt Brace College Publishers

Fort Worth • Philadelphia • San Diego • New York • Orlando • Austin •
San Antonio • Toronto • Montreal • London • Sydney • Tokyo

Publisher	Earl McPeek
Acquisitions Editor	David Tatom
Product Manager	Steve Drummond
Developmental Editor	Susan Petty
Project Editor	John Haakenson
Production Manager	Serena Manning
Art Director	Candice Johnson Clifford

Cover Image © Photodisc Inc.

ISBN: 0-15-503019-1

Library of Congress Catalog Card Number: 97-72836

Copyright © 1998, 1979 by Holt, Rinehart and Winston, Inc.

Address for Editorial Correspondence: Harcourt Brace College Publishers, 301 Commerce Street, Suite 3700, Fort Worth, TX 76102.

Address for Orders: Harcourt Brace & Company, 6277 Sea Harbor Drive, Orlando, FL 32887-6777. 1-800-782-4479 (in Florida).

Website address:
http://www.hbcollege.com

Harcourt Brace College Publishers may provide complimentary instructional aids and supplements of supplement packages to those adopters qualified under our adoption policy. Please contact your sales representative for more information. If as an adopter or potential user you receive supplements you do not need, please return them to your sales representative or send them to:

Attn: Returns Department
Troy Warehouse
465 South Lincoln Drive
Troy, MO 63379

Printed in the United States of America

7 8 9 0 1 2 3 4 5 6   039   9 8 7 6 5 4 3 2 1

The Master said, He who does not understand the will of Heaven cannot be regarded as a gentleman. He who does not know the rites cannot take his stand—The Analects of Confucius, XX, 3

I do not fear the habits, the politics, or the religion of any man anywhere in the world as long as he lives with an awe of God—Pope John XXIII

To Louise

PREFACE

Religion is a peculiarly human activity. No one has ever proved that other creatures than people engage in explicitly religious practices. The underlying assumption is that the human being is a uniquely religious animal, *homo religiosus*, religious man or woman to broaden the Latin tag for the idea. As such, universally, people seek to understand the deeper significance of their existence. Accordingly, in this book the human being is taken as the animal who understands and interprets her/his existence and experience in terms which transcend them. Because our world is now so largely desacralized by the postmodern mind and culture, we cannot say every person is religious. But we do say that relationship with the sacred is a matter that concerns every human being. This is consonant with a generally accepted working assumption about religious life, which is a development from modern theories: Since you cannot know with certainty, or prove, religious beliefs, you must make a "leap of faith" in your religious decision or commitment, whatever it is.

In talking about religion in these days you need to say something about your approach to the topic. That is true even though we are talking about religions themselves, not theories about religion in general, which are complex and hotly disputed. Just as in other academic and scientific disciplines, one's presuppositions and assumptions shape the treatment of the material. In an introductory text like this one, it is incumbent on an author to say something about "where he is coming from," as the saying goes. Without attempting, therefore, to state or defend a full theory, let me lay down some fundamental assumptions of my view of religion(s) which are the background for my writing.

Intellectually speaking, we live in what is called the postmodern world. Huston Smith "suspects" that it is not possible for humanity to live in a world without any focus, and "that a will-to-order and orientation" is fundamental in the human makeup. From him I borrow his description of the general intellectual situation in which religious studies must work. Smith has " . . . argued that the distinctive feature of the contemporary mind . . . is its acceptance of reality as unordered in any objective way that man's mind can discern. This acceptance separates the Postmodern Mind from both the Modern Mind, which assumed that reality is objectively ordered, and the Christian mind, which assumed it to be regulated by an inscrutable but beneficent will."[1]

---

[1]Huston Smith, *Beyond the Post-Modern Mind* (Wheaton, Illinois.: Theosophical Publishing House; Second Quest ed., 1989). p. 16.

The next relevant fact about our current cultural climate is that many significant differences among religions are obvious to any intelligent observer. The term for this is pluralism; it expresses the idea that when you look carefully at religions you realize that they really are many (plural) and different from one another. It is true that there is no system or scholarly agreement on how to decide which are true or false which in turn makes it hard to generalize, to form ideas that can be applied to all religions.

The whole category religion is problematic nowadays. The late crown prince of religious studies, Mircea Eliade[2], implies the transcendent/spiritual character usually ascribed to religion, and assumes that there is something substantively real and worthwhile about it. I supplement this borrowing from Eliade with my own brief description—it is not really a formal definition—of religion as a broad term denoting the vast collection of data under that word: the connection or relationship between humanity and a transcendent/spiritual world, domain, reality, person, or power.

Beyond the scholarly arguments about what religion is, there is general agreement on the primacy of rational, accurate depiction or reporting of the phenomena, the things that take place. Such description is what scientific investigators do when they observe, analyze, and describe a particular religion. There are the immediate visible customs and ceremonies which the adherents follow in that faith. And there are also the invisible and intangible ideas and meanings which lie back of the words spoken and acts performed. What is asked of us, both teachers and students, is to be impartial and detached enough to be scientific about it, on the one hand, and on the other to feel sympathy with and understanding of the people and their customs.

In light of these current theological and religious trends, this revised edition addresses some changes in the theory and content of religions since publication of the first edition. Although the original East/West contrast, structure, and substance is the same, some revision and clarification of my approach has been added, and the effect of contemporary political and social upheavals on religion, especially in China and Russia, is discussed. In place of the brief outline of five ancient religions, I assess the significance of Native American and African American religious movements. The new importance of feminist scholarship and religious concerns is noted in several contexts, and the emergence of "Black Theology" is cited as an example of the "hermeneutic of suspicion" in various forms. Contemporary issues affecting the three Western religions have been noted. All chapters have been carefully scanned for corrections and emendations where needed, and supplementary material has been revised.

---

[2]Mircea Eliade, *Patterns in Comparative Religion*, Rosemary Sheed, trans. (New York: Sheed and Ward, 1958). p. xi.

Acknowledgments

I am grateful to several reviewers for their helpful criticism: Donald N. Blakely, California State University, Fresno; Kenneth D. Hines, Carroll Community College, Maryland; the Reverend Bradford L. Karelius, Saddleback College, California; L. J. Tessier, Youngstown State University, Ohio; and the Reverend Conan H. Timoney, Catonsville Community College, Maryland.

I have enjoyed the full support of the editorial staff of Harcourt Brace, and wish to extend my particular thanks to Candice Clifford, John Haakenson, Serena Manning, Susan R. Petty, and David Tatom for their assistance, encouragement, and forbearance.

A NOTE TO THE READER ABOUT COMPARISONS

If the first purpose of this book is to describe the seven major religions, the second is to provide a basis for comparing them. Because of length limitations, it was not possible to devote a great deal of space to explicit comparisons. Some comparisons are noted, of course, but readers must do most of this work themselves. Fortunately, the arrangement of this book makes the process a simple one.

In drawing comparisons we ask in what ways are the items being compared the same and in what ways are they different. For example, football and baseball are alike in both being games that involve the use of a ball, but they differ in the kind of ball that is used and in what is done with the ball: It would be difficult to bat a football or to kick a baseball. In order to make comparisons, then, the items must have aspects in common that we can compare. Otherwise, as the popular saying puts it, we have problems when we try to compare apples and oranges. This book facilitates comparison by providing explicit, uniform bases of comparison.

Each of the religions is analyzed—taken apart for the purpose of study—and described—facts are assembled under each heading—in the same way. They are all treated in terms of their history ("Origin and Development"), sacred writings ("Literature"), fundamental beliefs ("Tenets"), the ways they worship ("Ritual and Worship"), and their moral and social rules and forms of organization ("Ethics and Institutions"). This uniform method of presentation is followed as consistently as possible throughout the book. As is noted in Chapter One, the first two are introductory and secondary categories; the last three present the essential substance and content of each religion and are, therefore, the more significant areas for comparison. The reader will find data that facilitate comparisons simply by using the book—even without making a conscious effort to make the comparisons explicit. This is true because the classification system of the book is itself an implicitly comparative method. One could make a matrix, thus:

	Origins	Literature	Tenets	Worship	Ethics and Institutions
HINDUISM	No one founder Aryans, etc.	Vedas, Upanishads etc.	Brahman-Atman *Karma*	Bhakti, and *puja* to the gods	Caste *Dharma*
BUDDHISM	Buddha, 6th cent B.C., etc.	Pali Canon *sutras* *shastras*	*Trikaya* nonself, four truths	Veneration of Buddha	Wheel of the law; *sangha*
ETC.	ETC.				

This is possible only because of the arrangement of the book according to basic, significant, religious categories. This arrangement enables the reader to isolate questions for explicit comparison without having to go through the whole chapter page by page or consult the index and laboriously locate the pages noted. To compare the view of the Godhead or the ultimate reality of a faith, for example, find the section "Tenets" and read about the god or gods (if any; see Hinayana Buddhism and Confucianism). All the religions treated in this book include some kind of ethical system, but the systems differ in their premises and objectives as well as in the way they operate. The reader need only consult the various sections on "Ethics" for making a comparison. A study can be made of the founders of religions, for example, simply by finding in the "Origins" section a clearly marked subsection on the founder.

Even if it were possible to include more comparisons in the text, that would not really satisfy all readers. The point of comparison is to provide a basis for judgment or evaluation, and different people have different concerns and employ different criteria in their comparisons and evaluations. Religious belief is perhaps the ultimate private and personal decision. No impartial study, such as this one tries to be, can possibly settle that question for any one person: One must decide for oneself which road to take. The study of religion, at least in a nonsectarian public school or college, does not and cannot make such final judgments. This necessity for freedom of personal judgment and decision, from the side both of the individual and of the science or study, reflects the present situation in both philosophy and religious studies. In both fields there are no final answers or decisions provided by the science or discipline. At most the discipline provides certain guidelines and methods, but it does not establish a consensus on basic questions in the way the physical sciences do. Rather, the "autonomous individual," which is the modern Western human being, must make his or her own decision about where the truth lies. It is hoped that this book provides a format that encourages scientific comparison as a sound basis for reasoned personal judgment and decision making about these classic religious traditions.

TABLE OF CONTENTS

PART 2

Four Eastern Religions, or Salvation East   35

Chapter 3
HINDUISM   37

Chapter 5
CONFUCIANISM   166

Chapter 6
TAOISM   **210**

PART 3
Three Western Religions, or Salvation West   239

Chapter 7
JUDAISM   241

Chapter 9
ISLAM   353

PART 4
Concluding Comparative Essay   399

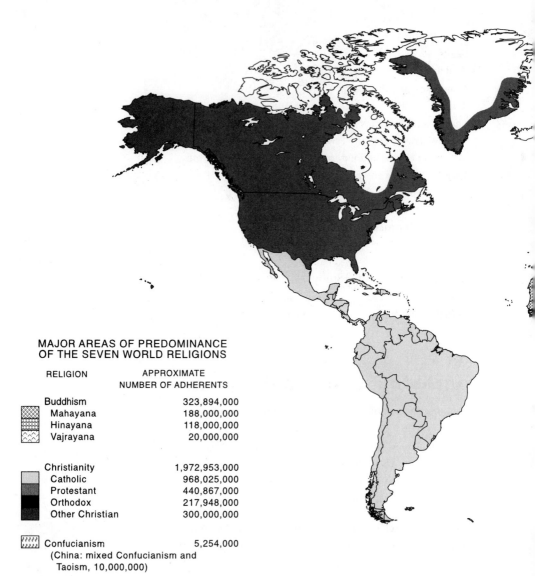

MAJOR AREAS OF PREDOMINANCE OF THE SEVEN WORLD RELIGIONS

RELIGION	APPROXIMATE NUMBER OF ADHERENTS
Buddhism	323,894,000
Mahayana	188,000,000
Hinayana	118,000,000
Vajrayana	20,000,000
Christianity	1,972,953,000
Catholic	968,025,000
Protestant	440,867,000
Orthodox	217,948,000
Other Christian	300,000,000
Confucianism	5,254,000
(China: mixed Confucianism and Taoism, 10,000,000)	
Hinduism	780,548,000
Islam	1,099,634,000
Sunni	830,000,000
Shia	180,000,000
Judaism	18,000,000
North America	7,500,000
Europe	3,500,000
Israel	4,500,000
Other	2,500,000

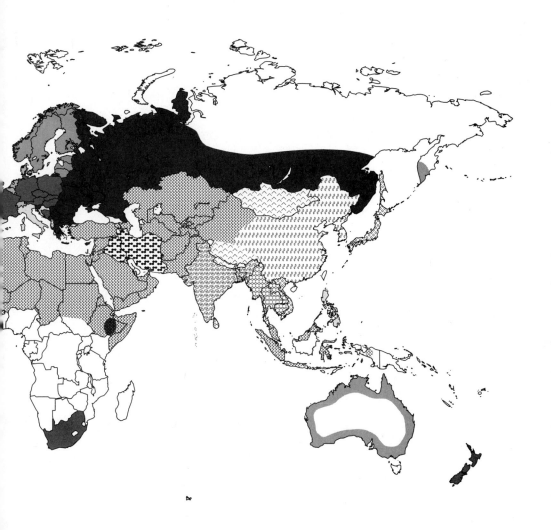

PART ONE

Preliminary Topics

Part I includes an introductory essay on the method and arrangement of the book and a chapter on some religious traditions other than the seven covered in Parts II and III. The introductory chapter is a nontechnical examination of two difficult scientific questions that are currently receiving wide attention: What is religion, and how does one study it? I do not attempt to justify, but simply to explain as clearly as possible, how this book analyzes and describes religion. The fundamental premise is that religion is the way human beings in this world relate themselves to another world, to the supernatural or transcendent order that is presupposed in religion. The categories, or parts of the subject, that constitute the method of analysis used throughout the book are identified in Chapter One.

Chapter Two briefly outlines some theories about ancient prehistoric religion, and describes two significant contemporary American religious traditions as examples of how religion has functioned in our national life. The five categories defined in Chapter One and applied in Chapters Three through Seven are not used in Chapter Two. It is hoped that the discussion of Native American and African American experience will help to clarify and justify the definitions and methods to be explicitly used later in the book.

Chapter 1

INTRODUCTION

Shiva-Vishnu Temple, Livermore, California. Front entrances, under construction, 200 × 200 square feet. Main sanctuary to be completed in 1999 at a total cost of nearly $10,000,000. There will be four towers dedicated to the two Gods. Religious pluralism works from East to West as well as West to East.

Henry Adams, a historian, and John LaFarge, an artist, went to Japan in 1886. For Adams the journey was a kind of spiritual recuperation from the blow of his wife's suicide. LaFarge was making the trip for a specific purpose. He was designing a fresco for The Church of the Ascension in New York and was looking for, he said, " 'certain conditions of line in the mountains.' Before he set off, LaFarge was asked by a reporter why they were going to Japan. 'To find Nirvana,' was his answer. To which the newspaperman replied: 'It's out of season.' "[1] They thought they were too late, but they were actually one hundred years too early: Today Nirvana is "in season" for many people seeking spiritual reality at home or abroad. This book is intended as a map of the different ways to Nirvana or its counterpart offered by seven world religions.

Take as our reason for study the mountaineer's well-known reply to the question, "Why climb the mountain?": "Because it is there." Whether one is a believer or nonbeliever, religion is an important aspect of human life: it is there.

HOW ARE WE TO APPROACH THE SUBJECT?

I wish we did not have to ask this question, because it raises so many problems. But in talking about religion these days, one must say something about one's approach to the topic. That is true even though we are talking about religions themselves, not theories about religion in general, which are complex and hotly disputed. Just as in other academic and scientific disciplines, one's presuppositions and assumptions shape the treatment of the material. That is especially true of religion in its dealing with the invisible world of gods and spirits. Two hundred years of doubt and skepticism have ushered in new challenges to faith, such as the "death of God." First sadly announced by Nietzsche's "madman" in 1887, the phrase now expresses a key aspect of much current discussion about religion. The word for these academic exercises is "hermeneutics," *interpretations* of religion. Although it is not, in an introductory text like this one, necessary to delineate a full hermeneutic, it is incumbent on an author to say something about "where he is coming from," as the saying goes. Without attempting, therefore, to state or defend a full theory, let me lay down some fundamental assumptions of my view of religion(s) that are the background for my writing.

Intellectually speaking, we live in what is called the postmodern world. Take as the starting point of our perspective Huston Smith's statement about the present situation:

> I have argued that the distinctive feature of the contemporary mind . . . is its acceptance of reality as unordered in any objective way that man's mind can discern. This acceptance separates the Postmodern Mind from both the Modern Mind, which assumed that reality is objectively ordered, and the Christian Mind, which assumed it to be regulated by an inscrutable but beneficent will.[2]

Smith concludes his diagnosis with his personal view and statement. He "suspects" that it is not possible for humanity to live in a world without any focus, and "that a will-to-order and orientation" is fundamental in the human makeup. From him I borrow his description of the general intellectual situation in which religious studies must work.

The next relevant fact about our current cultural climate is that many significant differences among religions are obvious to any intelligent observer. The term for this is *pluralism*; it expresses the idea that when you look carefully at religions you realize that they really are *many* (plural) and *different* from one another. At the outset it must be stated: The simplistic attitude that the differences do not matter because "they are really all alike" is not an acceptable answer to the problem. It is true that there is no system or scholarly agreement on how to decide which are true or false; that, in turn, makes it hard to generalize, to form ideas that can be applied to all religions. Pluralism, moreover, is the place in religious theory where the central philosophical issue of the past 200 years—since Immanual Kant—appears: epistemology, theory of knowledge, *how* we *know*. That is the huge unsolved intellectual quandary for all branches of scientific inquiry, including religious studies. We are not going to try to explain it fully or to solve it, but it is always there in the background. Here, then, are some fundamental ideas and theories that are operative in this book.

BASIC DEFINITIONS, THEORIES, PRESUPPOSITIONS

The whole category "religion" is problematic nowadays. We follow the late "crown prince" of religious studies, Mircea Eliade, who wrote *The Sacred and the Profane*, an early book, the subtitle of which is *The Nature of Religion*. We invoke his dichotomy as our way of denoting the area or field of religion. "The sacred," Eliade writes, "always manifests itself as a reality of a wholly different order from 'natural' realities.... The first possible definition of the sacred is that it is *the opposite of the profane*"[3] (italics added). Although this is only a negative definition, it implies the transcendent/spiritual character usually ascribed to religion, and it assumes that there is something substantively real and worthwhile about it. I supplement this borrowing from Eliade with my own brief description—it is not really a formal definition—of *religion* as a broad term denoting the vast collection of data under that word: *the connection or relationship between humanity and a transcendent/spiritual world, domain, reality, person, or power*.

Religion is a peculiarly *human* activity. No one has ever proved that creatures other than people engage in explicitly religious practices. The assumption that underlies the preceding description is that the human being is a uniquely religious animal, *homo religiosus*, "religious man or woman" to broaden the Latin tag for the idea. As such, universally, people seek to understand the deeper significance of their existence. Accordingly, in this book the human being is taken as the animal who understands and interprets her/his existence and experience in terms that transcend them. Because our world is now so largely desacralized by the postmodern mind and culture, we cannot say every person is religious. But we do say that they are all creatures who ask, think, talk, and decide about religion; relationship with the sacred is a question that concerns every human being. This is consonant with a generally accepted working assumption about religious life, which is a development from modern theories: Because you cannot know with certainty, or prove, religious beliefs, you must make a "leap of faith" in your religious decision or commitment, whatever it is.

Another essential concept—also basic in Eliade's work—is "phenomenology." The underlying meaning is carried by the Greek root word for "show" or "be seen," and the modern theoretical meaning includes the earlier implication of a contrast between what is seen or manifested in the world and the real substance or nature of these things. For us, the essential point is that that contrast must be kept in mind, because we are describing the facts phenomenologically or as appearances, apart from a judgment about their full nature or significance. A conference at Princeton a number of years ago on "The Study of Religion in Colleges and Universities" said: "A phenomenology of religion . . . intends to be an investigation into the structure and significance of facts drawn from the vast field of the history of religions and arranged in systematic order."[4]

The stress is on *description*. Beyond the scholarly arguments about what religion is, there is general agreement on the primacy of rational, accurate depiction or reporting of the phenomena, the events that take place. Such description results when scientific investigators observe and analyze a particular religion. There are the immediate visible customs and ceremonies which the adherents follow in that faith. And there are also the invisible and intangible ideas and meanings underlying the words spoken and acts performed. Harvard professor Wilfred Cantwell Smith uses the history of religions to frame a view of religion as a combination of personal faith on the part of the members, and "cumulative tradition" seen in the history of their religion. However religion is studied, it is a highly complex mix of data. What is asked of us, both teachers and students, is to be impartial and detached enough to be scientific about it, on the one hand, and on the other to feel sympathy with and understanding of the people and their customs.

Let me summarize this sketchy picture of the complicated intellectual puzzle over how to treat religion(s). Most scholars recognize two basic modern approaches to the problem: the cultural/linguistic and the experiential/expressive. In the first, the key to understanding is found in the total cultural complex of beliefs, customs, and practices characteristic of a religion. The second finds and stresses a more specific subjective and personal experiential core as the common factor in all religions. Although these approaches are not mutually exclusive, individual researchers usually consider one or the other as their primary method. If necessary to do so, therefore, I would classify myself under the cultural/linguistic label.

FIVE PRINCIPAL DIVISIONS

Description, giving the facts, that is our aim. But which facts are we to give? The amount of data, the volume of information or material that could be assembled about any religion is staggering. So rich and varied are the customs and beliefs of even the simplest of the major religions that we would be overwhelmed by the sheer mass of information. Therefore, selection from among the mass of data is essential. We will use a few simple and general headings or classifications as a basis of selection, and we will follow them as much as possible.

Before we set out our headings, two points must be made. First, we cannot entirely avoid some kind of segmentation as a way of handling the subject. Second, such division or classification does imply some judgment about the nature and character of religious phenomena. In other words, we cannot be completely neutral in our description, because analysis involves at least implicit evaluation of what is significant about the phenomena.

For each religion, we will describe the phenomena under five major categories: origin and development, literature, tenets, ritual and worship, and ethics and institutions. The first two are preliminary and secondary; the last three are the essential or substantive aspects of the religion. Through them we will try to get at what the religion means to the people who believe in it.[5]

Origin and Development

The first two divisions serve as our preliminary sketch of the religion and are subordinated to the three major descriptive dimensions. Taking history in its simplest sense of a chronological record, we are concerned with it only as it helps us to see what the facts are now by looking at the record of the past. The historical sketch of origins includes some important matters and major facts, but history for its own sake is not important to us. We are concerned with the history of a faith only as it shows how the religion began, grew, and changed in assuming its present shape. That is why our term is "origin and development."

Literature

The literature is important to us only as it increases our understanding of the larger faith. This is not to deny the intrinsic significance and interest of sacred writings, but to put them in their place as part of our study. For us the literature is a record of and source for beliefs and practices, and therefore, like origins, literature is subordinate to the three principal substantive categories. In those major categories we will often refer to the scriptures, because they are the source or justification for much of the theory and practice of any religion. Under literature we include not only the sacred scriptures but also associated writings that enlarge upon the basic sacred books. We will give a general summary and some details about them for each religion, classifying and describing the most important portions. Many excellent and inexpensive collections of sacred writings are available, so that we do not quote extensively from these sources. But because one cannot gain an understanding of the religions without being familiar with the scriptures, it is recommended that the student pursue related readings.

There is a problem about holy books construed as revelation, that is, as coming from or inspired by God in order to reveal himself to human beings. Let us say something about this category of revelation. Our handling of the difficult question raised by different holy books, each claiming to be a revelation from God, is consonant with or follows from our general descriptive but nonevaluative approach. This is what these scriptures say about this matter, and we cannot determine the final truth nor adjudicate among them. At the same time, there is a more positive basis for the significance of the scriptures than such an agnostic view might at first suggest. First, revelation is taken as revelation from the divine level or transcendent order to a human being—it is not simply a discovery or attainment by a human agent. The correlate of divine revelation is the inspiration of the human being, but the divine self-disclosure is primary. Second, revelation is not in a vacuum. For something to be a revelation it must "reveal" meaningful truth to some person or group, and the response of the person or group is part of a total revelation-and-response pattern. Third, revelation is construed not simply from the bare words or statement but from the meaning the message has for the religious community. The meaning carried by the words is the important thing. The modern technical phrase for this is a "nonpropositional" view of revelation, in which the meaning in context is the substance of the revelation. The fourth point follows from the third: In the different traditions, the nature of the two poles or relata (things related) and the method of relation differ. In Judaism, the one and only God speaks to a specific person, Moses, the word for Israel; in Hinduism, what emanates from the divine is heard by a *rishi* (seer), who then declares the message to all who listen. Thus different religions have different kinds of revelation and scriptures, according to the different divine and human poles.

Although we do not take a "literalist" or word-for-word position, neither do we deny the meaning and value of the record borne by these books. We make use of modern scientific study of these scriptures, holding that such study when properly used does not destroy, but rather enhances, their meaning. Nevertheless, the sacred writings of each tradition are accepted at face value for the purposes of describing the religion. When treating the myth, history, and doctrine that are found in the literature, we take them as they come, but remember that they are simply part of the picture. The reader is asked, therefore, to be both objective about, and yet sympathetic and open to, the message of these holy books.

Tenets

"Tenets" is a plural form because it covers a wide range of topics. Under this inclusive heading we put the whole array of beliefs and doctrines that are fundamental to the meaning and content of a faith, the invisible and immaterial but powerful ideas that shape the visible and tangible elements. The meaning of the Latin infinitive *teñere* is "to hold," and this is the key to the religious significance of the word and our use of it. That which is held to, which must be guarded and kept as essential, is a tenet of the faith. Tenets are the intangible truths to which the members of a faith hold fast—what they are convinced of, what they keep as essential and basic, such that they must not let them go. One might ask, why not use "beliefs" instead of "tenets"? The reason is that we need a word with a more general and less intellectual and theoretical connotation than "belief" carries. Particularly at the deeper levels of religion, there are convictions that are not fully articulated as beliefs nor embodied in symbols, although they may be expressed in actions, like the Buddhists' practice of always going clockwise around a stupa or pagoda.

Included under this broad rubric, then, is the wide area of more or less theoretical expressions denoted by more specific terms, such as "myth," "doctrine," and "symbol." Religious myths are stories or legends that carry a religious or spiritual truth and meaning that is significant for a particular group. They embody religious truths that have a deeper meaning than can be fully rationalized or expressed in factual records or scientific formulae; they are more like poetry than prose, more like painting than photography. Above all, although they are not literally or factually true, they are held as spiritually and religiously true. In presenting the myths of a religion we do not attempt to assess their value or truth; our concern is their meaning and significance in the religion. Whether they are factually accurate in an objective, empirical sense is not the question, even if it could be determined. Therefore, it must be understood from the outset that our straightforward description of the myths of a religion does not imply that we judge them either true or false. We try to state the myths fairly clearly, and accurately, but no judgment of their objective truth value is intended or attempted. Fortunately, both the function of myth as carrying ultimate meaning and its peculiar and distinctive form are now generally acknowledged.

Doctrine is the more formal theoretical expression of religious truth and meaning, systematic and rationalized or organized in some way. It has various purposes, which can best be grouped under two headings—those that apply to the members or initiates, on the one hand, and those that apply to the unbelievers and outsiders, on the other. For both groups, however, doctrine serves to explain, to clarify, to direct and guide, through intellectual formulation in words and ideas, the rational understanding and thus the action of the person addressed. Those familiar with Western religious traditions will think of doctrine as theology or dogma, especially important in Christianity, where the dual purposes of instruction for the faithful and apologetics for the nonbeliever or inquirer are clearly seen.

Another important element of tenets is religious symbolism. Symbols differ from signs in general in not being arbitrary or merely conventional. A sign like a traffic signal could use different colors, say purple and gold, instead of red and green, or red could mean "go" and green "stop." But a symbol participates in and is dependent on the reality or event it symbolizes; the form is determined by the fact or meaning to which the symbol refers. Symbols are psychologically powerful signs that come out of the experience and history of a culture and point to an ultimate and transcendent reality. They are physical or material in form, but of wide variety, and apart from the meaning they carry they may be quite ordinary physical objects. To the birds, a wayside cross in Poland or the colossal Buddha image at Kamakura represents just another roosting place; but the symbol is potent to people who see it. The people connect the cross or the statue with the original cross or Buddha. That is the way a symbol works. Like myths, symbols try to say the unsayable.

Ritual and Worship

By ritual we denote not only the forms of worship but a wide range of acts, usually performed according to a pattern, that are significant in a specifically religious sense. (Sometimes the word "cultus" or "cult" is used by social scientists to denote the system of rites in a religion.) Rite or ritual takes other forms than the strictly religious. In a sense, the French almost compulsive habit of shaking hands whenever one person greets another is a rite. Religious ritual has even more of the compulsive or obligatory character than such merely social ritual. And just as shaking hands expresses by the physical act one's inward wish to establish rapport with the other person, so it is in religious ritual. Wach points out, "*Cultus,* then, or practical expression of religious experience, is a total response of the total being—intense and integral—to Ultimate Reality, in *action.*"[6]

Associated with the words and actions of ritual are the places, such as churches or temples, where they are performed. Ritual may, however, be performed anywhere, according to time, like the Muslim's prescribed prayer five times a day wherever he or she may be. This example also reminds us that ritual may be either personal and solitary, like the Bedouin's prayer in the desert, or communal, like the Jewish Sabbath prayer at the synagogue. Some forms of ritual, like the meditations of a Zen monk, involve no outward expression at all once the posture is assumed, and the direction and intent are not in terms of worship of a divinity but attainment of what is perhaps most broadly described as a mental state or condition. Clearly, from the examples given and others the reader can easily provide, custom or habit, repetition, and more or less of form is of the essence of ritual. As both prophets and professors have often pointed out, this occasions the danger that ritual may become mechanical, external, or even insincere and distasteful. Yet religion without ritual, in spite of the protests of those who decry all rituals as mere ceremony, would be religion only for abstract, disembodied intelligences like the mind—things of science fiction. So long as people have bodies and live in physical space and time, embodiment of religious feeling or meaning in ritual would seem to be an indispensable element of genuine religion. The life of any society would be immeasurably impoverished by its disappearance. We hope to suggest some of the richness and variety of religious ritual in the pages that follow.

Ethics and Institutions

Our final descriptive category is ethics, the usual term in philosophy and religion for the study of standards of moral conduct. One problem will be to differentiate ethics from ritual, inasmuch as they are similar in both being matters of practice or conduct. They differ in that ritual relates to strictly religious duty and custom, whereas ethics describes the practice enjoined upon believers in their relations to other people and their conduct in the world at large. In practice, the problem is to keep ritual from dominating and determining ethics, as the Hebrew prophets saw.

The ethical areas will be extended to cover some of the organized social or institutional workings of religion, the relation of the religion to and its effect on the society or culture at large, as well as the influence of the culture on the religion. The theoretical basis for this aspect is provided by Tillich's dictum: "Religion as ultimate concern is the meaning-giving substance of culture, and culture is the totality of forms in which the basic concern of religion expresses itself."[7] The crisis for religion today is in its relation to secular or nonreligious culture. In the modern Western world, religion is simply another compartment or division within the total secular cultural complex. This makes religion one among several aspects of a culture and tends to rob it of its power as ultimate and transcendent. Many Western students are attracted to Asian religion because they feel that in the East religion retains some of its potency in dealing with ultimate and transcendent reality. It is not, they feel, simply another department or aspect of life on the same level with the other aspects, as it is in the West. Whether that is true or not is another question.

OTHER ASPECTS OF RELIGION

Of course, these headings do not by any means cover or include all aspects of seven normative religious systems; both breadth and depth have had to be curtailed. We do not have space or time for consideration of the wider social or institutional effects or workings of religion, nor for psychological study in depth of the religious experience itself. Neither do we attempt to decide whether or not the people live up to their religion. There is always a gap between preaching and practice in any area of human life, and even though it is more obvious in religion, we are not going to open that box. Even *homo religiosus* errs.

ORDER OF THE CHAPTERS

A final word is in order about the arrangement of the chapters. Chapter Two of Part I introduces the reader to traditions different from the major ones of our study. The four Eastern religions are covered in Part II, and three Western in Part III. As probably the oldest continuous culture and religion, Hinduism is treated first, followed by the other members of the Eastern group. There is a natural progression from Hinduism to Buddhism, which arose in India before spreading to other Asian lands, including China and Japan. The two indigenous Chinese systems then form a contrasting pair to conclude four Eastern religious traditions. Although Islam is not in every sense a Western faith, it belongs with the other two because all three are from the same Biblical root. Within the Western tradition it makes sense to start with Judaism, because it is the oldest and the matrix of Biblical religion, followed by the two others in chronological order. As the youngest, then, Islam is treated last. There is no attempt to trace any sort of overall development or relation except the obvious historical progression in some cases, and the chapters are otherwise essentially independent of each other. Readers may therefore take them in any order they prefer. In a concluding comparative essay, Part IV, I speak more personally than in the rest of the book.

NOTES

1. Denys Sutton, "Cathay, Nirvana, and Zen," *Apollo* (August 1966), p. 154.
2. Huston Smith, *Beyond the Post-Modern Mind* (Wheaton, Ill.: Theosophical Publishing House; Second Quest ed., 1989), p. 16.
3. Mircea Eliade, *Patterns in Comparative Religion*, Rosemary Sheed, trans. (New York: Sheed and Ward, 1958), p. xi.
4. Paul Ramsey and John F. Wilson, eds., *The Study of Religion in Colleges and Universities* (Princeton, N.J.: Princeton University Press, 1970), p. 256.
5. The three-fold typology of religious phenomena has been developed by Joachim Wach. See his *The Comparative Study of Religion* (New York: Columbia University Press, 1958). As used in this book, it is essentially a heuristic (interpretive) device, a way to divide the subject for analysis and discussion.
6. Wach, pp. 97 and 98.
7. Paul Tillich, *Theology of Culture*, Robert C. Kimball, ed. (New York: Oxford University Press, 1970), p. 42.

USEFUL BOOKS

Religion and Religions

al Faruqi, Ismail Ragi, and David E. Sopher. *Historical Atlas of the Religions of the World.* New York: Macmillan, 1974.

Ammerman, Nancy Tatom, and Wade Clark Roof. *Work, Family, and Religion in Contemporary Society.* New York: Routledge, 1995.

Bellah, Robert N. *The Broken Covenant (American Civil Religion in Time of Trial).* Chicago: University of Chicago Press, 1992.

Bruce, Steve. *Religion in the Modern World (From Cathedrals to Cults).* New York: Oxford University Press, 1996.

Eliade, Mircea, ed. *The Encyclopedia of Religion.* New York: Macmillan, 1986. The definitive modern reference work, of 16 volumes, with hundreds of authors.

————.*The Eliade Guide to World Religions.*
    Edited by Eliade's successors after his death, this book is a digest of his three-volume *History of Religious Ideas.*

HarperCollins Dictionary of Religions. Ed. Jonathan Z. Smith. San Francisco: Harper-Collins (with the American Academy of Religion), 1995.

Monroe, Charles A. *World Religions: An Introduction.* Amherst, N.Y.: Prometheous Books, 1995.

Peters, Ted. *GOD—The World's Future (Systematic Theology for a Post Modern Epoch).* Minneapolis: Fortress Press, 1992.

Sharpe, Eric J. *Understanding Religion.* London: Duckworth, 1983.

Methodology and Comparative Studies

Anthropological Approaches to the Study of Religion. Ed. Michael Banton. A.S.A. Monographs 3. London: Tavistock, 1969.

Beyond the Classics (Essays in Religious Studies and Liberal Education). Ed. Frank E. Reynolds and Sheryl Burkhalter. Atlanta, Ga.: Scholars Press, 1996.

Capps, Walter H. *Religious Studies (The Making of a Discipline).* Minneapolis: Fortress Press, 1995.

Contemporary Approaches to the Study of Religion. Ed. Frank Whaling. 2 vols. I: The Humanities, 1984; II: The Social Sciences, 1985. Berlin: Mouton.

Geivett, R. Douglas, and Brendan Sweetman, eds. *Toward Revision in the Scientific Study of Religion; Contemporary Perspectives on Religious Epistemology.* New York: Oxford University Press, 1992.

Hammond, Phillip E. *The Sacred in a Secular Age.* Berkeley: University of California Press, 1985.

Skorupski, John. *Symbol and Theory (A Philosophical Study of Theories of Religion in Social Anthropology).* London: Cambridge University Press, 1983.

Wach, Joachim. *The Comparative Study of Religions.* Ed. Joseph M. Kitagawa. New York: Columbia University Press, 1969.

Chapter Two

PREHISTORIC RELIGION
AND TWO AMERICAN TRADITIONS

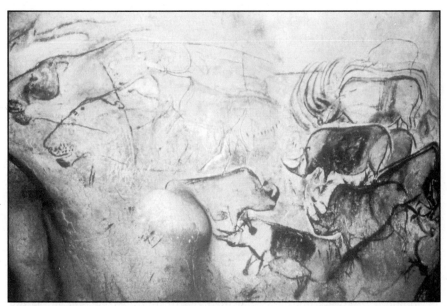

Twenty-thousand-year-old cave painting of rhinoceros from the Paleolithic era, found near Vallon-Pont-d'Arc, Ardeche River canyon in the Rhone-Alps region of central-south France, in December 1994.

(AP Photo/Jean Clottes/AP/ Wide World Photos, New York.)

OUTLINE

I. Prehistoric religion.
   A. Death and the afterlife: Archaeological evidence suggests early human-types observed some form of religion during burial rites.
   B. Hunting rituals: Early hunters may have ritualized the hunt during the Stone Age.
   C. Cave art: Cro-Magnons leave a record of the "sorcerers" and their animal prey.
   D. Fertility rites and figures: Early sculpture and printings reveal the importance of goddesses as the guarantor of crops, animals, and humans.

II. Two American religious traditions.
   A. The Native American struggle for religious identity: Native Americans' cultural and religious systems are challenged by the infusion of European colonists.
      1. Black Elk's picture of Indian religion.
      2. The new story of the second half of Black Elk's life.
   B. The faith of African Americans: The civil rights struggle is rooted in emotional, spiritual, and religious issues.
      1. "I'll Overcome Some Day."
      2. Martin Luther King, Jr., apostle of freedom.
      3. Coretta Scott King—Martin Luther King's personal faith.

———

One should not say that religion begins with death or human experience of death, but it is a fact that the earliest remains of *Homo sapiens* show evidence of some kind of ceremonial treatment of the dead. How religion began is not a problem we will deal with, although the first modern students of religion did try to explain its origin. Because they were following the evolutionary theory as a model for scientific research, they were much concerned with the origin of, in the sense of what gave rise to, religion.

Let us look briefly at religion in prehistoric times, and at two distinctive groups in American religious life. The chapter is included in Preliminary Topics because it points to religion as an aspect of human life from the beginning of human culture, and in American religious history. The three topics are intended to start us thinking about how pervasive and complex are religious phenomena. In addition, I express my conviction that the hostile view of religion as outmoded and dying is mistaken. Religion today is not disappearing, obsolete, or meaningless, but has become universal in scope while remaining infinitely basic, complex, and various in character and manifestation. So-called "other"—

either ancient or modern—religions can no longer be dealt with simply by contrasting them with traditional Western religions and describing them in Western terms. Religious belief, life, and action can only be seen and understood if they are treated as unique and distinct—and utterly fundamental—parts of human culture from its beginning. Thus the reality of religion is lost whenever human yearning for the divine is completely separated from the stuff of the world, in either its practice or—our concern here—the study of it. Above all, religions must not be *reduced* to something else, by treating data about religion as if it were "nothing but" a subheading under some other area of scientific study.

The word *prehistoric* will be used here to describe times and cultures that existed before there were any written records. The word *primitive* formerly implied a negative contrast to *modern* ideas and techniques, whereas proper current scientific usage makes the term purely descriptive of technologically less-developed societies, whether ancient or modern. Accordingly, it is used in this book rarely, and only in the scientific sense. Our first subsection here, then, concerns religion in prehistoric times. The two following sections will discuss Native American and black or African American religion as parts of American history and culture. Their experience and traditions are valuable to us in understanding some things about religions and the way in which religions have been and are studied and described. It also helps that these two important and distinctive groups of people are more or less familiar to us as Americans.

PREHISTORIC RELIGION

We assume that the prehistoric peoples who left no written record were human beings. The so-called (in earlier terminology) "cave man" and the "savage" are like us in their fundamental humanity. This means that they, like us, "understood and interpreted their existence and experience in terms which transcended them," and this leads inevitably to some kind of religious attitude. To be sure, there are profound differences between them and us. The most obvious are the technological differences that permit us to do such things as race around in great, heavy vehicles with enormous loads over smooth roads or in the air, while they walked, carrying their burdens on their backs. Deeper-seated are the theoretical or conceptual differences that put us in separate worlds of ideas and make our task of understanding them enormously difficult. Yet, it is generally agreed that religion was found among all peoples.

When we look at religion in prehistoric cultures we must narrow our descriptive categories drastically, because what little can be deduced from the evidence has mainly to do with ritual and worship. Whatever theoretical component, in the form of belief or conviction, there may have been is almost completely lost to us, so the tenets of prehistoric religions, as well as their ethical and social aspects, are purely conjectural. Our only knowledge of such matters is derived from study of cultural assemblages, collections of human bones, tools, weapons, and other artifacts (objects made or fashioned by human beings) that are found embedded in different levels of the earth. Such materials obviously give very little specific data; they provide a record of religious life only insofar as the physical materials themselves indicate the practice of some sort of ritual or worship activity. From these slight bits of evidence, as summarized by scientists in the field, we can conjecture a few things about prehistoric religion. Inasmuch as dating these events is problematic at best, we cite only approximate dates.

Death and the Afterlife

The early human beings whose slight and pathetic remains have been found in scattered spots of this wide earth must have believed or felt something about their life and death. As far back as the Paleolithic or Old Stone Age of primitive human types known as Neanderthals, there is some evidence of ceremonial treatment or interment of human bodies. For instance, in some of the earliest remains only the skull and lower jaw have been found, and not other bones, suggesting that these were given special treatment as the home of the spirit. This and other curious evidence, such as indications that the brain had been extracted and a cup had been made from the skull, point to burial customs and beliefs about death and the afterlife that we would probably call religious. Apparently there was belief in survival after death, as evidenced by the position in which bodies were interred, the presence in the burial place of ornamentation and tools, and the fact that bodies were interred in layers of reddish powders, symbolic of life.

In geological terms, the finds described above come from deposits of the most recent part of the Glacial or Ice Age, which have been extensively excavated and studied in Europe. In later eras, the Middle and New Stone Ages, there continues to be some evidence suggesting prehistoric customs and beliefs about death and the afterlife. In comparatively recent but still prehistoric ages, specific burial places in prepared graves and tombs from many parts of the globe yield more abundant evidence of the attention our human ancestors devoted to burial practices. It is assumed that these practices indicate some kind of religious behavior.

Hunting Rituals

It is possible to interpret the evidence summarized above as indicating belief in an afterlife. By contrast, other prehistoric ritual practices centered around maintaining physical life in this world. Survival meant having food, clothing, and shelter, and for most of the peoples concerned here these necessities were obtained by hunting. Evidence suggesting rituals surrounding this activity comes from findings of very primitive human types of the Old Stone Age who lived perhaps as long as 200,000 years ago. The courageous hunters who fought the cave bear of the European Alps, then and later, left great bear skulls that had been manipulated to interlock bones in a way that could not have been natural, and there is evidence to suggest sacrificial rites. Some students see these discoveries as positive evidence of ritual practices connected with hunting and perhaps of a deity associated with a bear cult.

Cave Art

More famous and more definite are paintings of prehistoric people discovered in the last century. These paintings are the artistic creations of the Cro-Magnons, the human types that developed in the last glacial age about 35,000 years ago. Largely centering around hunting, cave art has been found in three areas, mainly in southern France and northern Spain but extending into central and eastern Europe and western Siberia. Most of the paintings on the walls and ceilings of the caves are of animals, and many of them are of high artistic quality. What interests the student of religion is their purpose and meaning.

In most of the scenes of the hunt the human figures are portrayed only schematically while the animal figures are quite realistic, perhaps indicating a concern with animals rather than people. It is assumed that the art served ritual or magic purposes in connection with the hunt; in many cases the animal figures in the cave show that they were struck by actual stones, spears, and arrows. But whether the art itself represented a form of magic or involved religious ceremony and meaning is not clear. One consensus among authorities is expressed in the title given to the most famous single figure, from the Trois Frères cave in France, one of more than fifty instances of a human being dressed in animal skins. Human figures depicted in this way have been dubbed "sorcerers," and the Trois Frères figure is known as the "Dancing Sorcerer" or the "Great Sorcerer." It is considered typical of cave art and an instance of primitive religion. The fact that the caves were not used for daily living is further evidence that the activities which took place in them were of a ritual or ceremonial nature.

Fertility Rites and Figures

Prehistoric artists also reflected religious ideas in their selection of both animal and human procreation as subject matter. (Still later will come religion devoted to making fertile the fields, crops, and stock of the early farmer.) Among the cave paintings are clear representations of the copulation of animals of the chase, evidently expressing concern about the supply of hunted species. There are also some paintings depicting human sexual intercourse.

The other widespread and significant religious art form is sculpture—human fertility figurines. In these, personal traits are largely ignored while female sexual organs are emphasized or exaggerated. Therefore most scholars interpret them as mother goddess or fertility figures, naming them "Venuses." Male figures with erect phallus are found especially in northern European

deposits; these date from the later period known as the Neolithic. These artifacts are taken as evidence of the religious belief and practice of prehistoric
peoples.

An important new aspect of modern religious studies is dramatized by the
widespread presence of these female divinities as ancient religious artifacts. At
the same time, women scholars are among the leaders in study of the phenomena. This fact fits here because the key archaeological evidence is the preva-
lence of goddess figures. And that is taken as evidence of the popularity and
importance of the goddess. Anne L. Barstow boldly states: "Goddesses have
been worshiped since earliest times, far longer than have male deities." For
this claim Professor Barstow cites as evidence the female figurines found from
Siberia to Africa, from India to Ireland, and in our New World. She—the goddess—must therefore, says Barstow, have been worshiped under many names,
prefiguring such great goddesses as Ishtar, Cybele, Isis, Demeter. The goddess
was nevertheless one, as seen in her central power expressed in various ways.
The basic aspect of the varied goddess figurines seems to have been her essential femaleness; whence the Paleolithic images have been called Venus figures.
Barstow writes: "Preeminently, she was the symbol of fertility, the guarantor of
crops, animals, and humans."[1]

TWO AMERICAN RELIGIOUS TRADITIONS

The two following sections are in part intended to alert readers to the fact that
the ordinary understanding of religion in the United States makes mainline
white churches the characteristic type of our religious life. The unfortunate result of that limited view, in both popular and intellectual understanding, ren-
ders other religions less important. In order, then, to broaden our perspective,
we include brief descriptions of two significant American groups that have
been outside the standard denominations. (Those more familiar traditions will
be discussed in later chapters.) These two following sections are not detailed
or comprehensive scholarly treatments. They are, rather, brief summary statements about the religious sagas of two distinctive and important minority communities in the mosaic of American culture. In that context, their common aspect is that both of them are stories of the *struggle* of a particular group to
actualize its integrity and status as a religious community and culture.

The Native American Struggle for Religious Identity

Although the term "Native American Religions" properly designates both
North and South American indigenous traditions, we are here dealing only
with the North American, hence our title is in the singular form. Similarities between North and South America can be cited. Lawrence E. Sullivan, director of
the Center for the Study of World Religions at Harvard, quotes a scholar who is
a member of the Mescaloro Apache tribe, and who, Sullivan says, "goes so far

Mr. Chairman, the pride of the Picaris pueblo and the pride of all people who knew him.
(From Native Americans, p. 181. Photographs by Joseph C. Farber. Text by
Michael Dorris. Thomas Y. Crowell Co., New York © Michael Dorris.)

as to say that in Native American communities, religion is culture and culture is religious through and through."[2] (That statement goes back to a dictum by Paul Tillich in his work on religion and culture: "Religion is the substance of culture, and culture is the form of religion.")

In Chapter One we indicated the importance of this concept: religion as expressive of the fundamental ideas and values of a society. For description and discussion of Native American religions, I take it as axiomatic. It provides a broad generalization applicable to the many different tribes included under that heading. The scholars agree that there is no one single or simple detailed and specific model or type that fits all American Indian tribes. But scholars also say that, in spite of their manifold variety, each one of them embodies and expresses the fundamental beliefs and accepted religious customs—what sociologists call the *mores*—of their society. Putting those two ideas together—variety of specific patterns, yet similarity in their cultural function—this book takes one person's spiritual story and treats it as an example of Native American religion.

From the time of the first European explorations and colonization, the native peoples of both North and South America have had literally to fight for their lives and cultural survival. They have been subjected to both physical and intellectual dominance by their so-called discoverers and colonizers. As Lawrence Sullivan has explained in *Icanchu's Drum*, the white European reporters and recorders used Western intellectual concepts and terms in their writings about the New World. Although this was not necessarily or deliberately a method of subjugation, it worked, and still works, to shape the "natives" according to the views and terminology of the invasive/dominant ethos.

In the United States, we are more or less familiar with the long, often sad, history of the relations between Indians and whites. Sometimes there was harmonious coexistence and mutual respect, but the pressures of the rapid spread of colonizers and pioneers over the land led to tragic misunderstandings and strife. Add to that the fact that the mistaken policies of civil and military officials, or vicious misuse of government powers by selfish interests, produced disastrous events and circumstances for Indian Americans. That history must be kept in mind in our discussion of Native American religious life.

Vine DeLoria, Jr., author of a number of incisive books on Indian religion, contrasts the civil rights movement of black Americans in the 1960s with the Indian activism of the 1970s. He emphasizes the need to realize that the two struggles for liberation were different in significant ways. He writes:

> Was not the sacking of the BIA headquarters [1972] and the occupation of Wounded Knee the final spasm of the rugged 1960s when any type of change was considered obsolete but malignant? Perhaps it was the last hurrah of an era when people could thumb their noses at established authority without fear of painful reprisal. But the Indian incidents must . . . be seen within the context of the Indian experience in this nation's history and in that context the Indian movement raised an entirely different kind of question—that of religion—rather than equal enforcement of the law.[3]

The Native American struggle was by the whole people, a collective group effort by many participants and numerous tribal chiefs and leaders. Thus it is not correct to single out one or two as distinctive heroes and heroines, for there were countless unknown Indians, and many chiefs, who participated. Thus, our selection of one person to carry the story is not meant to make him the great protagonist, as in a literary epic. His name was Black Elk, and he is the spokesman in the best known book about Indian religion, *Black Elk Speaks*. The choice is based first on the fact that central aspects of the whole story come through in his words, and he is essentially a religious figure in life and in the narrative. The other reason for our choice is that Black Elk's later life well into the twentieth century brings a striking example of religious pluralism and the problems it engenders both for the participants and for scholarly interpreters.

BLACK ELK'S PICTURE OF INDIAN RELIGION

From Black Elk's story as told to John G. Neihardt we take a few salient points about the religious life of the Oglala Sioux.[4] During their final tribulations, as Native Americans tried to preserve their traditional ways at the end of the nine-teenth century, Black Elk strove to save his people from the encroachment of white settlers and the increasing attacks of U.S. troops. That is the essential context and claim here: that Black Elk's genuine concern, total sincerity, and utter honesty shine through his personal testimony. Thus our summary based on *Black Elk Speaks* is not a monograph or ethnographic report on Sioux religion; for that there are innumerable valuable anthropological studies of all kinds to be found in any good library. Take Black Elk's memoir, if you will, as testimony, personal affirmation. And use a current term for images generated on the Internet, "virtual reality," to characterize the content of his visions. It is then up to you to wrestle with your interpretation and assessment, for we are not going to use the technical terms and theories applicable to *Black Elk Speaks*.[5]

All through his long life, Black Elk was a man of visions; they came and went, but they marked him as a seer among his people. The contents and actors in his visions were ordinary objects of his experience, but their actions and words, and his acts and movements, were what we would term miraculous or wonderful. His Great Vision recorded in Chapter III of *Black Elk Speaks* took place when he was 9 and suddenly fell ill, then was caught up and transported through the air in a little cloud. There followed visions of horses, presentation before the six Grandfathers, and promises of powers; in the center of the earth "bloomed the holy stick that was a tree, and where it stood there crossed two roads" (p. 29), and much more. Above all, Black Elk was promised that the nation would live, but that great dangers and afflictions were to come. He was told he would go back, with power, to his home tepee. He then woke up and learned he had been ill for 12 days (pp. 37–47).

Subsequent visions were likewise related to tribal concerns, including bison hunting and fights with other tribes. Always, however, they were his personal visions; this places him in the shamanic tradition of native peoples. Dr. Michael Harner of the Foundation for Shamanic Studies, in a lecture at the Asian Art Museum of San Francisco (September 8, 1995) described the shaman as one who has experience of other worlds during a spiritual journey. Harner says that the phenomena are at least 30,000 years old, and he credits the late, great Mircea Eliade with rehabilitating its study through his pioneering book, *Shamanism*.

Black Elk's Indian view of the cosmos, the total world of nature and people, is taken as an example of a significant difference from Western ideas of history and change. Another book of Eliade's, *Cosmos and History*, 50 years ago brought this view to the attention of the intellectual world. In his preface Eliade declared: "The chief difference between the man of the archaic and traditional societies and the man of the modern societies with their strong imprint of Judaeo-Christianity lies in the fact that the former feels himself indissolubly connected with the Cosmos and the cosmic rhythms, whereas the latter insists that he is connected only with History." Eliade adds that for the archaic person, history is a "sacred history" that can be repeated indefinitely through ceremonies that preserve, renew, and reactivate the cycles of human life.[6]

On two occasions Black Elk was instructed by his voices to perform traditional sacred ceremonies. When he was 17, he was told by an old medicine man that he must fulfill the duty laid on him during his first Great Vision: "You must do what the bay horse in your vision wanted you to do. You must do your duty and perform this vision for your people upon earth. You must have the horse dance first for the people to see" (p. 165). With the advice and help of Bear Sings and Black Road, with much preparation and many participants in complex ceremonies and maneuvers, it was done. Afterward Black Elk felt very happy, "for I could see that my people were all happier" (p. 178). Likewise, a year later, when U.S. troops forced the Oglala Sioux onto their reservation at Pine Ridge, Black Elk called for the Heyoka ceremony, and afterward the people felt happy. In these ritual acts Black Elk seems to have been manifesting what Eliade refers to as "nostalgia for a periodical return to the mythical time of the beginning of things, to the 'Great Time'" (p. xi).

In what might be called his "discourses," Black Elk often referred to an idea voiced—for whatever reason—by many American college students: the superiority of "circular" over "linear" thinking. After the Heyoka ceremony, he went to live on the reservation, and was unhappy that his home was a *square* log house. He said:

> You have noticed that everything an Indian does is in a circle, and that is because the power of the World always works in circles, and everything tries to be round. In the old days when we were a strong and happy people, all our power came to us from the sacred hoop of the nation, and so long as the hoop was unbroken, the people flourished. . . . This knowledge came to us from the outer world with our religion. Everything the Power of the World does is done in a circle.

Black Elk applied this idea to the wind and the birds, to human life, to their tepees, and he lamented that, by the loss of their "circular" ways, "our power is gone and we are dying." He added, "But there is another world" (pp. 198–200). That was his epitaph for their vanishing culture, and the key to his faith.

All was not over for Black Elk. He received power to perform cures according to the Sioux version of the rites practiced in many tribes. With Buffalo Bill's touring show, he traveled in the United States and England from 1886 to 1889. On December 29, 1890, the terrible and infamous "Butchering at Wounded Knee," as the chapter is entitled, was visited on the men, women, and children by the soldiers. "And so it was all over, . . . a people's dream died there, it was a beautiful dream." So wrote Black Elk.

THE NEW STORY OF THE SECOND HALF OF BLACK ELK'S LIFE

Black Elk died on August 17, 1950. The book of his life in the nineteenth century has been a deservedly favorite text in religion classes for many years. For much of the time neither teachers nor students knew or cared about his new, full, satisfying work and life after the Oglala Sioux came to terms with their reservation existence. Since the mid-1980s, however, there has been discussion about the fact that in the twentieth century he became a Roman Catholic and served as a catechist. The bare facts are simple. On the Pine Ridge Reservation in South Dakota he was known and loved simply as Nick Black Elk, a devoted catechist of Holy Rosary Catholic Church and mission. His adoption of Catholic Christianity in 1904 was voluntary and rational, after familiarity with the church and faith. The problems for some Indian activists and academic purists have arisen from doubts about his sincerity and whether his active Christian service somehow compromises his Indian credentials. The issues and facts in this matter have been documented and analyzed in a number of texts and critical studies. The best is that of Michael Steltenkamp.[7]

In the debate among Native Americans about how to deal with such problems of pluralism and syncretism, outsiders can only state their opinions. For ours we appeal to an author who wrote about these matters before the recent controversies. Joseph Epes Brown, in *The Spiritual Legacy of the American Indian*, reminds us that a pervasive theme of their traditions has been that "the immediately experienced natural environment may communicate to human beings the totality of that which is to be known . . . of the sacred essence of being and of beings." We have seen this in Black Elk, whose "personal and tribal experience assure[d] the intensification and continuity of participation in the sacred." Thus he could "adopt and adapt new expressions of values into the sacred fabric of [his] own religious culture." We follow Brown's conclusion "that American Indian living religions have the right to a legitimate place along side the great religions of the world."[8]

The Faith of African Americans

Some clues for understanding African American religion may be taken from native African religion, if we follow the work done by scholars in that extensive field. Consider the following quotations from such a source, referring to African society: "In the traditional context religion cannot be a purely personal affair; the relation to the sacred is, first of all, a communal one. . . . In times of colonial oppression and rapid social change, ritual symbols have also served to create and reinforce new religious and political movements."[9] Assuming that these two characteristics may be applied to African American religion, they constitute our starting point. The African American story in the civil rights revolution of the 1960s was largely a communal and religious movement. Having been documented in countless sociological studies, that fact is presupposed in this description of the black struggle that forever changed the racial composition and attitudes of American society. The focus, nevertheless, of our summary assessment is on the charismatic Baptist minister, Martin Luther King, Jr., because of his leadership of the essentially spiritual battle for the soul of the American people.

Of course, the concrete issues of the civil rights battle concerned formal and informal laws, regulations, and policies at all levels of American society. The substance of those matters was played out in human terms by people in their physical circumstances and actions. As in any such conflict, however, the deeper issues and forces were emotional, spiritual, and, finally, religious. (Unwitting testimony to this fact is the present spate of interracial sitcom TV programs, dramatizing such events in their newer, current forms of human interaction.) Most of the things that we will say here about Martin Luther King and the civil rights story are familiar facts, discussed in an extensive literature, so we will not spend time on documentation, but simply assemble relevant points.

"I'LL OVERCOME SOME DAY"

In 1916, Charles A. Tinsley, pioneer composer of gospel music, published a song titled "I'll Overcome Some Day." The first stanza goes:

The world is one great battlefield,
With forces all arrayed,
If in my heart I do not yield
I'll overcome some day,
I'll overcome some day,
I'll overcome some day.

Amalgamated with the words and tune of the spiritual "I'll Be All Right," the song became "We Shall Overcome," the anthem of the civil rights movement sung by millions of people in the 1950s and 1960s.[10] It symbolizes for us the faith that filled African American churches at that time.

That faith is the single most important factor in the civil rights victory. It is no accident that "We Shall Overcome" was the marching song of the movement, for such music was—and still is—the emotional and liturgical center of the black Christian churches. Voicing the ultimate confidence of a people who for 200 years lived under white oppression and the suffering and fear that engendered, their faith *had* to be so expressed, for it was twofold. First, such music permitted people, individuals, souls to verbalize loudly, fully, and without shame or embarrassment their despair at their circumstances and the impossibility of any full end to the troubles that discrimination, segregation, injustice, and cruelty laid on them. Second, music was the vehicle, the means for *affirming*—in exuberance and joy—their robust common knowledge of and trust in the Lord Jesus Christ, who himself had suffered, and died, and risen again, to be forever their Savior, each one and all together, in this world and the next. *Amen!* and *Hallelujah!*

Like the Native American ordeal, the saga of black America was an old, sad story. Yet unlike the Native American story, which was often obscured by callous neglect and sentimental romanticism, the story of black America was known to anyone who cared enough to look closely at the realities. To be sure, there were elaborate social and political customs, which sanctioned the imposition of a new form of racial discrimination known as segregation. For that, a complex collection of laws and ordinances existed at all levels of the American political system that provided a veneer of legality—if not morality—to cover the nakedness of blatant racism.

Beginning in colonial times, that unsystematic pattern had developed throughout the nation, differing according to regional and local situations, but always there is some form. After the Declaration of Independence, the Revolution, and the Constitution, the contradiction between American ideals and political realities became more obvious to intelligent and honest observers. Thomas Jefferson, for example, freed his slaves in his will. After the Civil War, there were a dozen years of confused "Reconstruction" in the South, which ended when federal troops were withdrawn in 1877. To many decent people in both North and South, American racism was more or less of an embarrassment and a shame. But it was also generally accepted as an unfortunate aberration that they hoped would somehow be ameliorated—"sometime." Only the more sensitive and conscientious of white citizens studied and agitated against it, in colleges and churches where such unconventional opinions were tolerated. Meanwhile, the "realists" of all stripes saw to it that any sort of dangerous concrete policies and actions in the real world were coldly and mercilessly crushed. For that, there were sophisticated tactics of political and judicial control and corruption not usually involving violence or bloodshed, from the top. From the bottom, in some areas the rednecks and the yahoos were permitted to threaten, molest, beat, and lynch "uppity niggers" of all ages. It worked.

After the Civil War, when they were allowed to establish their own churches, African Americans quickly organized many new denominations, following the American pattern for such associations. Thus, most black Americans found their spiritual and social homes in the church. Living within the system, they were able to find a measure of security and accomplishment in the white world. For their deeper moral and personal lives, the church offered religious meaning and sustenance, but it was a segregated community, and thus limited in its wider context. Within that enclave, the black Christian minister had an important and significant position. He—there were no women clergy in the earlier days—did pastoral work among his flock, led worship and ritual, and served as intellectual and spiritual leader through his preaching and teaching. Of course, black people had all kinds of relationships with whites in the normal social and personal intercourse of their community. In addition, some black professionals and leaders could and did have status in the white culture as representatives of blacks in necessary dealings with the dominant culture.

Toward the end of the nineteenth century, black protest movements began to appear in such places as Tuskeegee Institute, Alabama, where Booker T. Washington organized black professionals to promote black education and self-improvement. He believed in cooperation with white liberals and with the black church, and his stance embraced assimilation or accommodation with the ruling caste. A more radical approach, critical of that kind of passivism, was espoused by W. E. B. Dubois, who helped found the NAACP (National Association for the Advancement of Colored People) in 1909. Not until after

World War II were there real cracks in the segregationist pattern, when President Truman in 1949 desegregated the armed services and the civil service. In the 1950s, although there was a pervading ferment of urgency for reform among the thinkers and leaders of black America, there was no focus, no plan, only a desperate search for an effective agenda.

MARTIN LUTHER KING, JR., APOSTLE OF FREEDOM

Commentators say it began December 1, 1955, in Montgomery, Alabama, with Rosa Parks's refusal to move to the back of the bus and her arrest for violation of the city segregation code. King had been pastor of Dexter Avenue Baptist Church since September 1, 1954; having completed his thesis during the following spring in Montgomery, he received his Ph.D. from Boston University School of Theology in June 1955. Dr. King was busy and happy in his pastorate, married to a bright, attractive, educated wife. Being the son of a prominent Baptist minister and having been an assistant to Dr. King, Sr., at Ebenezer Baptist Church in Atlanta, he was poised for success in the ministerial career he had chosen. That simple fact is the first major point in this summary of the African American civil rights revolution: Martin Luther King, Jr., was a Christian minister.

After December 1 the Montgomery bus boycott began, and Dr. King, as pastor of a leading church, was swept into the campaign. The rest, as we say, is history, from which we extract a few key points to make our case for the primacy of religion in that cultural upheaval. Item: "Although their exact numbers may never be known, from 1962 to 1965 in the South ninety-three churches, most of them rural, were bombed or burned."[11] Axiom: What their enemies think of and do to a group is a realistic measure of them.

The mood of desperation in the entire national African American cultural community at that propitious moment in 1955 was referred to in a previous paragraph. Perspicuous analysts of the events that began then see Dr. Martin Luther King, Jr., as the person who became the man of the hour by meeting that need for what I have called "an effective agenda." Lerone Bennett, Jr., has well stated the dilemma that confronted the black activists of the time, and why King proved, in time, to have the answer:

> King must be seen as a leader who solved a technical problem that had worried Negro leaders for decades. As a powerless group dominated by a powerful majority, Negroes could not stage an open revolt. To go into the streets under those conditions with open demands for change was suicidal. As I have indicated elsewhere, King and the sit-in students solved the technical problems by clothing a national resistance movement in the disarmingly appealing garb of love, forgiveness, and passive resistance.[12]

That is a valid statement in general historical terms, but it must be supplemented here lest it be misinterpreted.

It is easy for an advocacy group to adopt, as a *method* or technique, the *use*—in the bad sense of that expression—of Christian terms and beliefs, making the faith secondary to the cause. This must be said, because these days all sorts of "good causes" are touted as *Christian* concerns. They may or may not be such; if the Christian faith and church are merely means-to-an-end, no matter how good that end may be, Christianity is being *used*. And that is fatal to Christianity, because no one may, or can, *use* God.

In challenging such current "instrumentalism"—the misuse of religion to promote ideology—it is good to have support from Harvard. Three essays in a recent issue of *Religion and Values in Public Life* address these questions; following are brief quotations. Referring to Martin Luther King's "reinvention of Christianity in modern America," Gerald Early writes: "King created the metaphor of the dream for theological reasons—to give both blacks and whites hope that the race problems in America could be solved. It was his achievement to give men hope—the condition or state of being on the way." Gary Dorien writes: "Progressive Christianity cannot attribute divine sanction to any ideology, including democratic socialism, without implicating itself in idolatry. It must come into progressive political engagement on its own terms and with its own eschatological reservations" ("Beyond the Twilight of Socialism"). William Martin warns, in an excerpt from his book, that "nothing gives more comfort to the hardened sceptic or unbeliever than to have religious leaders chasing around the country invoking God's name on behalf of what are clearly secular causes."[13] Our documentation of the faith of Dr. King comes from the biography written by his wife, Coretta Scott King, speaking in intimate, personal terms.

CORETTA SCOTT KING: MARTIN LUTHER KING'S PERSONAL FAITH

When Dr. King received the Nobel Prize for Peace in 1964, nearly 10 tumultuous years had elapsed since Montgomery, and his concept of and devotion to nonviolence had fully matured. The Nobel Prize is itself the most famous and visible testimony from international opinion to his total dedication to peaceful means in the struggle. Mrs. King's view is reiterated in her book: Martin was dedicated to nonviolence from his youth, and he often voiced it to his own family. She writes that Dr. Jahn, who read the Nobel citation and presented the medal, declared in part: "Dr. King has succeeded in keeping his followers to the principle of nonviolence." When the Kings' home in Montgomery was bombed in 1955 shortly after the beginning of the bus boycott, a mob of outraged black citizens gathered there. Dr. King's calm words to them expressed the Christian basis of his nonviolence:

> My wife and my baby are all right. I want you to go home and put down your weapons. We cannot solve this problem through retaliatory violence. We must meet violence with non-violence. Remember the words of Jesus: "He who lives by the sword shall perish by the sword." We must love our white

Fruits of the civil rights struggle: King Center in San Mateo, California. Planned by black and other community organizations and federal agencies. Opened in January 1969. Occupies half a block in former city park. Includes offices, meeting rooms, auditorium/dining room, swimming pool, craft areas, courtyard, and parking lot. Total ethnic inclusion/clientele.

(Ward J. Fellows.)

brothers, no matter what they do to us. We must make them know that we love them. Jesus still cries out across the centuries, "Love your enemies." This is what we must live by. We must meet hate with love."[14]

The corollary of King's nonviolence was his invocation of Christian love, unsentimental realism. The basis for that was his confidence in God's ultimate victory of life over death, in Jesus Christ. For him these were essential, personal verities—not pious platitudes. Coretta King remarks how her husband described the kind of "love" that he meant in his sermons:

> The third kind of love was agapé. This meant understanding redeeming goodwill toward all men. It was disinterested love in which the individual sought not his own good, but the good of his neighbor. It was not weak or passive, but love in action. It was the kind of love Martin aspired to give his enemies.[15]

The final notable element in the personal faith and public utterances of Martin Luther King was his confidence in the ultimate victory of the civil rights movement. This confidence was expressed in the NAACP's slogan in the early 1960s, "Free by '63." In that also, Dr. King's faith was derived from Christian teachings, under the theological term *eschatology*, the doctrine of the "last things" that follow from the resurrection of Christ. Among the "last things" are included, despite the sufferings and defeats of the righteous, victories of justice and peace in the world, like civil rights.

For that we invoke perhaps the most dramatic and moving of all Preacher King's rhythmic, resonant, Baptist-style perorations, in which he was caught up in what black church people themselves call "whopping." Its title alone still has power to move those who exult in that and other unforgettable moments when the faithful—including thousands of whites—responded with joyous shouts to the triumphant cadences of the apostle of freedom. By 1963 the movement had gathered momentum and force all across the nation, bringing recruits and new voices, including that of President Kennedy. A "March and Demonstration for Jobs and Freedom" was organized, to include all elements of the new national call for action. On August 28, the largest such demonstration ever seen in Washington, D.C.—over 200,000 blacks and whites—marched from the Washington Monument and assembled in front of the Lincoln Memorial to hear speeches.

Lerone Bennett, Jr., writes: "King turned his eyes now from the paper on the lectern to the crowd before him, from the strife of the battle to the victory ahead." Again and again King repeated the phrase, "I have a dream . . . ," for several hopes, including that his children would one day not be judged "by the color of their skin but by the content of their character." With the public address system almost drowned out by the roar of the crowd he faced, King's strong baritone voice at full power concluded with the inclusive dream he always carried:

> When we let freedom ring, when we let it ring from every village and every hamlet, from every state and every city, we will be able to speed up that day when all of God's children, black men and white men, Jews and Gentiles, Protestants and Catholics, will be able to join hands and sing in the words of that old Negro spiritual, "Free at last! Free at last! Thank God almighty, we are free at last!"[16]

Some freedom did come in the next 5 years. But gradually the theme changed to the purely pragmatic "Black Power." The civil rights crusade lasted from 1955 to 1968. Martin Luther King was murdered in Memphis on April 4, 1968. African American Christianity had forever changed the American world, for the better.

NOTES

1. Anne L. Barstow, "The Prehistoric Goddess," in Carl Olson, *The Book of the Goddess: Past and Present* (New York: Crossroad, 1983).
2. Lawrence E. Sullivan, "Teaching About Religions Native to the Americas," in Mark Jurgensmyer, *Teaching the Introductory Course in Religious Studies* (Atlanta: Scholars Press, 1991).
3. Vine DeLoria, Jr., *God Is Red* (Golden, Colo.: North American Press, 1972), p. 47.

4. *Black Elk Speaks, Being the Life Story of a Holy Man of the Oglala Sioux*, as told through John G. Neihardt (Lincoln, Neb.: 1961). Quotations and citations from *Black Elk Speaks* in this chapter will be noted in the text by parentheses enclosing page numbers.

5. Cf. Richard Busse, "Black Elk Speaks in the Introductory Course," *AAR/SBL Religious Studies News*, Vol. 3, No. 1 (February 1995), pp. 5-8.

6. Mircea Eliade, *Cosmos and History* (New York: Harper and Row, 1959), pp. vii, viii.

7. Michael F. Steltenkamp, *Black Elk, Holy Man of the Oglala* (Norman: University of Oklahoma Press, 1993).

8. Joseph Epes Brown, *The Spiritual Legacy of the American Indian* (New York: Crossroad, 1993), pp. 26, 27.

9. Benjamin C. Ray, *African Religions* (Englewood Cliffs, N.J.: Prentice Hall, 1976), p. 17.

10. Mark A. Noll, *A History of Christianity in the United States and Canada* (Grand Rapids: William B. Eerdmans, 1992), pp. 427, 428.

11. C. Eric Lincoln and L. H. Mamiya, *The Black Church in the African American Experience* (Durham: Duke University Press, 1990), p. 97.

12. Lerone Bennett, Jr., *What Manner of Man* (Chicago: Johnson Publishing Co., 1968), p. 60.

13. *Religious Values in Public Life*, The Center for the Study of Values in Public Life at Harvard Divinity School, Vol. 4, No. 4 (Summer 1996), pp. 3, 5, 7.

14. Coretta Scott King, *My Life with Martin Luther King, Jr.* (New York: Holt, Rinehart and Winston, 1969), pp. 12, 129-130.

15. Ibid., pp. 58, 59.

16. Bennett, *What Manner of Man*, p. 284.

USEFUL BOOKS

Frankford, Henri, et al. *Before Philosophy*. Baltimore, Penguin Books, 1966.

Lessa, William A., and Evon Z. Vogt, eds. *Reader in Comparative Religion: An Anthropological Approach*. New York: Harper and Row, 1972.

Maringer, Johannes, ed. *The Gods of Prehistoric Man*. Trans. Mary Ilford. New York: Alfred A. Knopf, 1960.

Native American Religions

Brown, Joseph Epes. *The Spiritual Legacy of the American Indian*. New York: Crossroad, 1993.

DeLoria, Vine, Jr. *God Is Red*. New York: Grosset and Dunlap, 1973.

Driver, Harold D. *Indians of North America*, rev. ed. Chicago: University of Chicago Press, 1969.

Hosie, Frederick E. *Encyclopedia of North American Indians*. Boston: Houghton Mifflin,

Hultkrantz, Ake. *The Religions of the American Indians*. Berkeley: University of California Press, 1981.

Josephy, Alvin M., Jr. *Red Power (The American Indians' Fight for Freedom)*. Lincoln: University of Nebraska Press, 1971.

Sullivan, Lawrence E. *Icanchu's Drum; An Orientation to Meaning in South American Religions*. New York: Macmillan, 1988.

African American Religions

Du Bois, W. E. B. *The Souls of Black Folk*. New York: Dover, 1994. There are several paperback editions of this classic.

Franklin, John Hope, and Alfred A. Moss, Jr. *From Slavery to Freedom*, 7th ed. New York: Alfred A. Knopf, 1994.

Frazier, E. Franklin. *The Negro Church in America*. New York: 1974.

Garrow, David J. *Bearing the Cross. Martin Luther King, Jr. and the Southern Christian Leadership Conference*. New York: William Morrow, 1986.

Gates, Henry Louis Jr., and Cornel West. *The Future of the Race*. New York: Alfred A. Knopf, 1996.

King, Martin Luther, Jr. *I Have a Dream (Writings and Speeches That Changed the World)*. Ed. James M. Washington. San Francisco: Harper San Francisco (HarperCollins),

Ray, Benjamin C. *African Religions: Symbol, Ritual and Community*. Englewood Cliffs, N.J.: Prentice Hall, 1976.

PART TWO

Four Eastern Religions, or Salvation East

The arrangement of this book in two major parts devoted to Eastern and Western religions reflects the underlying theme of the book. That pervasive topic, comparison of East with West, was suggested in the Preface and is made explicit in the concluding chapter. The definition of religion as human relationship to the transcendent entails that the important, distinctive facets of religion are those which denote aspects of that relationship. The most inclusive and significant feature is salvation, the attainment of spiritual wholeness that comes from establishing the proper relationship with the divine or supernal reality. The final point of the concluding essay is that Eastern and Western religions see salvation in different terms. This contrast is implicit in Chapters 3 through 9. The "hidden agenda"—the underlying but unspoken question—of Part 2 is, therefore, "Salvation East." The reader should be reading between the lines and using our comparative areas to discern the pattern of the four Eastern faiths in terms of the problem and the solution of salvation.

Following that clue or theme—salvation—we begin Part 2 with a discussion of Hinduism, because it is the archetype (first model) of Eastern salvation. If we may use an ancient and literally "honorable" (Sanskrit *arya* means "noble") term that was misused and perverted by Adolf Hitler, this is the "Aryan" version of salvation, to be contrasted with the "Semitic" or Western. Buddhism, which comes out of Hinduism, then appears as the fully developed, universal, mature paradigm of Eastern religion or salvation. For all the differences and the tension between Hinduism and Buddhism, they pose and solve the problem of human relationship with eternal being in essentially the same fashion. The Chinese religions move closer to the Western model in both their diagnosis and cure of spiritual illness, and thus lead us in that direction, athough the final comparison leaves them in the Eastern camp. Some general aspects of Chinese religion that are relevant to both Confucianism and Taoism are included in the first part of Chapter 5, Confucianism.

USEFUL BOOKS

Listed here are a few books that are useful for several of the four Eastern Religions described in Part 2.

Chan, Wing-tsit, et al., comp. *The Great Asian Religions, An Anthology.* New York: Macmillan, 1969.

de Bary, Wm. Theodore, ed. *Introduction to Oriental Civilizations* Series. New York: Columbia University Press. The series includes:

1. Basham, A. L., et al., comp. *Sources of Indian Tradition.* 2 vols. 1964.

2. de Bary, Wm. Theodore, et al., comp. *Sources of Chinese Tradition.* 2 vols. 1964.

3. Tsunida, Ryusaka, et al., comp. *Sources of Japanese Tradition.* 2 vols. 1964.

Muller, F. Max, ed. *The Sacred Books of the East.* 50 vols. Oxford: Clarendon Press, 1870–1900.
The first great collection of English translations, most of which are still standard. Usually abbreviated as SBE.

Parrinder, Geoffrey. *Introduction to Asian Religions.* New York: Oxford University Press, 1976.

Rhadhakrishnan, Sarvepalli, and Charles A. Moore. *A Source Book in Indian Philosophy.* Princeton: Princeton University Press, 1970.

Chapter 3

HINDUISM

Kandariya Mahadeva Temple, Khajuraho [Courtesy, Har Bans Singh].

© B.B. Madhiwalla/Dinodia Picture Agency, Bombay, India.

OUTLINE

I. Origin and development of Hinduism, the religion of India.

    A. Aryan invaders from the West brought their own gods when they conquered the Indus Valley peoples *ca.* 1500 B.C.E. That early epoch is called the Vedic Age, from the Vedas, hymns to their gods first spoken or written by seers or *rishis,* who are looked back to as spiritual guides.

    B. By *ca.* 500 B.C.E. Hinduism proper appeared, combining old and new elements in the basic writings, theories, gods, and practices, which have greatly developed since then but have not essentially changed in their fundamental pattern.

II. The sacred writings of Hinduism are divided into two main parts:

    A. *Shruti* or "heard," by unknown *rishis*; most important are:

        1. The Vedas proper: *Rig Veda, Sama Veda, Yajur Veda, Atharva Veda.*

        2. The Upanishads, compilations of spiritual knowledge and methods, used as the basis for later doctrines.

    B. *Smriti* or "remembered," by legendary authors. The epics, *Mahabharata*, including *Bhagavad Gita*, and the *Ramayana*, are the principal *smriti* works.

III. The tenets of Hinduism include great variety within or under one fundamental doctrine.

    A. The fundamental belief is in one inclusive spiritual reality that includes and yet is more than all things.

        1. The Brahman, or absolute, as the objective being and nature of all things.

        2. The Atman, Soul, or Self of all individual things.

    B. Various thinkers and philosophers elaborated these teachings in different ways and systems of thought.

    C. The one God-reality is known in many gods and goddesses. The most important are Brahma the creator god, Vishnu the preserver, and Shiva the destroyer, and various goddesses.

    D. The human situation is that all things are caught in *samsara*, an endless cycle of birth, life, death, and rebirth by transmigration, under the law of *karma*, the record and consequence of human actions.

IV. There are four *margas* or ways to God, constituting different life styles as ways to *moksha*, spiritual freedom: *jnana* (knowledge); *karma* (works); *yoga* (discipline); *bhakti* (devotion).

V. The ethical component of Hinduism is found in its function as the way of
   life for all people according to their different circumstances, called
   dharma.

   A. The caste system, religiously based social stratification, is the principal
      organ of *dharma*.

   B. The *ashramas* are four stages in life.

   C. There are four acceptable goals in life.

———

INTRODUCTION

The Place of Hinduism

For many reasons the Hindu tradition is fundamental for understanding Asian
religions, because it is a factor in their development. In analysis of religious
faith as abstract thought or theory, Hinduism is basic in terms of the modern
dichotomy between being and doing, between existence and action, between
what something *is* and what it *does*.

Of course the two are related to each other, and both are operative in any
functioning entity. Yet they can be distinguished from one another, and their
separate place and significance can be established. It is an ancient theoretical
distinction and problem. In the *Republic*, when Plato comes to discuss the
supreme Idea in his system, the Idea of the Good, he says he cannot tell us
what it *is*, but he can and does describe what it *does*. Since then, the dichotomy has figured in philosophy; in Martin Heidegger's thought, the problem of being is "the crux of the spiritual history of the West." In religion the dichotomy appears as a basic distinction that is both problematic in, yet
necessary for, explicating spiritual truth and applying it to the problems of the
world. Although it has not always been explicitly remarked and noted, it is fundamental and pervasive in religious belief.

Modern trends have increased the urgency for us to recognize and respect
the difference between being and doing in the various religious traditions of
our pluralistic culture. Both aspects belong in any profound religion, but—as I
said in discussing Martin Luther King's faith—the religious substance itself in
its essential nature must not become simply a tool or instrument *used* by religious and secular leaders. That is the temptation, and the corresponding weakness, of Western religion-as-advocacy; call it "instrumentalism." Philosophically, it derives from the very power of modern epistemology (theory of
Knowledge); Paul Tillich called it "knowledge of control." Arising from the legitimate concern for concrete ethical expressions of spiritual truths, it may and
sometimes does mutate into exploitation of religious institutions for partisan

purposes. Contemporary events provide vivid examples, and the concomitant disagreement about which ends are good and which are bad shows the complexity of the problem.

Here, then, is where the distinction becomes significant for the future of religion(s). The essence or existence of spiritual reality itself is primary, underlying the manifold values that may flow from it. Otherwise, the sacred and holy substance of true religion, which endures and works in manifold ways, will be dissipated and dissolved by human misuse of it in bloody conflicts. In Hinduism the priority of being over doing has been consistently maintained, not always as a deliberate and explicit dogma, but involved in both belief and practice. To be specific, we turn to one tradition in which it has been affirmed and manifested as a form of Hindu piety.

For our brief exposition of this school of thought we follow *Speaking of Siva*, A. K. Ramanujan's introduction to and translation of the *vacanas* (religious lyrics) of the Virasaiva sect, which flourished for several hundred years in the medieval period. Ramanujan selected one of Basavanna's poems to illustrate the beliefs of the sect, whose name means "militant or heroic devotees of the God Shiva," one of the three great gods of India.

The rich
will make temples for Siva,
What shall I, a poor man,
do?

My legs are pillars,
the body the shrine,
the head a cupola
of gold.

Listen, O Lord of the meeting rivers,
things standing shall fall,
but the moving ever shall stay.

From Professor Ramanujan's comments on the lyric we take several that express our point. "The poem draws a distinction between *making* and *being*. The rich can only *make* temples. They may not *be* or become temples by what they do. Further what is *made* is a mortal artifact, but what one *is* is immortal . . . ." Ramanujan lists four "polarities" between approved and rejected terms; one is "make:be." The Virasaiva movement was in part a protest of the poor and outcastes against the rich and the higher castes. As Ramanujan says, "The poem enacts this conflict. Lines 10–12 sum up the contrasts, asserting a universal; What's made will crumble, what's standing will fall; but what is, the living moving jamgama is immortal."[1]

Disregarding the infinite ramifications of the problem, we take from the Upanishads a classic instance of the flat assertion of the primacy of being. The text is full of statements that refer to a primal, spiritual unity of being itself as the origin and basis of all things. Svetaketu, a young brahmin, in the *Chandogya Upanishad* is instructed by his father. "In the beginning, my dear, this world was just Being (sat), one only, without a second."[2] Professor Hume, in his "Outline of the Philosophy of the Upanishads," speaks of the "conclusion of the abstract presupposition as to the nature and possibilities of the pure unity which these thinkers conceived of as the essence of reality and to which they press on as the great goal of all their speculations." He concludes his remarks by quoting from another of the Upanishads:

As a unity only is It to be looked upon—
This indemonstrable, enduring Being. (Brih. 4.4.20.)[3]

A persistent, fundamental element in Hinduism, this theme is both significant for understanding its prevailing nature, and important in the dialogues of religious pluralism.

"Oneness" is not the one word to describe the essence of Hinduism, but it is as close as we can get to a one-word characterization. For there is a strange and fascinating unity to this religion of the nation and people of India. The Indians who figure in this chapter are denizens of a great subcontinent, the veritable Indians, whom Columbus mistakenly thought he had encountered. Although not all of them are Hindus, since the separation of the Muslim states of Pakistan and Bangladesh, most of them are, and so Hinduism is one, at least, in being the religion of around 700,000,000 people of India. But it is so rich and diverse that it almost overwhelms the Western mind. Take two examples from a novel, before we turn to more formal data. In E. M. Forster's novel about East meeting West in India, *A Passage to India*, Dr. Aziz, a young Muslim doctor, takes a party of English friends on an outing. Miss Quested, one of the Englishwomen, and Dr. Aziz talk about Akbar, great Mughal emperor of the sixteenth century. She says: "But wasn't Akbar's religion very fine? It was to embrace the whole of India." Dr. Aziz replies, "Miss Quested, fine but foolish. You keep your religion, I mine. That is best. Nothing embraces the whole of India, nothing, nothing, and that was Akbar's mistake."[4] The outing has taken them to the "Marabar Caves." Later the sound of the echo in the caves becomes a symbol for the India which two Englishwomen want to understand and enter into: "Whatever is said, the same monotonous noise replies, quivers up and down and wails until it is absorbed into the roof. 'Boum' is the sound . . ." But the echo overwhelms them, just as it absorbed all sounds into one, by reducing everything to nothing; it seemed to murmur, "Pathos, piety, courage—they exist, but are identical, and so is filth. Everything exists, nothing has value."[5] The oneness is too much for the Western women. But to the Indians of the novel, the caves, the echo, and the oneness are fun, amusing, and friendly. Our task now is to describe more circumstantially this rich and fascinating faith.

ORIGIN AND DEVELOPMENT

It is sometimes said that the Hindus themselves have no sense of history. Certainly it is not a part of their religious consciousness, nor does it constitute their religion in the way that the meaning of history is central to Judaism and is a factor in the two other Biblical religions. Nevertheless we must outline the religious history of Hinduism, and it is the longest and most complex of the religions we are considering. Only China can compete with India for the title of the oldest, living, continuous culture. Let us take the word of a Chinese scholar, Lin Yutang, "that India was China's teacher in religion and imaginative literature, and the world's teacher in trigonometry, quadratic equations, grammar, phonetics, Arabian Nights, animal fables, chess . . ."[6]

The Indus Valley Culture

Among the elements of contemporary Hindu religion are some which probably come from the oldest known Indian culture, the Indus Valley civilization, which has been studied in excavations at Harappa on a tributary of the Indus, and Mohenjo Dara farther south of the main river. The religion of these early inhabitants, whose culture and economy are known from the excavations at Mohenjo Daro to have been comparatively advanced, included some features that appear later in Hinduism. Their sculpture and figurines include a portrait statue of what may have been a priest and many female figures of a fertility or mother goddess. The most famous and most intriguing artifact is one of a large number of small steatite seals: a male divinity, ithyphallic, seated in the cross-legged posture of meditation, ornamented, wearing a horned headdress, and with animal figures in the background. There is also evidence of cults associated with stone phallic symbols, with animal and tree worship, and with elaborate ritual bathing. Although the relation between these features and later Hinduism cannot be demonstrated, they suggest that the original culture dating from about 2500 B.C.E. to 1500 B.C.E., before the Aryan invasions, included ideas and practices that entered into the continuing tradition.

The Aryans

Beginning in about 1500 B.C.E. a different people, who called themselves *aryas* or "noble," and hence are known as Aryans, surged into the Indus Valley from the northwest. These Aryans were probably a division of the Indo-Europeans, who moved south and east into Europe and Asia for hundreds of years from somewhere on the boundary of Europe and Asia. The invaders were culturally somewhat less developed than those who were already there, but they had horses and chariots, and they conquered the native peoples. Although they never occupied the whole continent, their gods and customs were significant for the religious development of the entire land. The Aryan language belongs to the same linguistic family as classical Greek, Latin, and other European languages, and from it Sanskrit later developed.

Aryan religious concepts and practices centered around a pantheon of naturalistic or functional male deities, whom they worshipped at great outdoor sacrifices. The altars for these sacrifices have been discovered during modern excavations. Counting their wealth in cattle, Aryans also herded goats and sheep and cultivated barley, and this pastoral and agricultural life was reflected in their sacrificial system. Elaborate rituals were centered in the fire sacrifice of animals, clarified butter, and plants, or in the ritual preparation and consumption of the inebriating juice of the sacred soma plant. Wars among their own tribes or with the natives were frequent, although often they were limited to glorified cattle rustling, to judge from the fact that the literal meaning of one of the words for battle is *gabisti*, "seeking of cows." A large group of priests, with sacerdotal functions but without hierarchical powers, were skilled in the composition, memorization, and recitation of hymns. The later, written form of these hymns, known as the Vedas, constitutes the body of the basic literature. Among the Aryan gods, who are praised and saluted in many of these hymns, are some comparable to Greek deities, namely, Dyaus Pitar ("Father Sky") and Pritivi Mater ("Mother Earth").

The Vedic Age

This first religious epoch of India, before 1000 B.C.E., is known as the Vedic era, from the name of the body of ancient literature, the Vedas. Veda* is from a root similar to Latin *video*, "perceive or understand," hence meaning "knowledge." Although the religious system of the *Rig Veda** precedes Hinduism, the *Rig Veda* is the primary scripture of Hinduism, and Vedic religion is one of its major components. From the *Rig Veda* we take a few key names and ideas about the Vedic gods, whose Sanskrit name of *devas** or heavenly one suggests the Latin *deus*, god. Some of them no longer matter, but since all of them contributed to Hindu myth and cult, we shall discuss them here.

VEDIC GODS

Two important deities are Agni* and Soma,* complex characters as both nature gods and liturgical powers. Agni (fire, cf. Latin *ignis*) appears in the opening lines of the *Rig Veda* as the radiant one who is "king of all worship." Whatever sacrifice he encompasses on all sides "indeed goes to the gods,"[7] carried

---

*Terms followed by an asterisk at their first appearance are defined in the glossary at the end of the chapter.

skyward in the smoke and flame. Being essential to worship, he is further exalted as progenitor of mankind and the first sacrificial priest, a kind of connec-
tor between heaven and earth, and a symbol of the oneness of the other gods.
Less conspicuous than Agni, Soma, often associated with the more powerful
Indra,* is the god of the soma juice and sacrifice. His significance in the sacrifice also expands his importance, as a link between gods and humans.

Another pair of Vedic gods are Indra and Varuna,* competitors for the
honor of great god of the Vedic pantheon. Although Varuna (cf. Greek *oura-
nos* or "heaven," and god Uranus) is the favorite of many Western commentators, who find him a moral and exalted being, he is destined in the later literature "to sink to the level of a god of the waters, without special ethical
quality."[8] In the Vedas, however, Varuna, the sky god, competes with Indra,
and their competition is further seen in that Varuna represents another class of
gods than the *devas*. The class is called *asuras*,* and includes a group of sovereign gods, of whom Varuna is principal. The *devas* gradually oust the *asuras*
and Indra's prestige thus increases. By a strange evolution, in the later portions
of the Vedas the term *asura* means demon. It includes various subgroups of
gods who fight the *devas*. Varuna's claim to power is based on divine right and
the sovereignty of the law (Rita, cosmic order, truth), while Indra claims his by
his own might and force. As a lord of gods and people, Varuna is a universal
ruler, and he, with Mitra, a sun god with whom he is sometimes associated,
has the *maya*,* or occult power that controls the dawn, clouds, weather.
(*Maya* is a complex term that will later mean illusion or deceit.) Although his
associations with order make him a guardian against falsehood, Varuna nevertheless is feared for his omniscience and malevolence. Earlier, Indra was the
sovereign protector and terrible hero of the Aryans, more concrete and personal than Varuna or any other Vedic deity, invoked against their enemies. His
great adversary is Vritra, the dragon that encompasses the waters; by slaying
him Indra sets the waters free, and even reestablishes order in the world. In
this cosmic conflict Indra's self-confident power, his conquering will, his insa-
tiable appetite for food and drink, and his use of the thunderbolt weapon
forged by Tvashtar, architect and blacksmith, combine to produce a victory of
life and light, from which he goes on to unleash the powers of nature for humanity. Although at the end of the Vedic Age proper he is the greatest of the
pantheon, today Indra is only a shadow, having neither power nor worshippers.

A third pair of gods, Rudra* and Vishnu,* later became the great gods of
India. They enjoy far less acclaim in the *Rig Veda*, where only three hymns celebrate Rudra, and five or six are given to Vishnu. Rudra-Shiva, originally an
asura like Varuna, is a fearful and awe-inspiring figure, a fascinating and numinous god combining creative and destructive powers. But Shiva, meaning auspicious, is only an epithet of Rudra in the *Rig Veda*. Fierce and strong, Rudra is
even more ambivalent than the other gods, for he is described as wrathful and
a dreadful destroyer, and yet he heals and restores. Vishnu is known in the *Rig
Veda* for his three great strides, which serve to measure out the earth, sky, and

the unknown beyond, but little else except his stature as a sun god and creator of time prefigures the later Vishnu.

In the *Rig Veda* there is only one important celestial goddess, the maiden Ushas, the radiance of whose bared breasts brings the dawn. The sun god proper is Surya,* although he is conceived in different forms—a bird, a speckled bull, a great heavenly stone. Surya in another aspect as Savitar,* the awakener, wins immortality for man. The invocation to him is the most famous in the Vedas, the Gayatri* or "Savior of the Singer," used on many occasions, especially for Vedic study. "May we attain that excellent glory of Savitar the god: So may he stimulate our prayers."[9]

Many other gods, *rakshas* or demons, and various female and semidivine figures populate the *Rig Veda*. Those we have discussed are meant to suggest the rich mythology which underlies Hinduism, in which gods assume varied shapes and perform different functions, changing and developing and often trading traits or overlapping in their jurisdiction. Now one and now another is assigned many powers and addressed as chief, and yet no one of them is supreme. Although many of the deities reflect or personify powers of nature, they are not treated as the explanation of natural phenomena. They generally do not serve as what anthropologists call "etiological" myths, meaning myths that explain the causes and operations of nature.[10] So far as the Vedic hymns are concerned, the mythology appears to be subordinated to their ritual and sacrificial use. The worshippers celebrate the chosen god, identify with him, sacrifice to him, and hope for help and blessings in return. In the later literature a more developed and expanded mythology does appear. We shall now summarize the ideas and significance of the later portions of the *Rig Veda* and other books in the transition to Hinduism proper early in the first millennium B.C.

TRANSITION TO HINDUISM

Several aspects of late Vedic religion are identified by modern scholars as keys for understanding the gradual transition to Hinduism. First, there is a new note of skepticism on the one hand and speculation on the other, in which the principal theoretical tendency is toward some kind of unity through the subordination of all the gods and powers to one deity or to an inclusive hypothetical monism (a system of thought centered on *one* idea or reality). Second, ritual performance and theological rationale make for an elaborate sacrificial system, and there is a corresponding growth in the power of the priests, who had long since enjoyed a special status. In these developments there is continuous interaction between the Indus Valley and other original cultures with the intrusive Aryan force, which continues to expand and to move eastward. Although the date of its origin is obscure, the stratification of society into the caste system had by now begun, so that mythological explanations of its origin appear in the later Vedas. We now enlarge on the development outlined above, as far as they enter into that picture of a developed Hinduism, which is our object.

THE SEARCH FOR UNITY

Along with the gradual decline of the great Vedic gods, there are found in the *Rig Veda* several strands of speculation about a more ultimate source, meaning, and order of the universe. The so-called "Creation Hymn" (X. 129) asks what was before being or nonbeing, air or sky? Only the One was there, which came into being by *tapas** (austerity) and *kama** (desire). Yet:

Who knows for certain, Who shall here declare it?
Whence was it born, and whence came this creation?
The gods were born after this world's creation:
Then who can know from whence it has arisen?[11]

Persons familiar only with Western monotheism should note line three of the stanza. Despite the hymns which celebrate specific gods, this will be the real answer in Hinduism—something given, unexplainable, and ultimate is there, before and beyond the gods themselves. Nevertheless certain specific figures are candidates for supremacy in other creation hymns. Vishvakarman, as the maker of all things, the father who fashions the world, is celebrated in X. 82, which likewise asks about: "That which is earlier than this earth and heaven, before the Asuras and gods had being, . . ."[12] In hymn number 121 of the tenth book, the singer is looking for that being who is truly entitled to be worshipped, the question being reiterated at the end of each stanza, "What god shall we adore with our oblation?" Only the true author and creator of all is entitled to such honor; who is he? He is the Golden Germ or Seed, according to one hymn, who supported the earth, gives breath and strength, established the sun, beheld the waters, was the one God above the gods: "O Prajapati,* none other than thou hast encompassed all these created things."[13] "Lord of creation or of creatures" is this Prajapati. Zaehner says that "the fusion of theism and monistic pantheism which is so utterly characteristic of Hinduism here appears for the first time."[14]

THE SACRIFICIAL SYSTEM

Associated with this speculative search for the unknown god is elaboration and development of the sacrificial system and theory, with an interesting application of the formula which appears in Greek philosophy and other systems of thought—the parallel between the microcosm (small world) and the macrocosm (big world). The macrocosm is the universe and the deities; the microcosm is humanity and the human scene. The element common to both is sacrifice—in the *Rig Veda*, an attempt to gain the help or blessing of the gods through the hymns, prayers, and sacrificial elements, for the worshipper. But the sacrifice changes into a mysterious operation in which the early sacrifice recapitulates the heavenly in such a way as to compel the gods to act for men as they once acted in the cosmic realm. Expressive of this is a famous hymn known as the *Purusha Sukta* (X. 90). The god Purusha* is humanity personified. Subject as the hymn is to subtle exegesis by the scholars, detailed commentary on it is difficult. It tells of the sacrifice of the superhuman figure, from whom came the gods, yet they sacrifice him and thus bring things into being. The most cryptic line, in stanza sixteen, expresses this paradoxical state of affairs thus: "With the sacrifice the Gods sacrificed the sacrifice."[15] In effect, this is a rationale for the sacrifice performed by the priests: earthly sacrifices repeat or reenact the cosmic sacrifice and renew the creative powers active there; the rites are potent and efficacious by themselves.

Now in all this the correct performance of every detail of the ritual becomes all important, hence the priestly function was needed at every point in the ceremonies, and the power of the priests correspondingly increased. By this time the system of caste had begun. Because of the priests' knowledge and control of the rites and formulas, the priestly or brahmin*[16] caste was thus firmly established. It is only a step from the efficacy of the ceremony to the efficacy of the ceremonial words and ritual acts. In any case, the priest was indispensable, because the complexity and solemnity of the rites made it impossible for the layperson to know and perform them properly.

A hymn from the *Rig Veda* (X. 68), which expresses this trend, celebrates the god who is the personification of prayer, Brahmanaspati, as the bringer of cattle, and he was also described as the father of the gods. In the *Sama** and *Yajur Veda** and the Brahmanas,* the tendency to multiply and complicate ritual sacrifice is clearly seen, for these works are all subordinated to the *Rig Veda*, and they are concerned in one way or another with sacrificial ritual and the functions of the priests. They gradually formed schools or orders, and the Brahmana was the teaching of the order. A priest had to master the Brahmana as well as know by heart the Veda of his order. Although commentators agree that the Brahmanas are tedious and verbose, they signalize the supremacy of the brahmin caste and the elaboration of, and emphasis on, sacrifice as the essence of religion. Prajapati appears again in the most famous, the *Satapatha Brahmana*, to explain the origin and power of the sacrifice, and the fire and horse sacrifice are compared to the cosmos itself. In terms of the different *margas** or ways to salvation which we will want to identify, this period brings forth the first, the way or *marga* of works: The gods bless those who serve them and sacrifice to them; religion is a matter of the proper word and deed. The way of asceticism and renunciation, which may be said to characterize all of Hinduism as an underlying mood, will also fit under this heading of works.

Jainism

Two great new religious systems emerged and broke off from Hinduism, which continued to develop its basic pattern. The two so-called heterodox systems of Indian thought are Buddhism and Jainism. Buddhism will be the subject of a chapter in this book, but Jainism can only be mentioned in this brief summary.

Beginning at the same time as Buddhism, about 500 B.C., Jainism looks back to a series of leaders or teachers, human beings who became pure souls. The truth which enables one to cross over the ocean of recurring births in this world (*samsara**) is provided by them. They are called *tirthankaras* or "ford-makers" because they lead people across the stream of existence, and they are also called *jina* or "conquerors" for their spiritual victory. Mahavira, a slightly older contemporary of Gautama Buddha, was the twenty-fourth and greatest of these tirthankaras or jinas. But what they have conquered is not so much the world as themselves and their passions; for in Jainism the way of austerity and renunciation is carried to its extreme. Mahavira and the other heroes even surpass the gods and gain omniscience by following the Jain maxim "*Ahimsa Paramo Dharma*"—"harmlessness is the supreme religion." Ahimsa or nonviolence is their fundamental ethical principle.

In their view there is no need for gods in the origin and cycles of the universe or in the nature and spiritual history of human beings. Their metaphysical cosmos has two kinds of entities, soul and matter, of which earthly beings are a combination. By right belief, knowledge, and conduct, pure soul and therefore liberation from matter are attained. A measure of the extremity of their austerities is the fact that in the first century A.D. the Jain community split over the question of wearing clothes; one group now does and the other does not wear clothes (usually only within the monastery.) They remain a small (about 2 million) but respected minority in India. Their extreme measure of asceticism and nonviolence in their preoccupation with liberation from *samsara* serve to remind us that deliverance from *samsara* becomes the main problem for most forms of Hinduism in the following centuries. The essential Hindu response to the problem appears in the Upanishads,* and we now turn to this period of the history.

Hinduism

After about 500 B.C.E. decisive changes effecting a transition from Vedic religion to Hinduism in the current sense took place. The new ideas were varied and complex doctrines centered around *samsara, moksha,** karma,** and Brahman.** (These terms are briefly defined here and will be discussed later.) *Samsara*, with its emphases on transmigration and rebirth of souls in one round of life after another (sometimes termed "metempsychosis"), called into question the sacrificial system and the gods, inasmuch as they could not free one from endless cycles of life. To gain freedom from transmigration, including not only earthly existence but also heavenly, a more ultimate release was deemed necessary, in *moksha* or liberation. By one's *karma*, literally action, in the past, a person's present status—body, mind, birth, position, character—has been determined; but one's present action and experience create new *karma*, which determines one's future. As the famous scholar Deussen put it in a classic phrase, as fast as the clock of retribution runs down, it winds itself up again. Together with these key ideas there emerged a new,

Bathing Ghat, Varanasi

(© Ashvin Mehta/Dinodia Picture Agency, Bombay, India.)

unifying concept that included both the gods and the worlds—for they too become subject to cyclical destruction and rebirth—in a total, cosmic reality, absolute and ultimate, Brahman.

THE SEERS WHO COMPOSED THE UPANISHADS

In the attempt to achieve release by some other means than sacrifice or ritual and duties, there developed the practice of renunciation of the world and commitment to an ascetic life as a hermit in the forest or as a beggar-wanderer about the land. Out of this life came meditation and speculation as the essential occupation of the religious seekers, apart from concern about their daily life or even the ritual itself. While earlier speculation had elaborated the theory and practice of the sacrifice, attention was now directed beyond the sacrifice to the meaning and truth which underlay the rites and to which they were directed. In this way, theory and truth apart from ceremony and practice became the focus of religion for those who were so minded, and a division which marks all developed religions emerged: between the internal, theoretical, ultimate meaning and the external, practical, immediate custom, ceremony, or way. Of course, it is not a final or clear division, for one merges into the other. Yet it will mark Hinduism especially, with what someone has characterized as the contrast between the *dharma** (law, truth) of the educated and the *dhastur* (custom) of the masses. But such a contrast is inevitable, and it is mentioned here not to denigrate Hinduism but in the interest of accuracy, lest anyone should think that all of Hinduism is speculation about the infinite. A similar contrast between the sophisticated and the primitive levels character-izes most religions. (For these more primitive practices we will sometimes use the anthropological term usually applied to them, which is "folk religion.")

These speculations, first expressed or taught principally in the Upan-ishads, are not a unified and consistent system. The teachings of different schools and thinkers over several centuries are found in the Upanishads, and they are inconsistent and even downright contradictory. What they reflect in any unified way is a general agreement on the nature of the religious question and a more or less consistent type of solution. The problem they address is *samsara*, which is conceived as insoluble in the old terms. To meet this situa-tion, the Upanishads propounded a principle or reality called Brahman, gram-matically a neuter noun, which expressed the essence of the world-soul pre-sent in all things. It has been pointed out by many scholars how the various forms of the Sanskrit root *brih* enter into these terms of Hinduism. The San-skrit for what we term Brahman, as above, is *bŕahman* (bŕah-man, accent on the first syllable), literally holy utterance or prayer. Spelled the same, but ac-cented on the second syllable, *brahmán* denotes the one who speaks or car-ries the sacred word, what might be called the pray-ér. Obviously the literature termed Brahmana is related to them, and there is some connection with the god Brahmanaspati, who was the priestly group's candidate for supreme god. As a supreme and abstract principle, then, Brahman is identified with the power in prayer. When some genius saw that the sacred power in a person, the microcosm, was identical with the sacred power of the macrocosm, and that both were *atman** or self, it was an easy step to what is called the Brah-man-Atman* equation, the fundamental Upanishadic doctrine. Since then, Hindu religious thought has revolved around the problem of the human soul in relation to the eternal soul, which somehow encompasses all things. Out of this era comes, then, the prototype of the second way or *marga* of religious life: *jnana,** or the way of knowledge. Not by the sacrifice, nor by doing one's duty in life, but by knowledge of the truth of Brahman, is the way to *moksha* found.

CLASSIC HINDUISM

The classic age of Hinduism, centered in several centuries before and after the time of Christ, emerges from these great movements of religious evolution. The heterodox systems (Buddhism and Jainism) are called heterodox because they deny the two essential dogmatic presuppositions of Hinduism proper: Brahminism, with all it connotes, not simply of caste but of spiritual reality and regimen; and the sanctity of the Vedas. Conversely, however else they differ, the orthodox Hindus of every level in traditional Hinduism do not question Brahminism and the Vedas. (Modern developments modify and weaken adher-ence to these traditions, especially in regard to caste, but do not deny them.)

Although Hinduism proper gradually rejected Buddhism and Jainism, it was affected by them, and the brahminic sacrificial system was challenged not only by the warrior-nobles who had long contested primacy with the brahmins, but also by merchants and other groups. By the second century B.C., the Vedic gods were yielding to Shiva and Vishnu, who became the great gods of popular Hinduism, as they are to this day. During the same period images and temples rose both literally and figuratively to the central place that they still hold in India, and the basic patterns of the iconography (meaning of various aspects of the image) of the gods—their appearance, posture, dress, ornaments, distinctive symbols—became fixed in traditions that held almost unchanged until modern times. In literature it was the time of the great epics, the *Mahabharata** and the *Ramayana.** In them the two great avatars or incarnations of Vishnu—Krishna* and Rama*—are celebrated. They become the focus of the third great *marga* or way of *bhakti** or devotion to one's chosen god. Another form of literature which shows us another aspect of developed Hinduism goes under the generic term of *dharmashastras* or lawbooks, of which the best known is that of Manu. *Dharma*, the way of life, the rules and forms of conduct, is a key term of Hinduism. Hinduism is, above all, *dharma*. For example, from the code of Manu we can know that by about C.E. 200 all widows, even virgin child-widows, were forbidden to remarry; that was part of dharma for women until modern times.

THE MIDDLE AGES

This is a conveniently flexible term to denote the centuries between the classic age and modern times. During the Middle Ages the intellectual substance of Hinduism continued to develop, while popular piety expanded and proliferated in many directions. The earlier formulations of learning in these times were the six systems of philosophy or schools of thought which are considered orthodox. The sixth century C.E. saw the invasion, with attendant destruction and rapine, by the Huns, but after that, until the Islamic aggression and empire beginning around C.E. 1000, the land was mostly free from foreign invasions. Buddhism had been developing for centuries in India, and now expanded into other lands, but in the later period it began to decline in India. Worship of the god Shiva,* represented by the phallic symbol called the *linga,** and of Vishnu, represented by an image, developed, and the third great sect, which looks to the female or *shakti** forms of Shiva, arose. In all of them *bhakti* or adoration was one of the most important elements. This was also the time when great, systematic teachers commented on and expanded the teachings of the sacred books, especially the Upanishads. The best-known teachers are Shankara,* Ramanuja,* and Madhva,* each of whom founded enduring systems of philosophical Hinduism.

After about C.E. 1200 the great fact of Indian life and history was the rise and dominion of the Islamic empires in northern India. There was much destruction of Buddhist and Hindu temples, images, and religious schools, and killing or dispersion of the monks and priests. From these terrible shocks Buddhism almost completely disappeared or was absorbed into Hinduism. Although Hinduism survived, the bitter strife of Hindu and Muslim also survives to bedevil India. The usual date assigned by the historians for the end of the Islamic regime known as the Mughal Empire is 1761, and it can serve as an arbitrary dividing line for us, to mark the end of more than a thousand years of vintage Hinduism.

SIKHISM

Out of the interaction of Hindu and Muslim came Sikhism; we shall describe it briefly in this separate section. The word *sikh* means disciple in the language of the Punjab, where most of the more than 20 million Sikhs live. The founder was Baba Nanak, a Hindu who became a disciple of Kabir, the Muslim follower of Ramananda, in the fifteenth century. It is said that as a boy Nanak protested against caste when the time came for the initiation rite of the sacred thread of his caste. For some time he adopted Muslim monotheism, but later rejected Islam. As a wandering preacher, he proclaimed the one God whose worship would free one from the cycles of *samsara*, blending Hindu transmigration and Islamic monotheism. Nanak died in 1538 and nine other gurus* or teachers followed him, until the tenth, Gobind Singh, decreed that henceforth the *Granth Sahib* (Holy Book) should take the place of an earthly leader. During those years the peaceful way of Nanak was changed, by conflict with the Muslim Empire, into a fellowship of militant worshippers of the one God, and disciples of their gurus. Traditionally, in India, they still wear the five *k's*, which are the mark of the Sikh warrior: the *kes* or uncut hair; the *kachh*, knee-length shorts; the *kana*, iron bangle; the *kirpan*, dagger or sword; the *khanga* or hair comb. In actual practice, they are generally distinguished by the turban, which is often worn even in Western lands. The five *k's* also have spiritual significance, and the religious life of the devout Sikh centers on devotion to God and to the *Granth Sahib* which is enshrined in the golden temple at Amritsar.

MODERN HINDUISM

Indian religious life from the eighteenth century on was marked by interaction of the traditional elements we have outlined with predominantly Western and, in religious terms, Christian influences. The British regime shaped the political and economic structure of modern India, but the traditional culture provided the substance of daily life for the people. For the most part Hinduism went on as before in the villages and among the populace. The notable and definable specifically spiritual movements were few, and they directly affected only a few people. More pervasive, but impossible to estimate, were the effects of Western science, education, ideas, customs as they impinged more or less on all of India. Stimulated by, and in reaction to, these Western ideas, a number of indigenous Hindu reform movements arose in the late nineteenth and early twentieth centuries. Politically, they opposed the caste system and other forms of repression; religiously, they espoused modernization and strengthening of traditional Hindu values. Among the leaders of those groups were such men as the poet Tagore. The most famous of such people was Mahatma Ghandi, who led India in a spiritual crusade against un-

The Golden Temple, housing the Sikh Granth Sahib, *Amritsar*

(Ward J. Fellows).

touchability, the lowest or "outcast" level, which reduced millions of Indians to poverty and excluded them from participation in the traditional spiritual life. Before and after World War II, Ghandi's "satyagraha" program of Hindu nonviolence against the British Raj led to their agreement to the independence of India. His follower Nehru carried on his work and led India's new government.

Those years of essentially spiritual struggle by millions of Indians have led to India's present position as the largest democracy in the world. Although those accomplishments should not be denied, many injustices and problems still haunt India. Feminist commentators hold that despite their dignified status, women's passivity and submissiveness continues. One says, "For awhile those visionaries managed to redirect Hinduism, in some instances they did infuse it with a new spiritual vision." But the reformers met tough opposition and were ambivalent about women's rights. "The ambivalence toward women is clearly seen in the writings and past actions of such luminaries as Tagore, Ghandi, and Swami Prabhuprada."[17]

In the United States, probably the best known religious movement to come out of India is the Vedanta Society. Its roots go back to Ramakrishna Paramahamsa (1836–1886), whose eclectic mysticism and personal charisma drew many followers from around the world. His follower Vivekananda, a brilliant high-caste and well-educated Bengali, dazzled the international Parliament of Religions at Chicago in 1893. He was the organizer of the Ramakrishna mission in India and the Vedanta Society in the United States. From its temples in American cities, the Society carries on worship and instruction in Advaita Vedanta.

More recently, the heavy immigration of Hindus has led to organization of Hindu temples in the United States. About 15 years ago, the Shiva-Vishnu Temple, "Hindu Community and Cultural Center," was organized in Livermore, California. Now members are completing sculptural work on the temple, and plans are being finalized for the Community Center/Assembly Hall. Total construction costs will exceed $10 million. The temple's name joins the two great gods of India, and a recent newsletter speaks of the members' intent to combine "poojas [worship] with the idea of serving the Hindu communities representing different parts of India." In their buildings they also express the union of variant Hindu forms, for the architecture combines the North and South India styles. Thus they unite elements that, in India, are usually separated in different temples. Five resident priests from India, several of whom are married and have families, conduct daily traditional services as well as special ceremonies for many families.

THE SCRIPTURES OF HINDUISM

Inasmuch as some of this literature has already been mentioned for its significance in our historical survey, we will avoid as far as possible the difficult question of dating the works by simply taking them in rough chronological order. To an orthodox Hindu, questions about date and authorship do not matter anyway, because the significant distinction is between *shruti** or "heard" and *smriti** or "remembered" writings. We therefore follow that division for our discussion of Hindu scriptures. *Shruti* and *smriti* texts are alike in being part of the sacred tradition, but they differ in certain ways.

Shruti

These works are not ascribable to specific human authors, but only to the *rishis** or seers in general, and they are considered "revelation," which is the word often used to define *shruti*, although the literal meaning is "that which is heard." They are revelation in that although they are not necessarily divine as coming from God, they are in some sense supernatural and therefore authoritative. Revelation as it is applied to the Bible of Western religions usually denotes the personal God as the source, and is directed to a particular person as the recipient, who then speaks to people for God. Hindu *shruti* is more impersonal both in the source, a generalized supernatural agency, and the human recipient, an unknown sage whose essential function is to hear "that which is heard." There are four principal divisions of *shruti* writings: the four Vedas, Brahmanas, Aranyakas,* and Upanishads.

THE VEDAS

In the narrow sense of the word, the Vedas include not all of the *shruti* literature, but only the four Vedas proper, which are usually then called the Samhitas (collections). A simple list shows the source and use in the sacrificial system of the three basic Vedas, each collection being ascribed to a different group of priests and being used in a different way in the ritual: *Rig Veda* is composed of *riks* or praises recited by the *hotri* or sacrificer. *Sama Veda* is a collection of *samas* or chants by the *udgatri* or singer. *Yajur Veda* includes *Yajus* or sacrificial formulas intoned by the *adhvaryu* or working priest. The *Atharva Veda** includes charms and spells.

THE BRAHMANAS

These were the compilations of the teachings of the different orders of priests, usually called by the traditional name of the school. Accordingly there is a Brahmana corresponding to each school, and, because each school had its own special Veda, the Brahmanas can be correlated with the four Vedic *samhitas*. The Brahmanas or treatises contain stories, etymological expositions, and comments about passages in the Vedas, in praise of the passage and against any opposing view. Out of their speculative searching came the later profound views of ultimate truth and reality, and they "evolved the interpretative scheme, regularly used later in the Upanishads, according to which things are understood in three aspects: divine, natural, and subjective."[18]

Sometimes included as part of the Brahmanas, and sometimes not even given separate mention, are the Aranyakas or "forest treatises," compiled from the meditations and reflections of those who literally "took to the woods" in pursuit of sanctity and insight in the later Vedic Age. Their main significance in our survey is their association with the forest dwellers, whereas the Upanishads are associated with the wanderers and ascetics, called *sannyasis*.

THE UPANISHADS

Western thought has tended to focus on the Upanishads as the most important and typical literature of Hinduism, because they are more abstract and universal in their appeal, less parochial and Indian, and perhaps more open to the Western mind. They also express or embody one of the basic Hindu ways of spiritual attainment, the way of *jnana* or knowledge, and this commends them to many minds. But then it should be recognized that they are not simply intellectual exercise or academic speculation, but are meant to be significant religious truth in personal and living terms. This concern is seen in the fact that the earlier Upanishads are often preoccupied with their corresponding Veda and Brahmana, trying to extract the spiritual meaning and significance from the ritual. By contrast, the later Upanishads go more directly to the doctrine, apart from the sacrificial system. The very name itself, Upanishad, expresses the practical and devotional aspect of Upanishadic thought, for the Sanskrit *upa-ni-sidati* is "to sit down with someone for something," or *upa* (near), *ni* (down), and *sad* (to sit). The name also connotes the secret or esoteric character of the teaching, which is supposed to be transmitted only to the sincere and qualified hearer. Sometimes the Upanishads are called Vedanta,* meaning literally "the end of the Vedas," in the sense of the fulfillment, the supreme truth of the Vedas. The term is later extended to apply to works of commentators and thinkers like Shankara, who came later but claim the authority of the Upanishads for their views. Although a large number of Upanishads can be listed, only about 15 are considered important enough to appear in the modern translations.

The one point of agreement among learned commentators is that it is impossible to summarize the full range of thought expressed in the Upanishads. The philosophy of the Upanishads is not a consistent development of basic doctrines, but only the repetition of certain themes, elaborations on the earlier Vedas, and speculations about an ultimate reality that is more accessible by esoteric wisdom than by sacrificial ritual. Nevertheless some salient characteristics are discernible, and the central doctrinal point is the concentration of religious meaning and transcendent reality in the absolute and ultimate, the Brahman. Whether by way of humanity itself and the deepest immanent spirituality of the human soul, or by way of the objective totality of existence which transcends and includes all specific elements, the end is the same: the One, the All, the Absolute, the Brahman identical with the One, the Self, the Soul, the Atman.

Although specific dating of separate works is not possible, there is general agreement that the *Brihadaranyaka Upanishad* is the earliest, dating from about the ninth century B.C., that the *Kena Upanishad* is near the middle, about the time of Buddha, and the latest, like the *Mundaka Upanishad*, may have appeared around the fourth century B.C. The doctrine of the transmigration of souls appears clearly in the Upanishads for the first time, coupled with the distinctive notion of *karma*. There is a development in the Upanishads toward a philosophic monism which culminates in the *Mandukya Upanishad*. This monism is combined in some of the later works—especially the *Svetasvatara Upanishad*—with tendencies toward theism and pantheism (god in and through all things) which presage the more immediate personal religious concern of later literature.

In several of the Upanishads the mystic syllable Om,* often used as a symbol of Hinduism and familiar to many Americans through the popularization of Hindu meditational techniques, is explained. Expanding the "o" to "a" and "u" together, to make "aum,"* the *Mandukya Upanishad* relates the four states of mystical consciousness to Om as a symbol for the ultimate reality and totality. It is both a visual and audible mystic symbol for the divine in Hinduism.

Smriti

The second major division of the body of Hindu literature includes works that are part of the sacred tradition but do not have so much authority as the *shruti* or revealed writings. They are described as *smriti* or "remembered" by human authors to whom in some cases they are specifically ascribed. Whereas the human agent is anonymous and passive, simply hearing the revealed wisdom of the *shruti* texts, the *smriti* authors actively "remember" the traditional wisdom embodied in their works, and many of them are

Portable altar to Sheni (Saturn), Mysore. Sheni is the most malevolent of the star deities; the bird is his vehicle; the bell is for advertising. Horizontal bidhuti *markings on the priest's forehead show that he is a Shaivite. Payment of a small fee guarantees protection against Sheni's evil influence. Anthropologists call this "apotropaic" religion. Educated Hindus deprecate this practice.*

(Ward J. Fellows)

named. We include epics, *puranas,* dharma shastras*, and *agamas** under this heading.

THE EPICS

The two epics are the *Mahabharata* and the *Ramayana*, composite works from the classic age of Hinduism. They can be compared with the Greek classics of Homer, the *Iliad* and the *Odyssey*. The *Mahabharata* is like the *Iliad* in being the story of a great conflict between two peoples, and the *Ramayana* resembles the *Odyssey* as a story of suffering in exile. In each of them the most important god character is an *avatar** (incarnation) of Vishnu: Krishna in the *Mahabharata* and Rama in the *Ramayana*. Above all, both epics are dramas of the conflict between good and evil. They are familiar to all Hindus and to people in many other parts of Asia; the *Ramayana* especially is part of the culture of Southeast Asia.

THE MAHABHARATA AND THE BHAGAVAD GITA*

As the longer work, of 100,000 slokas or two-line stanzas, the *Mahabharata* in its entirety is not so familiar as the shorter *Ramayana*, but its importance is such that it is called the fifth Veda. Covering a vast range of events and topics, the *Mahabharata* is long and complex. The story describes the background, occasion, climactic battle, and end of the war between the two great ancient Hindu clans, the Kauravas and the Pandavas, issuing in the victory (*jaya*) of the Pandavas. The section known as the *Bhagavad Gita* or "Song of the Lord" Krishna is the best-known and loved Hindu scripture. It is a kind of gospel of Krishna, in which the hero Arjuna is counseled and aided by Krishna, who is revealed in his terrible glory and yet responds to the lowliest who show him devotion. In purpose and in form it is a contrast to the theoretical and esoteric Upanishads; the author intended it as a manual of devotion in which the insights and truth of the Upanishads would be made available in warmer and more human terms. No other book, it is said, has so firm a hold on the faithful Hindu of the literate and educated classes. In it, moreover, the way to *moksha* is open to all castes, not restricted to the three upper castes or only brahmins, as it is by much traditional Hinduism. The occasion of the *Gita* section is the start of the great battle, when the two armies face each other. Leader of the Pandavas is Arjuna; his charioteer is Krishna. Sanjaya, charioteer of the blind King Dhritarashtra of the Kauravas, relates the action and the words of Arjuna and Krishna, which are the substance of the *Gita*. In Eliot Deutsch's translation, Dhritarashtra speaks: "What did the sons of Pandu and my men do, O Sanjaya, when, eager to fight, they gathered together on the field of righteousness, the Kuru field."[19]

At first Arjuna was so overcome with grief at the thought of the war between kinsmen that he told Krishna he could not fight. But Krishna chides him to follow his *dharma* (duty) as a warrior and set the battle in array: "Yield not to this impotence, O Partha (Arjuna), for it is not proper of thee. Abandon this petty weakness of heart and arise, O oppressor of the foe."[20] Arjuna is reminded of the meaninglessness of death and life in the face of the eternity of the spirit:

> He who thinks that this (soul) is a slayer, and he who thinks that this (soul) is slain; both of them are ignorant. This (soul) neither slays nor is slain.
>
> It is never born, nor does it die, nor having once been, will it again cease to be. It is unborn, eternal and everlasting. This primeval one is not slain when the body is slain.[21]

In the ensuing dialogue Krishna enlightens Arjuna about action: Act without "attachment" to the action; you are responsible for the action but not for the result. Devotion to Krishna is enjoined, but the *Gita* harmonizes the three ways: work, devotion, and knowledge.

The other great epic is the *Ramayana*, centered around the other principal avatar of Vishnu, Rama. The *Ramayana* is a simpler work than the *Mahabharata*, both intellectually and dramatically. But the total work is important for devotees of Rama, whereas it is the *Gita* excerpt that matters most in the saga of the Bharatas. The *Ramayana* is about one fourth the length of the *Mahabharata*. It tells the dramatic, moving, and deeply human story of Rama and his wife Sita,* supported by Rama's faithful brother Lakshman.* So that his father can crown another son as ruler for 14 years, Rama voluntarily goes into exile. The demon King Ravana kidnaps Sita and imprisons her in his castle. With the help of Sugriva,* the monkey king, and his general Hanuman,* Rama rescues Sita and vanquishes the demons. Restored to power, he tests Sita's virtue and finds her faithful. Rama and Sita are the ideal man and woman of Hindu culture, and Rama is adored as the embodiment of righteousness or *dharma* in his victory over vice and evil at all levels. The *Ramayana*, in innumerable forms and variations, is popular throughout India and beyond.

THE PURANAS

These are scriptures of popular Hinduism, including in their full compass a huge mass of material on many topics in 18 principal and 18 lesser *puranas*. Originally they arose as expansions and explorations of the Vedic teachings for the common people, containing mythology, cosmogony, and genealogies of gods and dynasties. In time they were augmented by miscellaneous information about places and types of worship and pilgrimage, and then by manuals of vows, devotions, and such practices. All in all they are the bible of semipopular religion, a kind of do-it-yourself manual of the richness and variety of Hinduism. The *Bhagavata Purana*, from about the ninth century A.D., glorifies Vishnu, and Shiva is the subject of the corresponding *Suta Samhita*.

THE DHARMA SHASTRAS

The works on *dharma* in the sense of law or conduct and morality first appear in the epic period around the time of Christ. The principal works are *The Laws of Manu* and Kautilya's *Artha-Shastra*. The first is the most authoritative exposition of custom and law, dealing not only with religion but also politics. Kautilya's treatise is devoted to statecraft and administration, both theory and practice, especially for monarchy, which he preferred.

LATER POPULAR DEVOTIONAL AND SECTARIAN LITERATURE

Much popular literature appeared, centered around Shiva, Vishnu, or Devi the Goddess, and in some instances associated with a philosophical school. A modern counterpart of the *puranas* are the sectarian scriptures called *agamas*. Most recent of all are numerous didactic works in English whose publication began with the nineteenth-century revival of Hindu self-consciousness.

TENETS OF HINDUISM: VARIETY IN UNITY

The oneness of Hinduism shows most clearly in the fundamental conviction, already seen in the history and literature, of inclusive and pervasive spiritual reality as the *one* ultimate nature or being of the entire cosmos. This is a unique characteristic of Hinduism in all its forms and levels and in every era, and it shapes all aspects of the religion. In the theoretical or doctrinal area it means that the primal spiritual unity of all phenomena is presupposed in all systems of thought and all forms of belief. It is explicit in the literature and the systems of thought right up to modern times. We could quote modern interpreters of Hinduism like Ramakrishna, recent contemporaries like Sri Aurobindo (1872–1950), and living pundits like Krishnamurti in a consistent affirmation of the one, ultimate, spiritual reality. As it is, we can only outline a few important theoretical expressions of this fundamental doctrine, and then turn to its manifestation in the many gods of popular Hinduism. But even the naive devotee of Kali knows that the image is not the reality and that back of the goddess there is ultimate spiritual being.

The Brahman or Absolute: The Brahman-Atman Equation

A grammatical device is helpful for the Western reader in discovering the difference between the one personal God of Biblical thought and the ultimate impersonal reality in Indian thought. The definite article "the" used before "Brahman" helps to do this; the ultimate reality and being of Hinduism is *the* Brahman. Several scholars from within the Indian tradition advocate this usage; one says: "The word *brahman* is not a proper name but is like the word Absolute. Etymologically it means 'ever-growing' (*brh* = to grow, to expand). For this reason it is right to put the definite article before it as before Absolute."[22] The same reasoning justifies use of the article before the subjective correlate of the Brahman, the Atman or Self. Together they constitute what has been called by interpreters "the Brahman-Atman equation."

THE BRAHMAN

The Absolute Being of Hinduism is one, is many, is personal, is impersonal, is everything, is nothing, is red, is green, is good, is bad, is the world, is emptiness. As the *Svetasvatara* Upanishad in a poetic version says:

> Thou art woman, Thou art man,
> Thou art the youth, Thou art the maiden,
> Thou art the old man tottering with his staff;

Thou facest everywhere.
Thou art the dark butterfly,
Thou art the green parrot with red eyes,
Thou art the thundercloud, the season, the seas.[23]

Perhaps such an array of seemingly contradictory predicates can serve to suggest to Western readers the complexity and difficulty of our task. But let us begin with the supreme reality as the one, the unity, the impersonal, the Brahman. Back to the Vedas must be our first assignment, back where the search for unity began. Often quoted is the passage from *Rig Veda* I. 164, 46: "They call him Indra, Mitra, Varuna, Agni, and he is heavenly nobly-winged Garutman. To what is one, sages give many a title: they call it Agni, Yama, Matarishvan."[24] Add to this the passage from the creation hymn that was quoted in our history section, with its implied unknown reality beyond the gods. This sense of ultimacy, primacy, the ineffable, gives to all Hindu theology its flavor of mysticism, and makes the Brahman real in spite of being finally unknown and utterly transcendent. The Brahman is first of all the ultimate fact, the ineluctable (unavoidable, inevitable) datum of the world and all experience. The idea of impersonal ultimate Being that is the source of becoming, or of the unchanging that remains when all else changes, is not peculiar to India, but the root idea has been more fully elaborated, and then incorporated more centrally, in philosophic Hinduism than anywhere else. The paradoxes are not avoided, but affirmed: "Other indeed, is it than the known, and moreover above the unknown." "It is conceived of by him by whom it is not conceived of."[25] Elsewhere it is described as beyond both being and nonbeing.

The paradoxical, absolute, impersonal, and unitary Brahman emerges in the Vedas, takes formless form in the Brahmanas and Upanishads, and is philosophically elaborated in the schools, especially the Vedanta, and by Shankara. Although the Brahman is not explained or discussed in the same way by all these sources, there are some common elements in their writings. They find that life and death are not final, because the ordinary world is changing and unreal. Krishna's reminder to Arjuna came from the *Katha Upanishad*:

If the slayer think to slay,
If the slain think himself slain,
Both these understand not.
This one slays not, nor is slain.[26]

Not even religion is true and eternal, says the *Mundaka Upanishad*, and it leaves one in the round of rebirths: "Finite and transient are the fruits of sacrificial rites. The deluded, who regard them as the highest good, remain subject to birth and death."[27] Beyond the sacrifice in all its form, and religion of all varieties, there is a reality that transcends and unifies all phenomena. Writes Shankara in c.e. 800: ". . . the entire complex of phenomenal existence is considered as true as long as the knowledge of Brahman being the Self of all has not arisen; . . . Hence, as long as true knowledge does not present itself, there is no reason why the ordinary course of secular and religious activity should not hold on undisturbed."[28] The Brahman is the essential reality, then, and the differences among phenomena are simply aspects of the absolute.

NIRGUNA AND SAGUNA BRAHMAN   We read in the *Brihadaranyaka Upanishad*:

> The form of this Person (Purusa) is like the golden colored robe, like the wool of a white sheep, like the Indragopa beetle (a red shining beetle), like the flame of fire, like the white lotus flower, like the sudden lightning. The glory of the man who knows this will be like the sudden lightning flash. Now, the instruction is: Not this, not this (neti, neti). The meaning is: There is nothing other than the Brahman.[29]

The instruction in the Upanishad is the often quoted negative side of the un-knowable Brahman, what is called *nirguna* Brahman, or the Brahman without attributes: *neti, neti.* It cannot be identified with any one specific thing, for it is beyond and includes all things. Yet it is possible and true to speak of the Brah-man with attributes, *saguna* Brahman This is a key dogma of the Vedanta by way of Shankara, whom we quote again. (He refers first to *saguna* and second to *nirguna* Brahman.)

> Brahman is apprehended under two forms; in the first place as qualified by limiting conditions owing to the multiformity of the evolutions of name and form (i.e., the multiformity of the created world); in the second place as being the opposite of this, i.e., free from all limiting conditions whatever.[30]

Nevertheless another familiar saying does ascribe three key attributes to the Brahman, and they are usually quoted in their Sanskrit form: *sat, chit,* and *ananda,** or being, intelligence, and bliss. For this formula there is no early *locus classicus*; the three are often applied one or two at a time, but not all at once, in the writings. In comparison with Western religions, the most notable feature of the threefold description is the absence of an explicit moral or ethi-cal category. As we shall see, the God of the Bible is first of all a moral law-giving deity, a righteous God of goodness. Brahman as pure cosmic Being is es-sentially beyond good and evil.

THE ATMAN

But now we must stress what is an essential feature of Hindu thought that we have not so far discussed: the doctrine that the world soul and the human soul are one. Most religions assume that there is an affinity, a relation, between the soul and God; that is, soul is what relates a human being to God. In Hinduism, however, this relation is fundamental, both in philosophical theory and reli-gious practice, for different reasons than in Western thought. In the West the soul is always part of the created order and therefore separate from and subor-dinate to God. In India God and the human soul are on the same level, of the same nature, fundamentally one. Quoting the *Brihadaranyaka Upanishad* the Hindu can say, "*Aham Brahma asmi*," "I am Brahman," that is, "I am God." My wife and I were once helped to occupy our rightful seats on the train from Gaya to Varanasi by a brahmin businessman from Bombay. In the ensuing conversation during the slow ride, the brahmin casually remarked, "After all, I am God." That was startling to a Westerner, even one who knew what he meant. The Jew, Christian, or Muslim would not dream of saying that. *But the point and purpose of Hindu religion is realization of this oneness:* To miss this is to lose Hinduism, to be ignorant of it is to be uninformed about the religious situation according to Hinduism.

An ancient story makes precisely this point; it is often quoted, but without noting that the situation of the modern reader is exactly like that of the boy in the story—he is missing the point until he learns the oneness of the human person *as a soul* with the divine person. The story is in the *Chandogya Upanishad*, where the boy Svetaketu is instructed by his father.

The young Brahmin Svetaketu returns home at the age of 24, conceited and complacent, after 12 years' study with his teacher. But his father shows him that he does not have the knowledge "by which we know the unknowable." The father, Uddalaka, tells him of the One existence in the beginning who projected the universe out of himself and entered into every being. "All that is has its self in him alone. Of all things he is the subtle essence. He is the truth. He is the Self. And that, Svetaketu, THAT ART THOU."[31] Asked to tell more, Uddakala continues: Creatures are really all one existence but do not know it; as the waters are ignorant that they are one though the rivers flow East or West, so creatures know not their oneness with the subtle essence of the world. The invisible essence of the fig tree seed gives rise to the tree and to all things; as the salt which is dissolved in water is yet there to the taste, so the Brahman is in the body as its existence. The refrain at the end of these and other illustrations is the same: *tat tvam asi*, "that thou art."

This teaching is fundamental for intellectual Hinduism, for the way of knowledge, and for the ground of popular Hinduism, *bhakti*, or the way of devotion. Its importance cannot be overestimated. The theme is stated in many forms and with variations in the Upanishads, and enters into later Hinduism as one of those truths so basic that everyone accepts it without question. Brahman-Atman are one and indivisible, two aspects of the one ultimate reality. As the Brahman, the one God is all that is objective and transcendent reality, while as the Atman or Self, the one God is the personal, subjective reality of consciousness and personality. In Western terms this is monistic pantheism: *One* idea explains and includes all things, and all (pan) is god (theism) or god is all. There are different ways of explaining and developing this doctrine in the philosophical literature of the Hindu tradition and we now turn to a brief discussion of some major thinkers and theories.

The Six Schools of Philosophy

The Six Schools of Philosophy is the usual label for six schools of thought that are not so much pure philosophical systems in the Western sense as technical religious treatises that continue and expand the subject matter and approach of the Upanishads to the goal of spiritual liberation. They are one in accepting the

Shiva and Parvati. Modern popular poster. In the foreground is a linga-yoni.

(Ward J. Fellows.)

authority of, and interpreting, the Vedas—and hence are called orthodox—and in being termed *darshanas** or intuitions of truth. In form they resemble the Western philosophical practice of one philosopher discussing the work of an earlier one, and then another discussing the second one's work on the first, and so on. In each school there is a collection of brief, aphoristic sayings called "sutras," concise statements of the Upanishad's essential meaning, assembled by compilers or formulators. There follow commentaries on the sutras that involve further glosses, exposition, modification, and development. The result is a very complex and specialized system of thought, which has many strata. Usually the six schools are paired in three sets, and are named according to the author of the sutras.

NYAYA* AND VAISHESHIKA*

Nyaya and Vaisheshika are analytic in method and atomistic in metaphysics. "Nyaya" designates that which moves toward a conclusion, logical proof as the method of knowledge; Gotama, third century B.C.E., is the author. The name of Kanada is attached to the Vaisheshika or atomistic theory.

SAMKHYA* AND YOGA*

These are paired because they accept the same doctrines of matter and spirit. Kapila's Samkhya postulates two fundamental categories of reality, *purusha* or spirit in the form of eternal individual souls, and *prakriti** or matter as the potentiality of nature for different forms of existence. Its theory of spiritual development is especially significant because it contributed to Hindu thought the doctrine of the three *gunas** or constituents of matter: purity (*sattva**), passion (*rajas**), and darkness (*tamas**). When one understands that the one's spirit is distinct from matter, one gains spiritual emancipation as a pure spiritual unit. Associated with Samkhya is the Yoga* school, and they have similar philosophical views except that Yoga accepts God, while Samkhya is agnostic, that is, does not know whether or not there is God. The Yoga system of disciplining body and mind through exercise and contemplation distinguishes it from Samkhya and forms the basis for the development of yoga* as a characteristic Indian way of spiritual attainment. (The content of Yoga is described in the section on ritual.)

MIMAMSA* AND VEDANTA

The third pair are two systems of *mimamsa* or inquiry. Their names are confusing because together they are called "Vedanta," meaning the end of the Vedas, but in actual practice it is the later or Uttara Mimamsa which is known as the Vedanta proper. The Purva Mimamsa writers are mostly atheistic, and they do not use the *Vedanta Sutra* or *Brahma Sutra* of Badarayana, which is the basis of the Uttara Mimamsa. Purva Mimamsa worked out the theory of sacrifice in such a way that the ritual was considered effective by itself, apart from the divine powers. Uttara Mimamsa or Vedanta was developed by the three great commentators Shankara, Ramanuja, and Mahdva. All three are commentators on the *Brahma Sutra* of Badayarana. In different ways they stress the underlying divine reality beyond the external world of events.

The Advaita of Shankara   Shankara lived in the eighth century A.D. His system is called Advaita or Non-Dualism because the Brahman, the eternal subject, is the inclusive and unitary reality of all things. All apparent objects or separate things, therefore, are the product of human ignorance. The Self is never to be known as manifold or different; all supposed differences come from ignorance. Knowledge gives the true and unchanging reality which is devoid of form and not in contact with anything. Moreover, it follows that there is only one Self, and spiritual liberation is to know the identity of my self with the Self. This is the knowledge way of liberation; all that is needed is for the supposedly individual soul to know that it is actually the True, the Real, the Self, and it becomes the Self. The admission, however, of levels of knowledge, and the relative reality of phenomena in the Brahman with attributes, left the way open for Shankara and his followers to practice ordinary religion in the phenomenal world.

Ramanuja's Qualified Non-Dualism or Vishishtadvaita   Vishishtadvaita is contrasted with Shankara's Advaita, of which Ramanuja, three centuries later, was highly critical. Again and again Ramanuja attacks Shankara's proofs of absolute monistic substance which depend on the assertion that all differences are a product of ignorance. He argues that there are different attributes of consciousness, and that the very discussion of different views shows that reality is affected with a difference. Rejecting a theory of threefold levels of one kind of reality which Shankara had elaborated, Ramanuja held that there were actually three different *kinds* of reality: God, souls, and matter. He says:

> The entire complex of intelligent and non-intelligent beings (souls and matter) in all their different estates is real, and constitutes the form, i.e., the body of the highest Brahman . . . The outcome of all this is that we have to cognise Brahman as carrying plurality within itself, and the world, which is the manifestation of his power, as something real.[32]

A devout follower of Vishnu, Ramanuja made room for devotion to a personal lord who was truly the Brahman. Two different ways of relating to this personal God gave rise to the two groups, known as the "monkey hold" and the "cat hold" schools. The baby monkey holds onto its mother while being held and carried, just as each soul must actively cooperate in its salvation. But the mother cat carries the kitten by the scruff of the neck, while the kitten itself does nothing; likewise the soul is delivered by God's grace, not its own effort. A comparable difference between "works" and "grace" appears in Christianity.

Madhva's Dualism, Thirteenth Century   To further emphasize the fact that *advaita* is by no means the only or the orthodox Hindu philosophical view, there is an explicit dualism, propounded by Madva. Not only is each soul distinct in nature from God, but from every other soul as well, and from nature. There are also differences among persons in spiritual knowledge, and stages or levels of salvation for souls. Both Madhva and Ramanuja were Vishnuites (followers of Vishnu) and were more anxious than Shankara had been to preserve a place for personal relation to God through devotion. The Brahman-Atman equation of the six schools and Shankara's commentary provided the form for the intellectual and religious understanding of the three upper castes in the centuries that followed. Ramanuja and Madhva provided doctrines that gave more room for devotion to the many gods of popular religion.

Forms of the Divine: The Hindu Pantheon

Not only the uneducated worship the gods; sophisticated scholars enshrine Shiva or Vishnu in their home altars, and the poet Tagore was a devotee of Kali. To them, the specific gods are but different names and forms of the ultimate spiritual reality. But there are a variety of myths that provide the popular rationale for the innumerable gods of the Hindu pantheon. No one, however, is troubled by the contrast between abstract monism and what must be technically characterized as polytheism (many gods), nor by the competition between Shiva and Vishnu, because in the end there is only the one encompassing divinity. The abstract oneness and theoretical ultimate reality and primacy of God is not what is expressed in the myths, however; it is the age-old conflict of good and evil that is the pervasive theme of the indescribable variety of Hindu mythology. Both the numinous quality and the ethical character of the godhead in Hinduism are found in the myths, where the power and might of the gods are seen in their victories over evil demons, whose terrible power is otherwise invincible. We will soon see that Vishnu comes forth for the "preservation of good" and the "destruction of evil." In that war—for such it is—the gods as champions of good can be excused for some deceit and immorality, because all is fair in war. The individual gods, moreover, and above all the images in their profusion and variety, are but soldiers or instruments in the victory of good God over evil demons. As such, they are not the ultimate reality, even for the simplest peasant, and the physical images are expendable and may be insulted or destroyed if they fail to serve the worshipper's needs. Westernized Hindus in modern temples use "idols" to denote images, for example, of the "nine planetary idols."

TRIMURTI:* THE HINDU TRINITY

The gods are many and various, but a few dominate the pantheon. What is called a trinity (Trimurti) exists, although the term is misleading when taken in its Christian sense, for the three are not "one God in three Persons," and their unity is as three aspects of the supreme divine reality. In principle, Brahma* is the creator god who functions only at the beginning of a *kalpa* to bring forth the new universe, Shiva is the destroyer, and Vishnu is the preserver. For purposes of worship these distinctions do not hold up, however. Brahma has almost no worshippers, and there are only one or two temples for him. Shiva and Vishnu are the great gods of India, far from their Vedic origins, rich in attributes and functions, celebrated in countless myths, generalized and impersonal so that various symbols and representatives are necessary to their cult.

Shiva, the Destroyer

Shiva Mahadeva* (Great God) is the richest in attributes, the most complex and many-sided divine personality of the world. The awful and terrible side of Shiva is expressed in his wildness and fierceness; he shows himself as destroyer in his liking for burial grounds and his necklace of skulls. Yet he is the ascetic, having matted hair and his body smeared with ashes. When Kama, the god of love, tried to tempt him from his meditations, Shiva consumed him with one glance from this third eye of wisdom. On the other side is Shiva Nataraja, the Lord of the Dance, who dances out the creation of the world. As the reconciliation of opposites he occasions some of the exuberant erotic temple sculpture through his male–female dualism. The explicit phallic symbol, the *linga*, or the combined *linga* and *yoni** (female symbol) of his dual nature are the usual symbols in home or temple for Shiva *bhakti*. Being so transcendent and sublime, he shows himself only through his female consorts (*shakti*).* Some devotees of his *shakti* or female energy in the *shakti* cults practiced various customs, including deliberate physical sexual union without orgasm, to symbolize the union of Shiva and Shakti, the reconciliation of opposites. The chief female consorts of this side of his personality are Kali* and Durga,* the Mother Goddess in her fearful and wild forms, and the cult is known as "left hand" Shaktism. There is a "right hand" or more conventional Shaktism of the Mother Goddess Mahadevi,* as Uma* (light) or Parvati* (daughter of the mountain). Around all these figures there is a rich collection of myths, which are familiar to most Hindus, whether or not they count themselves devotees. An interesting feature of Hindu iconography is that pictures of the deities must always be youthful in appearance; they are depicted as strikingly beautiful.

Vishnu the Preserver   The title is significant, for Vishnuities hold—contrary to the Shaivites* (worshippers of Shiva)—that nothing is destroyed, because sheer being is the only ultimate reality. Although things may change form, their essence is indestructible. It follows that Vishnu is the supreme deity, that his function is preservation, and that for this reason he becomes in effect a savior. With him there appears in Hinduism the idea of active, divine grace manifested in god-figures on earth, *avatars*, which literally means "descent" (of Vishnu) but is usually translated as "incarnation."

From the Bhagavad Gita comes a text for these appearances of the god. Says Krishna in the Bhagavad Gita:

> Whenever there is a decay of righteousness and a rising up of unrighteousness, O Bharata, I send forth Myself.
> For the preservation of good, for the destruction of evil, for the establishment of righteousness, I come into being in age after age.   *(4:7, 8)*[33]

Ramanuja articulates this Hindu doctrine of grace, and so does the *Bhagavad Gita*. (The obvious comparison is with Jesus Christ, but he is the unique Son of the Father whereas there are numerous *avatars* of Vishnu, and there are not the same doctrinal problems about the *avatar* as we will see there are for the God-man.) There is no problem about the descent of the *avatar*, for all gods move freely about the entire unitary cosmos. Nor is there a problem about the reality of the divine figures on earth, as there is for Jesus, because the essential substance of all beings is spiritual and it is the earthly figures that are in some sense lacking in full reality as compared to divine fig-

Somnathpur Star Temple, Mysore, c.e. 1268. (Courtesy, Har Bans Singh)
(© Pramod Mistry/Dinodia Picture Agency, Bombay, India.)

ures. Hindu gods do not blink or sweat; and their feet do not touch the ground.

The iconography of Vishnu gives him four arms, usually carrying the four symbols: conch shell, mace, discus, sword or bow; blue is his color; his vehicle is the eagle-winged Garuda.* His character is above all that which tradition assigns him as preserver and a lover of righteousness.

Lakshmi* or Sri, his principal wife-consort, is subordinate to him in conventional fashion; as the goddess of prosperity and good fortune she is honored in many households. But it is through his two great avatars that he is known and worshipped. Of them, Krishna is the more complex, being not only the charioteer of Arjuna, but also the lover of Radha* and the cowgirls *(gopis)*,* symbolizing the union of the soul with god. In many scenes his childhood, like a Jesu bambino, is depicted, and the best-known image is that of a graceful flute player. His worship in temples also produced beautiful erotic images as symbols of the divine act of love uniting soul with god. The other principal *avatar* is Rama. He and his wife Sita, known and loved for their romantic idyll, are the ideal man and woman of Hindu culture, pure and faithful and righteous. They appear on innumerable modern devotional posters, often with Hanuman, the monkey god. Of the two avatars, it is Krishna who is enshrined in most of the thousands of Vishnu temples, which are found in all parts of India, where he is often portrayed as the supreme god, with Brahma, seated on a lotus, issuing from Vishnu's navel. The "Hare Krishna" movement found in the United States is a modern expression of devotion to Krishna.

OTHER GODS AND GODDESSES

Another popular god, Ganesha,* a son of Shiva and Parvati, has the head of an elephant. One account of how he acquired the elephant head tells that as a boy he was guarding the door while his mother Parvati bathed, with orders to admit no one. When Shiva came home he was so enraged at being told he could not enter that he cut off Ganesha's head. Then, moved by Parvati's grief, he substituted the only available head, which happened to be that of an elephant. Many armed, Ganesha is the remover of obstacles, and is invoked at the beginning of any undertaking. A modern cult god of the first order is Surya, the sun god, invoked three times daily by practicing Brahmins. Other gods are Kubera* of wealth and Kama of love; Vedic gods who survive in name at least are: Indra, Agni, Yami, Vayu,* and Varuna.

SHAKTI: THE FEMALE ENERGY OF THE GODDESS

The female deities, forms of Mahadevi the Mother Goddess, are important as the focus of the third great *bhakti* movement, Shakti *bhakti*. Some of them have been mentioned as consorts of the great gods, but they are goddesses in their own right. The patroness of learning, wisdom, and song, the gracious Sarasvati,* Brahma's wife, is honored early in each year. Durga is worshipped as a beautiful ten-armed woman who stands on the buffalo demon whom she has slain. Kali acquired a taste for blood when she had to drink the blood of a demon she had speared, to prevent the blood from reproducing him. However, devotional posters still show her black and nude with a necklace of heads, standing on Shiva's inert body to show that without the exuberant *shakti* Shiva is powerless. Uma or Parvati has been mentioned as Shiva's wife; a legend about her voluntary death on a sacrificial fire in defense of Shiva's dignity was used to justify the practice of widows dying on their husbands' funeral pyres. The English term, "suttee," for this practice was from *sati*, virtuous woman; the custom has long been officially outlawed.

Since the 1980s there has been a movement of scholarship directed to the Goddess in her innumerable forms; at the same time, new female gurus and goddess figures have arisen in India. A key work in this development is an anthology on Rahda and the cowgirls, the Preface of which sets the contrast with the "patriarchal" *trimurti* of Brahhma, Shiva, and Vishnu.

> Yet even as this formula was being articulated, Brahma's actual position was tenuous, and as Hindus of later centuries reflected on their tradition they deleted him from the trinity and filled his place with what had been omitted: the Goddess. They ranked her power (*sakti*) alongside that of Visnu and Siva. . . . The special nature of the hegemony of the Goddess (the very terms, biased toward hierarchy, seem inadequate: "supremacy," "hegemony") forces us to rethink the range of roles she plays in Hindu religion.[34]

That is too large an order for us to fill, but we should at least confront the general question of sexuality in Hindu religion.

Any intelligent Westerner who looks at Hindu art, or travels to India, or even reads this book realizes that Hinduism has its own form of that universal, pervasive human factor. A distinction useful for stating the situation appears in studies by women scholars. They locate the problem for a patriarchical culture in the very *sakti* (power) of the female. As consort, wife, or even sexual partner in tantric customs, the woman is rendered tractable and benevolent by *dharma*. But the goddesses, independent and heroic in their own right—for example, Durga killing the buffalo demon—are uncontrolled and hence potentially dangerous. This ambivalence attributed to female nature is expressed in rules of *dharma*. One scholar says:

> Alongside the negative cultural valuation of sexuality and menstruation embodied in the fact that sexual intercourse renders one impure, and that a menstruating woman is impure and treated like an untouchable, there is a positive valuation. This positive valuation is expressed by the term *auspicious*. . . .[35]

This analysis and term help us to understand the place of the Goddess in Hindu religion: auspicious, inauspicious, or both. In her conclusion, Marglin writes:

> At the beginning of this essay I spoke of the power of life that females possess in the Hindu world; I might more accurately speak of the power of life and death. This power, called *sakti*, in its benevolent aspect covers all that is called auspicious and in its malevolent aspect all that is called inauspicious. But we are confronted by a single process, which in its unfolding may be positively or negatively valued or even both at times.[36]

The World

The external world does not matter to Hinduism in theological terms, for—whatever it is—it differs from the ultimate spiritual reality which does matter. Sir Charles Eliot writes: "It is remarkable that Indian thought, restless and speculative as it is, hardly ever concerns itself with the design, object, or end of the world."[37] The reason is that the world is born, not made or created out of nothing like the Western Biblical world. The absolute source does not "create" a separate world in the sense of Western Biblical creation; rather, as pure and unitary *Being* it *becomes* something discrete and specific, it manifests itself as the empirical world, the context for separate selves. Philosophical Hinduism has a kind of personal God for this purpose, who appears in the literature: Ishvara,* the Lord, a personal God correlated with *saguna* Brahman, Brahman with attributes. In popular and mythological terms the creator is Brahma. From some primal stuff, or from a worn-out universe thrown in the cosmic salvage bin, a new world is brought forth by Brahma the Creator, according to the *puranas*. Hence Hinduism does have a chronology, for in time the world is born and dies, and begins again, in cycles, just like human souls but on a vaster scale. It is a cyclical or "pulsating" universe. Derived from the *Vishnu Purana*, the accepted time scheme says four *yugas* or ages constitute a *maha yuga*.

The years of different *yugas* vary, but a *maha yuga* includes 12,000 divine years, each one 360 human years in length, a total of 4,320,000 years, constituting a single cosmic cycle. A thousand of these make a *kalpa*,* 4,320,000,000 years, when there is a great dissolution and re-creation. We are living in a fourth or *kali yuga*, when righteousness has been reduced to one fourth of the virtue prevailing in the first or golden age; it is a time, therefore, of extreme human wickedness and misery. But when it ends the *krita yuga* of gold will return. There is also a mythology of space in Book II of the *Vishnu Purana*, and popular religion assumes there are three worlds, the earth, the sky of the stars, and the infinite heavens.

Mythology supplies myths for other major natural phenomena, which enter into ritual practices of the common people. Each god has a particular animal as his vehicle, the best known being Nandi,* the white humped bull of Shiva. In fact almost nothing in the world has escaped the omnipresent religious meaning that Hinduism brings to all phenomena as part of the one great inclusive God reality.

Perhaps the most persistent, erroneous generalization about Hinduism as a whole is that it considers the world as nothing but *maya* or illusion. In the *Rig Veda*, *maya* means "supernatural powers" or "artifices," while the Upanishads develop the *maya* or cosmic illusion doctrine of the world as the projection out of Brahman the illusion-maker. In terms of Advaita, the world is illusory because people take it as real apart from Brahman, when in truth the only reality is Brahman, and therefore anything that is treated as *separate* reality is, as such, illusory. In Shankara's view, *maya* arises from *avidya** or ignorance. He classifies knowledge as higher knowledge, of Brahman, and lower, *avidya*. For those who do not have the higher knowledge of the unity of the *atman*, the phenomenal world is real. Furthermore, Shankara defines two kinds of existence corresponding to the two kinds of knowledge: empirical and metaphysical existence. Empirical existence is real to the empirical self, and as a fact of consciousness the phenomenal or empirical world has a kind of existence for everyone. But those with higher knowledge know that only the One is real, all is Brahman. On the other hand, the world is not unreal to the multitude of followers of Samkhya and Ramanuja. The usual metaphor for the evanescence of appearances is the waves of the ocean, which ebb and flow from the one body of water, which remains ever the same. Note that the waves are dependent on, or are a manifestation of, the water, but not the reverse. Smoke and heat arise from the fire, depend on it, are real while they exist, but are not the lasting fire which produces them. Such figurative views of the nature of the empirical world are quite general.

The Human Situation

For all Hinduism, everything is held to be subject to the fact or reality of *samsara*, the round of endless life and death of all sentient beings. The *Maitri Upanishad* asked: "In this sort of cycle of existence (*samsara*) what is the good of enjoyment of desires, when after a man has fed on them there is seen re-

Brahma, Somnathpur Temple, C.E. 1268.

(Ward J. Fellows)

peatedly his return here to earth?"[38] This idea entered into Indian thought as a presupposition, an aspect of the world which everyone accepted, so that elaboration and defense of it were not deemed necessary. Let an authority speak of the contrast with Western religion:

> What most sharply distinguishes Hinduism, like its offshoot Buddhism, from the religions of Semitic origin, is its unquestioning acceptance of the doctrine of rebirth, reincarnation, or the transmigration of souls. Of this there is no trace in the Samhitas or the Brahmanas, and it is only when we come to the Upanishads that we first meet with this doctrine which was to become central to all Hindu thought.[39]

This discussion of *samsara* leads to the religious situation of humans in the world. The Westerner counts himself or herself unique, God's chosen among all his creatures, but the Hindu knows himself or herself as but one of many forms of life in the universe. The Upanishads declared that the vital essence in a human is the same as that in an ant, a gnat, an elephant, the three worlds, the universe. Then they said that this essential Atman is spiritual, that it is the same as the Brahman, and different from the empirical self. According to the Vedanta analysis, the human *atman* or self has three levels or aspects: the "gross body" or physical, separate, human body; the "subtle body," the total accumulated traits of individual character and personality; and the *atman* or soul proper, the eternal and unchanging spiritual reality of each individual as part of the total ultimate and universal Atman. At death the gross body is sloughed off, but the subtle body, which is bound by its *karma*, "transmigrates" across the borders of life and death and is reborn in another physical body. Only when one attains *moksha* (liberation) is one also delivered from the subtle body, and the *atman* is not reborn because it has merged with the one universal *Atman*. A simple diagram is sometimes used to illustrate this model of the self:

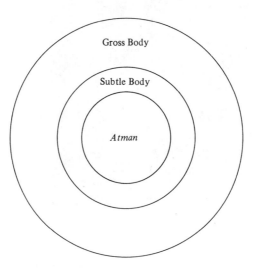

KARMA—THE SPIRITUAL BALANCE SHEET

What holds one in the cycle of transmigration is *karma*, literally action. The basic idea of moral responsibility is familiar in Western religious thought, but the way in which it works is peculiar to Indian thought. The familiar aspect of *karma* is that it is a law of moral cause and effect. Nothing could be more familiar to a person reared in the Judaeo-Christian tradition: Human acts have moral consequences; there are laws of God that apply to human actions; good acts bring good consequences and evil acts bring evil effects, sooner or later, to the doer. What is different about *karma* is the method or context of its operation—it operates as an ineluctable law of spiritual economy for one soul from one life to the next. Reborn souls come into the world laden with past *karma*, good or bad, and accumulate more *karma*, which is added to their balance for the next life. (Swami Shraddhananda of the Vedanta Society compares *karma* to trading stamps—for good deeds you get good stamps.) *Karma*, therefore, determines one's rebirth and hence one's caste. People are what they are, in personality and character as well as social caste, according to their past *karma*.

MOKSHA—THE GOAL OF SPIRITUAL LIFE

If all souls are held in *samsara* by *karma*, then the goal of spiritual life is *moksha*, freedom, liberation, or deliverance. Negatively, therefore, *moksha* is deliverance from *samsara* and *karma*; positively, it is attainment of union with or in God. Once again, the oneness of Hinduism is seen in the unifying force of a single spiritual goal for all beings, not just human beings but all sentient existents (existing beings), oneness with and in the absolute spiritual reality. This oneness served to unify the many gods, and it also unites the different ways to God in worship and the different ethical practices.

HINDU WAYS TO GOD

The religious life of the Hindu is directed to *moksha* as the inclusive religious goal. Therefore the aim of all Hindu worship and ritual is *moksha*, and the different forms of worship and service to the gods are but different ways to the one goal. Ancient scriptures and modern teachers agree that the different paths, including different faiths, all lead to God, just as winding rivers flow at last into one wide sea.

The Four Margas: Different Ways to One Goal

There are four standard Hindu paths or ways (*margas*) of religious life: *jnana marga*,* the way of knowledge; *karma marga*,* the path of works or performances; *raja yoga**, the way of discipline; and *bhakti marga*,* the way of love and devotion to a god.

JNANA MARGA—THE WAY OF KNOWLEDGE

Jnana marga is the way of attainment by intellectual means to the realization of oneness with the Brahman, as in *vedanta*, or to pure spirit of Samkhya. It is the characteristic way of the intellectual and professional classes.

KARMA MARGA—THE WAY OF WORKS

Karma marga or the way of action includes external acts like giving and observance of religious duties as part of one's *dharma* or duty in life. People

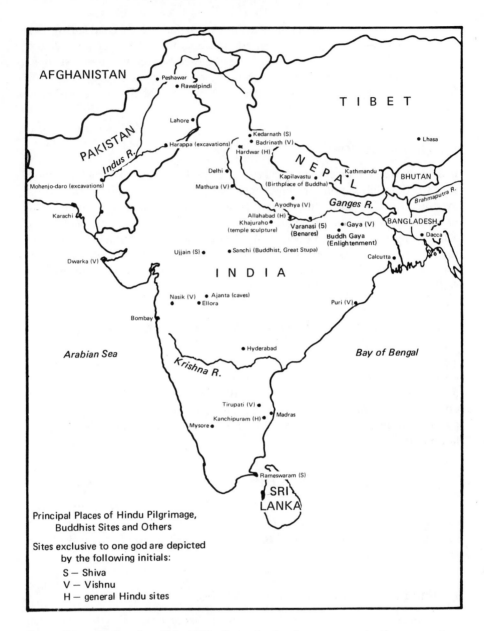

AFGHANISTAN

• Peshawar
• Rawalpindi

T I B E T

PAKISTAN

Lahore •

• Kedarnath (S)
• Badrinath (V)
Hardwar (H) •

• Lhasa

Harappa (excavations)

Indus R.

N E P A L

Delhi •

Kathmandu

BHUTAN

Kapilavastu
(Birthplace of Buddha)

Mohenjo-daro (excavations)

Mathura (V) •

Ganges R.

Brahmaputra R.

Ayodhya (V)

Karachi

Allahabad (H)
Khajuraho •
(temple sculpture)

Varanasi (5)
(Benares)

• Gaya (V)

BANGLADESH

Buddh Gaya
(Enlightenment)

• Dacca

Ujjain (S) •

• Sanchi (Buddhist, Great Stupa)

Calcutta •

Dwarka (V) •

I N D I A

Nasik (V) •
•

• Ajanta (caves)
• Ellora

Puri (V) •

Bombay •

Arabian Sea

Krishna R.

• Hyderabad

Bay of Bengal

Tirupati (V) •

Kanchipuram (H) •

• Madras

Mysore •

Rameswaram (S)

SRI
LANKA

Principal Places of Hindu Pilgrimage,
   Buddhist Sites and Others

Sites exclusive to one god are depicted
   by the following initials:
   S — Shiva
   V — Vishnu
   H — general Hindu sites

from all *varnas** and walks of life, from the businessperson to the peasant or laborer, may and do follow the way of works.

RAJA YOGA*—THE WAY OF DISCIPLINE

The discipline of mind and body is developed in the various systems of *yoga*. The word "yoga" is from the root *yuj*, meaning to join, yoke, or harness, but the term generally denotes certain methods used for attaining the desired unity with the Absolute. Sometimes all four ways are called *yogas*, and then what is known in the West as *yoga* is termed *raja yoga*. It includes elements of asceticism that go back to the forest dwellers of the Vedic age, and perhaps is Dravidian (pre-Aryan) in origin, as *tapas*, austerity. Yogic practices include mental discipline, prolonged meditation, and the extreme physical control and discipline of the body in *hatha yoga*. In the latter, breath, posture, and muscle control are used as means to attain immediate apprehension of reality in supersensuous states of mind. The classic literary and philosophic formulation of yoga theory and discipline is in the *yoga sutra* of Patanjali.[40] He gives the eight steps to *samadhi*,* trance or superconscious state. Abstention (1) and observance (2) are ethical prerequisites for practicing yoga; posture (3) and breath control (4) are aids to concentration and serenity of mind. *Hatha yoga** is the expansion of (3) and (4). The last four are the specific stages of: abstraction (5) or withdrawal of the senses from the objects; fixed attention (6) of mind on a specific thing; contemplation or meditation (*dhyana*) (7) leads to concentration (*dharana*) (8). The fulfillment is *samadhi* or yoga proper, when the self realizes its pure and eternal nature.

BHAKTI—THE WAY OF DEVOTION

Bhakti, stressing devotion to a god, is the most popular and varied path. But followers of the other ways may also include devotion to a chosen deity (*ishtadevata**). The focus of *bhakti* as adoration is Bhagavan,* the adorable, a god to whom adoration is directed, and the term *bhagavata** (devotee) is used in all the *bhakti* schools of Vishnuism. Practicing and popular Hinduism includes, therefore, a multitude of personal gods, some of which have been mentioned. Because in most instances devotion to the god is the devotee's only way of worship, we will be outlining, in effect, the *bhakti* pattern of faith, love, commitment, and service to a god or gods, which is characteristic of Hinduism.

Bhakti (from the root *bhaj*—to participate in or share) is not the same as the Vedic sacrifice, for both the outward acts and the inward intention are different. The cults of the images began as Vedism declined, developed in the years from about 500 to 1200, and assumed their modern form in the medieval period under the Muslim empires. There are two clues to the rationale of the enormously varied and constantly changing patterns of *bhakti*. First, in accordance with Hindu concern to escape to the timeless realm of the gods, the aim of the individual worshipper is realization and experience of her underlying unity with the gods. The seventeenth-century poet Tukaram wrote: "Step by step he supports me: . . . I have found an assured place in him, and the world I have left void . . . In this mortal world I have joined the pervading spirit."[41] Second, the pattern of worship is set by the god. The Hindu's main idea of worship is that each god is to be worshipped in accordance with the god's own wishes, because whatever the command of the god is, it must be on his or her terms that one experiences the delicious rapport. However, neither of these principles provides any objective criteria; hence new customs proliferate and personal variations within the prevailing culture pattern are possible. In practice, the operation of iconographic and liturgical traditions provides stability and conformity for the countless variants of deities and festivals.

PUJA*

There are different methods and levels of devotion, but the principal expression of *bhakti* is *puja*, what we would call worship, and it is directed to the image of the god. It is the central point of external religious activity, and is an individual experience even when the worshipper is in a crowded temple or at a great festival. The educated Indian, at least, would say that the image is but a symbol and a means to an end, and the adoration of the formless is what is expressed. The diversity and variety of *bhakti* are enormous, and there is very little organization or custom to provide regularity except for the calendar, which determines festivals, feast days, auspicious occasions, and propitious moments. The sheer amount of religious activity is staggering to a Westerner, because it includes in some way almost everything.

Puja in the home is in a room reserved for that purpose if possible, with an image or symbol in the shrine, perhaps a *yantra* or *mandala*—a mystic symbol or design—for those who use it. Fire and water will usually be used in the *puja*, the image being anointed with water or *ghee*,* and perhaps offered food, with flowers and leaves, which, as Krishna said in the *Gita*, by themselves are effectual when brought with devotion. For the devout who have the freedom to do so worship begins at dawn, after which there is ceremonial sprinkling and sipping of water on the river bank or in the Puja room, with breath exercises, prayers, repetition of the Gayatri, and so on. At midday there are more prayers and offerings to the Lord. In the evening there is a simpler procedure on the same order. Five offerings each day are prescribed, to the gods, *rishis*, forefathers, lower animals, and guests. Perhaps only few people fulfill the full list of such obligations, but the partial outline suggests how much is expected of the upper caste devout. In practice, and for the lower castes, *puja* is simpler, but at least some gesture of performance will usually be made each day.

There is a temple in each town, and hundreds of them in the city, of course differing in size and splendor. Usually temples are chiefly devoted to one of the two great gods. The image is the center of the temple *puja* and is bathed and dressed ceremoniously each day, offered food and flowers, sung to, and perhaps carried in a procession. The temple may also serve as a dormitory for pilgrims and devotees; anyone may stay for three days. People prepare themselves for worship by ablutions, food restrictions, body postures, and other practices, all part of ritual purity, which is a preoccupation of the Hindu at all times.

FEASTS AND FESTIVALS

Durga is the focus of a nine-day celebration in October, and Divali, the festival of lights, comes about the same time. Krishna's birthday falls during an August–September fortnight, and Rama's on a movable date in March or April. Holi, in honor of Kirshna, is another spring festival. Local celebrations abound.

PILGRIMAGES

Instead of listing pilgrimage times and places, we would like to give readers some idea of the flavor of a pilgrimage through a specific example. The following excerpts are taken from a vivid, century-old description of the Car Festival of Jagganath,* at Puri, Orissa, sacred to Vishnu under his title of Jagannath, the Lord of the World. (A car for a god or goddess is an elaborately decorated platform on wheels; such cars are used in all kinds of religious celebrations in India.) Pilgrims of all castes flock there, because caste divisions were traditionally disregarded in the worship at the great temple built in the twelfth century A.D. All year pilgrims travel hundreds of miles to Puri, but they inundate it for the Car Festival, when the images are carried about the city. The English word "juggernaut" is derived from the inexorable movement of the car, but the passage refutes the idea that devotees deliberately committed suicide under the wheels.

> For weeks before the Car Festival, pilgrims come trooping into Puri by thousands every day. The whole district is in a ferment. By the time the great car has risen to the orthodox height of forty-five feet, the temple cooks make their calculations for feeding 90,000 mouths. The vast edifice is supported on sixteen wheels of seven feet diameter, and is thirty-five feet square. The brother and sister of Jagannath have separate cars a few feet smaller. When the sacred images are at length brought forth and placed upon their chariots, thousands fall on their knees and bow their foreheads in the dust. The vast multitude shouts with one throat, and, surging backward and forward, drags the wheeled edifices down the broad street towards the country-house of lord Jagannath. Music strikes up before and behind, drums beat, cymbals clash, the priests harangue from the cars, or shout a sort of fescennine medley enlivened with broad allusions and coarse gestures which are received with roars of laughter by the crowd. And so the dense mass struggles forward by convulsive jerks, tugging and sweating, shouting and jumping, singing and praying, and swearing. The distance from the temple to the country-house is less than a mile; but the wheels sink deep into the sand, and the journey takes several days. After hours of severe toil and wild excitement in the July tropical sun, a reaction necessarily follows. The zeal of the pilgrim flags before the garden-house is reached; and the cars, deserted by the devotees, are dragged along by the professional pullers with deep-drawn grunts and groans. These men, 4200 in number, are peasants from the neighboring fiscal divisions, who generally manage to live at free quarters in Puri during the festival. . . .
>
> In a closely-packed eager throng of a hundred thousand men and women, many of them unaccustomed to exposure or hard labour, and all of them tugging and straining to the utmost under the blazing tropical sun, deaths must occasionally occur. There have doubtless been instances of pilgrims throwing themselves under the wheels in a frenzy of religious excitement. But such instances have always been rare, and are now unknown. At one time several unhappy people

were killed or injured every year, but they were almost invariably cases of acci-
dental trampling. The few suicides that did occur were for the most part cases of
diseased and miserable objects, who took this means to put themselves out of
pain. The official returns now place this beyond doubt. Indeed, nothing could be
more opposed to the spirit of Vishnu-worship than self-immolation.[42]

The chief pilgrimage place for Shiva *bhakti* is the banks of the Ganges river at
Varanasi (Benares), for the Ganges is his river, although Vishnu claims the
heavenly source. Varanasi is the most holy of the seven sacred cities, and
everyone has seen pictures of the bathing and burning ghats or great stone em-
bankment steps which line the Ganges there. A typical myth accounts for the
power of the river to wash away sins. Once Shiva, angered because Brahma
grew a fifth head to prove his superiority, cut off the head of Brahma. But
Brahma is a brahmin, and to kill a brahmin is a heinous sin, so Shiva was forced
to roam the world seeking deliverance from his guilt and from the head which
he carried in his hand. When he bathed in the Ganges at the site of Varanasi his
sin was forgiven and he was delivered from carrying the head, so he decreed
that the city and temple to be built there would be his own residence. To die
there and to have the corpse cremated on the burning ghat and the ashes
thrown in the river bestows *moksha* on the soul of the dead.

Rural and village life, which means the life of most of India, has its own
rhythm of worship, ruled by the seasons and crops. Family and private ceremonies are saved up for times when work is light. In a typical village in central
India, *bhakti* includes a number and variety of observances throughout the
year. The examples that follow give only a brief sampling. The Nine Goddesses
(Naudanga) are worshipped on nine nights at the end of September and first of
October, with the principal village festival of Naumi (ninth) on the ninth day.
On Naumi homage is paid at all the 44 shrines in this typical village of about
1,000 people—including the shrine of the Smallpox Goddess, the Shaivite and
Vishnuite temples, the Lord of the Village Gates (east), and the shrine of Gane-
sha as patron of blacksmiths.[43]

Special personal or family observances include *shradda** rites for deceased
parents, which are performed once a month for a year after death. There are
sacramental occasions for birth, and for "taking the thread" or religious initiation for boys of the three upper castes, and for marriage and death.

Of formal religious organization there is almost none. Nevertheless, there
are three principal divisions of temples and worshippers, corresponding to the
three chief gods: Shiva, Vishnu, and Shakti. Usually, each temple is principally
devoted to one of the three, although there may be side altars to the others. Individual Hindus, likewise, usually count themselves as devotees of one of the
three for their personal worship and devotion: Shaivites, Vishnuites, and Shak-
tas* (devotees of Shakti). Vishnuites mark their foreheads with white lines in
the form of a "V"; the mark of Shaivites is three horizontal white lines on the
forehead. Thus, in effect, there are three divisions of Hindu worship, in spite
of the fact that there are no formal organizations or structures, but only customs and conventions, corresponding to the three.

Celestial couple, Vishnu and Lakshmi. Kandariya Mahadeva Temple, Khajuraho.

(Ward J. Fellows)

RELIGIOUS PERSONAGES

Although priests are associated with every temple, they do not constitute a hierarchy or have any special status. The priest and his assistants are in charge of the technical aspects of the temple worship and are responsible for the regular *puja* ceremonies. Usually they are householders, but sometimes the priest is a *sadhu* (holy man) who has settled down. Some families will have their own priest, or hire one for special occasions, and such priests are not looked down on. But neither they nor the temple priests are given special honor or privileges. Some priests are brahmins, but many are from lower castes.

A *guru* is a teacher, a personal spiritual instructor. A *sadhu** is a more general term for a holy man of no specific order, while a *sannyasi* is above all a renunciate who is following some specific discipline. The *swami* is associated with a religious order by formal ties and vows, and the term usually denotes one who has attained formal ordination of some kind. Many holy men, *gurus*, *swamis*, and *yogis** from India are found today in the United States, practicing and promoting their form of meditation or way of deliverance. They vary, of course, in the type as well as the authenticity of their spiritual life and message.

ETHICAL AND SOCIAL ASPECTS OF HINDUISM

Where shall we find the ethical component of Hindu religion? It has been pointed out earlier that the Hindu divine, unlike the ethical monotheism in the Judaeo-Christian Bible, does not include a specific morality. So whence is goodness, what are good and evil, in the One which is all of Hinduism? The poet of the British Empire, Rudyard Kipling, wrote about "the road to Mandalay, where the flying fishes play" as a place "where there are no Ten Commandments." That has led some Westerners to conclude that there is no morality there, which is a mistake. They think that the only possible basis for morality is the commandment of God, because that is the basis in the Bible. Ethics are an important part of life in India, in spite of there being no Ten Commandments. They permeate the culture and are not separated from other mores. There is no word for "religion" in Hindi, because religion is not a separate compartment but pervades all of life. The whole of religion is concerned with conduct, because it is more a way of life than a doctrine about the divine or a system of ritual.

In its ethical and social institutions the oneness of Hinduism is again the key to understanding it: Whatever carries you toward the One spiritual-God-reality is good, and whatever carries you away from God is evil; that is, whatever aids you to reach *moksha* is right, and what hinders you from *moksha* is wrong. This formula is not to be found in so many words, but it is the logical and existential heart of Hindu morality. It serves to explain the classic story of the holy man in 1857 who, in echo of *tat tvam asi*, said calmly to the British soldier who bayoneted him, "And thou also art He." And it explains the sect of Thugs who once made ritual murder, human sacrifice, to Kali, until the larger *dharma* for all was invoked to end the practice. Ritual murder and acceptance of violent death, strange as they may seem to Westerners, were part of *dharma* for those Hindus. And thus at the end there is one word to epitomize religion in India—*dharma*. Sometimes Hinduism is referred to as *Sanatana Dharma*, eternal *dharma*. The *Mahabharata* is called a *dharma shastra** (lawbook) because it includes much about the duties of each level of society and serves as a traditional ethical guide.

True Life for All Hindus: *Dharma*

In this final section the oneness of Hinduism is to be found in *dharma* as the good way of life for every person according to his or her station. Here is a definition of *dharma* from a book written by Hindus: "Righteousness, duty, law, the path which a man should follow in life; one of the four ends of man."[44] It connotes the general ideas of honesty, decency, respect, and care for others, responsibility and duty which are incumbent upon all persons regardless of their position in society. But in addition *dharma* is what is expected of you in your specific situation or place, as a soul among souls seeking spiritual freedom or at least a better life and higher caste in your next reincarnation. There is a striking parallel with the Greek word *dike*. Just as *dike* or justice was the good way of life for the members of the different orders in Plato's *Republic*, so *dharma* is in Indian society. As Plato's justice provides a formula that is adaptable to each level of his society, so *dharma* provides a flexible standard of duty that applies to different people and different circumstances. It is a kind of early form of "situation ethics," in which one's individuality, career, and circumstances are factors in determining what is proper for each person in a given context. This solves, for example, dilemmas such as some idealistic Western young people face when there is conflict between various personal and social responsibilities and commitment to some form of radical political or religious cause. The *ashramas** distinguish between the householder's responsibilities and the *sannyasi's* renunciation; in Hinduism, not all are called to renounce the world. Both the life of renunciation and the way of "action without attachment" taught in the *gita* are open to a Hindu. There are, moreover, four different and acceptable goals in life. We deal now with these two sets of four specific ethical norms, but first we discuss caste, because a person's caste largely determines his or her *dharma*.

CASTE

First, what is caste, religiously speaking? Caste is the ancient religiously based system of social stratification in India. It is theoretically based on *karma*, because *karma* determines one's level at birth; one is born into a certain caste, the same as one's parents, depending on one's previous *karma*.[45] There are myths that explain and justify caste. The "Hymn to Purusha" in the *Rig Veda* (X. 90) says that from the sacrifice of, and by, Parusha were born the castes: his mouth, the brahmin; the kshatriya,* his two arms; his two thighs, the vaishya*; and the shudras,* from his feet.

The general structure looks like this: the brahmins, the smallest and top caste, enjoy many privileges and bear heavy spiritual responsibilities; they are usually educated, and often found in the professions, banking, and so on. Traditionally they were the priestly caste, but of course they are not now all priests by occupation. Second are the traditional warriors and nobility, the kshatriya. There are perhaps twice as many of them as the brahmins and they have customarily occupied positions more managerial and military than professional or academic. The vaishya are traditionally small shopkeepers, farmers, clerks. These three are the "twice born" who are expected to begin study of the Vedas under a teacher, at a certain age depending on their caste.[46] At that

Pilgrimage procession, Kanchipuram. Sri Ekambaranadhar Devasthanam, Shaivite, Temple. The occasion is celebration of the healing from disease of the boy with garland. The loin-clothed priest or sadhu in the center is in charge, probably from the village.

(Ward J. Fellows)

time they "take the thread," which is literally a loop of string, worn over the left shoulder and hanging diagonally across the body and down to the right of the waist, except as changed for a few special occasions. Fourth are shudras, the many millions of laborers of all kinds, traditionally forbidden to study the Vedas. But what has created the problem for India is the existence of millions of outcasts, pariahs, or untouchables, in the old vernacular. Theoretically, they must literally not come near the higher castes. For example, they may now enter temples in Calcutta, but although twice-born castes present their offerings at the altar in person, untouchables must hand them to the priest for presentation, while they stand outside the railing around the sanctuary. In the image given by Ghandi and new laws they are *harijans*, God's children, but customs change slowly.

The actual structure is much more complex, with most lower caste Hindus finding their place in an elaborate and detailed system of subcastes according to economic function or job. In this complex picture, caste really means subcaste, of which there are thousands. The four major traditional class levels are more accurately labelled *varnas* (from color) and operate through the subcastes. The term *varna* points to the probable origin of caste in the color pattern of Vedic times, the Aryans being lighter skinned than the indigenous Dravidians, or Dasyus as they were contemptuously termed. Now, however, it is only *jati* or birth that determines caste, and there is no absolute correlation between *varna* and color. In sociological terms, Hindu caste displays four characteristics: (1) *jati*, birth, one's parents, determines one's caste; (2) one's occupation or job choice is limited by one's caste; (3) commensality or eating only with members of one's caste level is practiced; (4) endogamy, marriage within the caste, is expected.

The religious aspect of this situation comes from the sanction provided by sacred custom and tradition through the operation of *karma* as the supposed explanation for one's caste. One's level of society at each rebirth has been determined, according to the theory, by one's past *karma*, hence each person is morally responsible for his or her own present status. Thus there is no social-moral problem raised by the inequities of social stratification at birth. Only on this basis can India's almost unanimous acceptance of the *varnas* be explained. The theoretical religious use of caste is that if one follows one's *dharma*, one will be reborn in a higher caste, and the higher castes have greater moral restrictions and more exacting religious duties. The brahmin who fulfills his *dharma* can expect to attain *moksha*. Hence the members of the lower castes hope to be reincarnated in a higher caste. The ambiguities and injustices in operation of the caste system expose it to much criticism, but traditional Hinduism still accepts and defends it.

The Four *Ashramas*

The literary or scriptural substance of what can be called the formal Hindu ethical system developed during the classical period. Embodied in popularized verse form, the norms are called *dharmashastras*, the best known being *The Laws of Manu* from which we will be quoting. Another part of *smriti* literature which indirectly provides ethical ideals are the epics, the *Mahabharata* and the *Ramayana*.

From *The Laws of Manu* came the four orders or *ashramas*:

"The student, the householder, the hermit, and the ascetic, these (constitute) four separate orders." (VI. 87)[47] *The Laws* specifies the age at which a boy is to begin his study of the Vedas under a teacher, following rules of chastity and obedience. When he has studied three Vedas, or two, or even one, and kept the rules, "having bathed, with the permission of his teacher, and performed according to the rule the rite on returning home, a twice-born man shall marry a wife of equal caste who is endowed with auspicious (bodily) marks." (III. 4)[48] Manu recognized the economic dependence of the three other orders on the householder, which is therefore the most excellent. But "when a householder sees his (skin) wrinkled, and (his hair) white, and the sons of his sons, then he may resort to the forest,"[49] with or without his wife. Last of all, ". . . having passed the third part of (a man's natural term of) life in the forest, he may live as an ascetic during the fourth part of his existence, after abandoning all attachment to worldly objects."[50]

Manu's explanation of a person's duties is arranged according to the four castes, much of it in terms of what kinds of work one may engage in without suffering ritual defilement or even losing caste. Manu writes only about males. He considers women as a separate category of being, for whom he legislates after he has dealt with the castes. Two apparently contradictory rules about

Nandi, Chalmundi Hill, Mysore. With Shaivite priest and devotees.

(Ward J. Fellows)

women appear in *Manu*: "Women must be honored and adorned by their fathers, brothers, husbands, and brothers-in-law, who desire (their own) welfare."[51] There are other provisions like this one: "In childhood a female must be subject to her father, in youth to her husband, when her lord is dead to her sons; a woman must never be independent" (V. 147).[52] Yet Indian women enjoy many freedoms and have much influence in both family and public life.

The Four Goals

Another system of ethical norms, apart from the obligations of one's stage in life or one's caste, are the four traditional accepted aims or goals of life (*purushartha*): *dharma, artha,* * *kama, moksha*. The four are not mutually exclusive; *dharma* applies all through life, *artha* and *kama* must not be pursued without regard for *dharma*, while *moksha* is the final goal for all.

DHARMA

Dharma is usually named first. In the context of the four *purushartha*, the more general sense of moral duty and obligation in terms of virtue, honesty, righteousness is denoted by *dharma*, in contrast to the more specifically religious aim of *moksha*. It is in the epics that the highest literary expression of *dharma*, beyond the lawbooks, is found. In each of them exalted ideals of human conduct are expressed in dramatic and moving language. The epic legends are part of Indian culture, so that the most illiterate villager knows them, along with the traditions of his local gods. Many Indian films depict the lives and adventures of the gods, and thus this modern art form is able to utilize traditional items of the culture in a meaningful way. The goatherd can discuss with the carpenter (same subcaste) how well the movie actress played Sita.

ARTHA

Providing a place for legitimate worldly concerns is *artha*, the second goal, the science of material gain or profit. It is embodied in literature like Kautilya's *Artha Shastra*, sometimes described as a treatise on diplomacy and politics.

KAMA*

In third place comes *kama*, the pursuit of love and pleasure. The *Kama Sutra of Vatsayana*, a discussion of sexual enjoyment, has become familiar in the United States. Sexuality in Hindu religion is a symbol for the union of opposites in spiritual reality. The full range of physical pleasure is recognized, while love is also spiritualized as devotion to the god. India also produced aesthetic speculation and theory, and there is Hindu love poetry in Sanskrit of great beauty.

MOKSHA

We have already suggested that *moksha*, the fourth end, expresses the most fundamental and inclusive Hindu spiritual goal, as a culmination or fulfillment of the other three. Although the fruits of the other three, even of *dharma*, are transitory, *moksha* is not simply endless but timeless, even beyond or out of time.

Ethics in Practice

The saint who attains *moksha* has gone beyond the pull of the gravity—as it were—of *karma* and *samsara*, into the timeless realm where worlds begin and end. When Pandit Nehru, who had guided nationalist India before and independent India after her freedom, died, he was cremated on the Shanti Ghat (The Steps of Peace) on the bank of the Jumna at Delhi. Although in his personal life Nehru was a secularized Westerner, that did not matter to the people. In his life he stood for political freedom, and in his death he attained spiritual freedom. Such is the faith of Hinduism, and it was expressed by the multitudes who witnessed his final liberation from the bonds of physical and transitory phenomena. As the flames from the sandlewood pyre rose into the air, the more than a million mourners cried out "*Panditji amar rahe*" (Panditji has become immortal).

Nehru was associated with quite a different kind of Hindu, Mahatma Ghandi, whose tomb is not far from Nehru's. Being asked, near the end of his life, what he considered the essence of Hinduism, Ghandi said that all of Hinduism was contained in the first verse of the *Isha Upanishad*, which he translated in these words:

> All this that we see in this great universe is permeated by God.
> Renounce it and enjoy it.
> Do not covet anybody's wealth or possessions.[53]

Ghandi's life work, second to the struggle for independence, was rehabilitation of untouchables and removal of the injustices of caste. It was fitting—if one may use the word in the context—that he was killed by a member of a fanatical orthodox Hindu sect opposed to change. When he was struck down, his last words were: "Ai, Ram; Ai, Ram."[54] That is to say, "O, God; O, God."

SUMMARY

Hinduism is the religion of India, and our clue to understanding it is "oneness," the spiritual oneness which unifies a varied subcontinent of 700,000,000 people. The present religion has a 4,000-year history beginning with Aryan invaders who brought their gods with them and introduced new elements into the ancient culture. After 500 B.C.E., out of the interaction of new and old, came a religion with both one single, eternal, spiritual reality known as Brahman, and many individual gods with particular and more or less limited characteristics and powers. This religion was first articulated by seers or *rishis*, whose writings, known as the Vedas, provide the basis for later doctrines and speculations. It was administered by a priestly group called brahmins, who became the top level in a social system of grades, levels, or "castes." The basic writings, theories, gods, and practices of this essential Hinduism were established by C.E. 500, although there continued to be developments and refinements of the basic pattern. An extensive sacred literature accumulated, based on the Vedas, which were explained and amplified theoretically in the Upanishads. Two great epics, the *Mahabharata* and the *Ramayana*, expressed the more specific traditions and customs of the faith, and complex systems of technical religious speculation and philosophy were developed.

Fundamental to Hindu belief about the world and the divine powers is the conviction that one inclusive and pervasive eternal spiritual reality supports and extends throughout all temporal events and separate beings, including gods and human beings. This reality is Brahman, and the essence of religion is to know that all people, including oneself, are *atman* (self or soul), identical with the objective, spiritual, absolute Brahman. There are, however, many individual gods. The principal ones are: Shiva the destroyer, known usually through his female consorts (*shakti*) or the phallic symbol of his power; and Vishnu the preserver, known mostly in his *avatars* or incarnations Krishna and Rama.

The religious problem or situation of humanity is created by the fact that all soul entities, and thus human souls, are continually reborn after death, in a new physical body, by a process of transmigration. This cycle of rebirth, called *samara*, is maintained through *karma*, a law of spiritual action. *Karma* serves as a spiritual balance sheet which has determined one's present status of being and thus caste, and works to determine one's future birth. The aim of religion, therefore, is to attain *moksha*, which is both freedom or liberation from the rounds of *samsara* as well as the attainment of one's true oneness with and in the absolute spiritual reality of Brahman.

There are four different *margas* or ways toward *moksha*, and these constitute the framework for different customs of Hindu ritual and worship. One may elect to follow the way of knowledge, works, yoga, or devotion. The last, *bhakti* or devotion, provides the substance of most Hindu worship (*puja*) at temples and shrines. There are various occasions for public festivals, pilgrimages, and celebrations, and the obvious personal occasions such as marriage, which are marked by religious ceremonies. But in all of these ways, customs, and occasions there is one aim or goal: *moksha*, spiritual freedom through union with the one divine and universal absolute spiritual reality.

The oneness of Hinduism in ethical and social terms is provided by *dharma*, the law of righteousness and duty for every person according to his or her circumstances. Inasmuch as the point of *dharma* is the one, same end or fulfillment of *moksha*, it serves to guide all people toward the realization of human spiritual nature in union with the divine spiritual reality. Whatever carries you toward *moksha* is right and good, and vice versa. Under *dharma* fit the caste system of four *varnas*: brahmin, kshatriya, vaishyu, and shudra; the four *ashramas*, stages or orders of life; and the four goals (*purushartha*), each of which is a legitimate ethical guide and rationale.

NOTES

1. A. K. Ramanujan, *Speaking of Shiva* (Hammondsworth, England: Penguin Books, 1973), pp. 20, 21.
2. Robert E. Hume, *The Thirteen Principal Upanishads* (Oxford: Oxford University Press, 1972), p. 241.
3. Ibid., p. 39.

4. E. M. Forster, *A Passage to India* (New York: Harcourt, 1924; Modern Library ed., n.d.), p. 145.

5. Ibid., pp. 147, 149.

6. Lin Yutang, ed., *The Wisdom of China and India* (New York: Random House, 1942; Modern Library ed., n.d.), p. 3, 4.

7. Herman Oldenberg, *Sacred Books of the East,* Part II, Vedic Hymns (Oxford: Clarendon Press, 1897), XLVI, 1.

8. A. Barriedale Keith, and Albert J. Carnoy, *The Mythology of All Races,* Vol. VI, *Indian and Iranian,* Louis H. Gray, ed. (New York: Cooper Square Publishers, 1964), p. 85.

9. *Rig Veda*, III, 62:10.

10. It is possible to construct a creation myth from scattered references in the *Rig Veda.* See Jack Finegan, *Archeology of World Religions* (Princeton: Princeton University Press, 1970), p. 23.

11. A. A. Macdonell, *Hymns of the Rig Veda* (London: Oxford University Press, n.d.), p. 19.

12. R. T. H. Griffith, *The Hymns of the Rig Veda,* Vol. II, 3rd ed. (Benares, India: E. J. Lazarus, 1920-26), p. 498.

13. Edward J. Thomas, trans., *Vedic Hymns, Wisdom of the East* (London: John Murray, 1923), X, 121:10.

14. R. C. Zaehner, *Hinduism* (New York: Oxford University Press, 1966), p. 41.

15. Thomas, *Vedic Hymns,* X, 90:16.

16. The common American spelling is used for the caste.

17. Theodora F. Carroll, *Women, Religion, and Development in the Third World* (Philadelphia: Praeger, 1983), p. 36.

18. V. Raghavan, in *The Religion of the Hindus,* Kenneth W. Morgan, ed. (New York: Ronald Press, 1933), p. 407.

19. From *The Bhagavad Gita,* trans. Eliot Deutsch (New York: Holt, Rinehart and Winston, 1968), p. 29.

20. Ibid., p. 36.

21. Ibid., p. 39.

22. P. T. Raju, in *The Great Asian Religions,* Wing-Tsit Chan et al., comps (New York: Macmillan, 1969), p. 31.

23. Swami Prabhavananda and Frederick Manchester, trans., *The Upanishads, Breath of the Eternal* (New York: New American Library, 1948), p. 124.

24. Griffith, *Hymns,* I, 164:46; vol. I, p. 227.

25. Hume, *The Thirteen Principle Upanishads,* "Kena Upanishad," pp. 335, 337.

26. Ibid., "Katha Upanishad," II: 19; p. 349.

27. Prabhavananda and Manchester, *The Upanishads,* p. 44.

28. George Thibaut, trans., *The Vedanta Sutras,* SBE (Oxford: Clarendon Press, 1896), XXXIV, Part I, p. 324.

29. Wing-Tsit Chan et al., comps., *The Great Asian Religions* (New York: Macmillan, 1969), p. 47.

30. Thibaut, *The Vedanta Sutras,* Part I, p. 61.

31. Prabhavananda and Manchester, *The Upanishads,* p. 69.

32. Thibaut, *The Vedanta Sutras,* Part III, pp. 88, 89.

33. Deutsch, *The Bhagavad Gita,* p. 55.

34. John Stratton Hawley and Donna Marie Wulff, eds., *The Divine Consort: Radha and the Goddesses of India* (Boston: Beacon Press, 1986), p. xi.

35. Frederique Appfel Marglin, "Female Sexuality in the Hindu World," in *Immaculate and Powerful*, Clarissa W. Atkinson et al. (Boston: Beacon Press, 1985), p. 40.
36. Ibid., p. 55.
37. Sir Charles Eliot, *Hinduism and Buddhism*, vol. I (New York: Barnes and Noble, 1934), p. 46.
38. Hume, *The Thirteen Principal Upanishads*, p. 413.
39. Zaehner, *Hinduism*, p. 57.
40. See Sarvepalli Rhadhakrishnan and Charles A. Moore, eds., *A Source Book in Indian Philosophy* (Princeton: Princeton University Press, 1973), pp. 467ff.
41. Fraser and Maratha, "The Poems of Tukaram," in *A Primer of Hinduism*, J. N. Farquhar, ed. (London: Oxford University Press, 1912), p. 141.
42. W. W. Hunter, *Orissa* (London: Smith, Elder and Co., 1872), pp. 132-134.
43. Adrian C. Mayer, *Caste and Kinship in Central India* (Berkeley: University of California Press, 1960), pp. 100ff.
44. Kenneth W. Morgan, ed., *The Religion of the Hindus* (New York: Ronald Press, 1953), p. 407.
45. For a scriptural explanation of the relation between caste and karma, refer to *Garuda Purana*, Chs. 113, 115.
46. Refer to *Laws of Manu*, II, 36.
47. G. Buhler, trans., *The Laws of Manu*, SBE XXI (Oxford: Clarendon Press, 1886), p. 214.
48. Ibid., p. 75.
49. Ibid., p. 198.
50. Ibid., pp. 204-205.
51. Ibid., p. 85.
52. Ibid. (V.147), p. 195.
53. Zaehner, *Hinduism*, p. 180.
54. "Ram" is the modern vernacular for Rama.

Topics and Questions for Study

1. Trace the development of the present Hindu religion, showing how the nature gods brought by Aryan invaders fit in with older elements and gods of a different kind, to produce a new blend.
2. What is the relation between the many gods and the primal reality, Brahman, and how do they differ from the one God of monotheism?
3. Discuss the nature of the soul as divine, yet caught in the world and time. How does it unite with absolute Brahman, and how do the different Hindu philosophies explain these things? Why can the Hindu say "I am God"?
4. Describe the different strands of Hindu sacred writings. What instructions do they give for becoming godlike?
5. Comment on the private or individual nature of Hindu worship. What does one do in *puja* (worship)?
6. Outline the various different ways to God, and describe the friendly competition among gods and their worshippers over which god helps most.
7. What is the religious basis and function of the caste system, and why is it one of the two essential dogmas of Hinduism?

8. Where do you find the moral or ethical aspect of Hinduism? Why do Westerners have a hard time locating it?
9. Discuss sexuality in Hindu religion: How and why does it differ from Western religion's treatment of human sexuality?
10. What is the one word for the one religion with such bewildering variety and seemingly strange customs?

USEFUL BOOKS

Babb, Lawrence A. *Redemptive Encounters: Three Modern Styles in the Hindu Tradition.* Berkeley: University of California Press, 1986.

Basham, A. L. *The Wonder That Was India.* New York: Grove Press, 1959.

Dimmitt, Cornelia, and J. A. van Buitenen. *Classical Hindu Mythology, A Reader in the Sanskrit Puranas.* Philadelphia: Temple University Press, 1978.

Eck, Diana L. *Darsan: Seeing the Divine Image in India.* Chambersberg, Pa.: Anima Books, 1985.

Hawley, John Stratton, and Donna M. Wulff, eds. *The Divine Consort: Radha and the Goddesses of India.* Boston: Beacon Press, 1986.

Kiriyanna, M. *Essentials of Indian Philosophy.* Bombay: George Allen and Unwin, 1973.

Kinsley, David R. *Hinduism: A Cultural Perspective.* Englewood Cliffs, N.J.: Prentice Hall, 1982.

Knipe, David M. *Hinduism.* San Francisco: Harper and Row, 1991.

Klostermaier, Klaus K. *A Survey of Hinduism.* 2d ed. Albany: State University of New York Press, 1994.

O'Flaherty, Wendy Doniger. Introd. *Hindu Myths.* Hammondsworth: Penguin Books, 1978.

Radhakrishnan, Sarvepalli, and Charles A. Moore, eds. *A Source Book in Indian Philosophy.* Princeton: Princeton University Press, 1957.

Sen, K. M. *Hinduism.* Hammondsworth: Penguin Books, 1969.

GLOSSARY

An approximate pronunciation of some words is given in parentheses following the word, using a simple phonetic system without any technical devices, and with no claim to expert accuracy. Accent is not noted, but the rule of thumb is to accent the last long syllable, or the antepenult (third from the end) if there is no long syllable.

advaita (ud vie tah): Non-Dualism or monism, especially that of Shankara

agamas: a series of later Hindu scriptures

Agni (ugh nee): Vedic god of fire

ananda (ah nun duh): bliss, joy, or happiness; an appellation of Shiva used in names of teachers

Aranyakas (ah ran yah kahs): "forest books," Vedic speculations about sacrifice

artha: material wealth and prosperity; one of the four goals

ashramas (ahsh rum uhs): the four stages of life: student, householder, hermit, wanderer *(sannyasi)*

asuras (ah sur uhs): earlier, spirits of natural forces; later, Vedic demons

Atharva Veda (ah tarh vuh vay duh): fourth part of the Vedas; charms and incantations

Atman (aht mun): the Self, subjective correlate of the Brahman

Aum: expanded form of "OM" mystic syllable, which see

avatar: "descent" or incarnation of a god in the world

avidya (ah vid ya): ignorance, especially about the self and world

Bhagavad Gita (bug uv ud ghee tah): "Song of the Lord"; popular favorite part of the *Mahabarata*

Bhagavan (bah guh vun): "the adorable One"; any god of *bhakti* worship

bhagavata (bah guh vuh tuh): devotee, especially of Vishnu as Krishna

bhakti (buk tee): religious devotion to a deity

bhakti marga: the way of devotion, as one of four ways to deliverance

Brahma (bruh may): the creator God of the Trimurti

Brahman (bruh mun): earlier, the sacred prayer word-knowledge-power; later, the Absolute, Ultimate Reality, Spiritual Being and Principle

Brahmanas (brah mun uhs): *shruti,* Vedic, priestly books of sacrificial ritual

Brahman-Atman: combining form of Absolute as objective-subjective Self

brahmin (brah min): member of the top ("priestly") caste now used in English

darshana: view of life or system of thought; one of the schools of thought

deva (day vah): Vedic divine being

dharma (dhar muh): righteousness or duty, following cosmic moral order; one of the four goals

Durga: a female form of Shiva; the Distant One

Ganesha: god with elephant head, son of Shiva and Parvati.

Garuda (gah ru duh): bird god, vehicle of Vishnu

Gayatri Vedic prayer to the sun

ghee (ghee): made from butter by melting it and pouring off the liquid, which is the ghee

gopis (go pees): cowgirls, lovers of Krishna in Bhagavata Purana

gunas (goo nahs): "qualities"; three elements of matter: *sattva, rajas, tamas,* which see

guru (goo roo): spiritual teacher, qualified by insight

Hanuman: monkey hero (not the god) of the Ramayana, although a deity of popular Hinduism

hatha yoga: extreme physical discipline system of spiritual deliverance

Indra: Vedic god of war and storm

ishta-devata (eesh tah deh vuh tuh): the chosen, personal god for *bhakti*

Ishvara (eesh vuh ruh): "Lord," hence Brahman as personal

Jagannath (jug un uth uh): the image of Krishna in the temple at Puri; "Lord of the World"

jnana (jnah nuh): true knowledge of supreme reality

jnana marga: one of four ways of deliverance, by knowledge of reality

Kali (kah lee): the "dark" or "black" and fierce form of Mahadevi the Mother Goddess

kalpa: an aeon or cycle of creation and destruction of a universe

kama: love, pleasure, sensuous enjoyment; one of four goals

karma: the law and record of moral action and consequences

karma marga: the way of "works," one of four ways of deliverance

Krishna: one of two chief avatars of Vishnu

kshatriya (kshah tree yah): traditional military and ruling group, second of the four castes (varnas)

Kubera (koo bare uh): god of wealth

Lakshman (luck shumhn): brother and companion of Rama in the *Ramayana*

Lakshmi (luck shmee): consort of Vishnu and goddess of wealth and good fortune

linga: phallic symbol for Shiva

Madhva: philosopher, thirteenth century, school of dualism *(dvaita)*

Mahabharata (mah hah bah rah tah): epic which includes *Bhagavad Gita*

Mahadeva: "the Great God," title of Shiva

Mahadevi: the "Great Goddess," "Mother Goddess," personification of Shiva *shakti*

marga: path, way, or method of salvation

maya (mah yuh): illusion, phenomena as misunderstood in human ignorance

Mimamsa: one of the six schools of philosophy

moksha (moke shah): emancipation or liberation from the bonds of phenomena, *samsara,* and rebirth, one of the four goals

Nandi: sacred bull, vehicle of Shiva

Nyaya: one of the six schools of philosophy

Om (ohm): the most holy mantra or sacred sound, symbolizing the gods and Vedas, and embodying all sounds

Parvati: gracious and pure consort of Shiva

Prajapati (pruh jah pah tee): "Lord of creatures," in the Vedas a creator god

prakriti (prah krrih tee): matter, ultimate primal stuff of the cosmos; contrasted with *purusha*

puja (poo jah): worship of the image of any deity

purana (puh ran uh): "old," one of the divisions of *smriti* literature, popular religious lore

purusha (puh roo shah): consciousness, subject as contrasted with objective matter *(prakriti)*; cf. Purusha, cosmic person of the Vedas

purushartha: the four permissible goals or ends of human life

Radha (rahd huh): queen of the cowgirls, Krishna's *shakti*

rajas (rah jus): one of three *gunas,* namely, active power, passionate quality

raja yoga: one of the four ways of deliverance: by discipline

Rama (rah muh): one of two chief avatars of Vishnu; hero of the *Ramayana*

Ramanuja (rah mah noo jah): ca. 1100; philosopher; qualified Non-Dualism (Vishish-tadvaita)

Ramayana (rah mah yuh nuh): the epic poem about Rama; "Adventures of Rama"

Rig Veda: the first division of the Vedas; stanzas of praise

rishi: sage, seer of truth recorded in the Vedas

Rudra (roo druh): Vedic storm god, precursor of Shiva

sadhu (sahd hoo): "leading to the goal"; general term for a holy man

samadhi (sum ahd hee): concentration; in Yoga, the eighth and final stage

Sama Veda (sah mah vay dah): third of the Veda collections

Samkhya (sahm khyah): one of the six schools of philosophy

samsara (sum sah ruh): the cycle of transmigrations through successive rebirths

sannyasi (sun yah sih): one who has renounced the world and entered the fourth phase of life as a wandering ascetic

Sarasvati (sar ahs vah tee): goddess of wisdom and learning, and wife of Brahma

sat-chit-ananda (saht cheet ah nahn dah): the Absolute as being, intelligence, bliss

sattva (suht twa): one of three *gunas;* pure quality

Savitar: the sun

Shaivite (shy vite): follower of Shiva

Shakta (shuk tuh): devotee of Shakti

shakti (shook tee): female power or force of a god; the Mother Goddess as personification thereof; consort of a god, especially Shiva

Shankara: ca. 800, philosopher, Non-Dualism, *advaita*

shastra: a book of divine authority, especially a law book

Shiva (she vuh): member of the Trimurti, usually called "the Destroyer"

shraddha: rite in memory of ancestors

shruti (shroo tee): "heard" literature, sacred or canonical as divinely derived

shudra (shoo druh): lowest of the four castes *(varnas)*, mostly laborers and peasants

Sita (see tah): wife of Rama

smriti (smree tih): "remembered" literature of sacred tradition

soma: a hallucinogenic plant, used in Soma ceremony

Soma: Vedic god of *Soma* sacrifice

Surya: Vedic sun god

Sugriva (soo gree vah): king of the monkeys, who befriended Rama; Hanuman was his prime minister

tamas (tah mus): one of three *gunas*; dark quality, heavy, dull

tapas (tah pus): austerity, practiced as means to deliverance

Trimurti: the triad Brahma, Shiva, Vishnu treated as one

Uma (oo mah): goddess of light; another name of Parvati, consort of Shiva

Upanishads (oo pun ish uds): fourth division of *shruti* literature; philosophical and mystical

Vaisheshika (vie sheh she kuh): one of the six schools of philosophy

Vaishnavite (vie shnuh vite): worshipper of Vishnu

vaishya (vie shya): third rank of caste *(varna)* levels; merchants, artisans, farmers

varna: one of four major classes or castes

Varuna (vah roo nuh): Vedic sky god

Vayu (vah yoo): Vedic wind god

Veda (vay duh): "knowledge"; basic *shruti* literature; primary corpus of Vedic literature

Vedanta (ved ahn tuh): "end of the Vedas"; applied to teaching of the Upanishads, especially Shankara's *advaita*; one of the six schools of philosophy

Vishnu (veesh nu): one of two major deities of modern Hinduism, usually designated the "Preserver"

Yajur Veda (yah joor vay duh): second division of four Vedas, sacrificial formulas

yoga: "yoke" or union with God; a discipline as means to that union

Yoga: one of the six schools of philosophy

yogi: one who practices yoga

yoni: stylized symbol of female genitals

Chapter 4

BUDDHISM

Head of Buddha. Thailand, seventh century A.D.

OUTLINE

I. Buddhism is a family of religious traditions deriving from Gautama Buddha, who lived in India during the sixth century B.C.E., who attained enlightenment by his own efforts, and who showed others the way. Over the centuries three major divisions developed.

   A. Hinayana follows the earlier discipline for monks in the monastery as the true path, with lay persons helping then, and is now found in Southeast Asia.

   B. The Mahayana developed other means of enlightenment which allowed all people, and not just monks, to enter on the path to Nirvana, the Buddhist goal. They are now mainly in Japan, since the suppression of religion in China.

   C. A later variation of Mahayana is the Vajrayana of Nepal and Tibet.

II. The scriptures of the three main divisions differ markedly.

   A. Hinayana uses the "three baskets" of early sermons, stories, and so on.

   B. Mahayana writings develop Buddha theory and metaphysics.

   C. The Vajrayana has its own "thunderbolt" writings.

III. The beliefs of Buddhism are presented in a twelve-point "catechism" as a way of covering the varying doctrines. Some of the twelve are:

   A. In place of God there is Buddha. Three major views or kinds of Buddha can be described:

      1. Human Buddhas like the historical Gautama.

      2. Bodhisattvas, who have the Buddha nature and are entitled to enter Nirvana, but who defer doing so in order to teach others.

      3. Cosmic Buddhas, who are like God in their "cosmic" significance and nature and in actively helping people toward Nirvana.

   B. Buddha's way is a "middle way" between pleasure-seeking and self-denial.

   C. The fourfold truth about life is that there is suffering; it comes from desire; thus, to end suffering, end desire; and to end desire follow the eightfold path.

IV. The goal of life and of religious practice, and hence worship and ritual, is to overcome *karma*, escape from *samsara* and rebirth, and attain Nirvana. There are various ways to do so, but meditation is the basic method of overcoming the desire and ignorance which keep us from Nirvana.

   A. In Hinayana this is done by monks in the monastery.

   B. Mahayana has a program for anyone to seek enlightenment by moral life, study, and contemplation.

V. Buddhist ethical and institutional life is guided by the *dharma* of the Buddha and motivated by desire to promote and share his enlightenment.

   A. In Hinayana the monks follow a stricter rule than the laity.

   B. Japanese Mahayana has three major divisions expressing different solutions to the problem of how to attain enlightenment:

      1. The way of faith in the Amida Buddha who brings believers to his Pure Land.

      2. Nichiren's adherence to the *Lotus* scripture brings enlightenment.

      3. Zen is the way of supreme determination and disciplined meditation as the way to "do it yourself."

VI. Recent developments in Japan, China, and Tibet since the Cultural Revolution of the 1980's, especially China after Tiananmen Square 1989 and in the 1990's.

INTRODUCTION

Buddhism is the Western name for the complex of religious faith and practice which derives from the historical Gautama Buddha, born a Hindu in the sixth century B.C.E. Both in doctrine and organization it is a universal religion, including adherents in most countries of Asia and now finding a ready ear among many in the West. Estimates of the number of practicing Buddhists range upward from about 200,000,000, but millions more are touched by Buddhist culture. Such wide diversity in beliefs and customs exists among the various national and doctrinal divisions that the unifying factors are hard to find, and the three major branches are often studied and described separately. In keeping with our attempt to stress the basic factors of the religions we study, we will not emphasize the divisions, but the fact that they differ in many respects must be recognized at the outset.

Buddha is the central symbol and reality of Buddhism, because he embodies the way of thinking and living which is common to the various branches of Buddhism, namely, an analysis and description of human existence as conditioned by desire and ignorance, and a method for attainment of spiritual freedom through voluntary human effort. Giving this ancient faith new appeal in the West is the rediscovery of the human situation as limited and conditioned, in contrast to the confident autonomy of Western women and men for hundreds of years—a confidence which is now rapidly vanishing. Buddhism is a twofold faith: On the one hand it describes the human predicament in existential terms, and on the other it offers a rational method of spiritual freedom through human insight, effort, and—in some of its branches—faith.

ORIGIN AND DEVELOPMENT OF BUDDHISM

The Buddha

What Buddha looked like, no one now knows. Does it matter? Not to the Buddhist. Buddha images are stylized symbols, not realistic portraits, and we must be content with the traditional image both in the literal physical sense and the biographical. Scholars recognize and accept the fact that the description of the founder of any religion is to some extent an interpreted and official version; so it is with Buddha. It does not mean that there is necessarily any deliberate distortion or falsification in the picture, nor are we required to search for some kind of pure, original, true life. We can and do distinguish among different strands in the tradition and evidence, but all of the records and legends are relevant to what the religion makes of the founder, which is our concern. No matter who tells the story, however, it should be understood that the scriptures do not give us a clear and continuous "life of Buddha" in the modern sense.

The human figure whom we have been discussing was born in India, the traditional site being near Kapilavastu* in the northeast, now included in Nepal. The exact date is a problem; modern scholars say 567 or 563 B.C.E., although a few Buddhist traditions date the birth in the seventh century B.C.E. Born into the aristocratic Sakya tribe of the Gautama clan, Buddha's father was a kshatriya nobleman or king named Suddhodana, and his mother was Queen Maya. However, tradition makes Buddha not simply a human being who originated the religion, but a divine preexistent personage who came to earth. According to this view, therefore, he was not properly Buddha, the awakened or enlightened (from *budh-ta*, past participle of "awake"), until after he achieved enlightenment. Before that he was a Bhodisattva,* a being destined to be a Buddha. As such, his antecedents are traced through various legendary predecessors, and he himself had vowed to be a Buddha in aeons past, when as the brahmin Sumedha he saw Dipamkara, his twenty-fourth predecessor, who proclaimed of him:

Behold ye now this monk austere,
His matted locks, his penance fierce!
Lo! he, unnumbered cycles hence,
A Buddha in the world shall be.[1]

BIRTH AND EARLY LIFE

The conception and birth stories are found both in the sacred books of the earliest Buddhists and in some later traditional texts. According to them there was

---

*Terms followed by an asterisk at their first appearance are defined in the glossary at the end of the chapter.

a supernatural conception, somewhat comparable to the Virgin Birth in Christianity, in which the Buddha himself, as a superb white elephant, "walked around his mother's couch, with his right side toward it, and striking her on her right side, he seemed to enter her womb. Thus the conception took place in the Midsummer Festival"[2] In precisely the correct number of months the delivery took place, his mother standing up and the child, "flashing pure and spotless, like a jewel thrown upon a vesture of Benares cloth," was received on a golden net held by four angels. His given name was Siddhartha;* Gautama was the family name; Sakyamuni denoted him as sage of the Sakya clan. In due time he became Buddha, the Aware, Awake, or Enlightened One.

Of the child various signs and portents were reported, principally a warning to his father that if Buddha saw the "four signs" he would forsake his aristocratic position and retire from the world when he was 35. Although legend enhances the luxury in which Prince Siddhartha was reared, there is little doubt that he enjoyed the privileges of a kshatriya family of rank. Thus in due time he came to maturity, married, and enjoyed the luxuries and amusements with which his father surrounded him in order to circumvent the seer's prophecy. Nothing, however, could prevent the fulfillment of his vow, made ages before, that he would be a Buddha, and the gods themselves arranged the signs for him to see as he drove his chariot in the park: "a decrepit old man, a diseased person, a dead body, and a monk."

RENUNCIATION

Deeply moved in his spirit by these things, by a divine messenger, and by the appearance of the palace dancing girls in their exhausted sleep, "some with their bodies wet with trickling phlegm and spittle; some grinding their teeth, and muttering and talking in their sleep; some with their mouths open; and some with their dress fallen apart so as plainly to disclose their loathsome nakedness,"[3] he resolved to go out. Although his wife had given birth to a son, Rahula ("impediment"), he paused only to look at them, and went out in the spirit of Indian renunciation, accompanied by his charioteer and on his horse, both of whom he soon sent home.

The scriptures next tell how Gautama sought instruction from two gurus but found them no help; then for six years of terrible austerities he tried the way of asceticism and self-torture of the flesh, likewise to no avail. At last he gave up these methods, determined to use what food he needed to learn the secret of life, and resolved "Let my skin, my sinews, and bones become dry, and welcome! and let all the flesh and blood in my body dry up! but never from this seat will I stir, until I have attained the supreme and absolute wisdom."[4] The tree under which he sat is called the *bodhi** (wisdom) tree; a lineal descendant of it now grows in the same spot, by the temple erected there. With his back to the Bo-tree and facing east, he sat down "cross-legged in an unconquerable position." The *Jataka*,* from which we have been quoting, recites the temptations by the god Mara* and his army, all of whom Buddha

Prag Bodhi, the Mountain of Austerities. Seen from the banks of the Nairanjana River near Buddh Gaya, India.

(Ward J. Fellows)

vanquished that same day. A later source, Ashvagosha's *Buddhacarita, The Acts of the Buddha*, reports the enlightenment itself the same night, the Buddha having put himself into trance, in four stages during the four watches of the night, the date being full moon of the month Visakha (April–May).

ENLIGHTENMENT

In the first watch, the recollection of his own series of successive births and that of others led him to the conviction of the insubstantiality of this world of *samsara*. With the heavenly eye that he acquired in the second watch he surveyed the world and saw that rebirth depends on *karma* and that no resting place is to be found in this insubstantial world. He saw the causes of the round of life and death, gained knowledge, passed through the eight stages of insight, and became tranquil in the third watch. When he reached the state of all-knowledge in the fourth, the whole world rejoiced with him. He stayed under the tree in what is called the Bodhi-Seat seven weeks while he considered and decided to transmit his truth to the bright, uncomprehending world. At the Mahabodhi temple in Buddh Gaya, India, which marks the throne (Vajrasana) of the enlightenment and is a place of Buddhist pilgrimage, there are seven holy places matching the seven weeks Buddha spent there.

The hymn that the Buddha uttered then expressed his joy at having discovered the source of this illusory world of misery, in terms startling to the Western mind when it is realized that he is speaking of sentient existence:

O builder! I've discovered thee!
This fabric Thou shalt ne'er rebuild!
Thy rafters all are broken now,
And pointed roof demolished lies!
This mind has demolition reached,
And seen the last of all desire![5]

Less startling are other utterances, from the *Buddhacarita*, which expressed his purpose and the point of Buddhism. To a medicant (beggar holy man) who recognized him as enlightened and asked who was his teacher, the Buddha voiced the Buddhist insistence on your own effort:

> Quite by myself, you see, have I the Dharma* won. Completely have I understood what must be understood, though others failed to understand it. That is the reason why I am a Buddha . . . Having myself crossed the ocean of suffering, I must help others to cross it. Freed myself, I must set others free.[6]

From a section of the *Sutta Pitaka* comes a phrase that seems like a perfect metaphor for the work of all saviors such as the Buddha.

And for this blinded world I'll cause
The drum of deathlessness to beat.

Or, as another wording has it: "I will beat the drum of the immortal in the darkness of this world." Finally, there is the Buddha's specific mission in terms of his own message, the complex Buddhist intellectual and philosophical formula symbolized by the Wheel of the Law or *Dharma*: "The Wheel of the Law has been turned, which has no extension, no origin, no birth, no home, isolated and free from matter."[7]

In the same source we find new honorific epithets applied to him now: "He became the perfectly wise, the Bhagavat, the Arhat, the king of the law, the Tathagata*. . . ."[8] Bhagavat or "Lord" is a Sanskrit term used by Hindu *bhakti* sects for their founder or special deity: An *arhat** is a saint, one who is free from craving and is enlightened; Tathagata is literally the "thus gone" or "thus come," and is the name Buddha most frequently used to describe himself. The "Light of Asia," as in the title of Arnold's poem based on one of the biographies of Buddha, had arisen in India 2,500 years ago.

Then began his active teaching of the doctrine, which lasted for 45 years. The canonical account says he went to nearby Sarnath, where he converted the five monks who had forsaken him when he gave up asceticism and took food in order to concentrate. This was his first sermon. Other traditions describe various meetings with different people; his followers soon numbered

60; the two chief disciples were Saripatta and Moggallana. The *Jataka* account ends with the donation by a merchant of the monastery of the Jetavana. About a year after the enlightenment, then, the order of monks, the *Sangha*,* was established. Two other notable disciples were Ananda, described as the beloved disciple and Buddha's relative, and Devadatta, the Buddhist Judas. Legend says that in the summer rainy season Buddha would stay with the monks at some place of retreat, while during the rest of the year he went on a preaching tour in northern India, at least for the first 20 years or so. An order of women followers or nuns was established, not without some misgivings on Buddha's part and only under eight strict rules. Rules and regulations increased as the numbers of monks grew, and gifts from laymen added to the number and wealth of the monasteries. In the older Buddhism, the *Sangha* is one of the Three Jewels: the Buddha, the *Sangha*, and the *Dharma*—in them, the monk declares, "I take my refuge." Wearing the traditional yellow robes of the Asian mendicant, Gautama and the monks begged for their food, and the monks became a permanent aspect of life in southeast Asia.

In about his eightieth year, Sakyamuni, having long since been fully enlightened and having reached Nirvana,* at last died and entered the ultimate Nirvana without any bodily basis, sometimes called Paranirvana.* (Nirvana is the Buddhist equivalent of *moksha*.) Although the records vary and radical critics may question the historicity of Gautama, the impression one gets from the Buddhist literature is not of a mythical but of a real figure with great power and consummate spiritual insight. He is austere and forbidding as he leaves his loving wife and grieving father, and as he lives among the monks who always treat him with awed respect. Yet at the same time a winsomeness is seen in his unassuming willingness to talk with any seeker, and a true spiritual concern dominates all his dealings with people, while never does he give way to hatred, anger, or contempt for a fellow being. Above all one is convinced by the canonical legends of his spiritual power and charisma, and of the ineluctable will and mental concentration which carried him to supernal wisdom.

The Councils

During his lifetime Buddha had continued to exercise leadership and to provide instruction, but even then there had been some disruptions and divisions among the monks. After his death, problems and pressures increased, and in the second and third centuries of the order, the fifth and fourth centuries B.C.E., subsects emerged. In response to such problems, the First Council of monks had convened immediately after the Buddha's death, according to a record compiled 100 or 200 years later. The Second Council was held 100 years after Buddha's death, at Vasali, where 10 rules softening the rigor of the order were condemned. By the time of the Third Council (247 B.C.E.) the process of division had proceeded so far that even the concern of the great Buddhist emperor Asoka, who according to tradition convened it, could not arrest the split. At rate intervals since then there have been other councils, for example, a rival third

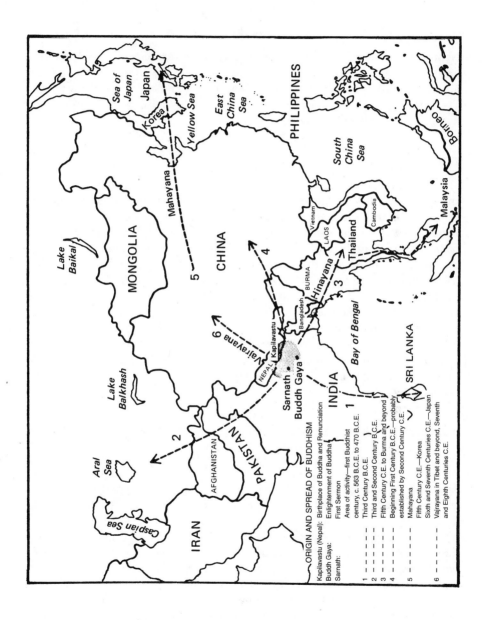

ORIGIN AND SPREAD OF BUDDHISM

Kapilavastu (Nepal): Birthplace of Buddha and Renunciation
Buddh Gaya: Enlightenment of Buddha
Sarnath: First Sermon

Area of activity—first Buddhist
century, c. 563 B.C.E. to 470 B.C.E.

1 – – – – – – Third Century B.C.E.
2 – – – – – – Third and Second Century B.C.E.
3 – – – – – – Fifth Century C.E. to Burma and beyond
4 – – – – – – Beginning First Century B.C.E.—probably
              established by Second Century C.E.
5 – – – – – – Mahayana
              Fifth Century C.E.—Korea
              Sixth and Seventh Centuries C.E.—Japan
6 – – – – – – Vajrayana in Tibet and beyond, Seventh
              and Eighth Centuries C.E.

council under King Kanishka in the first century. The Sixth Council, of Southeast Asian Buddhism, met at Rangoon in 1954, commemorating 2,500 years—according to their chronology—since Buddha's enlightenment.

Divisions of Buddhism

None of the subsects and schools of the early centuries remain, except the two great divisions; therefore we must pass over most of the controversies and outline the growth and change of Buddhism from about the third century B.C.E. The three chief schools that comprise most of Buddhism are Hinayana,* Mahayana,* and the later Vajrayana.*

TERMINOLOGY

The usual figurative meaning given the terms are: Mahayana, "great vehicle," and Hinayana, "lesser vehicle," from the literal meaning of *yana** as a wagon or cart. The doctrine or *dharma* of the Buddha may be thought of as a ship or vessel—hence vehicle—that carries believers across the sea or river of *samsara* to Nirvana on the farther shore. There is truth in the implied comparison: the Mahayana as great in the sense of large enough to carry many across, and the Hinayana being lesser in the sense that it is a way for the few who enter the full discipline of the *Sangha*. The term "doctrine of the elders" or Therevada,* which they themselves prefer to Hinayana, stresses the originality, age, or priority in time of their school. This we do associate with the earlier literature and customs, but we will use the customary term, "Hinayana." The third vehicle, latest and least numerous of the three, is called Vajrayana, "the vehicle of the Thunderbolt" or *vajra*, a development of certain Mahayana elements, mainly in Nepal and Tibet.

THE DIVISION BETWEEN HINAYANA AND MAHAYANA

The scientific problems of these historical developments are complex, and any summary explanation is tentative and inconclusive. Conze makes the monk Sariputra the catalyst of the division, because Sariputra shaped the teaching and life of the *Sangha* and decided which aspects of Buddha's teaching should be stressed. "He dominated the Buddhist community in the sense that one section of the community adopted his interpretation, and that another section formed their opinions in conscious direct opposition to it."[9] The program which Sariputra determined was the pattern of monastic life designed to produce the *arhat*, a kind of Buddhist saint who—by the threefold program of moral discipline, concentration or trance, and wisdom—overcame all attachment to life and achieved the exalted state of enlightenment. As centuries passed, however, the distinction between monks and laity lost its significance when even monks no longer achieved arhatship, and they were charged with selfishness in their pursuit of Nirvana. The ideal of the *arhat* gave way to the

Buddha, Yasodhara, and Rahula. Gandhara sculpture, third century A.D.

ideal of the Bodhisattva, according to which anyone might become a Buddha. A new theory about the nature of the world, stressing what is called "emptiness"—the lack of any definable properties of things—also developed. (Both of these will be discussed more fully under Tenets.)

Hinayana   The most important political and social factor in the early history of the faith was the career of the Emperor Asoka as a Buddhist. At about the time of Alexander the Great, the first great Indian emperor, Chandragupta of Magadha, ruled all northern India. His grandson Asoka was crowned about 270 B.C.E., and conquered large territories to the southeast in a war whose horrors so revolted him that he gave up further military campaigns, and, as Vincent A. Smith says in *The Oxford Student's History of India,* "for the rest of his life he devoted himself to winning 'the chiefest conquest, the conquest by the Law of Piety or Duty (dharma),' "[10] He is supposed to have convened the Third Council in about 240 B.C.E., but his real furtherance of Buddhism was in his own life and administration, guided by a sincere devotion to the *dharma.* Using his power to spread the message, he ordered stone pillars and standing rocks to be inscribed with edicts proclaiming, and adjuring obedience to, the law. Throughout India some of these inscriptions are still to be seen. With humanitarian measures and economic policies he attempted to improve the life of the people, and he organized a system of missions which carried the wisdom of the Buddha to Sri Lanka, South India, Hellenic areas of Syria, Egypt, Macedonia, and beyond. Buddhism was on its way as a world religion.

Although Asoka began the process, the diffusion of Buddhism beyond India took many centuries. At first, of course, it was monks' religion, Hinayana, and, although elements of Mahayana and of Hinduism played a part at times, Hinayana is today the Buddhism of Southeast Asia. In Sri Lanka Buddhism flourished for centuries, and it was there that the teachings were first put in written form; although there have been times of decay and retreat from Buddha, the land is still full of Buddhist stupas* and holy places, and Buddhism is the chief religion. If Asoka's missions reached Burma they had little effect, for it does not seem to have been until about the fifth century C.E. that Buddhism took firm hold in Burma. Influences from Mahayana teachings and from China entered into the development, but Hinayana was the dominant movement by the eleventh century, and has remained so in spite of some alliances with other cults which have tended at times to dilute Buddhist tradition.

The Buddhist man-made mountain of sculpture at Borobodur in Indonesia testifies to the past glories of Buddhism there, but when Islam came, the faith of the Buddha was overwhelmed. Like Indonesia's Borobodur, Cambodia's Angkor Wat still stands as a monument to the mixed Mahayana and Hindu cult which prevailed for several centuries; now the prevailing form in Cambodia is Hinayana. So is it in Laos. Thailand follows Sri Lanka and Burma as the third principal Hinayana country, probably having been led into it soon after the great Laotian migration about six centuries ago. Vietnam has many Buddhists, but the Unified Buddhist Church is officially banned, and in 1995 their number two leader was imprisoned for criticizing communist rule and maintaining an independent Buddhist church. In all the countries mentioned, the dominant Buddhist tradition now, whatever the variations over the centuries, is this Hinayana or Sinhalese (from Simhala, the ancient name) Buddhism, which came to fruition in Sri Lanka after Asoka's missions. Few monarchs in history have been so honored for their personal piety and have so significantly helped to nurture religion by their public policy as Asoka.

India itself gradually swallowed up or pushed out the *dharma* of the Buddha, and today there are Buddhists only in Himalayan border states or hill country, and in Bhutan and Nepal. There are Buddhist places of pilgrimage in India, and recently a kind of Buddhist revival has been attempted. From the first, Buddha himself disregarded caste in the *Sangha*, and Buddhism has consistently denied the religious status of caste. Probably this was one reason for its ultimate rejection in India. Another theological difference was the Buddha's rejection of the authority of the Vedas and his denigration of the Vedic gods. On the other hand, much of the fundamental Buddhist literature and philosophy was written in hybrid Sanskrit by Indians, and the *Sangha* itself was not foreign to Hinduism with its tradition of asceticism and contemplation. It was in India, therefore, that the fundamental ideas and practices of the faith took form and the basic scriptures were composed, and even after that India shared in the development.

Mahayana   The waning of zeal within the *Sangha* and corresponding pressures from the laity have been mentioned as psychological or sociological factors, and the shift from Gautama Buddha as a paradigmatic (ideal example) human figure to a Bodhisattva savior has been briefly suggested as a doctrinal factor in emergence of the Mahayana. New views also developed from the ideas, found in Hinayana scriptures, that Buddha came to earth from the Tushita ("contented") heaven, and that from there would also come, someday, the great future Buddha, Maitreya.* Mahayana expanded this teaching into doctrines of great Buddha heavens and many heavenly Buddhas. A summary of these three factors (teachings of heavenly realms and Buddha beings, Bodhisattva doctrine, personal and social forces) as formative of Mahayana is given by Saunders:

> In this apocalyptic heaven and in the cult of the Maitri Buddha which belongs to the same era we may see evidence that, the attainment of Arhatship having ceased, men were constrained to find satisfaction in contemplating either rebirth in a new era of enthusiasm or in a Paradise beyond this vale of tears. And the divine figures of Amitabha* and Avalokitesvara* embody no doubt, while they help to inspire, the new ethical ideal of service and compassion which are one of the hallmarks of the new movement; . . .[11]

But no simple definition of the division between Hinayana and Mahayana has ever been possible. The clue to it might be found in the two sets of scriptures, which embody the differences, if one could but master them! A famous Chinese pilgrim, I-ching (C.E. 635–713), after a long sojourn in India and return to China, was asked the unanswerable question: What is the difference between Hinayana and Mahayana? His reply, pointing to the scriptures as the place to find the answer, if that is possible, has become legendary: "Those who worship Bodhisattvas and read Mahayana *sutras* are called Mahayanists, while those who do not do this are called Hinayanists."

Tradition and history agree that although Buddhism in China began at about the beginning of the Christian era, coming from India at first, it did not gain wide acceptance until the fourth and fifth centuries, when the translator Kumarajiva turned out an enormous amount of literature. This was only a foretaste of the vast body of literature produced by the Chinese themselves once Bodhidarma began the expression of the faith in terms of Chinese thought. In succeeding centuries Buddhism developed characteristic Chinese forms of much complexity and variety. During the T'ang dynasty, seventh to tenth centuries, it was strongest, but intermittent restrictions then and later, and competition with the indigenous Taoism and especially Confucianism, prevented it from becoming more than one of the three faiths of China. There was a strong Buddhist revival in the second half of the nineteenth and first half of the twentieth century, but under the Communist regime its scope was severely limited.

The movement spread to Korea in the fourth century and flourished from about C.E. 700 to 1400, when a new importation of Confucianism eclipsed it except among the inhabitants of a few mountain fortresses; the common people also retained remnants of faith. From Korea, Buddhism entered Japan in C.E. 538 or 552, and was established quickly because of royal patronage. The schools of Japanese Buddhism were derived from the Chinese, but have assumed distinctive Japanese form. Japan is now the principal Mahayana country.

Vayrayana   Historically and geographically Vajrayana is Tibetan Buddhism, but the Chinese occupation has crushed it there. It is related to Hinduism through what is known as tantrism. Tantras* are scriptures describing the rituals, spells, and formulas of certain sects which followed magical and other unconventional practices. One element of this tantric Hinduism was Shaktism, the female energy cult. The characteristic Vajrayana sects were Left Hand Tantric groups, whose Buddha theory included female counterparts to the Buddhas, called Taras or "Savioresses." Their iconography symbolized the union of the soul with Buddha by stylized copulating *Yab-Yum* or "Father-Mother" couples, representing a Bodhisattva and his consort, in Nepalese and Tibetan mandalas* and images. Both of the divisions described below were reformist movements of certain aspects of this tantric Buddhism. Modern adherents of Vajrayana disclaim all explicit sexual interpretations and practices of the tantric cult, and find in it profound discipline and spiritual meaning in distinctive philosophical treatises.

Padmasambhava* in the eighth century was the main agent for the introduction of this Buddhism into Tibet. The distinguishing institutional feature of Tibetan Buddhism and culture is the monastic orders of the monks or *lamas*, wherefore Tibetan Buddhism is often designated as "lamaistic Buddhism." Most familiar to Westerners are the great fortress-like monasteries shown in photographs of the country, some of them of great size. Certain aspects of tantric and monastic Buddhism led to reform movements and divisions, and today there are two principal orders of monks. The larger reform movement is known as the Gelugpa or "Yellow Hat" school, headed by the Dalai Lama. After the occupation of Tibet by China, repression of the Buddhist monks became so severe that the *lamas* were forced to flee, and in Tibet Buddhism is now almost completely repressed and is officially vilified, pictured as morally corrupt and socially reactionary. The Dalai Lama has headquarters in India now. Representatives of the other group, the Nyingmapa or "Red Hat" school, have established centers at several places in the United States. Preserving more of the tantric elements, they are known for their scripture, the *Bardo Thodol* or *Book of the Dead*, describing the pilgrimage of the soul through 49 days between death and rebirth.

BUDDHIST SACRED WRITINGS

The first fact about Buddhist literature is its sheer, staggering volume. It would be impossible for any one person to know the full body of works. Even a brief descriptive list of the texts, languages, and scripts involved is a scholarly nightmare. The second fact is that there is a great difference between the two schools in size and complexity of the respective bodies of literature. The (Hinayana) Sinhalese Canon proper, apart from extensive commentaries, was estimated by the late Professor Rhys Davids at about twice as much matter as the Christian Bible. The Mahayana Canon, however, includes translations from San-

The Bodhi Tree and Temple. Buddh Gaya, India. The spot under the tree where Buddha attained enlightenment is now marked by a marble altar.

(Ward J. Fellows)

skrit, and original works in Chinese, Tibetan, Japanese, and other languages, numbering into thousands of parts. This suggests the problems one has in making a summary description of the series of libraries or different collections which have grown up around the Buddhist *dharma*. Some of the Mahayana are comparable to Hinayana documents, but on the other hand the distinctive and important Mahayana works have no exact parallel in the earlier literature because they are considered extensions and elaborations of it.

Many modern translations and collections of parts of this material are available. The first standard English series was the same as that for other Asian religions. *The Sacred Books of the East*, 50 volumes edited by F. Max Muller, was originally published beginning in about 1880 by the Oxford University Press, and has now in part been reissued by other publishers. The definitive English collection of Hinayana works has been that which the Pali Text Society has produced over the past 60 years.

Hinayana Scriptures

THE PALI* CANON

Pali is the language in which a portion of the Buddhist scriptures are written. These scriptures constitute the Pali Canon of Hinayana writings. Historical theories about their origin vary, but tradition says that Asoka's missionary to Sri Lanka was his own son Mihinda, who brought the scriptures with him, and who had perhaps grown up using the Pali dialect, a mixed literary form of discourse. In Sri Lanka, Pali became the language which the Buddhists used, perhaps in deliberate rejection of the classical Sanskrit of the Hindu scriptures, and Pali itself later died out in India where it had begun. When Buddhists from Sri Lanka went on to Burma and Siam, they carried with them Buddhism and the Pali Canon, as well as commentaries and additions to it. When the works from India were lost, it was the unbroken succession of scholars using Pali in Sri Lanka and Burma, most of them Buddhist monks, who preserved this literature. Of these monastic commentators the greatest was Buddhaghosa, a convert from Hinduism, author of the *Path of Purity* and the one most responsible for the preservation of the canon in Pali.

THE TRIPITAKA*

The texts of this literature are called the *Tripitaka*, because they are divided into three *pitaka*, literally baskets, still used in moving earth and for construction in India. Hence the name refers to a tradition handed down. The first is called the *Discipline Basket (Vinaya Pitaka*) because it contains rules and ordinances for the monks in the *Sangha*. Five separate subdivisions are included in it, some of them rather dry and special reading, but some being lively narratives of the life and teaching of Buddha. Usually the second is known as the *Sermon Basket (Sutta Pitaka*)*. It is the most interesting and significant for understanding the philosophy and folklore of early Buddhism, because the sermons and lectures of Buddha, or one of the chief disciples, bear on questions which we still ask about the doctrine. *Sutta* is actually Pali for the Sanskrit *sutra*, in Hinduism a short saying or aphorism, but in Buddhism a brief story or verses about one subject. In the third *pitaka*, the metaphysical treatises (*Abhidhamma Pitaka*), are seven sets of scholastic explanations of doctrines. All of the *Tripitaka* reflects its oral origin, the Buddhist homiletical style, and the peculiarities of the language, in the repetitions and formalities of the *sutras*. Probably it circulated in oral tradition for centuries before being put in writing no earlier than the time of Asoka; the third basket is unanimously pronounced a later work than the other two.

Mahayana Scriptures

CHINESE, JAPANESE, AND KOREAN SCRIPTURES

Strangely enough, the Pali Canon has not been translated into Chinese. The Chinese Buddhist Canon comprises translations of the so-called Hybrid Sanskrit or Northern India *Tripitaka* and many Mahayana Buddhist texts. With the exception of a few key writings by the founders of modern Japanese schools or branches of Buddhism, the Japanese collection, like Japanese Buddhism, is based on the Chinese. Because of the decline of Buddhism in China and the emergence of Japan as the principal Mahayana country, the modern collections have been done there. The fruit of centuries of scholarship and devotion by Chinese and Japanese monks is the latest and most critical Japanese edition of the scriptures, with other materials such as drawings and catalogs: the *Taisho Daizokyo* of 100 volumes, printed from 1924 to 1934. During the 1980s the Korean Canon was published in 14 volumes, under the editorship of Lewis Lancaster of the University of California, Berkeley.

SPECIFIC WORKS

Even for Chinese and Japanese Buddhists, the sheer bulk of the collection required them to have some method of selecting which volumes they would use. This was usually determined by what school or sect they belonged to; they would use the scripture favored by or produced by their school, usually two or three of the important books. Some ancient scholars wrestled with the insoluble problems of classifying or even harmonizing the total corpus in some kind of system. All we shall attempt is a list and short explanation of a few titles that recur most frequently in collections, or that are referred to by many Buddhists, or that modern scholars consider unique or significant for understanding Buddhism. One helpful distinction is that between basic teaching or text (*sutra*) and commentary teaching or treatise (*shastra*).

   The Expanded Discourses (Vaipulya Sutras) teach the doctrine of the heavenly Buddhas and Bodhisattvas as part of an "expanded" (beyond Hinayana interpretations) exposition of the law. The Buddha is usually the speaker, seated in a prominent place, surrounded by a great assemblage including divine beings, accompanied by theophanies of light illuminating other worlds. Probably the most important is *The Lotus of the True Law (Saddharma-pundarika*)*, in which essential Mahayana teachings are presented clearly and simply using poetic and parabolic language. Nearly all Mahayana refer to it, and the T'ien-T'ai sect in China and Nichiren* in Japan make it their chief work. Another major group or class of scriptures is *Discourses on the Perfection of Wisdom (Prajnaparamita* Sutras)*. As a noun, the *paramita* or "perfection" is feminine in gender, and is often addressed or apostrophised as "she," Perfect Wisdom. Two of the best-known *sutras* in this group are the *Diamond Cutter (Vajracchedika*)* and the *Heart (Hridaya*)*, which has a short and a long version. One example of the *shastras* is *The Awakening of Faith*, attributed to Ashvagosha (a different Ashvagosa from the author of the *Buddhacarita*). It is a commentary on Mahayana topics and includes various Mahayana doctrines.

   The distinctive popular forms of Mahayana, although they may ultimately rest their doctrine on the *sutras* and what they find implicit in the *Tripitaka*, have their own favorite scriptures which were translated into Chinese and later into Japanese. One such key work has been mentioned, *The Lotus Sutra*. Others in this category of works basic to Mahayana practice and doctrine are three Sanskrit works, the larger and the smaller *Description of the Land of*

Kuthodaw (Royal Bounty) Pagoda, Mandalay, Burma. Begun in 1857, housing 729 marble tablets carved with text of the Hinayana scriptures as decided by the Fifth World Buddhist Council at Mandalay in 1871

(Ward J. Fellows)

Bliss (Sukhavati-vyuha), and the *Meditation on Buddha Amitayus (Amitayur-dhyana)*. They are fundamental books for the largest group of Chinese and Japanese Buddhists, the worshippers of Amitabha Buddha, the Pure Land schools. In them faith and devotion to the Amitabha Buddha and recitation of his name are enjoined as the way to gain eternal peace in the Pure Land of Bliss, which is described in all its glory. The *Meditation (Amitayur-dhyana) sutra* gives instructions for gaining visions of the Pure Land. For Zen there is the *Sutra of the Sixth Patriarch*, or *Platform Sutra*, of Hui-neng (died C.E. 713), the only Chinese work to be honored as a Mahayana *sutra* or scripture of the canon itself. The Tibetan Canon comprises the Sanskrit *Tripitaka* and over 200 volumes of commentary.

TENETS

As we turn to what Buddhists believe about the world, spiritual life, and human beings we encounter Buddha's injunction that there are many such "questions which tend not to edification." In the *Sutta Pitaka,* Malunkyaputta, an ascetic, asks the Buddha why he has not elucidated certain questions. In reply Buddha states in the repetitive fashion of the sermons:

> I have not elucidated, Malunkyaputta, that the world is eternal; I have not elu-
> cidated that the world is not eternal; I have not elucidated that the world is in-
> finite; I have not elucidated that the world is finite; . . . that the soul and the
> body are identical; . . . that the soul and the body are not identical. . . . [and
> so on]

This kind of speculation, he says, does not tend to edification about the funda-
mental religious problem of "cessation of misery."[12] Buddha was saying two things: first, that speculation about purely theoretical questions does not "tend to edification," that is, does not help us understand or answer the real spiritual problem of human suffering, and therefore he has not dealt with such theoretical questions; and second, that practical help with what in modern terms could be called the "existential" problem of suffering is what people need, and that he has explained the cause and cure of this suffering.

Nevertheless, the Buddha's strictures have not prevented Buddhists from constructing an abundance of theories and doctrines, some related to the "cessation of misery" and some being philosophical views about the nature of this world and human knowledge of it.

Actually, Buddhism is the most determinedly theoretical of all the religions we consider in this book, because in it theory or rational explanation is neces-
sary for the bare statement and meaning of the scheme of salvation, and not simply for defense, apologetics, or theological elaboration of the doctrines. The philosopher Alfred North Whitehead said: "Buddhism is the most colossal example in history of an applied metaphysic. Christianity took the opposite road. It has always been a religion seeking a metaphysic, in contrast to Buddhism which is a metaphysic generating a religion."[13] Some scholars dispute Whitehead; in any event, it is not a criticism but purely a descriptive contrast. Surely the amount of sacred literature testifies to the attempt to state the doctrines in theoretical form, which is the essence of theology.

The task is difficult, because we are going to try to systematize the unsystematic. There is no official formulation, no promulgated orthodoxy, no

summary of doctrine for us to appeal to. There are the wide differences among the three vehicles, the variety of schools and sects, the changes and variations through time. We search for the unity and meaning of the vital *dharma* of Buddhism. Just as *dharma* was the one word for the totality of Hinduism, so the *dharma* is the doctrine of the Buddha. "The dharma of Buddha consisted in teaching the true doctrine (*saddharma*) of man's beliefs and actions, and this exists in the Buddha-word, the Doctrine."[14] We will list twelve key tenets in the form of a Buddhist catechism.

But before we begin it must be made explicit that there is no category for God in the list that follows, because there is no doctrine of God in Buddhism. The Western theist must not expect to find a figure like the God of the Bible or the Qur'an in the religion of Buddha. In Hinayana there simply are no gods, because the question of God would be one which did not tend to edification, and hence it would not be elucidated; God is neither affirmed nor denied. Buddha himself dismissed the Vedic gods, and his *dharma* after him had no place for them because they were transcended by Buddha. In Mahayana the Buddhas become a kind of God, or take the place of God, but the term is not applied to them because their significance is not as transcendent beings but as embodiments of *dharma*, of wisdom, of the truth about the world and human destiny. There is no place for God as the Supreme Being in the Buddhist scheme of things or in Buddhist philosophy, because there is no permanent being or reality of things, there is no ontology (positive theory of existence) to be the ground for God. Some of the functions or work of God are, however, taken over in Buddha theory: the Bodhisattvas are saviors in a sense, and the cosmic Buddhas not only pervade their Buddha world but dispense grace to their believers. In place of a section on God, therefore, we begin with the closest thing to God, which is Buddha.

The Catechism

Of course there is not really a general Buddhist catechism; this is simply a way to present twelve key doctrinal points. In all except number one the list of items included will be derived from some Buddhist source. The flowering of Buddhist literature coincided with the scholastic phase in India, which delighted in such lists, and they found all through Buddhist scriptures—three of this, four of that. We will not stress the catechism (question-and-answer) form, except to introduce each of our numbers. We repeat that this list is simply a device for covering a number of doctrinal points and does not claim to be canonical or official. However, each collection of six or seven, and so on, is from the scriptures.[15]

ONE BUDDHA

What is "the one"? The Buddha. Whether it be the human Gautama Buddha or the celestial Buddha Amitabha, of Infinite Light, Buddha is first, the source and center of Buddhism, number one. Of that there is no question. But what or who Buddha is, is a problem. Buddhists solve it by having their own interpretation, their own Buddhology or Buddha doctrine, to fit their form of Buddhism; but there is no single inclusive theoretical structure to cover all types or instances of Buddha. Buddha theories are so many and varied in content and approach that we cannot describe them, but must impose an external and arbitrary descriptive system of classification. Recognizing, then, that there are many different ways of viewing or describing Buddha from within Buddhism itself, and not claiming anything but an interpretive or descriptive function for our categories, we suggest three main types or kinds of Buddha figures or images: the human or *manushi* Buddha, Bodhisattvas, and cosmic Buddhas. Westerners must put aside their prejudice against images, for the image and the Buddha reality are not opposed, not separable, but somehow fused. One must enter as far as possible into the complex feeling and understanding of the Buddhist believer for whom the image is not a realistic representation of the man Buddha, but a stylized image of the ideal enlightened one, an iconic metaphor for the infinite wisdom, truth, and compassion of the eternal Buddha.

The Human or Manushi Buddha   The historical Buddha is important for all Buddhism, although he is described or regarded in different ways. For instance, no Buddhists would deny that Gautama Buddha was seen in the world and attained enlightenment, but there have been those who denied that he was actually human. Thomas says, "Buddha was held by some to be supramundane in all respects, and hence not subject to the same conditions of existence as ordinary human beings, a view quite parallel to the Christian heresy of docetism."[16] Most Hinayana Buddhists believe that Siddhartha actually was born, did go out, and did attain enlightenment by his own efforts. And although divine epithets are also applied to him and he is an eternal being, he is not "a god in the sense of the originator of the universe or its ultimate reality."[17] In one place, the *Angaturra Nikaya*, Buddha replies to the Brahmin Don's questions with denial that he is a god and denial that he is a human being: "Take it that I am Buddha, Brahmin," he concludes,[18] meaning the awakened or enlightened one. As such, he could not be fully identified with gods, or with human beings in their limitations. This would seem to distinguish the human Buddha from both the Christian doctrine of Incarnation in Jesus Christ, who is both human and divine, and the Hindu *avatar* who is in some sense always a god even while on earth. Buddha is the supreme teacher, a historical being who differs from other humans who attain enlightenment, by being the discoverer, the pioneer, the supreme exemplar. Although he is human, then, his qualities and powers make him unique among all human beings.

It is above all as the enlightened one, an ideal to be followed by them, that the Hinayana monks see Buddha, and the *Tripitaka* expresses that view at all times. The Pali Canon says that he entered Nirvana at his death: "rising from the fourth trance, immediately the Blessed One passed into Nirvana."[19]

However, as he told Ananda before he died, that does not mean they have no teacher: "The Doctrine and Discipline, Ananda, which I have taught and enjoined upon you is to be your teacher when I am gone."[20] Buddha in Nirvana is beyond them, beyond all sensation and perception, beyond all space or nothingness, in the fourth trance; hence he hears no prayers and can answer none. He is their guide, their inspiration, their ideal; but he is not a god who hears, and heeds, and helps. Current art history uses "Sakyamuni" as the title for his various exemplary human lives.

Nevertheless the Pali Canon speaks at length of the preexistence of Gautama Buddha, and of other Buddhas, 24 former Buddhas being listed in the introduction to the *Jataka*. Under them he made his wish to be a Buddha during "four immensities and a hundred thousand world-cycles." Since Kassapa, the twenty-fourth, there have been no Supreme Buddhas except Gautama; another source reports that he prophesied that there will be another Buddha, Maitreya*, and listed 10 of the monks as future Buddhas. In the *suttas,* say Thomas, the term "Bodhisattva" appears, but not the doctrine that Buddhahood is a possible goal for everyone.[21] To the all-important Bodhisattva doctrine and pattern we now turn.

Buddha as Bodhisattva   The development of the Bodhisattva doctrine was the most important aspect of Buddhist thought between the time of Asoka and the beginning of the Christian era, although we know little about its beginnings. For the developed doctrine we must turn to Mahayana *sutras*, especially to the *Lotus of the True Law*, which is primarily concerned with the nature of Buddhas and secondarily with Bodhisattvas. The Buddha preacher is Sakyamuni the Tathagata, who teaches the one vehicle or career for all of winning full Buddhahood. The setting is a celestial drama of Buddha worlds and beings, with great theophanies and choirs of innumerable Bodhisattvas, all of whom have been pupils of the Tathagatha. The good news is that everyone has the Buddha nature, can teach others and attain Buddhahood. In the later chapters various specific Bodhisattvas are eulogized. The conclusion of the *Lotus Sutra* is the basic Mahayana doctrine of Buddha as a principle or reality, a theoretical and spiritual entity, as contrasted with the specific human individual Gautama in Hinayana, which was our first category. The Mahayana Buddha is first of all an ideal or personification rather than a specific person, a type or kind of person rather than a particular individual. This major Mahayana development is the ground for both of the second and third of our categories, which are Mahayana extensions or developments of the human Buddha who is significant for Hinayana.

That is the crucial step: Once Buddha is not simply the one Sakyamuni, the actual and single Enlightened One, but is a principle, a universal, neither one Buddha nor many, but the origin and source of all Buddhas—once that has happened there is a new Buddhism. It is not what his qualities are, whether he be divine or human, which constitutes the distinction. The difference between Hinayana and Mahayana Buddhology is that in Mahayana the Buddha is a principle, a type, a predicate, a universal, to use philosophic terms; whereas in Hinayana he is the *only* specific instance, the unique element in a unique class, defined—as in modern logical class calculus—by its membership and not by the qualities or predicates apart from the members. The mythical predecessors of the Buddha in the Pali Canon are not fully realized Buddhas like Sakyamuni. Insofar as they may foreshadow a universal or type they are only that, adumbrations of the Buddhas. In Hinayana he is the only instance or instantiation; Gautama is the only Buddha. In Mahayana, each Buddha is an instance of Buddhahood. Attempts to define the difference in other terms prove inadequate, because it cannot be done in terms of specific predicates, characteristics, qualities, or attributes. In Hinayana, Buddha is one, single, unique, *sui generis*, specific. What his characteristics or attributes are does not matter in distinguishing him from the Buddha of the Mahayana; many of the same characteristics or qualities can be applied to the Mahayana Buddha. But the Mahayana Buddha is a universal, a type, a class, having—it may be, as in Bodhisattva doctrine—an infinite number of instances or members. Moreover, all of them have the various marks, qualities, or attributes of the logical predicate, Buddha.[22]

A Bodhisattva is first of all, then, an embodiment in human form of the Buddha principle or truth. This is the basis of what we might call the metaphysical status of a Bodhisattva. The nature or being of a Bodhisattva is such that although he appears on earth he is not subject to the same conditioned existence as are unenlightened human beings who are still held by *karma* and ignorance in the chain of interdependent origination (see our "the twelve"). *Bodhi* means wisdom or enlightenment and *sattva* means essence or being, hence one whose essence has become wisdom. That is the nature of a Bodhisattva, the sort or kind of being of all Bodhisattvas.

The second mark of the class of Bodhisattvas is their function or task, what they do in distinction to what they are. In the Pali Canon a Bodisattva is one who is going to be a Buddha, like Gautama as Sumedha, and thus a Buddha-to-be. This idea is extended from the Hinayana context of preexistence to the Mahayana context of one who exists in the world, but who is entitled or qualified to be in Nirvana now, hence a Buddha-to-be. The reason why they voluntarily defer their deserved entrance into Nirvana is in order to help all beings toward enlightenment and Nirvana. In order to proclaim that all who manifest devotion to Buddha will be delivered out of sentient selfhood into Nirvana, they willingly defer their own entrance into Nirvana. In this their motive is compassion, for all Bodhisattvas embody the infinite compassion of Sakyamuni.

In the later chapters of the *Lotus Sutra* several noted Bodhisattvas are introduced. The self-sacrifice of Bhaishajyagura,* the Buddha of healing, is described. The grandeur and ubiquity of Avalokitesvara, the Bodhisattva of compassion and mercy, the Lord Who Is Seen or Who Sees Our World, are celebrated, and he is the most widely venerated Bodhisattva in Asia. In China he is known as Kuan-Yin* and in Japan as Shokannon, or Kannon for short. After C.E. 1100, many of these manifestations are feminine, but it is not true that

Kannon is always feminine, a Goddess of Mercy, as is sometimes mistakenly supposed. Samantabhadra* undertakes to be a protector to future preachers of the *dharma* after the Lord Buddha's Nirvana. Two other popular Bodhisattvas are Manjusri,* the embodiment of supreme wisdom as the Bodhisattva of meditation, and Vajrasattra or Vajrapani, "the Bearer of the Thunderbolt," indicating derivation from Indra and relation to Tibetan Buddhism. In Japan Kshitigarbha,* who shows compassion for souls after death, is known as Jizo and is widely venerated. Thus different Bodhisattvas manifest different aspects of the Buddha nature and are seen in countless temples.

Cosmic Buddhas   The third category of our simple typology of Buddhas is harder to describe and type. Some writers use the term "Dhyani Buddhas" or Buddhas of supreme meditation for this group, but other scholars object to the term. Perhaps a better classification is "cosmic Buddhas," connoting their distinctive supramundane status. They are celestial beings who, unlike Bodhisattvas, never appear on earth in human form. (Although Bodhisattvas are supramundane, they choose the kind of birth they will have, and appear on earth.) The principal cosmic Buddha is Amitabha (infinite light) or Amitayus* (immeasurable life) of the larger and smaller *Land of Bliss (Sukhavati-Vyuha)*, who will appear to the faithful when they die, and they will be reborn in that world of Sukhavati.* The later forms of Mahayana in China and Japan have several such Buddhas. Vairocana* in one form is a solar Buddha, a Cosmic Lord, whose body is the totality of material existence; he is the main focus of devotion for Japan's Shingon sect. Five are known to the Buddhists of Nepal; Vairocana, the Brilliant; Akshobya, the Imperturbable; Ratnasambhava, the Jewelborn; Amoghasiddhi, Sure Success; and Amitabha, Endless Light. All Buddhists recognize Maitreya, the Buddha-to-come at the end of the age, the great future Buddha. There is some similarity to the Jewish Messiah, to the second coming of Christ in Christianity, or the Mahdi in Islam.

The Three-Body or Trikaya* Doctrine   There is a Mahayana doctrine which is in effect a metaphysical theory about the nature or being of Buddhas, which means the body of the different forms of Buddha. Assuming different forms in different schools of thought and practice, it can be used either as a metaphysical (theory about the Buddha entity or being) or a theological (an explanation about divine operations) and religious formula. The first, ultimate, or true body, hence sometimes called the "truth body," is the *dharmakaya** or *dharma* body. As *dharma* it is the essence of all Buddhas, the permanent reality and truth of the teaching of Buddha which underlies all that exists and all expressions of Buddha. Serving as the "support" of the two others, the *dharmakaya* is independent of all things yet is the "thatness" of all things. The second, *sambhogakaya,** is usually translated as the body of bliss or enjoyment, because it is "that through which Buddha affords enjoyment of the doctrine in assemblies." That is, Buddha who appears to Bodhisattvas in celestial places

Shwe Dagon, Rangoon, Burma. The "Thursday Altar" for those with birthdays on a Thursday

(Ward J. Fellows)

and reveals to them divine truths which they all share and "enjoy" and who is himself adored by them, is Buddha in the *sambhogakaya*. Third is the *nirmanakaya** or transformation-body, the "body" of the historical Buddha and of any Buddha on earth, "that by which he works the good of all creatures." It is called "transformed" because in appearing as a human being Buddha is "transformed" from his true and eternal form as pure wisdom and truth into ordinary and limited existence.

The *Trikaya* served different purposes for different groups, but for all it was a convenient formula for harmonizing views of Buddha that otherwise would have conflicted, and it provided the basis for unifying all beings in the ultimate Buddhahood. In some ways it can be compared with Christian doctrines of the Person of Christ, which will be discussed. In both cases there is the necessity to explain the nature of a savior figure who is both divine and human, or supernatural and natural.

Some writers have tried to make Buddhism into a monotheism through the Adibuddha theory which appeared in Vajrayana in about the tenth century. The Adibuddha does appear in that system as a primordial Buddha being and the head of what might be called their "pantheon" of Buddhas; some Mahayanists even direct prayers first to Adibuddha. But neither in theory nor in the practice of Buddhism as a whole can Adibuddha unify Buddha theory or make Buddhism into monotheism.

TWO EXTREMES

What are "the two"? The two are the two extremes: hedonism (pleasure seeking) and asceticism (extreme physical self-denial). They come right out of the Buddha's own experience, and they are the first point in the first sermon in the Deer-Park following his enlightenment. Buddha's words were:

> These two extremes, brethren, should not be followed by one who has gone forth as wanderer:
> Devotion to the pleasures of sense—a low and pagan practice, unworthy, unprofitable, the way of the world (on the one hand), and on the other hand devotion to self-mortification, which is painful, unworthy, unprofitable.
> By avoiding these two extremes He who hath won the Truth (the Buddha) has gained knowledge of the *Middle Path* which giveth vision, which giveth knowledge, which causeth Calm, Insight, Enlightenment, and Nibbana.[*23]

The luxury and sensuality with which his father had surrounded him in the effort to prevent his renunciation brought him no peace; it was profitless. But neither did asceticism, which he imposed on himself, bring wisdom. The "middle way" between these two, the way of knowledge, leads to wisdom, calm, Nirvana. The resemblance to the Greek golden mean and Aristotle's ethics is not irrelevant; Buddhism is a rational way of practical wisdom, moderation, and self-control.

THREE CHARACTERISTICS

What are "the three"? Three characteristics of being: transitoriness, misery, and non-ego. Warren deemed them so significant that he put them as the foreword to his collection. We quote, omitting the repetitive alliteration:

THE THREE CHARACTERISTICS

Whether Buddhas arise, O priests, or whether Buddhas do not arise, it remains a fact and the fixed and necessary constitution of being, that all its constituents are transitory. This fact a Buddha discovers and masters, and when he has discovered and mastered it, he announces, teaches, publishes, proclaims, discloses, minutely explains, and makes it clear, that all its constituents are transitory.

Whether Buddhas arise, O priests, . . .
. . . all its constituents are misery. . . .
Whether Buddhas arise, O priests, . . .
. . . all its constituents are lacking in an Ego. . . .[24]

(Translated from the Anuttara-Nikaya (iii. 134.1))

The difficulty for us is not in understanding this intellectually or formally, but to comprehend that Buddha means it, and that it is the basis for Buddhist metaphysics and religion. All being, all existents, all of life, all things are characterized by transience, misery, and the absence of a self or ego. There is no doctrine of creation in Buddhism, no ultimate explanation or origin of things, no final or first cause; there simply are transient, miserable, egoless things. Although some modern Buddhists are for some reason apologetic about this doctrine, it remains basic to the faith. It describes the way things are in this world: To live is to suffer in a transitory world.

FOUR NOBLE TRUTHS

What are "the four"? The four Noble Truths. While Buddha did not elucidate some things he did elucidate others—the causes, the explanation, of human misery. It is perfectly straightforward, consistent with the three characteristics doctrine, and utterly essential and fundamental. It answers a twofold set of questions. On the one hand: What is it that ails mankind? What is the spiritual illness from which people suffer? From what does humanity need to be delivered? On the other: What is the cure? What is the medicine to heal the soul?

Again we quote from the First Sermon:

Now this, brethren, is the Ariyan Truth about *Suffering*;

Birth is Suffering, Decay is Suffering, Sickness is Suffering, Death is Suffering, likewise Sorrow and Grief, Woe, Lamentation and Despair. To be conjoined with things which we dislike, to be separated from things which we like—that also is Suffering. Not to get what one wants—that also is Suffering. In a word, this Body, this fivefold Mass which is based on *Grasping*, that is Suffering.

"Now this, brethren, is the Ariyan Truth about *The Origin of Suffering*:

It is that *Craving* that leads downwards to birth, along with the Lure and the Lust that lingers longingly now here, now there: namely, the Craving for Sensation, the Craving to be born again, the Craving to have done with rebirth. Such, brethren, is the Ariyan Truth about *The Origin of Suffering*.

And this, brethren, is the Ariyan Truth about *The Ceasing of Suffering*:
Verily it is the utter passionless cessation of, the giving up, the forsaking, the release from, the absence of longing for, this *Craving*.
Now this, brethren, is the Ariyan Truth about *The Way Leading to the Ceasing of Suffering*. Verily it is this Ariyan Eightfold Path, that is:
RIGHT VIEW, RIGHT AIM, RIGHT SPEECH, RIGHT ACTION, RIGHT LIVING, RIGHT EFFORT, RIGHT MINDFULNESS, RIGHT CONTEMPLATION.[25]

It can be stated formally thus:
All life is suffering (*dukkha**).
All suffering is from desire or craving (*tanha**).
But if there is no craving, there is no suffering.
So if you follow the eightfold path, there is no craving and hence no suffering.

FIVE SKANDHAS

What are "the five"? The five *skandhas*.* (As with three and four, there could have been other nominees for a place in the catechism, and for some of the others there will be many possible lists which we will have to omit. The object is to get as varied, comprehensive, and significant a spectrum as possible of the great body of Buddhist beliefs.) The five *skandhas* are "the five aggregates" which Buddha mentioned in "the four"; they are the components of the (illusory) self or person. This is Buddhist anthropology in the sense of doctrine of man or humanity, teaching about how the human being is to be described and understood. It is a unique Buddhist description or assessment of human nature, and its importance is great although its meaning or purport is rather paradoxical and obscure. The specific list comprises the five components of the self, and the doctrine which it points to is the nonself (*anatta**). The non-ego already appeared as the third of 'the three" characteristics of being.

The *skandhas* are collections or groups inasmuch as each of them is itself composed of many elements. These five *skandhas* constitute the human being, but there is no permanent self or ego, only a changing collection of these elements. The five *skandhas* remain during the lifetime of a person, but the composition of each of them is always changing. The problem of translation of these technical doctrinal terms is most vexatious here; we follow Thomas's translation of *The Majjhima Nikaya* list of the five *skandhas*: "body (*rupa*), sensation (*vedana*), perception (*sanna*), the aggregates (*sankhara*), and consciousness (*vinnana*)." The fourth, "the aggregates" is confusing because each of the five is a collection or group; the fourth aggregation designates certain mental factors, and the translators are reluctant to use any one English word. We use "mental constituents." The first *skandha* designates the physical body, the other four refer to one or another aspect of immaterial and essentially mental factors. A further source of confusion in the literature of this subject is the frequent translation of the first *skandha* as "form," meaning form of the body, its structure as a physical thing, which is analyzed in more detail into four components.

Let us hear what the sage Nagasena told the perplexed King Milinda, using "form," "sensation," "perception," "predispositions," and "consciousness" for the five, and meaning by "form" the physical form. Milinda asks what constitutes the sage himself, Nagasena, as a person. The king asks the question and the sage replies:[26]

"Is now, bhanta, form Nagasena?"
   "Nay, verily, your majesty."
   "Is sensation Nagasena?"
   "Nay, verily, your majesty."
   ". . . perception . . . ?"
   "Nay. . . ."
   ". . . the predispositions . . . ?"
   "Nay. . . ."
   ". . . consciousness . . . ?"
   "Nay. . . ."
   "Are, then, bhanta, form, sensation, perception, the predispositions, and consciousness unitedly Nagasena?"
   "Nay, verily, your majesty."
   "Is it, then, bhanta, something besides form, sensation, perception, the predispositions, and consciousness, which is Nagasena?"
   "Nay, verily, your majesty."

After using a metaphor of a chariot's components to show that no one of them is the chariot, he concludes:

"Even as the word of 'chariot' means
That members join to frame a whole;
So when the Groups appear to view,
We use the phrase, 'A living being.'"

Well, Milinda was satisfied by this explanation.

Buddhagosa put it in prose; speaking of different noun substantives, and coming to "tree," he says:

"tree" for trunk, branches, foliage, etc. in a certain relation, but when we come to examine the parts one by one, we discover that in the absolute sense there is no tree; in exactly the same way the words "living entity" and "Ego" are but a mode of expression for the presence of the five attachment groups, but when we come to examine the elements of being one by one, we discover that in the absolute sense there is no living entity there to form a basis for such figments as "I am," or "I"[27]

But now there is a practical problem, not "a question which tends not to edification." Buddhism keeps from Hinduism the ideas of *karma* and *samsara*. So it also has rebirth. But if there is no self, how can there be transmigration? What passes over from one life to the next, as the *atman* or soul does in Hinduism? Again, Nagasena answers with a metaphor: At night the flame of the torches of the first watch is not the same as the flame of the second, nor the third as the second; yet "through connection" as the second lit their torches from the first, and so on, there was only one light in each watch. "Therefore neither as the same nor as a different person do you arrive at your latest aggregation of consciousness."[28] The paradox remains. However, the doctrine of *karma* will serve to justify, for practical moral purposes, the reality of the continuing person. Eliot warns against Westerners interpreting the *anatta** doctrine as a kind of nihilism.

> It merely states that in all the world, organic and inorganic, there is nothing which is simple, self-existent, self-determined, and permanent: everything is compound, relative, and transitory. The obvious fact that infancy, youth, and age form a series is not denied: the series may be called a personality and death need not end it. The error to be avoided is the doctrine of the Brahmans that through this series there runs a changeless self, which assumes new phases like one who puts on new garments.[29]

SIX PERFECTIONS

What are "the six"? The six perfections. In the *Jataka* Sumedha saw the "ten conditions which a Buddha make," and there are several lists of six or ten in different traditions. The six perfections are the six acts which will bring a Bhodisattva to the full perfection of Buddhahood. He considers various stores of merit that he can accumulate for the benefit of those who wish to be delivered, and one of the stores is the merit of achievement through these six perfections.

Our text for them is from a Mahayana source, in the form of six questions asked by the disciple Subhuti of the Lord Buddha. "Subhuti: What is a bodhisattva's perfection of giving? . . . perfection of morality? . . . perfection of patience? . . . perfection of vigour? . . . perfection of concentration? . . . perfection of wisdom?"[30] The six perfections, then, are: giving, morality, patience, vigor, concentration, wisdom.

SEVEN FACTORS

What are "the seven"? The seven factors of enlightenment. Our "seven" is illustrative of the emphasis on meditation and concentration which characterized Buddhism from the beginning. In the *Sangha* the discipline was directed to the attainment of the same knowledge and enlightenment as Gautama himself had attained. Mental training and discipline in concentration were Hindu practices that Buddha found ready to be developed and applied by him for his own purposes. In the furtherance of this purpose to lead others to enlightenment, careful instruction and guidance were given to the monks, and out of this there came elaborate formal methods and categories of meditation and concentration. These remembered formulas form part of the early collections in the Pali Canon. In the later stages of the process the monk is to reflect on numerous lists of things and topics which help to direct the mind in the right direction. One of these lists is that of the seven factors of enlightenment.

In order to show the number and complexity of the meditational categories and techniques, and also to indicate that our numbers list is true to this scholastic aspect of Buddhism, we include an abbreviated quotation of the seven factors, taken from the *Majjhima Nikaya* of the *Sutta Pitaka*:

> And how, o Monks, must the Seven Factors of Enlightenment be practiced and cultivated that they effect the Knowledge that liberates?
>
> A monk, o Monks, practices the Awakening of Introspection, effected in solitude, effected by detachment, effected by renunciation, ending in finality:
>
> practices the Awakening of Penetration . . . ;
>
> . . . practices the Awakening of Energy . . . ;
>
> . . . practices the Awakening of Serenity . . . ;
>
> . . . practices the Awakening of Gentleness . . . ;
>
> . . . practices the Awakening of Concentration . . . ;
>
> . . . practices the Awakening of Even-Mindedness, effected in solitude, effected by detachment, effected by renunciation, ending in finality.[31]

EIGHTFOLD PATH

What are "the eight"? The Noble Eightfold Path. Twice four is eight: By the logic of Buddhism, the Eightfold Path is the fulfillment of the Fourfold Truth that was our number four, and hence these eight must be taken as following from the fourth truth—namely, the way to end craving or desire is by following the Eightfold Path.

> And what, O priests, is the noble truth of the path leading to the cessation of misery? It is this noble eightfold path, to wit, right belief, right resolve, right speech, right behavior, right occupation, right effort, right contemplation, right concentration.[32]

The eight are often broken up into three sections, thus: The first two are preliminary, referring to the Buddha's analysis of the human situation and his pointing the way for a person's resolution; the next three clearly have to do with proper moral behavior in speech and deed, and with the traditional Indian idea of certain occupations being inconsistent with the path of spiritual growth; the last three are the more specific Buddhist program of thought and mind control in pursuance of virtue and enlightenment. As amplified in the original source they already contained the germ of problems, doctrinal controversy, and philosophical elaboration. But as they stand they are the basic doctrine or *dharma* which all schools of Buddhism accept as fundamental. This is true even of some modern and more Westernized expressions of Buddhism in which the Fourfold Truth is not emphasized.

Following and sometimes quoting the original source again, let us see a little more about each one of the eight. The first is correct belief about the origin and cessation of misery, according to Buddha's Fourfold Truth. The second is resolving to renounce sensuality, malice, and harm to any creature, as a precondition to following the path. Three, four, and five are self-evident, although stated in Buddhist terms. The sixth refers to the will, resolution, and psychological force of earnest striving against evil and for good qualities.

> Whenever, O priests, a priest purposes, makes an effort, heroically endeavors, applies his mind and exerts himself that evil and demeritorious qualities not yet arisen may not arise; . . . and exerts himself that evil and demeritorious qualities already arisen may be abandoned; . . . and exerts himself that, meritorious qualities not yet arisen may arise; . . . this, O priest, is called right effort.[33]

It is a call to mind control by the will. The seventh is perhaps better termed "correct mindfulness," as indicating the content of the habitual attitude of mind. "As respects the body, observant of the body strenuous, conscious, contemplative, and has rid himself of lust and griefs"; the same attitude and formula is enjoined toward "sensation," "the mind," and "the elements of being."[34] In the eighth step, the program is stated in terms of the four *dhyanas** or trances of the meditation *sutras*, which can hardly be paraphrased and which are therefore quoted. The first "is accompanied by applied and discursive thinking," while the second "is devoid of applied and discursive thinking, born of concentration, rapturous and joyful. Through distaste for rapture, . . . he experiences with his body that joy. . . ." and attains the third Dhyana. Finally, "he dwells in the fourth Dhyana, which is neither painful nor pleasurable—in utter purity of evenmindedness and mindfulness."[35]

NINE INCAPABILITIES

What are "the nine"? The nine incapabilities. The nine exemplify the practical and empirical expression of spiritual life in moral conduct. The monk who has reached perfection is so self-controlled that he is incapable of performing evil deeds.

> The brother who is arahant, in whom the intoxicants are destroyed, who has lived the life, who has done his task, who has laid low his burden, who has attained salvation, who has utterly destroyed the fetter of rebirth, who is emancipated by the true gnosis, he is incapable of perpetrating nine things:
> 1. He is incapable of deliberately depriving a living creature of life.
> 2. He is incapable of taking what is not given so that it constitutes theft.
> 3. He is incapable of sexual impurity.
> 4. . . . of deliberately telling lies.
> 5. . . . of laying up treasure for indulgence in worldly pleasure. . . .
> 6. . . . of taking a wrong course through partiality.
> 7. . . . of taking a wrong course through hate.
> 8. . . . of taking a wrong course through stupidity.
> 9. . . . of taking a wrong course through fear.[36]

TEN REFLECTIONS

What are "the ten"? The ten reflections taken from a list of subjects of Meditation:

The following make forty subjects of meditation: ten kasinas, ten impurities, ten reflections, four sublime states, four formless states, one perception, and one analysis.

The ten reflections are: reflection on the Buddha, reflection on the Doctrine, reflection on the Order, reflection on conduct, reflection on liberality, reflection on the gods, the contemplation of death, the contemplation of the body, the contemplation of breathing, reflection of quiescence.[37]

It will be noted that the first three are the Triratna or three refuges: the Buddha, the Dharma, and the *Sangha*. The fifth, "on the gods," is interesting in relation to the problem of how to classify Buddhism in terms of theism, and so on. Thomas says, speaking of this very reflection:

It does not deny the gods, but it recommends remembrance of them only in order to recognize that they have reached their respective heavens by means of such faith, morality, and other virtues as the disciple himself possesses. They are not worshipped, they are not the basis of morality, nor are they the bestowers of happiness.[38]

ELEVEN STEPS

What are "the eleven"? Eleven steps or stages of the path to freedom. There are few canonical series of eleven, and this eleven is artificial because we omit the twelfth as the goal of knowledge that is reached by the eleven. It is the positive form of the chain of causation that will be our "twelve." Very few scholars have mentioned it.[39]

The point is that the "negative" form of the casual law or explanation of continued existence of human beings, which we will see in "twelve," is the only form generally known; it occurs in many versions and is an essential doctrine of Buddhism. But this "positive" causal sequence for *liberation* from *samsara* is hidden, unknown, rare. In Mrs. Rhys Davids' "Editorial Notes" to the Pali Text source, she says:

Yet more refreshing is it to find that oasis on p. 26 (XII, #27) where a causal sequence of joy and happiness for this once only is harnessed to the scheme! How might it not have altered the whole face of Buddhism to the West if that sequence had been made the illustration of the causal law! . . . Yet how it is hidden away in this book! How many students of Buddhism have ever seen it?[40]

The text states the pattern in both directions, and the positive form is brief, as follows, the preposition "with" denoting causal dependence:

faith with sorrow, joy with faith, rapture with joy, serenity with rapture, happiness with serenity, concentration with happiness, the knowledge and vision into things as they really are with concentration, repulsion with the knowledge and vision into things as they really are, passionlessness with repulsion, liberation with passionlessness, . . .[41]

From sorrow as the beginning arises faith, and so on, which brings one through the eleven steps to the goal: "knowledge about extinction [of intoxicants] . . ." As Mrs. Rhys Davids says, it is a strong and hopeful path to freedom.

TWELVE NIDANAS*

What are "the twelve"? The twelve *nidanas*. The *nidanas* are "causes," and hence they are commonly called a causal chain or nexus; the series is also known as "interdependent origination," and, in the Pali Canon, the "middle doctrine" "as avoiding the doctrine of *To on* ["the being"] on the one hand, and of nihilism or the denial of reality or existence on the other."[42] That is, the two are a view of the eternal existence of the self on the one hand, and a view of complete nonbeing, utter and absolute unreality or nothingness of the self, on the other. The *Nidanas* constitute an explanation for the continuous existence of sentient beings in spite of *anatta* or nonself, and *anicca** or impermanence. Furthermore, the doctrines of *karma* and *samsara* in Buddhist form are implied or involved here. Actually, this is the answer to Mrs. Rhys Davids's lament that the "negative" causal chain is the one found everywhere else in the scriptures: it serves to explain and justify the workings of *karma* and *samsara*, and the "existence" of the self—that is why it is the standing pattern.

Not death but rebirth is the enemy, in Buddhism, as in Hinduism. It is the life that is tied to this ceaseless round, from which the Buddha escaped by his own great achievement, and which others can cross over and thus reach the further shore, which must be transcended. Death is made a subject of meditation: "the ten impurities" of the "forty subjects of meditation" are "a bloated corpse, a purple corpse, a putrid corpse," and so on. But the point is not the horror of death but the horror of the futile and illusory existence which does *not* end in death, but begins again! It is no accident that an Indian religion produced a metaphor for the endlessness of recurrent life which has been often copied. It is worth quoting in full, with the moral, to clarify our understanding of *samsara* and the need to escape:

> It is as if, O priest, there were a mountain consisting of a great rock, a league in length, a league in width, a league in height, without break, cleft, or hollow, and every hundred years a man were to come and rub it once with a silken garment; that mountain consisting of a great rock, O priest, would more quickly wear away and come to an end than a world-cycle. O priest, this is the length of a world cycle. And many such cycles, O priest, have rolled by, and many hundreds of cycles, and many thousands of cycles, and many hundreds of thousands of cycles. And why do I say so? Because, O priest, this round of existence is without known starting-point, and of beings who course and roll along from birth to birth, blinded by ignorance, and fettered by desire, there is no beginning discernible. Such is the length of time, O priest, during which misery and calamity have endured, and the cemeteries have been replenished; insomuch, O priest, that there is every reason to feel disgust and aversion for all the constituents of being, and to free oneself from them.[43]

Ordination of a monk, Wat Bovornives, Bangkok. The novice is a young Australian who is taking temporary vows in order to study. The lay woman in the foreground has brought gifts for him in his life of poverty. Note begging bowl at right side.

(Ward J. Fellows)

That is *samsara*. *Karma* is the operation of the moral continuities that determine one's rebirth to another life in the rounds of *samsara*. To call it a "law" is to give it more of the status of a separate government or judgment as in Western religious terms. It simply is a fact, in Buddhism; the world simply is like that. Good actions have good effects that work themselves out in one or another lifetime, with evil actions having corresponding effects. Moggallana was one of Buddha's two chief disciples, but when he was murdered by highwaymen Buddha calmly told the monks that his death was suited to his bad *karma* from a previous existence, when he had murdered his father and mother.

There is no suggestion of a moral governor enforcing divine laws of reward and punishment after the fact. There is only the ineluctable operation of a total world system in which human destiny works itself out in moral terms. The operation of *karma* was described by Buddhaghosa in a simple verse:

A round of karma and fruit;
The fruit from karma doth arise,
From karma then rebirth doth spring;
And thus the world rolls on and on.[44]

The Buddha's *dharma* confronted this situation unflinchingly, described the human predicament in the Fourfold Truth, and provided a theoretical basis for understanding and using the system itself. This basis is interdependent origination, the twelve *nidanas*. Again we find that there is more than one list in the literature, which fact may help us to see that the total causal sequence matters more than the specific links in the chain. The undeniable fact that there are people who do suffer is explained as the working of cause and effect in a pattern that produces old age, misery, and death. To break that pattern, one must break the chain. Here is one of the many versions of the chain:

> That things have being, O Kaccana, constitutes one extreme of doctrine; that things have no being is the other extreme. These extremes, O Kaccana, have been avoided by the Tathagata, and it is a middle doctrine he teaches:
>   On ignorance depends karma;
>   On karma depends consciousness;
>   On consciousness depend name and form;
>   On name and form depend the six organs of sense;
>   On the six organs of sense depends contact;
>   On contact depends sensation;
>   On sensation depends desire;
>   On desire depends attachment;
>   On attachment depends existence;
>   On existence depends birth;
>   On birth depend old age and death, sorrow, lamentation, misery, grief, and
> despair. Thus does this entire aggregation of misery arise.[45]

The causal chain accounts for the life and rebirth of living souls, in spite of the nonself doctrine. By understanding this pattern of pain and then breaking the pattern, escape from desire and suffering is possible.

Metaphysical Systems

The Hinayana philosophic systems taught the impermanence of all things, both selves and objects, because they are nothing but momentary, shifting, changing collections of elements or *dharmas*. They did not, however, deny the reality of the elements themselves and of the series or collection. With Mahayana, however, this unreality of the world was extended to call into question any objective reality at all, for the Mahayana systems said, in various ways, that all *dharmas* are no things.

Two principal Mahayana systems of doctrine or metaphysics coalesced from the development of systematic thought about the nature of the world. Both of them serve the purpose of an ontology or theory of being or existence, even though as theories they deny the reality of ordinary existence. Their ultimate purpose or motive is religious, the attainment of Nirvana, and the systems are meant to be used for spiritual understanding toward that end.

THE MIDDLE DOCTRINE

One is known as the Madhyamika* (Middle Doctrine) and is associated with Nagarjuna* (*ca. c.e.* 100) and with the *Perfection of Wisdom sutras* which were mentioned in our literature section. It is sometimes known as the Void School, from *sunya,** "void" or "empty," but that name is misleading because it suggests complete emptiness or nothingness. The middle doctrine denies the two extremes of being and nonbeing only in order to affirm the reality of the void itself, which is void or empty of any and all *specific* qualities but somehow exists or is real. The definition or description of that reality, however, differs with different interpreters. In the principal texts there is not so much exposition of a doctrine as a puzzling and paradoxical method in which certain specific assertions of fact or principle are categorically pronounced and then are dogmatically denied or contradicted. This method can be seen in the *Diamond Sutra* and in Nagarjuna's *Examination of Causality*. The outcome of this writing is sometimes termed nonsense, in that contradictory statements are asserted and no significant true statement can be made because the senses give us only changing phenomena. Others call it a doctrine of relativism, and stress its positive function: "According to these philosophies, our understanding acceptance that 'all is empty' as measured by the standards of ordinary experience and logic is the necessary and sufficient condition of realizing that which is supremely true but inexpressible in terms of experience and logic."[46]

The substance of the doctrine is that reality is void or empty of the characteristics which it appears to have. A clear and simple summary is provided by Thomas:

> The old doctrine that there was no entity in a self beyond the elements that compose it was extended to things in general (*dharma-nairatma*). Existence consists of dharmas, things or objects, but what can be said of these objects? They are all impermanent and changing, and nothing can be said of them at one moment which is not false the next. They are as unreal as the atman itself.[47]

The point of Nagarjuna's philosophy is to destroy people's conceptual frames through which they try to explain everything. Through the methodological negation in this philosophy many Buddhists have mystical experience that is expanded in *prajna** (wisdom) texts.

MIND ONLY

The other principal Mahayana school is the "mind only" or "consciousness only" or Vijnanavada. Its chief literary sources are the *Lankavatara Sutra*, Ashvogosha's *Awakening of Faith*, and the writings of the traditional founders of the school, Asanga (*ca.* C.E. 500) and Vasabandhu. Everything is denied except consciousness (*vijnana*); hence the name "Vijnanavda." A key term of Ashvagosha's exposition is "thusness" or "suchness" (*tathata**): the absolute goal, principle, reality. "What is meant by the soul as suchness is the oneness of the totality of things, the great all-including whole. . . ."[48] "Suchness" was also expounded in the *Lankavatara Sutra* as Tathagata, hence Buddhahood and mind, but mind apart from all else. The essence of this suchness is mind or consciousness, and the goal of spiritual knowledge is to apprehend this truth and thereby be one with Buddha in Nirvana. All ideas come from the one store-consciousness (*alayavijnana**), and true knowledge is of this pure, undifferentiated mind, which is also the only reality. If we think we have true ideas of the world apart from those ideas, we are mistaken. Once we know that the only reality is the store-consciousness from which come all our ideas, we apprehend the truth.

The Oneness of the Absolute

There is a special kind of oneness that is suggested by or emerges from Mahayana doctrines, which is hard to define or analyze but which definitely counts in Mahayana spiritual life. It is the analogue of the ontological relativity of all existence in Mahayana philosophy. For although the parts or elements are unreal, the whole thing, the total complex of innumerable unreal collections, is ultimate reality. The total or whole of what taken separately is relative, *is*, is real and actual, as some kind of ultimate or absolute. Such statements as these express the meaning in metaphysical terms: "Samsara is Nirvana, because there is, when viewed from the ultimate nature of the Dharmakaya, nothing going out of, nor coming into, existence [samsara being only apparent]: Nirvana is samsara, when it is coveted and adhered to."[49] "This our worldly life is an activity of Nirvana itself, not the slightest distinction exists between them," says Nagarjuna.[50] The enlightened one is in Nirvana even in the midst of the world, because, to one who understands, both Nirvana and *samsara* lack any differentiated characteristics and all is one.

The same oneness is arrived at by the route of the Buddha nature. In the truth body (*dharmakahya*) there is also a kind of ultimate transcendent reality. Because sentient beings possess the Buddha nature—whether they know it or not—they are *potentially* one with the Buddha. The Bodhisattvas are *actually* one with the Buddha, even though they keep themselves from Nirvana, because they do not allow the apparent differences and discriminations of worldly existence to arise in themselves. This ill-defined but positive absolute pervades Mahayana through the character of Nirvana as beyond the relativity of existence and nonexistence, and of Buddha as an ultimate and absolute reality—for, to the Mahayanist, both of them are experienced or empirical facts.

RITUAL AND WORSHIP IN BUDDHISM

We are not able to say how many practicing Buddhists there are and exactly what they do in performance of their religious duties, but we can describe in a general way the theory and practice of ritual and worship in Buddhism. The central and unifying factor is again Buddha, but the difference between pure Hinayana and pure Mahayana is very wide. Some scholars say there is almost no cultus or worship in the Buddha's original program. We shall begin by discussing Nirvana as the goal or end of the religious practices for all Buddhists, and next we shall deal with meditation; then follow separate sections on Hinayana and Mahayana.

Nirvana, the Indescribable Final Good

Nirvana is the goal, the end sought, and all means toward that end are, in the broad sense of the terms, worship or ritual. Applying the term "salvation" to Buddhism, we find that enlightenment brings salvation; but then Nirvana is the ultimate blessedness which constitutes salvation, the beatific vision in Buddhism. Thus we get a kind of working or operational definition of Nirvana as the happy state or condition that is the goal or fulfillment even beyond salvation in Buddhism. But that does not give us the characteristics or description of Nirvana—what Nirvana is like. It is hard to do that because Nirvana connotes the ineffable, the indescribable, the transcendent realm sought in this pragmatic religion.

A few specific descriptive factors can be listed regarding Nirvana, but they are mostly negative. Etymologically, the word comes from the preposition *nir* used in a negative sense, and *va* for wind—hence calm, unruffled, and therefore extinct, like a fire or flame gone out; but this etymology is not a prominent aspect of the doctrine. In any case Nirvana is positively not annihilation, as early disputes recorded in the Pali Canon and Mahayana *sutras* make completely explicit. That which is ended is the hold of *karma* and the round of rebirth. When the factors that comprise the stream of individual existence have their interdependence destroyed and hence no longer originate, then Nirvana is attained. It is sometimes described as getting rid of the three fires—lust, anger, and sloth. More positively, it is a state most to be desired and utterly satisfying—somehow—to the discarnate and liberated soul, because the pattern of birth, suffering, unsatisfied desire, old age, and death has been utterly broken and transcended. Therefore it is deathless and changeless, but this refers to the quality of the experience more than to simple duration in time. The conqueror of grasping and attachment is free from what can be described in literary terms as "the pathos of temporality," that is, the melancholy sense of mortality that hangs over all our relationships, our achievements and possessions, our comings, and especially our goings when we know we will not see again these places and faces. Above all Nirvana is frequently described as a state of happiness and bliss uncontaminated by all attachment and dependence.

Although there are some problems about it, a distinction is usually made between Nirvana and Paranirvana. The distinction is found in *The Itivuttaka* in the Pali Canon: "Monks, there are these two conditions of Nirvana. What two? The condition of Nirvana with the basis still remaining and that without basis." Exactly what is meant by this is not made entirely clear, but it is defined as being with and without dependence on the five *skandhas*. It usually is taken to mean before and after physical death. In any event, it is a natural development of doctrine to explain how Gautama Buddha could have been in Nirvana while still alive, but now is totally beyond reach in some ultimate state. The actual state of the *arhat* after death was among the proscribed questions. In a long sermon in question and answer form with Vaccha, the wandering ascetic, Gautama repudiated all explicit answers to the following questions: whether or not the soul and body are identical; whether or not the saint exists after death; whether or not and where he is reborn after death. He says such questions are irrelevant, like asking about a fire which has gone out, "in which direction has that fire gone. . . ?"[51] All that we know, he insists, is that the saint is free from all attachments, has attained deliverance from what is called consciousness.

MEDITATION AS THE WAY TO NIRVANA

The fact that most Buddha images are seated in the cross-legged posture of meditation points to the central importance of meditation in the life of Buddha and for the disciple, both in Hinayana and Mahayana Buddhism. The Pali Canon often describes Gautama's meditation and is full of techniques and disciplines for concentration, which probably were taken over from Hindu yoga. Buddhists did not claim that the practice of concentration was original in Buddhism, but that they had the true method, right concentration. The objective was also different from Hinduism, not the attainment of the pure *atman* by stripping away all thought and feeling, but the creation of a new and higher state of mind, *panna*,* the Pali for Sanskrit *prajna*: wisdom, knowledge, enlightenment. Even when stillness is reached by the saint, the mind is not left behind or derogated in Buddhism; one is still mindful, but in the proper way. This is seen in the eightfold path: the culmination in the eighth step is a mental condition of pure freedom from all limitations.

However, Nirvana is not reached simply by analytical and discursive reasoning. Apparently the first disciples did grasp or attain at once, under Buddha's guidance and inspiration, *samadhi** (concentrative absorption). Later followers needed more time, understanding, practice, and skill in a discipline which is both spiritual and mental. Our seventh "Tenet," the seven factors of enlightenment, is an example of these techniques. Conze, in *Buddhist Meditation*, says that meditation includes mindfulness, concentration, and wisdom. Mindfulness is the initial and preparatory stage. The second stage is transic concentration or *samadhi*. (This term means "rapture" or "bliss" in Hinduism, and is a key word in Buddhism, the eighth step of the path being *samma-samadhi*.) Conze says: "Spiritual, or transic, concentration results less from intellectual effort than from a rebirth of the whole personality, including the body, the emotions, and the will."[52] To this stage belong the four trances, in which concentration is directed to an object, in which the *dharmas* themselves are the subject and substance of the pure mental and spiritual state or condition.

Meditation can be compared with prayer in Western religious practice. Both are means open to and initiated by the believer in relation to the ultimate reality, the divine. But whereas prayer is meant, in part, to address or speak to God, as a sort of transaction between two parties, meditation is essentially a personal, self-contained, subjective operation concerned with, but not really involving or implicating, the subject of meditation in the operation. Prayer is to God; meditation is about the divine or supernal reality.

Although the theory and in some ways the practice of later and Northern Buddhism differs from early and Southern Buddhism, both of them use meditation as the way to enlightenment; however, in Mahayana there are other distinctive ways to *samadhi* that are more popular.

MANDALAS AND MANTRAS*

Two aids for promoting *samadhi* are mandalas and mantras, which are especially important in Tibetan Buddhism and are sometimes used in other traditions. They have become familiar to Western students through the popularity of Nepalese and Tibetan Buddhism. A typical Nepalese or Tibetan mandala is in form *thang-ka*, literally "rolled up," being a painting on paper or cloth so that it can be rolled up. The painting is a diagrammatic representation of the universe in religious terms. Usually a large, central Buddha figure is surrounded by smaller Bodhisattvas or other deities and various symbols of key doctrines as decoration. They are arranged in such a way as to lead the mind of the one who meditates on the mandala to the higher nature of the Buddha and Buddha world.

Mantras are words or phrases whose utterance has spiritual potency. They are used as an aid for meditation and concentration, as well as memory devices and for spells against misfortune. The most famous is the "*Om Mani Padme Hum*,"* whose origin and meaning are disputed, but which comes out of Vajrayana. Usually it has been translated "Oh, the jewel in the lotus," and some authorities construe it as a reference to Avolakitesvara. Written on paper or wood and blessed by the lamas, the mantra is incorporated into a prayer wheel twirled by the holder or set as a windmill or water wheel. Then every rotation is considered a recitation of the mantra.

Ritual and Worship in Hinayana

"Do it yourself" is a modern phrase that expresses the Hinayana way to salvation. Texts for this adjuration to the monks by Sakyamuni are found all through the Pali Canon. At the point of death the Blessed One addressed the priests; the *Digha Nikaya* says: "And now, O priests, I take my leave of you; all the constituents of being are transitory; work out your salvation with diligence."[53] Until the effects of *karma* and the hold of desire are gone, one is bound to the wheel of *samsara;* but only the one who "swelters at the task" by himself can attain release. This is the message and method of Hinayana Buddism then and now. As a consequence, the true Buddhist in Hinayana countries is the monk, and there is a spiritual difference between the monk and the layman. But for both of them, in theory at least, religion is not a matter of help from a god who controls and dispenses salvation by grace without regard to individual *karma* and the *dharma*. Rather is it true that monks and lay people alike must strive by their own efforts to attain release. This is because Gautama is the only Buddha, and he is in Nirvana, having attained coolness, and is no longer moved by any desire, being constitutionally unable to hear or answer prayer.

We have now moved into the problematic area of the specific actions of the faithful, who often do not know the theory but only the custom, the actual practice. In practice, Hinayana is monks' religion, for only they can work at the job of meditation and discipline toward enlightenment. Yet they generally do not expect to attain it in this life, to be an *arhat*. That common expectation ended many centuries ago, perhaps early in the Christian era as Mahayana was developing, so that in practice it is almost an unattainable idea, although it is not theoretically impossible. Therefore only when Maitreya, the future Buddha, comes will believers gain enlightenment in the body. This tends to produce a somewhat relaxed mood in some monasteries, rather than the intense striving of those who must lift themselves by their own boot straps to the supernal realm.

In some countries of southeast Asia nearly a quarter of the men wear the saffron-colored cotton robe of the Buddhist monk. Some of them are only temporary monks, for in Hinayana countries it is customary for young men of good families to enter a monastery for a period of time. In Burma almost all Burmese boys spend at least a week there at the age of 15. "Young men of good family"—a phrase often used by the Buddha in the *Lotus Sutra*—in Thailand are temporarily ordained as monks, following the custom of spending the rainy season in a monastery. While there the young men observe the discipline, including begging for their food, to be eaten before noon. In some places small boys of four or five have their heads shaved and their "princely robes" replaced by the saffron robe in emulation of the Buddha's renunciation, and then they spend a night in the monastery. These temporary disciples recite "The Three Refuges," which have been the formula for entrance into the *Sangha* since earliest days.

Begging monk, Bangkok. Monks from Wat Bovor-
nives on their early morning begging rounds

(Ward J. Fellows)

THE THREE REFUGES

I put my trust in Buddha.
I put my trust in the Law. [Dharma]
I put my trust in the priesthood [Sangha]

The typical religious establishment in Hinayana countries is a walled compound or enclosure, called a *wat**. In Burma the central structure is usually a
combined temple and dormitory, having an elaborate, multistoried roof whose
ends are curved finials, the whole standing at least a few feet off the ground.
There is usually a large chamber with a high ceiling; this is a multipurpose
room—meeting place for study and assembly, dining room, dormitory if it is
not separate; at the eastern end is one principal Buddha image and altar with
flowers, flags, and candles. Within or outside there is a stupa or shrine which
houses a relic of Buddha, or a large outdoor Buddha image. In Thailand the
temples make more provision for public worship, having a kind of raised pulpit for a preacher in the middle of the hall. The altar furnishings may include

clocks as offerings. Burmese and Thai temples are lavishly decorated with color, mosaic, mirrors, and gold leaf. Hinayana monks are not sequestered. They make their begging rounds, officiate at religious rites in the temple and for lay people, perform community projects, provide most of the schooling, and undertake special devotions to help lay people gain merit, in addition to their morning and evening assembly for chanting praise of Buddha and *dharma*, and personal prayer and meditation. In Bangkok young men from around the world—including some Westerners—are temporary monks in residence at *wats* while studying at the Buddhist university, Mahachula.

To gain merit toward better *karma* and eventual enlightenment is the purpose of the lay person's religious life and duties. Traditionally most acts of merit were associated with the monks and monasteries: giving food (alms) to the monks, building a pagoda*, providing for the support of a monastery, making a pilgrimage to and circumambulating a stupa. From an early date relics of Buddha were enshrined in structures built specifically for that purpose and called stupas or pagodas. The earliest ones are solid structures that enclose or cover the relic, a remnant of the body of the founder. Of course few of them even claim to incorporate a veritable physical relic of the Buddha himself; most house some kind of derivative relic—from a disciple, scriptures, and so on. Stupas are the characteristic structure of Hinayana and Vajrayana.

Worship at shrines and temples is usually individual and personal, individuals bringing a flower or candle offering held between the hands as they bow and then seat themselves before the Buddha image to recite their traditional or personal verses or prayers. The object of these devotions is praise and veneration of the one Gautama Buddha as the pioneer of enlightenment. In modern times many lay people engage in various good works and charitable enterprises as more social and humanitarian forms of merit. Modern developments and the spread of education have brought an increase in study and appreciation of the more abstract aspect of Buddhism. It must be admitted, however, that much of the popular religious life in these countries is mixed with primitive customs and involves what the anthropologists call "apotropaic" Buddhism, the religion of magical protection against ills and evils in this present existence. Overall, the aim of Hinayana religious life is to live conformably to the Buddha's *dharma* and to strive for the attainment of his transcendent wisdom.

Mahayana Worship and Ritual

When we turn to Mahayana forms of religious activity, we find customs that more closely resemble the sort of worship of a divine being familiar to Western minds. In terms of worship and devotion, Buddha figures like Avalokitesvara, Amitabha, and Vairocana are great gods of Asia. We also encounter an even more complex history and diversity of theory and practice.

James Bissett Pratt, in his book *The Pilgrimage of Buddhism*, said that he was surprised to find (*ca.* 1928) that many Hinayana Buddhists were unfamiliar with the Fourfold-Truth formula. However that may be, Mahayana Buddhism tends to minimize it, and an expression of this is the fact that in Mahayana the three characteristics of being are as follows (note the significant omission of misery or suffering):

All that exists is impermanent.
All elements are selfless.
Nirvana is serenity, peace.[54]

The result of this doctrinal shift is that the locus of evil, the point of attack, the victory to be won is over ignorance rather than over the desire, craving, burning of existence. Generally, the Mahayanist is not required to emulate the strenuous and lonely exertion of the Buddha to win the *dharma*, but only to see the light.

Chapter 3 of the *Lotus Sutra* includes the famous parable of the burning house, a Mahayana polemic against Hinayana strictness, and a defense of the one vehicle over the three. The rich father whose great but decrepit house catches fire entices his children safely out of the house by promises of three kinds of carts, but actually gives to all the same great vehicle, the best one. The three are: the *yana* or vehicle of the *sravaka** (an immediate disciple of Buddha or one of his followers); the *pratyekabhudda** (one who gets enlightenment by and for himself); and the Bodhisattva. In the section on tenets we described the Bodhisattvas and cosmic Buddhas who people the Mahayana world and heavens. The *Lotus Sutra* proclaims that

There have been an infinite number of
Buddhas saving people.
There have been hundreds of trillion kinds,
whose numbers cannot be calculated.

All those who have done any works out of heartfelt seeking for the Nirvana of the Buddhas achieve Buddhahood, and

All people such as these,
By gradual accumulation of merits
And with an adequate sense of compassion,
Have already achieved Buddhahood.[55]

They will see an infinite number of such Buddhas.

Now, obviously such a religion has a different cultus from the Hinayana. To overstate it: In one nobody is saved, in the other everybody is saved. The *Lotus Sutra* provides one basis for this universalism in the countless Bodhisattvas. They appear in the world: "In the world he pursues his course for the world's weal, unstained by worldly taints."[56] But in addition there are the eternal or cosmic Buddhas, like the Buddha Amitabha who has his own realm or Buddha-land of bliss to which all the faithful are transported. The *Larger Sukhavati-Vyuha* or Description of the Land of Bliss includes 48 vows or promises on behalf of believers, each vow in the form of a negative conditional: If in my Buddha country such-and-such is not true, then may I not obtain enlightenment. It follows logically that because Amitabha, who was then the Bodhisattva Dharmakara, did become enlightened as Amitabha Buddha, the promises must be true. The eighteenth of these vows is considered the most important by the Jodo-Shinshu of Japan. It promises that those who after hearing his name meditate on him with serene thoughts will after death behold and worship him with untroubled thoughts in his Buddha land of bliss. In the other Amitabha scripture, the *Meditation on Buddha Amitayus* is the basis for the Amitabha formula: "Adoration to Buddha Amitayus." Repetition of the thought and words will bring one after death to the land of bliss. From there one can easily go on to attain Nirvana. The effect, in terms of religious practice, of both these doctrines is to provide a popular religious cultus embracing all believers on a basis of faith and devotion, and that is what happened in China and Japan.

SCHOOLS OF MEDITATION BUDDHISM

The Meditation schools go back to the formidable figure of Bodhidharma in sixth-century China. His personal character is shown by his having meditated for nine years seated facing a wall; Chinese and Japanese prints depict his fierce scowl of concentration and piercing eyes as he confronts a questioner or crosses the river on a slender reed. The Japanese term for the school is "Zen," in Chinese it is "Ch'an"* fromi Pali "*jhana*" for Sanskrit "*dhyana*." They are complex concepts connoting active contemplation or meditation directed to ultimate truth and meaning in the form of wisdom. The characteristics of Zen can be summed up in the teaching attributed to Bodhidharma. Like the Pure Land thinkers, he saw the Buddha nature in the heart of every man, and to find that nature in one's own soul is the greatest good and supreme wisdom. Prayer, study of books, ascetic discipline are only "the tracks of the bird which the hunter pursues but not the bird itself." The vision of the Buddha nature is attained through intuitive insight, and brings light and deliverance. After the seventh century the school of sudden enlightenment as opposed to gradual enlightenment became dominant in China. Its classic expression in *The Platform Scripture of the Sixth Patriarch*, a famous verse attributed to Hui-neng, contradicting an earlier verse by his opponent, is:

By no means is Bodhi a kind of tree,
Nor is the bright, reflecting mind, a case of mirrors,
Since mind is emptiness,
Where can dust collect?[57]

MAHAYANA DEVOTION IN JAPAN

Japanese Buddhism is almost completely derivative from Chinese, but it has distinctive sects, has retained its integrity and vitality, and now constitutes the center and strength of Mahayana Buddhism. In contrast to Chinese Buddhism, which was rarely consciously sectarian, Japanese has been vigorously sectarian. Many beautiful monasteries are found in Japan, in which the monks retain their traditions, although most of them, except Zen monks, do not regularly go out to beg for food. However, they perform religious and social work in the community and preach in the open in the cities. Lay people visit the monasteries for spiritual refreshment and study. In monastery temples prayers are conducted at least twice a day—morning and evening—and scriptures are recited. Public worship somewhat similar to Western communal religious services may be conducted on Sundays, including prayer, chants, sermons, and offerings. With hands in the Asian position for prayer, worshippers wear a small rosary around their wrists. In some temples candles are replacing the traditional incense sticks which are lit as an offering. The traditional temple is a light and airy wooden structure, with an altar having a golden Buddha image in the central place of honor, surrounded by flowers and other decorations and paraphernalia. Some temples have numerous Buddha figures, of different types depending on the sect, and a few have a pagoda on the grounds. Japanese Buddha iconography is very complicated. In the Pure Land temples the central act of worship is the recitation of the "Nembutsu"* formula, *Namu Amida Butsu,** reverence or homage to *Amida** (Amitabha) Buddha, in accordance with the injunction in the *Amitayur-Dhyana-Sutra.*

Special or occasional observances include various festivals. The ancient Bon or Obon is on July 15, an outdoor festival commemorating Buddha's death. The brightest and principal festival in Japan is the Hanamatsuri or flower festival on Buddha's birthday, April 8, in which children carry lotus flowers and ladle sweet tea over the head of the image of the infant Buddha. Water is poured over the image of Ojizosama, Japanese form of Bodhisattva Kshitigarbha, revered as a protector of young children in the afterlife, in whose behalf the image is also draped with red cloth. December 8 marks the enlightenment of Gautama. Most funeral and memorial ceremonies in Japan are Buddhist, and exorcisms of evil spirits are conducted by some sects. Marriage ceremonies may be Buddhist instead of Shinto, with which a resurgent Buddhism shares the very active religious life of Nippon.

ETHICAL AND INSTITUTIONAL ASPECTS OF BUDDHISM

The two complementary aspects of Buddhism are the intellectual and doctrinal forms we have described and the ethical and moral practices to which we now turn. In perhaps no other religion are they so completely interrelated and interdependent; the usual summary terms for them are wisdom and compassion. But the scriptural expression of the relation between thought and action is in the mutuality and equality of three factors: morals, mental training or concentration, and wisdom. In this formula the middle term serves to connect the two extremes, and a *Dhammapada** verse expresses this:

Not to commit any sin, to do good,
And to purify one's own mind, that is the teaching of (all) the Buddhas.

Morality and mental training lead to the wisdom taught by Buddha. Moral behavior is central to Buddhism, part of its rational and pragmatic solution to the human religious situation.

Underlying Principles

DHARMA

The fundamental theoretical component of Buddhist morality is derived from the total Buddhist law or *dharma*. It shares with many other religions or metaphysical systems the conviction that there is an underlying structure or order of the universe which includes human actions in their moral context. Thomas says:

> All Indian religions are dominated by a single conception, which goes back to pre-Indian times. In both Vedic and old Persian it is expressed by the same word meaning "law." It is the view that all things and beings follow or ought to follow a certain course prescribed for them. The course is based upon the actual nature and constitution of the existing world, through which the sun rises duly, the seasons return, and each individual part performs its own function.[58]

Note what the Buddhist *dharma* is not, however. It is not God's command or law, as in the Western Biblical religions; and hence Buddhist morality is not an ethic of sanctions (rewards and punishments) enforced by a divine ruler and judge. It is not tied to a social system or institutional structure, as Hinduism's ethic is related to caste and social patterns. *Dharma* is not a system or metaphysical entity or structure in its own right.

It simply is an empirical fact, says Buddha, that things are this way: there is suffering which depends on craving, and this leads to certain consequences. Buddhism does not know of, far less explicitly raise, the question posed by Plato in the Euthyphro: Is holiness simply a fact by itself, or do the gods decide what it is? But if the question were put, we can be sure of Buddhism's answer: The holy and just are primordial, actual, purely empirical facts, which are before and beyond any gods, who like any other beings can only see and discern, but not order and decree, what is good or evil.

The Causal Order   The idea of cause and effect is basic in Buddhism and is used in many Buddhist theories. Cause and effect—as seen in the Four Noble

Truths—produce human misery and keep human beings in the grip of *karma* and the round of *samsara*. Interdependent origination, the twelve *nidanas* in our catechism, is the way in which *karma* operates, through cause and effect, to hold people in unending cycles of *samsara*. As Professor Burtt has pointed out,[59] the causal chain guards against someone saying that because there is no self there is no moral responsibility, because this causal sequence provides the continuity through time which seems to be denied by the nonself teaching. The twelve *nidanas*, therefore, are the necessary theoretical basis for a system of positive morality; that is, one might object that *karma*, *samsara*, and nonself determine one's moral nature and excuse one from personal responsibility. But the causal chain explains moral responsibility and makes each person accountable for his or her own life.

That system of cause and effect is, therefore, the explanation of human misery. But another pattern of cause and effect can break the chain of *karma* and *samsara!* This is the gospel (good news) of Buddhism. The other or good causal chain delivers people from the bad causal chain. The good causal chain is the Buddhist law, the *dharma*, which is usually symbolized as the wheel of the law, and the wheel is the most characteristic Buddhist symbol. Buddha described himself at the outset of his ministry as "turning the wheel of the law." The wheel can also be used as a figure for *samsara*, the bad causal chain which operates through the *nidanas*. What we might call the gospel of Buddhism, then, is that people can stop the wheel of *samsara* by turning the wheel of the *dharma*.

UNIVERSALISM

From the beginning, there is a universalism in Buddhism in Buddha's practice of disregarding caste and seeking to lead all to *samadhi*. (Although he was worried about their effect on the *Sangha*, he admitted women as nuns and made no sex distinction in his preaching.) Universalism was extended, rationalized, and made more explicit in the Bodhisattva doctrines and literature of the Mahayana. In particular, there was a shift from preoccupation with individual enlightenment as the ideal of the *arhat*, to the Bodhisattva's fundamentally universalistic motive and operation. The Bodhisattva first of all seeks to bring others to the *dharma*, to Buddha, to wisdom, and will not be content until all beings are rescued; his merit is for the benefit of others.

The salvation of all beings is possible because in every one there is present the *bodhichitta*,* according to Mahayanist writings. The Buddha mind, which is supreme *bodhi* (wisdom), is the original essence of every mind. "As it is said: 'In each being there exists in embryonic form the element of the Tathagata, but people do not look through to that.' "[60] Morality itself is only possible because our minds have a spiritual affinity with the Buddhas. By morality and mental training the full expression of this inherent wisdom is possible, not so much an attainment as an uncovering and liberation of what is there already. In Mahayana meditation this is an essential presupposition; mind and morals enter in as necessary aspects of the full program.

Practices

We cannot actually separate "practice" from moral theory, and Buddhism does not do so. The threefold mutuality of morals, concentration, and wisdom makes morality simply the precondition in life and practice to *prajna*, but understanding is essential to the discipline; so they are, as we said, interrelated. To clarify, we now set out some specific practices enjoined in pursuit of the life and mind of supreme wisdom, *sambodhi*. One further clarification, however, is necessary in this context, lest anyone should apply certain categories often used in Western religion. Ethics or moral practices are not by themselves a sure way to salvation in Buddhism; it is not a doctrine of "works" because moral conduct by itself does not guarantee enlightenment, and wisdom or insight cannot be assured by performance of specific steps, even though the prescriptions of sets of steps abound in the religion of Buddha. After 40 years of service the "beloved disciple" Ananda was "still a pupil with much yet to be done" when Buddha was on his deathbed and promised him, "Soon shall you be made perfect." The Eightfold Path remains the prime guide to thought and action for all branches of Buddhism, and the end is right rapture or meditation.

VICES AND VIRTUES

The three primal manifestations of egotism are all kinds of lust, desire, and evil intention. The three roots of evil are greed (for pleasure), anger, and delusion. The five hindrances are: sensual desire, ill will, slothfulness and apathy, excitedness or vanity, and perplexity or doubt. There are eight great hells, depending on the sin. These lists can be expanded.

The five virtues are organs or faculties in the broader context of meditation practice: faith, vigor or exertion, mindfulness, concentration, and wisdom. Sometimes the five are called the cardinal virtues, but lists vary, and only three of them deserve the title, as found on nearly every list: faith, contemplation, and wisdom. The six perfections of our number six were the later form of ten perfections ascribed to the Buddha in the story of Sumedha: the future Buddha promised himself and his teacher that he would practice all ten of the virtues ensuring his attainment of Buddhahood. With the extension of Buddhahood to all Bodhisattvas in Mahayana, the six perfections became the goal for all followers of the path of Buddha.

METTA* AND KARUNA* IN BUDDHIST MORALITY

As a significant aspect of Buddhism and a point of comparison with other faiths, let us discuss *metta* (loving kindness or benevolence) and *karuna* (compassion). One of the seven factors of enlightenment that we discussed is an ethical norm: gentleness. Hinayana practice always stressed inoffensiveness, *ahimsa* or no-shedding-of-blood, nonviolence, on the part of the monks, although specific texts for it are hard to find. *The Collection of Discourses (Sutta Nipata)* includes the *Metta Sutta* or *Discourse on Love*, verses from which are often quoted as a prescription for outgoing love:

> As a mother at the risk of her life watches over her own child, her only child, so also let every one cultivate a boundless (friendly) mind toward all beings.
>
> And let him cultivate good will towards all the world, a boundless (friendly) mind, above and below and across, unobstructed, without hatred, without enmity.[61]

In practice one finds concern about taking the lives of creatures: There is a ceremony in Japanese Buddhism (Pure Land) of justification for fishermen who must take the lives of fish, and in the great memorial park at Mt. Koya south of Kyoto there is a monument, raised by the trade association for exterminator businesses, for the countless white ants (termites) which they are called to exterminate.

Metta is the more active expression of concern for human welfare in broad terms, putting others before oneself. *Karuna* or compassion is important not only in the ethical context but doctrinally and in regard to Buddhas. *Karuna* is an essential attribute of all Buddhas, especially as the motive for a Bodhisattva's deferral of Nirvana, and becomes a doctrine of positive or saving grace in Avalokitesvara, Amitabha, and Kuan-Yin. It was his compassion for the spiritual suffering of all beings, in their ignorance and desire, which moved Gautama to return to the world where he demonstrated enlightenment. The preeminence of the three Buddhas mentioned above arose from the gradual emergence of *karuna* as more important than *prajna* (wisdom) in Buddhist theory and practice.

In comparison with Confucianism, we will see that there benevolence or "human-heartedness" is the essential ethical norm, but it is more a matter of the correct attitude and lacks the active or outgoing element of *metta*. Although of course Judaism and Islam enjoin kindness toward other human beings, in these religions the virtue is not given the central place which it holds in Buddhism and Christianity. In both Buddhist compassion and Christian love there is the idea of active, outgoing, gratuitous (in the sense of not required, earned, or deserved) love from the divine or supernal toward human beings; and in both the believer is to emulate the divine love. The grace of God as love was manifested in Jesus, say Christians, and the Bodhisattvas manifest their grace in their activity and teaching out of *karuna*. Both Jesus Christ and Bodhisattvas are, therefore, savior figures; at this point they both resemble Hindu *avatars*. Differences arise in that while the Christian believer is called actively to *bear* the actual sufferings of others, the Bodhisattva, simply by living in the world, is suffering on *behalf* of others and is not called to suffer with them.

The more active element in Buddhism is taken by *metta*, as expressed in the quotation above. In both Christian and Buddhist ethics the motive for love is supplied by the grace and the example of the savior figures.

Practitioners of the Dharma

HINAYANA

Principles and norms require someone to apply them, to put them into practice or operation. There was first of all Gautama Buddha who lived and taught the *dharma*. After he had gone into ultimate Nirvana there was the *dharma* which he left as a guide. The practitioners of the full way were the monks of the *Sangha*, for whom there were the Ten Precepts. Lay people, who could not renounce the world and become *bhikkus** (disciples) on the way to arhatship, could practice the first five of the ten, hence the Five Precepts.

The traditional Hinayana code is as follows:

The ten precepts or laws of the priesthood.
Abstinence from destroying life;
Abstinence from theft;
Abstinence from fornication and all uncleanness;
Abstinence from lying
Abstinence from fermented liquor, spirits and strong drink which are a hindrance to merit.
Abstinence from eating at forbidden times;
Abstinence from dancing, singing, and shows;
Abstinence from adorning and beautifying the person by the use of garlands, perfumes, and unguents;
Abstinence from using a high or a large couch or seat;
Abstinence from receiving gold and silver; are the ten means (of leading a moral life).[62]

These remain the basis and fundamental rules. In the *Sangha* the number has been increased to over 200 in some orders, and first stress is put on sexual purity, as is perhaps natural for a celibate priesthood. From an anthology of Pali Buddhist verse comes this one, labelled by the translator "A Buddhist S. Anthony," and no doubt typical of the devout monk's attitude:

Fragrant with sandal-wood and garlanded,
  A girl was dancing gaily in the street
With softest strains of flute accompanied.
  I chanced upon my begging round to meet
The harlot, as she plied her shameful trade:
  "O Snare by Mara set, licentious jade"—
My gorge arose—my mind was free!
The Dharma's work behold in me,
Fruit of the Sage's husbandry.[63]

Ayudbaya, Thailand. People gain merit by paying the woman to free the birds from the cages. (At night the birds fly home to feed and roost. The next day they are taken out to be ransomed and freed again.)

(Ward J. Fellows)

There is no doubt that the monks' ideal of inoffensiveness, gentleness, and forbearance influences the life of Southeast Asia in that direction, even though the monks do not always practice it as a group when their interests are adversely affected. The author of a major anthropological study of Burmese Buddhism concludes that "the vast majority of them comply with the rule" when one excludes from consideration the "bogus" monks and considers those who are in the order out of conviction.[64] As we noted earlier, however, many monks do not really expect to attain Nirvana in the world. The underlying doc-trine is that we are living in a degenerate age, somewhat like the *kali yuga* of Hinduism. The effect on both monk and lay believers alike seems to be a kind of gentle melancholy.

MAHAYANA

The Mahayana ethical attitude was less narrow and restrictive than Hinayana, for various reasons, some of which have been suggested. Mahayana polemical tracts criticize the search for individual enlightenment as selfish, while Hi-nayana texts defend it as the true way to help the world by leading people to-ward Nirvana. In the *Lotus Sutra* and other works, the compassion of the Bod-hisattva is the motive and starting point for the deferral of Nirvana in order to help others reach it. (There was a precedent for this sort of self-sacrifice in the earlier scriptures. The *Jataka* includes "The Hare Mark in the Moon," which tells how the future Buddha was born as a rabbit and gladly jumped into the fire to provide food for a brahmin who needed it to perform his vows and yet could not break the precepts by destroying life.)

> A Bodhisattva resolves: I take upon myself the burden of all suffering, I am re-solved to do so, I will endure it. . . . I have made the vow to save all beings. . . .
> My endeavours do not merely aim at my own deliverance. For with the help of the boat of the thought of all-knowledge, I must rescue all these beings from the stream of Samsara, which is so difficult to cross, . . .[65]

Another aspect of Mahayana which broadened its appeal and partially ac-counted for its spread was the doctrine of "skill in means." A Bodhisattva at the seventh stage of perfection of wisdom is able to adapt words and teach-ings to fit people's needs by appealing to the relativity of all things accord-ing to the Madhiymika teaching of the void. Hinayana monks were ham-pered by their literalism about such prosaic matters as food and dress, while Mahayana adapted to fit conditions. For example, they disregarded the *vinaya* rule against the practice of medicine. Wright says that Ma-hayana Buddhism brought change to Chinese society in two major ways: first, "opposing a universal ethic to the long-prevailing familialism and par-ticularism"; second, "propagating the idea of the spiritual debt and the ex-piatory gift."[66] Nevertheless, Chinese Buddhism incorporated the Chinese emphasis on filial piety, as expressed in the *Meditation on Amitayus* used by both Chinese and Japanese Amitabha or Pure Land Buddhists. There a threefold goodness is enjoined on those who would be born in the Land of Highest Happiness in the Western quarter: "Firstly, they should act filially toward their parents and support them; serve and respect their teachers and elders; be of compassionate mind, abstain from doing any injury, and cultivate the ten virtuous actions."[67] The second goodness is to take the three refuges; third, to attain and promote the mind of wisdom. In practice,

Jizo (Kshitigarbha) images in the temple compound of Hierinji, Tokyo. Clothing is draped on the Bodhisattvas, who help the spirits of dead children into heaven. The evil witch snatches their clothes away, and they may not enter unclothed.

(Ward J. Fellows)

in both Chinese and Japanese Buddhism, heavy stress is laid on this first injunction to filial piety.

SIGNIFICANT NATIONAL DIVISIONS OF BUDDHISM

In general, for centuries any religion has been closely identified with the rulers and the culture of the country in which it is found, for obvious reasons. Hinduism, in its completely Indian character, was an extreme example of that. With Buddhism we must take account of the fact that it developed along many different national lines. That is the more typical pattern. Thus, it began its spread as a missionary religion—one that actively seeks converts—under the Emperor Asoka. Although students of religions look for the uniform factors in the various regional or national forms of a certain faith, they cannot ignore the variations in the beliefs and practices within one religion. International and national events and changes since 1980 have drastically altered the picture of worldwide Buddhism in certain areas.

Japan

Coming by way of Korea out of Chinese Buddhism, Japanese Buddhists developed their own sects, ritual, and iconography, while the ethical and social manifestations have profoundly influenced Japanese culture. Some historical facts to bear in mind are as follows. Traditionally, Buddhism began under royal patronage in the sixth century; the religion was specially valued for its stress on health and well-being and for its inclusive universalism. In the eighth-century Nara period many forms of Buddhism flourished, and the Heian era (roughly 800 to 1200) brought the transition to the modern forms, most of which were established or stabilized by about 1300. In the following centuries the amalgamation of Buddhism with traditional Shinto and a degree of subordination of religion to the state continued, although for the past 100 years and especially since World War II Buddhism has been more independent of state patronage and control. The three principal divisions of Japanese Buddhism that result from these 13 centuries of development are: Amida, Zen, and Nichiren. We comment briefly on each of them, appealing or relating so far as possible to relevant facts which have already been presented in this book.

AMIDA

This is the oldest and largest sect, served by professional clergy in a strong system of temples. The most common Japanese Buddhist temple is affiliated with one of the two principal subdivisions of Amida, Pure Land (Jodo Shin*) and True Pure Land (Jodo Shinshu). Jodo has about 4 million followers today and Jodo Shinshu claims nearly 10 million. Basing their teaching and ritual on the three Amitabha scriptures in the Chinese Canon, their worship centers on Amida Buddha and his Pure Land, using the Nembutsu formula (*Namu Amida Butsu*, Hail to the Buddha of Infinite Light). Honen in the twelfth century is the traditional founder of the earlier Jodo subdivision; his disciple Shinran (1173-1262) carried the doctrines further in the Jodo Shinshu. Both of them were learned men who studied at the Mount Hiei center of Tendai, the Japanese form of T'ien T'ai from China. Amida practices had been incorporated into Tendai and other monasteries and temples earlier; however, Honen and especially Shinran made the Amida and Pure Land doctrines far more explicit and practical than they were before. His stress on the inherent superiority of Amida over all other forms of worship and devotion led Honen to break away from Tendai.

Shinran made simple trust and reliance—"faith" in the usual sense—in Amida Buddha the only requirement for deliverance to Buddhahood and the Pure Land. He rejected the monastic vows and celibacy to which Honen had adhered. His reason for this was not merely freedom from celibate restrictions, but that celibacy was an admission of insufficient faith in Amida, an expression of egoism and dependence on what is referred to in modern Japanese religious discussion as "self-power." Amida Buddhism is contrasted with that, being called a way of "other power." The compassion and kindness of the believer, is, therefore, not simply the entrance into the Bodhisattva career, but an expression of gratitude for the gift of salvation from Amida.

NICHIREN

Taking its name from the founder in the thirteenth century, an aggressive counterreformer of the Shingon and Tendai Nara sects from which Honen and Shinran withdrew, Nichiren is the most intolerant among the usually tolerant Japanese sects. The founder harked back to the Eternal Buddha of the *Lotus Sutra* and also called for unifying of Nippon itself in the one and only true faith of the glorified Buddha of the *Lotus Sutra*, *Hokkekyo* in Japanese. Like Honen and Shinran in Amida Buddhism, he felt that few people could devote themselves to meditation, and like them he concentrated the faith and message of the sect in a simple slogan, which for Nichiren in its defiance of all other Buddhist groups sometimes becomes a battle cry: *Namu Myo Horengekyo,** "Hail to the Scripture of the Lotus of the Good Law." Through repetition of the chant believers are identified with the truth of the *Lotus*.

Its offshoot Soka Gakkai ("Value Creation Society") is an example of the postwar Japanese phenomenon of informal sects and voluntary lay associations, a development which began with the "new religions" in the nineteenth century. It combines Nichiren's dogmatic form of devotion to the Lotus with a practical philosophy of self-help and psychological positive thinking, happiness and success being the fruits of faith. Expelled from Nichiren Shoshu in 1991 over doctrinal disagreements, it is a lay organization with an estimated 2,000,000 members in Japan.

ZEN

Zen has been a popular form of Buddhism with Western intellectuals and mystics for a good many years, having been presented and promoted by the famous Professor D. T. Suzuki and supported by many occidentals. In terms of the religious issue just mentioned under Amida, it is the complete opposite: Zen is the ultimate expression of self-power, the most extreme form of the strenuous, disciplined concentration by which one attains *satori** (*samadhi*) by oneself. The Four Great Vows, recited after every service, express the determination of the Zen aspirant:

However innumerable beings are, I vow to save them;
However inexhaustible the passions are, I vow to extinguish them;
However immeasurable the Dharmas are, I vow to master them;
However incomparable the Buddha-truth is, I vow to attain it.[68]

Although it is very much colored by its Japanese development, it derives from the Chinese Ch'an or Meditation school, and from the teachings of Bodhidharma.

An instructive familiar tradition is that one day Sakymuni, while preaching or in answer to a question, held up a flower and smiled. Among the monks, only Kashyapa grasped the Buddha's meaning as the inadequacy of words to express the essence of the *dharma*. Zen has made this wordless tradition which Bhodidharma brought to China the center of its teaching and methods. It has stressed the transmission of the truth not by formal or merely rational instruction, but by direct intuitive grasp of the ultimate and inexpressible insight which those who already know have gained.

Followers are divided into two schools: Rinzai* teaches sudden enlightenment, and Soto* teaches that the process is gradual. Both schools insist that *satori* comes spontaneously and cannot be forced by sheer direct assault. Disciplined meditation while sitting cross-legged (*zazen*) has always been the core of monastic life for both sects. However, they also believe in utilizing secular arts in the cultivation of *satori*. Most of the adherents are lay persons. The distinctive methods are the question and answer (*mondo*) between master and pupil, and the riddle or *koan* used especially by Rinzai. The rationale of these methods is the necessity for direct communication of the illumination from master to pupil, not simply in a formula; the truth must come in a flash of insight; you either have it or you do not. In one sense Zen is the world's greatest "in-group"; those who have insight are in, everybody else is out. Public attention has been drawn to it also because of its unconventional use of (controlled) violence as in sword play and voluntary submission to the monitor's flexible board across the shoulders during group meditation sessions. There are still elements of the strict discipline which made it attractive to the samurai in the troubled Middle Ages.

The interest of the West in Zen has led to the establishment of Zen centers in the United States, where Americans can go for training in meditation and to join the order if they wish to and if they are accepted. The powerful attraction of the ancient faith can be heard in the chanting of the *Heart Sutra* refrain at several mountain retreats in California: "Listen to the Mantra, the Great, Mysterious Mantra: *Gate, gate, paragate, parasamgate, bodhi, svaha!* Gone, gone, gone, to that other shore; safely passed to that other shore, O prajnaparamita! So may it be."[69]

China

Organized religion in China was almost totally repressed during the Mao regime that began in 1949, except for some traditional practices under strict limits and controls by the government. After Mao's death in 1976, the 1980s saw a loosening of the extreme Marxist restrictions, and, since the events in Tiananmen Square in 1989, China has been a study in ambivalence about religion. On the one hand, there is a constant threat or practice of government repression and control; on the other hand, consider Professor Overmeyer's summary statement about religion in Chinese history:

> The study of Chinese religions is important not only in its own right, but as an essential element in the study of Chinese culture as a whole. Vast areas of that culture simply cannot be properly understood without the study of its religion, . . . In its actual practices, China was just as religious as any other traditional culture. . . .[70]

This ambivalence is pronounced in contemporary China and must be borne in mind while digging for some data on this question.

I use materials from my own files on the Citizen Ambassador Program, Religion and Philosophy Delegation from the American Academy of Religion, to the People's Republic of China in June 1994, of which I was a member. They are relevant to the topic and revealing of the current situation.

At Fudan University in Shanghai we met with people from the Philosophy Department. "Religion is defined narrowly, . . . as involving gods or God, an afterlife, and the supernatural." They regard Chinese culture as nonreligious, and make a distinction between religion and superstition. "Buddhism, Judaism, Islam, and Christianity are studied sociologically and as parts of Chinese history, philosophy, and culture. . . ." Religion is now viewed as compatible with socialism, and is studied as an aspect of Chinese culture.[71]

After lunch we visited the large and important Jade Temple, "closed during the Cultural Revolution but reopened in 1980 after the change in government policy to permit freedom of religion in accordance with the Chinese Constitution." We saw 50 novices in robes, with senior monks and nuns, enter to chant, and we toured the temple complex, which holds images of Sakyamuni, Guanyin, and other gods and guardians, before whom many people prayed and burned incense. Novices trained there go out to regional temples, and the abbot often received foreign dignitaries.

To supplement the preceding description, I offer the comments of the "Rev. —— Y——", head monk of the Dharma Realm Buddhist Association monastery in the San Francisco Bay area, who recently returned from a visit to his base in China. He was allowed to move about freely, but feels he must remain anonymous to protect himself and his organization from (possible) pressure by the Chinese government. His own Buddhist establishment is in a clean, modern building, with offices, a meditation room, and other facilities, in which, of course, the monks follow their regular practices. On a recent visit to the United States, their head monk from China was accompanied everywhere he went by an official of the People's Republic. I summarize Mr. ——'s comments about the present situation of Buddhism in China. (Readers must, however, decide for themselves how to evaluate these differing views.) Although there are 10 "showcase" or token temples, only a few of them are designated to teach the *dharma*. The others are in effect museums, with attendants who are paid by the state. Admission is charged and many things are for sale; regular temples do not do that. Most of the attendants are untrained lay people, although they may pose as monks. Only minor, routine services are allowed, and all major events must be scheduled and overseen by government officials. The *Sangha* has little power and is not really free to teach or study the *dharma*.

My visit to the Consulate of the People's Republic in San Francisco yielded no hard data, but I was given a booklet, *China*, with a section on "Population and Ethnic Groups" that included a little more than one page on "Religious Belief." The booklet listed a variety of religious and ethnic groups, and had a short section on Buddhism, including a list of four temples and eight lamaseries. The last paragraph states:

> The Buddhist, Islamic, Catholic, Protestant and Taoist organizations have been established at national and local levels, independently dealing with their own religious affairs. The religious groups and affairs in China are not subject to the directions of foreign powers.[72]

Unquestionably, Buddhism—like other religions—is alive and growing in China, in spite of some restrictions; at issue is how far believers are free to be themselves, and what the future holds for them.

Tibet

Nepal and Tibet are the traditional centers of Vajrayana, which we earlier described as one of the three principal divisions of Buddhism. Although Nepal is still an independent nation with a Hindu king, in which Buddhist life has not been forced to change drastically, we noted earlier the Chinese occupation of Tibet and the accompanying suppression of lamaistic Buddhism. Our comments are, therefore, directed at Tibet.

The Dalai Lama, leader of the Gelugpa school, has become the famous and charismatic symbol for the heroic struggle of Tibetan Buddhists to survive in the face of relentless Chinese persecution. He is thus the prime example of the clash between political power and religious devotion. Some commentators claim that as many as one million Buddhists have died from Chinese gunfire in massive uprisings and confrontations, or in prison or forced labor. Although such figures cannot be confirmed, neither can they be ignored. Without excusing them, it must be noted that the lamas dominated the social structure for several centuries, and thus the government fears their power.

For us, one point is the apparent driving concern of the Dalai Lama to bring the ancient texts and *dharma*-wisdom of the "thunderbolt vehicle" into creative relation with modern science and technology. This concern brought together the Lama and Robert Thurman, whom the Lama ordained in 1965 as the first Western Tibetan Buddhist monk; they each wanted what the other had. Rodger Kemenetz, in *New York Times Magazine*, called him—for various reasons he is no longer a monk—"the Dalai Lama's man in America." Kemenetz described their Buddhism as emphasizing "prostrations, visualizations, guru worship and deity yoga, in which the practitioner identifies with Tibetan deities as a path to higher states of consciousness.[73]

In Tibet itself the religion lives not just by the monks, scholars, and lamas, but by the heroism of the people themselves in their daily lives. And their religion includes much ancient lore and practices called "folk" or "popular" religion. That is why it survives in Tibet and can be carried into the larger world by the Dalai Lama and Robert Thurman.

SUMMARY

Buddhism is the name given to a family of religious traditions deriving form the *dharma* (law) enunciated and exemplified by Gautama Buddha in India about 600 B.C.E. It presents a view of all existence as characterized by transience, suffering, and no determinate essence of anything; it describes human beings as limited and ruled by ignorance and desire; and it offers a path to spiritual freedom through understanding and mental and moral action. Gautama, the originator of this tradition, after a great struggle attained to wisdom or enlightenment (*bodhi*) by his own unaided effort, which constituted him as *Budh-ta*, the awakened or the enlightened one. He then formed the *Sangha* (order of monks) who emulated him and aided in proclamation and dissemination of his spiritual insight and regimen. After his death in *Sangha* grew, and through the centuries there were several great Councils of representatives from all branches.

Gradually a division took place between the stricter program, where a limited number of monks followed the original program and discipline in the monastery, and a developed or expanded version of the spiritual way, which gave opportunity for more people to follow the path to enlightenment. For these two major divisions or ways the usual names are Hinayana and Mahayana, commonly translated "lesser vehicle" and "great vehicle." Hinayana is found in Southeast Asia, and Mahayana was for centuries widespread in China until suppressed by the present Chinese government, leaving Japan as the principal Mahayana country. A subgroup of the Mahayana formerly found in Tibet and Nepal continues in Nepal and outside Tibet and constitutes a third vehicle, the Vajrayana or Way of the Thunderbolt. There are great differences among these three divisions, particularly between the two major groups. They do agree that *karma* holds one in rounds of *samsara* until one gains enlightenment and thus reaches Nirvana, the spiritual homeland.

Each of the three vehicles has a distinctive sacred literature; the Hinayana canon consists of collected traditional oral stories about, and sermons or discourses of, Gautama Buddha; Mahayana and Vajrayana literature expanded and developed the traditions about Buddha, explaining their new Buddha theory and metaphysical teachings, in a voluminous body of hundreds of works in thousands of volumes. Included in these works are various classic formulations of Buddhist teaching, such as the Four Noble Truths: all life is suffering; suffering is caused by craving; to end suffering, end craving; to end craving, and hence suffering, follow the Eightfold Path of right:

belief, resolve, speech, behavior, occupation, effort, contemplation, and concentration.

All three ways take Buddha as their ideal and guide, and in every case their theory and practice are centered on him, but the development of the Buddha cult brought a much different view of him in the Mahayana. In Hinayana, Buddha is a human, paradigmatic figure who is venerated for his own spiritual achievement and teaching, but now being in Nirvana he is not available for prayer or direct help to believers, who must accomplish salvation by themselves. Buddha himself neither affirmed nor denied the existence of God, and there is no place or need for God in Hinayana. In Mahayana theory the Buddha cult transformed Buddha into a principle, concept, or type as the ideal expression of the Buddha spirit, and at least two general classes of Buddha figures appeared. The Bodhisattvas are by nature beings of wisdom who defer their earned entrance into Nirvana in order to perform their function of bringing all beings to enlightenment. Various celestial or cosmic Buddhas with distinctive spiritual attributes, although they do not appear on earth in human form as do the Bodhisattvas, are available to devotees through devotion and faith, to help them advance toward spiritual freedom.

The traditional, ideal program of Buddhist practice is threefold: moral conduct as the prerequisite, study and meditation as the means, and *samadhi* (concentrative absorption) as the fulfillment. Nirvana stands as the ultimate realization beyond even meditation, a kind of Buddhist spiritual homeland, transcending all else as the place of pure spiritual reality and enjoyment. The classic means to it is meditation, but the varieties of Buddhism include what are essentially systems of faith in certain Buddhas and their Buddha worlds, as other ways to Nirvana. Worship and ritual in Buddhism follow the Asiatic pattern of individual acts centering on veneration of Buddha as seen in an image. The typical Buddhist religious structure in Hinayana countries is a stupa or pagoda, housing a Buddha relic and/or images. In Japan there are temples with a wide variety of Buddha images, which are the focus of reverence and devotion.

Hinayana Buddhism is monks' religion, with the laity gaining merit (toward better *karma* and enlightenment) only by acts of merit, such as visits to stupas and other holy places, and by supporting the monks and monasteries. There is more direct participation in the ritual and activity of the temple by the laity in Japanese Mahayana. For although few Hinayana monks attain enlightenment, the Mahayana cult makes it possible in theory for everyone to reach Nirvana. Through the help of Bodhisattvas and celestial Buddhas who really serve as gods, whatever they are called, Mahayanists gain enlightenment, so that Avolokitesvara and Amitabha, for example, as the prime manifestations of *karuna* (compassion or mercy), are great gods of Asia.

In Hinayana the ethical aspect is grounded in the rules of *dharma* for monks and laity, while in Mahayana it is spelled out in the perfections which carry a Bodhisattva toward enlightenment. There is a strong universalistic stress on benevolent love, deriving from the boundless compassion of Buddha for all beings, which believers are to emulate. The institutional organization of Buddhism is through the monasteries or *wats* in Southeast Asia. Following a pattern somewhat like that of Christianity, with its organizational structures based on doctrinal differences, there are three major divisions of Japanese Buddhism: Pure Land or Amida, Nichiren, and Zen.

NOTES

1. Henry Clarke Warren, *Buddhism in Translations* (New York: Atheneum, paperback ed., 1968), p. 11. Originally published by Harvard University Press, © 1896.
2. Warren, p. 43. Note that he walks around the couch *clockwise*, "his right side toward it." This clockwise direction is always prescribed in the literature and followed in the actual practice of circumambulating a stupa.
3. Warren, pp. 60, 61.
4. Warren, p. 76.
5. Warren, p. 83
6. Edward Conze, selector and trans., *Buddhist Scriptures*, © Edward Conze, 1959. Penguin Classics, 1959 (Baltimore: Penguin Books, 1968), p. 53, 54.
7. E. B. Cowell, trans., *Buddhist Mahayana Texts. Sacred Books of the East*, Vol. XLIX (Oxford: Clarendon Press, 1894), p. 180.
8. Cowell, p. 155.
9. Edward Conze, *Buddhism: Its Essence and Development* (New York: Harper & Row, Torchbook ed., 1959), p. 91.
10. Vincent A. Smith, *The Oxford Student's History of India*. Revised by H. G. Rawlinson (London: Oxford University Press, 1962), p. 55.
11. Kenneth J. Saunders, *Epochs in Buddhist History* (Chicago: University of Chicago Press, 1924), p. 60.
12. Warren, pp. 117–122.
13. A. N. Whitehead, *Religion in the Making* (New York: Macmillan, 1926), p. 50.
14. Edward J. Thomas, *The History of Buddhist Thought*, 2d ed. (New York: Barnes and Noble, 1971), p. 13.
15. The list does not owe anything to the "Buddhist Catechism" of Colonel Alcott nor to the "Twelve Principles of Buddhism" offered by Christmas Humphries in his *Buddhism*. Both of them are formulations in the authors' own thoughts and words of one principle for each number. Mine follows the "Novice's Catechism" form of "the Four Aryan Truths," and so on.
16. Edward J. Thomas, *The Life of Buddha*, 3d ed. (London: Routledge and Kegan Paul, 1949), p. 215.
17. Thomas, *Life*, p. 107.
18. Edward Conze, et al., eds., *Buddhist Texts Through the Ages*, © Bruno Cassirer (Publishers) Ltd., Oxford, England (New York: Harper & Row, Torchbook ed., 1964), p. 105.
19. Warren, p. 110.
20. Warren, p. 107.
21. Thomas, *Buddhist Thought*, p. 167.
22. Needless to say, this is my own formula of how to interpret or understand the difference.

23. F. L. Woodward, trans., *Some Sayings of the Buddha* (London: Oxford University Press, 1973), p. 7.

24. Warren, p. xiv.

25. Woodward, *Some Sayings of the Buddha*, pp. 7, 8.

26. Excerpts and quotations which follow are from Warren, *Buddhism*, pp. 129–137.

27. Warren, pp. 133, 134.

28. Warren, pp. 148, 149.

29. Sir Charles Eliot, *Hinduism and Buddhism* (New York: Barnes and Noble, Inc., 1954), I, pp. 191, 192.

30. Conze, *Buddhist Texts*, p. 135.

31. Dwight Goddard, ed., *A Buddhist Bible* (Boston: Beacon Press, 1970), pp. 75, 81.

32. *Maha-Satipatthana-Sutta*, in Warren, pp. 373ff.

33. Warren, p. 373.

34. Warren, p. 374.

35. Conze, *Buddhist Scriptures*, p. 185.

36. T. W. and C. A. F. Rhys Davids, *Dialogues of the Buddha*, Part III, in T. W. Rhys Davids, ed., *Sacred Books of the Buddhists* (London: Pali Text Society, 1965), IV, p. 125.

37. Warren, p. 292.

38. Thomas, *Buddhist Thought*, p. 56.

39. Bhikshu Sangharakshita, *The Three Jewels* (Garden City, N.Y.: Doubleday, Anchor Books, 1970), develops it in Chapter 13, "The Stages of the Path."

40. Mrs. Rhys Davids asst. by F. L. Woodward, trans., *The Book of the Kindred Sayings (Samyutta Nikaya)*, Part II, *The Nidana Book (Nidana-Vagga)*, © Pali Text Society, Translation Series, No. 10. (London: Luzac & Company, Ltd., 1952), pp. viii, ix.

41. Mrs. Rhys Davids, *The Nidana Book*, p. 27.

42. Warren, translator's notes, p. 115.

43. *Samyutta Nikaya*, xv. 5, 6 in Warren, pp. 315–316.

44. Warren, p. 247.

45. Warren, p. 166.

46. E. A. Burtt, *The Teachings of the Compassionate Buddha* (New York: New American Library, Mentor Books, 1955), pp. 168, 169.

47. Thomas, *Buddhist Thoughts*, p. 218.

48. Lucien Stryk, ed., *The World of the Buddha* (Garden City, N.Y.: Doubleday, Anchor Books, 1969), p. 248.

49. Stryk, p. 270.

50. Stryk, p. 283.

51. *Majjhima Nikaya*, in Warren, p. 127.

52. Edward Conze, *Buddhist Meditation* (London: George Allen and Unwin Ltd., 1968), p. 20, *et passim*.

53. Warren, p. 109.

54. Sarvepalli Radhakrishnan and Charles A. Moore, eds., *A Source Book in Indian Philosophy* (Princeton, N.J.: Princeton University Press © 1957; Princeton Paperback, 1967), p. 345.

55. Wing-tsit Chan, et al., comp., *The Great Asian Religions* (New York: Macmillan, © 1969.) Second printing, 1970, pp. 200, 201.

56. Conze, *Buddhist Texts*, p. 130.

57. Goddard, *Buddhist Bible*, p. 502. Reprinted by permission of E. P. Dutton & Co.

58. Thomas, *Life*, p. 173.

59. cf. Burtt, *The Teachings of the Compassionate Buddha*, p. 86.

60. Conze, *Buddhist Texts*, p. 217.
61. V. Fausboll, trans., *The Sutta Nipata, The Sacred Books of the East* (Oxford: Clarendon Press, 1881), X, Part II, p. 24.
62. Warren, *Buddhism*, p. 397.
63. K. J. Saunders, trans. and ed., *The Heart of Buddhism* (London: Humphrey Milford, Oxford University Press, 1915), p. 42.
64. Melford E. Spiro, *Buddhism and Society* (New York: Harper & Row, 1970), p. 372.
65. Conze, *Buddhist Texts*, p. 131.
66. Arthur F. Wright, *Buddhism in Chinese History* (Stanford, Cal.: Stanford University Press, 1959), p. 75.
67. J. Takakusu, trans., *The Sutra of the Meditation on Amitayus, Buddhist Mahayana Texts* (New York: Dover Publishing Company, 1969), p. 167.
68. Daisetz Teitaro Suzuki, *Manual of Zen Buddhism* (New York: Grove Press, 1960), p. 14.
69. Goddard, *Buddhist Bible*, p. 86.
70. Daniel L. Overmeyer, Introduction to "Chinese Religions—The State of the Field" Part I; *The Journal of Asian Studies* 54, no. 1 (February 1995), p. 128.
71. Quotes and paraphrases from the *Journal* of the delegation.
72. Qin Shi, compiler, *China 1995* (Beijing: New Star Publishers, 1995), pp. 31, 32.
73. Rodger Kemenetz, "Robert Thurman Doesn't Look Buddhist," *New York Times Magazine*, May 5, 1996, p. 49.

TOPICS AND QUESTIONS FOR STUDY

1. Why does it not matter to the Buddhist what the historical Buddha really looked like?
2. What was the greatness of Gautama Buddha? Why is he the central figure of Buddhism? What did he accomplish? Is Buddha a savior figure or god?
3. Discuss the structure or organization of Buddhism—how did it grow and what are the divisions and differences? How and why are the scriptures taken as the indicators of those divisions?
4. Discuss the theoretical or philosophical character of Buddhism, as a religion in which thought and analysis are fundamental.
5. Why is there no God in Hinayana Buddhism? How are some kinds of Buddhas like God?
6. How does Buddhism describe the human situation? What does it say people need to overcome? How do people overcome these obstacles and what do they find if they succeed?
7. Buddhism views the human being as not having any permanent or unchanging self. Explain how this theory fits in with the belief that people are reborn again and again.
8. How would you rationalize and justify, in Western terms, the explicit sexual ideas and practices found in Vajrayana, and in the art of Nepal and Tibet?
9. What are some Buddhist observations or celebrations? What are the differences between Southeast Asian and Japanese Buddhism (same religion, but very different kinds of people)?

10. Outline the Buddhist philosophical views of the nature of the world of things and people. How do those views relate to the more strictly religious program?
11. What is the basis and nature of the morals of Buddhism? How is Buddhist "compassion" related to Christian "love" or "charity"?
12. Name the different kinds of Buddhas. What does each do for people? Why does a modern and educated Buddhist venerate the Buddha image and why would he or she resent your calling him or her an "idol-worshiper"?
13. There is a wide variety of schools of thought and methods of salvation or deliverance in Buddhism. Why and how are they simply different "ways" to the one end?
14. Explain how "turning the wheel of the law," which Buddha said he had done, might be described as "the gospel of Buddhism."

USEFUL BOOKS

Conze, Edward, trans. ed., with I. B. Horner, David Snellgrove, and Arthur Waley. *Buddhist Texts Through the Ages*. Oxford: One World, 1995.

Corless, Roger J. *The Vision of Buddhism—The Space Under the Tree*. Visions of Reality series. New York: Paragon House, 1989.

Cowell, E. B. et al., trans. *Buddhist Mahayana Texts*. SBE, 1894; New York: Dover Publications, 1969.

Dalai Lama. *The Path to Enlightenment*. Edited and translated by Glenn H. Mullin. Ithaca: Snow Lion, 1982.

deBary, William Theodore, ed. *The Buddhist Tradition—In India, China, and Japan*. New York: Vintage Books, 1972 *et. seq.*

Foucher, Alfred Charles. *The Life of the Buddha*. Edited and translated by Simone Boas. Westport, Conn.: Greenwood Press, 1972.

Gard, Richard A. *Buddhism*. In "Great Religions of Modern Man" series. New York: Washington Square Press, 1963. (Difficult reading, but much essential information about Buddhist doctrines.)

Harvey, Peter. *An Introduction to Buddhism—Teachings, History, and Practices*. Cambridge: Cambridge University Press, 1990.

Kitagawa, Joseph, and Mark Cummings, eds. *Buddhism in Asian History*. New York: MacMillan, 1988.

La Fleur, William. *Buddhism: A Cultural Approach*. Englewood Cliffs, N.J.: Prentice Hall, 1988.

Woodward, F. L., trans. *Some Sayings of the Buddha—According to the Pali Canon*. New York: Oxford University Press, 1973.

GLOSSARY

Abhidhamma Pitaka (ah bhee dahm uh pih tuh kuh): third basket of the *Tripitaka*; philosophical treatises

alayavijnana (ah lah yah vih gnyah nuh): storehouse consciousness

Amida (ah mee dah): Japanese "limitless," covering both Amitabha and Amitayus Buddhas

Amitabha (ah mee tah bah): Buddha of "infinite light" of the Western Paradise

Amitayus (ah mee tah yus): another name for Amitabha, "infinite life"

anatta (ah not uh): denial of a permanent self

anicca (ah nee chah): impermanence or change

arhat (are hot): one who has ended rebirth, attained enlightenment; a saint.

Avalokitesvara (ah vuh lah kit esh vara): Bodhisattva, "Lord who looks down" in compassion on each generation

Bhaishajyagura (bhai shah jyah gurah): the cosmic Buddha of healing

bhikkhu (bhih koo): Hinayana monk

bodhi (bo dhee): enlightenment, wisdom.

bodhichitta (bo dhee chee tah): Buddha mind or nature

Bodhisattva (bo dhee satt wuh): a Buddha-to-be, dedicated to bringing others to enlightenment

Ch'an: Chinese form of *dhyana;* meditation school of Buddhism

Daibutsu (die boot soo): a great Buddha image (Japan)

Dhammapada (dum mu puh duh): verses on Dhamma

dharma (dhur muh): righteousness, moral law or duty; but plural "dharmas" connotes "elements"

dharmakaya: body of truth or essence, highest of the three-body forms of Buddha

dhyana (dyaa nuh): (Jnana in Pali) supreme contemplation through meditation

dukkha (doo kha): suffering, "ill," or misery

Hinayana (hee nah yah nuh): "lesser vehicle," Southeast Asian Buddhism

Hridaya sutra: Heart Sutra (Mahayana): heart or essence of *prajnaparamita*

Jataka (jut uh kuh): birth stories of the Buddha

Kapilavasta (kah pih lah vus too): birthplace of Gautama Buddha

karuna: mercy, compassion

koan: a riddle whose solution is considered a way to enlightenment in Rinzai Zen

Kshitigarbha (kshi tih gar bha): Bodhisattva who vowed to deliver all people, especially children, and the wicked in hell (Ojizosama in Japan)

Kuan Yin: Bodhisattva Avalokitesvara in China; Kannon in Japan; sometimes female

Madhyamika (mahd yuh mee kuh): Mahayana school of philosophy which stresses the void (*sunya*)

Mahayana (mah ha yah nuh): "Great vehicle," second of two major Buddhist divisions: Tibet, China, Japan

Maitreya (my tray yuh): the Buddha yet to come

mandala (mahn duh luh): a symbolic diagram of the cosmos, usually centered around Buddha figures

Manjusri: Bodhisattva of wisdom and meditation

Mantra: a holy sound; ritual or devotional formula

Mara: personification of death and evil; the "Tempter"

metta: Loving kindness or benevolence

mondo: question and answer in Zen

Nagarjuna (nah gar joo nuh): second-century philosopher, founder of Madhyamika school

Namu Amida Butsu: the full invocation-phrase of Amida Buddha in Japanese Pure Land, usually known as "Nembutsu"

Namu Myo Horengekyo (nah moo meeyo hor engee keeyo): Nichiren logan of devotion to the Lotus Sutra

Nembutsu (nem boo tsu): see "Namu Amida Butsu"

Nibbana: Pali for "nirvana"

Nichiren (niche ihr enn): Japanese sect, and founder in thirteenth century

nidana (nih dah nuh): cause; the twelve nidanas—causal chain

nirmanakaya (nihr mah nah kah yuh): "transformation" or "manifestation" body in which Buddha appears on earth

Nirvana (near vah nuh): supreme goal or good, release from all craving and attachment

"Om mani padme hum": mantra, combining "Om" (Buddha), "mani" (jewel), "padme" (lotus), and "hum" (a petition for protection).

Padmasambhava (pahd mah sahm bhava): Indian monk who introduced Tantric Buddhism in Tibet, eighth century

pagoda: a stupa

Pali (pah lee): traditional literary language of India, in which Hinayana canon was written

panna (pahn nyah) (Pali for *prajna*): wisdom, intuitive insight

Paranirvana: The ultimate Nirvana at the end of earthly existence

prajna (praj nyuh) (Sanskrit): intelligence, wisdom

prajnaparamita: literally, wisdom gone to the other shore; supreme wisdom

Pratyekabuddha: a solitary Buddha, who does not help others; attains enlightenment by himself

Rinzai (rin zie): one of two major Zen sects; sudden enlightenment

Saddharma Pundarika: a sutra, Lotus of the True Law

Sakyamuni: Buddha as the sage of the Sakyas

samadhi (sum ah dih): "transic concentration," spiritual ecstasy

Samantabhadra: Bodhisattva of compassion

sambhogakaya: "enjoyment body" of Buddha in which he appears before Bodisattvas

Sangha (sang ha): order of Buddhist monks

satori (sah tor rih): Zen experience of enlightenment

Shin: largest Pure Land sect in Japan

Siddhartha: Buddha's given name

skandhas: the five aggregates which comprise the individual

Soto: the largest Zen sect; gradual enlightenment

Sravaka: a Buddha who gains enlightenment through hearing Buddha's teachings, but does not teach others

stupa: originally a burial mound for relic of Buddha; later developed into pagoda

Sukhavati (soo kuh vuh tee): the happy land of the Pure Land school, hence also the *Sukhavati Sutra*

sunya, or *sunyata:* emptiness, relativity, nonspecific character; Mahayana school of thought

Sutta Pitaka: Sermon Basket of scriptures

tanha: craving, desire, attachment

tantra: esoteric literature; see Hinduism, "tantric," sexual symbolism

Tathagata (tuh tah guh tuh): a title of the Buddha, probably "the thus gone"

tathata (tah taah tah): "truly so," thusness or suchness, the nature of *sunya*, ultimate reality

Therevada (ta ruh vah dah): "doctrine of the Elders," Hinayana

Trikaya (trih kah yuh): three-body doctrine of Buddha

Tripitaka (tree pih tuh kuh): the "Three Baskets" of basic scriptures of the Pali canon

urna: the jewel or other mark on the forehead of a Buddha image, the "third eye" of wisdom

Vairocana (vie row kah na): the Brilliant One, a cosmic Buddha

Vajracchedika Sutra (vaj rah keh dee kuh): "Diamond Cutter" *sutra*, important for Zen

Vajrayana (vaj rah yah nuh): "Thunderbolt Vehicle" of tantrism

Vijnanavada (vin-nya-na-vah-da): school of "consciousness only"

Vinaya Pitaka: Discipline Basket of Scriptures

wat: monastery complex of buildings in Hinayana

yana (yah nah): "vehicle" across the stream of *samsara* to deliverance; hence the "way" or method to enlightenment, as in "Vajrayana" etc.

zazen (zah zen): Zen meditation technique

Chapter 5

CONFUCIANISM

Confucius (Courtesy, Sheikh Publications, Inc. New York).

OUTLINE

   I. Religion in Chinese History.

       Back of the three traditional religions of China—Buddhism, Confucianism, Taoism—are centuries of nature and ancestor worship, and ideas of the importance of moral order in society.

  II. Origin and Development of Confucianism.

       A. Confucius, born 551 B.C.E., articulated what he considered to be the good and useful concepts and traditions from the past, and grounded them in Chinese concepts of Tao as the way of Heaven (T'ien).

       B. After his death his disciples carried on his work, and in the Han dynasty, *ca.* 200 B.C.E., the Confucian school of thought became the official doctrine and remained so through most of the succeeding centuries until about 1913. Various developments during those years did not essentially change its character.

 III   Literature of Confucianism.

       A. The five "Confucian Classics" are: *The Book of Changes*, *The Book of History*, *The Book of Poetry*, *The Book of Rites*, and *The Spring and Autumn Annals*.

       B. The "Four Books" are: *The Analects*, or Sayings, of Confucius; *The Mencius*, or book of the foremost follower; *The Doctrine of the Mean*; *The Great Learning*.

  IV. Although there are few, if any, explicit religious doctrines in Confucianism, there are some implicit essentially religious beliefs.

       A. Heaven as a transcendent moral force, the basis of ethics.

       B. *Jen* or goodness as the nature of Heaven.

       C. Tao or the good way of Heaven to be followed by ruler and subjects.

   V. Ritual and worship.

       A. The basic concept is *li*, propriety in the double sense of proper observance of religious ceremonies and proper moral attitude in conduct, with emphasis on sincerity and honesty in them.

       B. Ancestor worship was made part of Confucianism.

       C. The state cult was under direction of Confucian scholars.

       D. The cult of Confucius himself was especially for the scholars.

  VI. The ethics of Confucianism are its most distinctive and significant feature.

       A. Moral guidance is provided not by a set of rules, but by the moral person, the *chun-tzu* or "prince's son," who knows and practices the proper moral conduct in accordance with and reliance on the way of Heaven.

           1. The moral person has *te*, moral power or force.

2. The moral person is guided by *jen*, benevolence or "human hearted-ness," according to *chung* and *shu*, positive and negative forms of the golden rule.

B. Guides or norms are provided by:

1. Learning, the way to know the meaning of *jen* in practice.

2. Filial piety and the five relationships. (Confucianism is a mean be-tween the two extremes of license and fanaticism.)

RELIGION IN CHINESE HISTORY

The old formula for Chinese religion was "the three religions of China": the purely Chinese Confucianism, Taoism, and an adopted and naturalized Buddhism. For the past 1,000 years the most obvious fact about Chinese religious life was the complex interrelationships among these three, and a "typical Chinese" was one who made use of the three according to his need and the occasion. Thus a Chinese family might acknowledge the Buddha at a pagoda they passed on a journey, while the tablets of their ancestors were kept in the Confucian temple of their home city; and when someone died the funeral might be conducted by Taoist priests. Although this general picture may still be true for China as a whole, it has become problematic and complex during the years since World War II. In the previous chapter (Buddhism) we mentioned the Maoist suppression of religion, and the change since then to relative freedom but ambivalent official policies.

During the infamous Maoist "Cultural Revolution" of 1966–1980, study of religions and religious practices were banned, and many religious groups went underground. Official policy changed with the "People's Republic of China Government's 'Present Religious Policy: New Constitution of 1979'." Article 36 states:

> No state organization, public organization, or individual may compel citizens to believe in, or not to believe in, any religion, nor may they discriminate against citizens who believe in, or, do not believe in, any religion. The state protects normal religious activities. No one may make use of religion to engage in activities that disrupt public order, impair the health of citizens or interfere with the educational system of the state.[1]

Obviously, there is much room under these rules for differing interpretations of such phrases as "normal religious activities." In 1982 the Communist party issued a statement on their viewpoint and policy on religion, summarizing past experiences and lessons and stating their new official views. On January 31, 1994, the People's Republic issued new regulations governing religious activities of foreign nationals, and venues for religious activities.

At first the religions found the 1994 rules at least neutral, but the latest government moves are threatening. According to a Reuters' dispatch from Beijing, appearing in the San Francisco *Chronicle* of January 15, 1996, government authorities ordered "all places of worship to register with the government and warned of new problems in the practice of faiths permitted in the communist nation." This was occasioned by the rapid expansion of interest in religion, and official displeasure with "those who take advantage of religious resources to split the country." Other sources report charges of "splitism" made against Buddhist monks in Tibet. Chinese religious leaders are seriously worried about such new pressures on them. These political events must be included in an adequate understanding of Chinese religious life.

That the suppression of religion means the extinction of Chinese religious faith and life is another question, for the history of China includes previous eras of drastic repression which did not destroy religion. The religious aspects of Chinese life and character have endured for 4,000 or 5,000 years, and such elements are difficult if not impossible to eradicate. These ancient religious factors antedate both Confucianism and Taoism, and they must be outlined as a background for both. So we turn to a brief summary of some relevant facts about Chinese religion.

As in any culture, Chinese tell of their origins in prehistorical epochs. These theories or explanations are important, regardless of how factual or accurate they are, for understanding the culture and especially the religion. Among the figures assigned to the earliest times by Chinese tradition are three legendary emperors; Fu Hsi typifies the Hunting Era early in the third millennium B.C.E.; Shen Nang is the mythical founder of agriculture; and the first truly individual character is Huang Ti, the Yellow Emperor, who founded the first cities. They are followed by four other rulers, and then come Yao, Shun, and Yu, who are the first to be mentioned in the *Book of History*,* and whom Confucius considered model rulers. Yu is credited with draining away the waters of a great flood—the Yellow and other river floods have devastated China for thousands of years—and with founding the first dynasty, the Hsia (2205?–1765? B.C.E.). The last Hsia emperor lost what is called the Mandate of Heaven by his evil deeds, according to the *Book of History*, and he was overthrown by T'ang, the founder of the Shang dynasty.

Divination and Ritual Sacrifice During the Shang Dynasty

Modern archaeological study has focused interest on artifacts from this first historical regime, the Shang dynasty, usually dated about 1765 to 1122 B.C.E. Among items of religious significance are bones and tortoise shells; the people who used these for divination heated them until they cracked and then interpreted the cracks to answer questions. On some of the bones and shells inscriptions are found which are taken to be the earliest known examples of Chinese writing and which provide information about the deities they worshipped. These included ancestral spirits, elemental spirits of earth and other natural phenomena such as wind and river, Western or Dragon Mother, and Shang Ti,* a vague but dominant ancestor figure important in later developments. The other principal religious artifacts are bronze vessels of different sizes and shapes. They are called "ritual

Ceremonial wine vessel. Late Shang, 12th–11th century B.C.E. (Courtesy, The Asian Art Museum of San Francisco, The Avery Brundage Collection, San Francisco, California). Copyright © 1974 Asian Art Museum of San Francisco. All rights reserved.

bronzes" because it is assumed that they were used as part of the sacrifices to ancestral spirits. In both of these phenomena, divination and ritual sacrifice, we see a combination of the practical and mystical, people planning and acting to conduct ordinary affairs wisely, by taking account of the transcendent and mysterious forces of the supernal realm. This combination seems to be a characteristic of Chinese religion from the beginning.

The Duke of Chou

The end of the Shang was occasioned, like that of the Hsia, by the "misconduct" of the last emperor. The ruler of the kingdom of Chou to the West was Wen Wang. He and later his son Wu successfully resisted and then overthrew the last Shang emperor and established the Chou dynasty,* which lasted nearly 900 years, *ca.* 1100–221 B.C.E. The records report that Wu Wang was assisted by his brother, the Duke of Chou, and when Wu died the Duke acted as regent for a number of years during the minority of Wu's son Ch'eng. The Duke repressed a revolt against Ch'eng and when Ch'eng came of age voluntarily retired. For this he became a kind of legendary ideal ruler; people in later ages looked back to him through the pages of the *Book of History*. Confucius considered the Duke of Chou as an early precursor in the Way that he followed. Many important cultural advances were made during the years of the Chou regime, but it was the dynastic policy to divide the kingdom, and it gradually broke up into semi-independent states; ultimately a kind of feudalism developed. The last 250 years of the dynasty were so chaotic that the time is called "The Warring States," and the sixth century B.C.E., which saw the rise of Confucianism and Taoism, was a period of disintegration and disorder. The degradation and despair of the era formed the background for both these Chinese systems.

Decisive political change in China came with the founding of the first truly imperial—in power, extent, and administration—regime by the fearsome Ch'in monarch Shih Huang Ti in 221 B.C.E. His absolute reign lasted little more than 10 years and was succeeded by the Han dynasty in 202 B.C.E. which endured for 400 years. Since the establishment of the Han dynasty, the Chinese have styled themselves "Sons of Han," and the country has been a great nation state which they have called the "middle kingdom." Despite occasional interruptions, the various regimes maintained an imperial structure until the downfall in 1911 of the Manchu emperors or Ching dynasty.

Heaven: Shang Ti and T'ien*

It was during the Shang and Chou dynasties that certain fundamental religious phenomena appeared, and they should be mentioned because they were more or less permanent and general aspects of the total religious situation in China. Artifacts used in divination and ritual in the Shang dynasty have been mentioned as sources of our knowledge of these activities. Various written works also provide information about Chou religion, which is significant for understanding Confucianism and Taoism. G. F. Moore once described the religion of China as a union of nature worship and ancestor worship. These dual aspects from the Shang were extended and developed in the Chou, which includes the time of Confucius' life.

The most significant change was the elevation of Shang Ti to the position of a chief deity, independent and supreme, who made moral demands on the kings whom he chose to rule. The Ti were the deified spirits of the former kings of the ruling house of the Shang dynasty, and, to the Chou regime, Shang Ti was the highest of these Shang spirits. The Chou needed to substitute some other name than the founder-ancestor of the Shang dynasty as the heavenly ruler; since they had overthrown the dynasty they could not expect help from that dynastic divinity. Thus some kind of identification was established between Shang Ti and T'ien or Heaven, and the terms were combined to form Hao or Huang T'ien Shang Ti, that is, Shang Ti of Exalted or Imperial Heaven, supreme high or heavenly God, the supreme object of worship who was concerned for the entire Chinese people. As such, Shang Ti was no longer simply the supreme ancestral spirit of the ruling house, but the heavenly ruler to whom all earthly kings were morally responsible. He elevated or deposed kings, and the fall of the Hsia and rise of the Shang, followed by the fall of the

Yin-Yang.

Shang dynasty and rise of the Chou, took place, according to this interpretation, because the Mandate of Heaven (T'ien-ming*) was in each case lost by the old regime and inherited by the new.

In later Chou times, and usually in the *Book of History*, the term T'ien was used for God. Although some attributes of personality were ascribed to T'ien, it should not be equated with the personal God in Western monotheism, being more a universalized moral principle. An interesting and revealing aspect of this terminology is that in modern times Christian missionaries could not agree on the proper Chinese word to use for God. Protestants used Shang Ti or Cheng Shen, "true God," while the Catholics adopted the term T'ien Chu, "Lord of Heaven."

The Yin and the Yang

The *yin-yang** contrast goes far back in Chinese thought, pervades Taoism, and strongly influences Confucianism; yet its origins are obscure and there is no classic statement or formulation of the concept. It is a Chinese doctrine of interacting opposed or complementary forces or factors, working both in the production and the operation of all things and events. *Yin** connotes the passive, dark, cool, female, water, earth, moon, autumn, and winter, while *yang** signifies the active, light, hot, male, heaven, sun, spring, and summer. From the interaction of these forces in a cyclical fashion comes all growth and change. The Yin-Yang* was one of the six schools of thought, to which we will refer later. It will be obvious, when we come to Taoism, that it is a central metaphysical characteristic of the Tao*, the way and reality of Taoism. Although it is not mentioned in the *Analects** or by Mencius*, *yin-yang* was incorporated into Confucian theory in the Han era by Tung Chung-shu and became a permanent element in later Confucianism.

Ritual and Ethics Before Confucius

Sacrifices to spirits were still essential after the exaltation of T'ien, and the ritual system in which the kings performed the principal rites, assisted by the nobles, followed the pattern which was to continue for thousands of years. New methods and ceremonies of divination were developed, as seen for example in the *Book of Changes** (*I Ching**). The spirits were everywhere and were to be invoked and appeased at all times, and this superstitious aspect of popular religion permeated the religion of the masses. Both beneficent or kindly (*shen**) and maleficent or evil (*kwei**) spirits were active.

It was, however, the moral elements, which had been slight in the Shang but developed in the Chou era and were reflected in the classics, that were significant for the development of Confucianism. Social, political, and economic conditions deteriorated after the end of the Western Chou dynasty in 771 B.C.E. Warfare, civil strife, violence, and suffering afflicted all levels of society, but especially the poor, peasants, and other lower classes. As seen in some of the poems of the *Book of Odes or Poetry**, despair and doubt increased as troubles grew. The ethical and spiritual significance of the rituals tended to be lost because rituals were subordinated to policy and expediency and were used as ways to control the spirits and powers. These circumstances are the background of Confucius' effort to reinterpret the ancient literature and reconstitute the rituals on their proper basis, namely, the ethical principles or order that were considered the framework of human life and history.

ORIGIN AND DEVELOPMENT OF CONFUCIANISM

In Western terms Confucianism is one of the eponymic religions; that is to say it takes its name from its founder. But in Chinese terms Confucianism is not so much a distinct religious system, but rather one of three forms or institutions for the expression of human religious needs: Ju Chiao*, Shih Chiao*, and Tao Chiao*, or Confucianism, Buddhism, and Taoism in Western terms. Ju Chia* (without the "o") is the school or "ism" of the cultured or intellectuals, but these persons might also make use of Buddhist or Taoist monks and rites on special occasions such as funerals. Confucianism and Taoism are usually spoken of as the two chief schools among the six principal schools of thought or philosophic systems from among the many that arose in the fifth through third centuries B.C.E. The idea of religious affiliation in the sense of deliberate choice or adherence by a believer to one tradition did not begin to operate in Chinese culture until C.E. 1000. But even then the Chinese said that the three religions were one, and except for a few Confucianist purists who despised the other two, most people used or patronized whichever form or school fitted their needs at the time.

Confucius

Confucius was a historical figure whose life and work played the decisive role in initiating and determining the development of the movement which bears his name; in this sense he is the founder of Confucianism.

SOURCES

The *Analects* is the best single source for understanding Confucius as a real personality, through his own writings. But a wide variety of materials would have to be consulted in order to construct a proper biography, and we will not attempt to do that. The Confucian classics reveal the tumultuous times and events that were the background for his life and work, and the *Book of Mencius* includes much about him. The following brief account is a summary of essential facts about Confucius as a human being and the originator of the school that bears his name.

LIFE

Kongfuze, whose name Latinized by the early Jesuit missionary scholars to Confucius, means "Kong the master," his family being the Kong, was born in a winter month of the year 551 B.C.E. in the small state of Lu, in the town T'sou, which was near the modern city Ch'u-fu of Shantung Province. His father was, some say, the commandant of T'sou district; at any rate it is probable that his family was among the lesser feudal nobility. But his father died when Confucius was quite small, and he grew up in humble and straitened circumstances, according to his own words in the *Analects*, and had to make his own way. Tradition relates that as a boy he enjoyed play-acting with his friends in imitation of the sacrificial ceremonies, and that somehow he acquired an education. A summary outline of chief events in his own development as given in the *Analects* says:

> The Master said, At fifteen I set my heart upon learning. At thirty, I had planted my feet firm upon the ground. At forty, I no longer suffered from perplexities. At fifty, I knew what were the biddings of Heaven. At sixty, I heard them with docile ear. At seventy, I could follow the dictates of my own heart; for what I desired no longer overstepped the boundaries of right (II, 4)[2]

Apparently he was married quite young and had a son and two daughters, the son being specifically mentioned in the *Analects*. But little more is known of any family life, so it is thought that perhaps the marriage did not last. Although

Altar, Confucian Temple, Tainan. Plaque to Confucius (Ward J. Fellows).

he became a sage, a scholar, and a teacher, he did not spend all his youth in study and work, for he seems to have had some opportunity to indulge in archery and music, the pursuits of young aristocrats. Nevertheless he was by no means a typical creature of his times, but a man who early thought for himself and went his own way.

He was ambitious to be of real service in a government post and to work for the improvement of the condition of society. The small state of Lu managed to survive to the end of the troubled and strife-torn Chou dynasty, perhaps because Lu was founded by the great Duke of Chou and was honored as the inheritor of the ancient culture and ceremonies. Actually, conditions within Lu were better than in many other parts of the empire. Although some traditions tell of his holding significant posts in Lu, the reliable evidence is that Confucius never held the kind of position he wanted and of which he felt himself capable. The truth seems to be that he was not really fitted for the political life of his time, when there were more than the usual pressures for dishonesty, flattery, and ruthless practices, while he was uncompromising in principles and outspoken in speech.

Thwarted in a political career, he turned to study and somehow became in effect a teacher, although teaching was not then organized or professionalized. Certain parallels between Confucius in China and Plato in Greece about a century later have often been remarked: Both were thwarted statesmen who turned to training political leaders. While unsuccessful in direct political influence and not holding important office, both established seats of learning for the inculcation of fundamental principles of good government, and young men of high ideals heard them gladly. The number of Confucius' students was not great; in the *Analects* 20 or 30 are mentioned, two others appear in the *Book of Mencius*, and tradition says there were 70.

By the force of his personality, the purity of his motives, and the clarity of his mind, he created an environment of learning in which young men from different backgrounds studied the classics and discussed how to govern a state well. As the wisdom of the teacher became known and the reputation of the school increased, some of the disciples were given positions of authority by princes who were afraid to hire the master but wanted the skill of the pupils. He was given a position of some kind, around 500 B.C.E., in which he describes himself as "following after" the Great Officers of Court. Probably this means that he was "Leader of the Knights," a kind of police magistrate. Although he thought (or hoped) that his insights would be used and his opinions consulted on important matters, the position turned out to be a sinecure, without responsibilities or power, and he resigned it.

Soon after this disappointment Confucius undertook, although he was nearly 60 years of age, a journey away from Lu in search of a state and ruler who would heed his teachings and give him employment. Some of his disciples accompanied him, and he was evidently accorded honors and supported with a stipend in some of the states he visited, which were all within what are now the provinces of Shantung and Honan. In others he was not welcomed but was treated with hostility. Indeed at one point an attempt was made on his life by a disgruntled nobleman, and the little company was in dire straits for awhile. Undoubtedly he was at other times encouraged by the deference paid to his opinions and hoped that he would gain a significant permanent post which would enable him to put his principles into practice. One or two petty officials with limited authority did make offers of administrative positions, and Confucius' yearning for recognition is shown by his giving these offers active consideration in spite of the fact that they were really beneath his dignity.

Meanwhile certain of his pupils had achieved prestige in Lu, and out of genuine affection and respect for him they prevailed on Confucius to end his more than 10 years of voluntary exile and return. But although his travels seemed to have been in vain, they too contributed to his wisdom and prestige as a sage and thinker for the ages and not simply a functionary in an obscure Chinese province. Everywhere he went he maintained his integrity, spoke out firmly against evils and for the ancient virtues, and exemplified his teaching by his conduct. Although at the time it seemed to have been a futile adventure, it helped to make him the supreme teacher of China.

He was 69 when he returned to Lu, according to tradition, in 483 B.C.E., and little firm information about his last years is available. He seems to have devoted time to working on records and information gathered during his travels and perhaps to have continued work on the classics, especially editorial work on the *Book of Poetry*. But his principal effort was the further instruction of his students and the refinement and summary of his teaching. When first his son and then his favorite disciple Yen Hui died, he mourned more than he would have earlier, and the tragic death of his most distinguished follower,

Ssu-Ma Niu, and of the intrepid Tzu-lu in defense of his chief in Wei, further grieved and weakened him. There is no reliable account of his death. From the *Analects* come three brief anecdotes and sayings which give us some picture of his attitude toward death. When Confucius was seriously ill (but not in his terminal illness), Tzu-lu arranged a display of the disciples as if they were high officials gathered around a great dignitary. But Confucius rebuked this display, asking if he could deceive Heaven, and stated his confidence that the disciples would give him decent burial (IX, 11). Again when the master was very ill, Tzu-lu asked about performing the Rite of Expiation, and Confucius said that he had done his kind of praying long ago (VII, 34). A third quotation perhaps expresses his resignation to his destiny, shortly before his death: "The Master said, The phoenix does not come; the river gives forth no chart. It is all over with me" (IX, 8). Waley's notes explain that these events would be deemed portents of a Savior.[3] In 479 B.C.E., Confucius died.

According to Mencius, the disciples mourned him for the canonical three years of mourning of a son for his father, living in huts which they built near his grave. As the news of his death spread through the states, the men of worldly power and so-called realism began to apotheosize the man whom they had feared, ignored, or laughed at during his lifetime.

THE WORK OF CONFUCIUS

In later centuries Confucius became, for awhile, a god; but he was not a god. We are talking about "Confucianism," but he was not the founder of an organized religion. He was not a zealot or fanatical reformer with a panacea. Sober and circumspect, he was not a visionary, a mystic, or a religious enthusiast. Yet he was a man with a vision, a man with a goal and purpose; he had zeal, and he offered an essentially religious way to the good society. That is, he proclaimed that truth and virtue are the basis of good government.

What such a man thought about himself is perhaps as good a clue as we can get to what his task or function in life was. *Analects* IX, 5 is cited as the crucial statement of Confucius' idea of his purpose in life:

> When the Master was trapped in K'uang, he said, When King Wen perished did that mean that culture (*wen**) ceased to exist? If Heaven had really intended that such culture as his should disappear, a latterday mortal would never have been able to link himself to it as I have done. And if Heaven does not intend to destroy such culture, what have I to fear from the people of K'uang? (IX, 5)

The passage requires elaboration in order for its significance to be appreciated. The occasion was the perils he encountered in his exile, which we mentioned. Wen was the first king of the Chou empire, whose practice of *wen*, the arts of peace, qualified him to replace the Shang emperor. Heaven willed that the culture of Wen should prevail and now wills that Confucius should live, because Confucius is the one chosen by Heaven to preserve and transmit that culture.

Another passage in the *Analects* expressive of this conception of himself as a transmitter of tradition says: "I merely try to describe (or carry on) the ancient tradition, but not to create something new. I only want to get at the truth and am in love with ancient studies" (VII, 19).[4]

In pursuit of this purpose of preserving, refining, and transmitting the best of the ancient culture, Confucius first of all lived the part, practiced it himself. Like Socrates in Greece, he personified the ideal of wisdom which he professed. In this he was like many religious reformers, whose living and practicing their faith is their most notable service and effective teaching. The picture that comes out of the *Analects* is of a warm human figure who cared first of all about virtue and the ancient forms and ceremonies which were meant to express those virtues. "These were the things Confucius often talked about: Poetry, history, and the performance of ceremonies."[5] One reason he never gained high position was that when he was asked for advice by rulers he always spoke bluntly in terms of their need to stop acting selfishly and cruelly and to begin practicing virtue and doing good for the people. He sharply criticized the corruption, cynicism, and incompetence of the hereditary rulers and officials. The measure of his character is the honor which he gained after death and the movement which bears his name.

But he would not be so honored if his only concern had been to maintain a dead or fixed tradition. In teaching his disciples and adjuring the rulers he gave new meaning and power to traditional wisdom. It was this innovative, if not revolutionary, interpretation and application of tradition which made him the founder of something new. The exact nature of his contribution is disputed. Confucius carefully and purposely made use of tradition; let us borrow Huston Smith's term to describe Confucius' practice: "deliberate" tradition. He did it on purpose. But he did not simply and uncritically take *all* tradition, as if whatever was old was good. Instead, he selected what was good, true, and useful. To understand Confucius' work, therefore, we must describe this selective tradition. But first it is necessary to summarize the later development of Confucianism.

The Confucian Movement

Inasmuch as there was never a formal, institutionalized, and organized Confucianism, one should not look for a simple pattern of growth from small beginnings to great size, which is a success story in Western terms. There is simply the development of the *Ju Chiao*, the faith or cult of the intellectuals or the cultured, involving theoretical formulations by the disciples and later philosophers of a more or less distinctive and self-conscious school or group. The background for this developed Confucianism was a period of strife both in political and intellectual terms. Politically, the "Warring States" fought among themselves for supremacy until their unification in 221 B.C.E. In the fifth to third centuries B.C.E. there were many competing philosophies, usually grouped in six major schools of thought, including Confucianism as the School of the Intellectuals and Taoism.

MENCIUS

The 70 disciples were widely scattered after Confucius' death. Although many of them became teachers and government ministers in the service of feudal lords, Confucianism as a system of thought was in apparent decline for 100 years. During that time, nevertheless, the followers of Confucius probably began their work of collecting and editing the pre-Confucian works. Almost exactly 100 years after Confucius' death Mencius or master Meng was born; he studied under pupils of Confucius' grandson Tzu-Ssu, and is the greatest of Confucius' followers. He considered it his task to oppose opponents of Confucianism, especially Mo Tzu*, the latter being the founder of the Mohist* school. We place Mencius as the first major thinker after Confucius who shaped the development of the Confucian school. In many ways the course of his life was similar to that of Confucius.

EMERGENCE OF THE CONFUCIAN SCHOOL

The unification of China under the great Han dynasty brought a need for officials and administrators from the scholar class, and the Confucian group had trained men who could fill the need. Under their influence the empire embraced Confucianist principles for guidance of policy, and the emperor Wu-Ti about 100 B.C.E. adopted Confucianism as the state cult and doctrine. The emperor served as high priest and the literati became masters of ceremonies. Thus a kind of state Confucianism for political and religious practices was established. Although influenced and changed somewhat by Taoism and Mohism, Confucianism became the official school and remained the dominant theoretical and religious position of the government and among the scholar-administrators until 1905, when the civil service examinations based on the classics were dropped. Confucius' theory and practice in selecting students was according to ability and not nobility of birth. This equalitarian practice gave Chinese officialdom new blood throughout its history.

THE CULT OF CONFUCIUS

Meanwhile a cult about Confucius himself had grown up. After Confucius' death the disciples who settled in the vicinity of his tomb began the practice of offering sacrifices there several times a year. From this developed the cult of Confucius. We give Hodous' summary.

> The first emperor of the Han dynasty visited the tomb of Confucius. In C.E. 441 a temple was erected at Chu-fu the place of his tomb. In 505 one was erected at the capital. This was canonization. From now on honors multiplied. Tai Tsung of the Tang dynasty (C.E. 618–906) put the cult on a new basis. In 630 he decreed that all districts in the empire build temples to Confucius with statues of the Master dressed in royal robes. This universalized the cult. In 647 he made the Confucian Temple the Hall of Fame for scholars and officials.[6]

Titles accorded to Master Kong were: Supreme Teacher (665), King (735), Supreme Saint (1013). However, tablets replaced the images of Confucius in most temples after 1530.

Contemporary Confucianism

We must note the present position of Confucianism within the general religious situation in China as described at the end of our previous summary of Chinese religious history. This brings us to the fundamental question that has always divided both Confucianists themselves and scholar-observers of it: Is Confucianism a religion, or is it an ethical system, simply an intellectual and cultural movement? Historically, such a difference existed among all the big three of China. The Chinese had two words for them: Described as religious organizations, they were called *Chiao*, but construed as different schools of thought and cultural ways, the term was *Chia*. This was more of a problem for Confucianism than for the other two, and now it is central to Confucianism's nature and survival.

For the following material I again refer to the Journal of Professional Activities cited in discussing Buddhism. Our group spent two full days in Qufu. The destruction wreaked on the 2,000-year-old shrine by the Red Guards of the Cultural Revolution has been more than restored. The traditional Confucian decoration was quite subdued compared to the bright Chinese decoration we saw in moving freely among the refurbished historical structures. Everything, from the mound memorials for Confucius and his immediate family to the extensive park-like cemetery for many descendants, is open to the public. This is part of the active rehabilitation—perhaps propagandistic—of Master Kong. The People's Republic has embraced and exalted the memory of its own native sage and spiritual leader.

Our delegation interviewed four professors from the Confucius Research Institute and the Confucius Cultural Institute of Qufu Normal University, and met with scholars from the Confucius Foundation. Their remarks probably reflected the necessity to avoid any kind of improper opinion on delicate social, political, and economic policies impinging on the issue of Confucianism as a religion, but we felt their comments were sincere. The Journal of Professional Activities for our group reported on parts of the discussion:

> Mr. Luo said, some scholars say Confucianism is a religion. He thinks it is not a religion because Confucius taught no strict religious beliefs and stressed the priority of this life and world over the "other" one. . . . Mr. Luo said Marx and Confucius were both great philosophers, but Marx is greater (and more relevant) because his ideas were developed in an industrial society rather than an agricultural one. Mr. Li added that the relationship between Marxism and Confucianism "is a real problem." Both are still considered useful in helping to build the modern Chinese society; the question is how to make them cooperate, especially given what seems to be a renewed, more widespread interest in Confucianism among the Chinese in recent years.[7]

A careful analysis of and judgment on the present situation by Professor de Bary puts it in context and clarifies the issues. He reminds us that a whole generation of Chinese grew up ignorant of and opposed to the Confucianism that is now being promoted as the new basis for economic and cultural society. Therefore, he writes:

> Only with the reinstatement of some genuine Confucian culture, and the reading of basic texts in the school and college curriculum . . . could Confucian learning be articulated to the level of literate discourse so that it could have any significant influence on educated Chinese today, as well as on those who might participate in higher level decision making or policy formulation.[8]

LITERATURE OF CONFUCIANISM

The generic term for the canonical scriptures of all three Chinese religions is *ching*, usually translated "classic," but in practice "the classics" is taken to mean the Confucian books in particular. The original meaning of *ching*, like all Chinese concepts, is derived from a concrete or specific thing: *Ching* at first meant the warp of woven fabric, that is, the longitudinal threads on a loom into which the many cross threads are woven back and forth.

One of the legends about Mencius and his mother, who worked so hard for him to be educated, illustrates the importance of the *ching*. His mother was still supporting him by weaving; although he was grown he was continuing his studies. When he got home one day his mother asked how he was getting along. He gave an indifferent reply as if it did not matter, whereupon she took a knife and cut straight across the warp of the weaving on her loom. Being shaken from his indifference by this extraordinary act, he asked what it meant, and she pointed out how his indolence was doing to his own life what she had done to her weaving. The play on words implied in the legend is that just as the *ching* or warp carries the body of the fabric, so the classics (*ching*) provides enduring threads or guides for the Confucian virtues and morality. Moreover, "study" for Confucius, Mencius, and the *ju chia* for nearly 2,000 years, meant study of the classics, devotion to them, learning from them. Perhaps sometimes it was too slavish memorization of them, but the *ching* were the long threads on which the fabric of Confucianism was woven.

A host of complex technical questions cluster about the classics. However, one thing is distinctive of them: They are *not* considered divine revelation. In this they are unlike such books as the Bible, the Koran, the Vedas, and so on. Most important is the problem of authorship, and specifically the question of whether or not Confucius himself wrote or edited them. Although the judgment of most modern scholars is generally against the Confucian authorship, the traditional ascription of some of them to Confucius as editor if not author should not be casually dismissed. In any event they were probably collected, edited, and interpreted by Confucius' followers, and in this sense they are the work of the Confucian school and are the classics of Confucianism. Although the list of

An altar, temple in Taipei. Three figures and three plaques (behind glass) are Longevity, Achievement, Posterity (Ward J. Fellows).

classics technically includes 13 works, we follow the standard pattern in our list of Five Classics and Four Books* as the most important. (We list the Chinese names first for the Five Classics or *Wu-Ching*, because they are so commonly used.)

The Five Classics

I CHING

A work that has gained some popularity in recent years in the occident is the *Book of Changes (I Ching)*, an ancient text dating from early in the Chou dynasty. It is a manual for divination or fortune-telling, using 64 sets of hexagrams or six-line figures. Sixty-four is the number of possible combinations of undivided (———) and/or divided (— — —) lines arranged in six rows. The body of the *Book of Changes* is clearly pre-Confucian, but "came in Han times to be considered one of the Confucian classics, despite the fact that Confucius and all the great early Confucians had scorned the practice of divination."[9] The appendices were added in Han times.

SHU CHING*

The Book of History is termed by Lin Yutang "documents of Chinese democracy," because of the concern for the people manifested in those documents or records; they are attributed to governments from about 3000 B.C.E. to the

Chou. Confucius may have played a part in editing them, and their spirit of civic virtue and devotion to Heaven make them truly part of the Confucian canon. In all there are 58 chapters, not all authentic.

SHIH CHING*

A collection of 305 ballads, satires, love songs, and other forms of poetry, the *Book of Poetry* is sometimes called the *Book of Odes* or *Book of Songs* because of the variety of its contents. Confucius may have worked at editing them, and seems certainly to have been familiar with and fond of such a collection. Many of them carry the universal human themes of all great poetry. Translator James Legge's heading to this poem, which dates from perhaps 800 B.C.E., refers to the author as "some officer in a time of disorder and misgovernment":

> Small is the cooing dove, But it flies aloft to Heaven. My heart is wounded with sorrow, And I think of our forefathers. When the dawn is breaking and I cannot sleep, the thoughts in my breast are of our parents.[10]

LI CHI*

In the expanded canon there are three texts dealing with *li** or ritual. This one is important for the theoretical views it expresses, as well as the details of rituals. It was probably put together in Han times, and is called the *Book of Rites.** Several key passages of Confucianism are found in it.

CH'UN CH'IU*

*The Spring and Autumn Annals** is often attributed directly to Confucius because of a reference in *The Book of Mencius*. But critics doubt this and note the *Analects* never mentions it. It is a matter-of-fact record of events in Lu from 711 to 481 B.C.E.

The Four Books

Whereas the Five Classics are all traditionally attributed to the time of Confucius or before, the Four Books come from Confucius' time or after. The great neo-Confucianist Chu Hsi grouped them as the Four Books in the twelfth century, and they formed the basis of Confucian education in succeeding centuries.

THE ANALECTS

This is the name which James Legge gave to this collection of sayings attributed to Confucius. The Chinese name for the book is *Lun Yu*, meaning "selected sayings." No other Chinese work except the *Tao Te Ching* has been the subject of such careful translation into English, and it deserves the attention. Yet there are many problems about its authenticity, and it undoubtedly contains extensive sections that are not from Confucius himself. However much or little of it may be genuinely ascribed to Confucius, it is "Confucian" in the best sense, in its cumulative force as a picture of Confucius and a true book of wisdom.

THE BOOK OF MENCIUS

His Latinized name, from Meng Tzu or Master Meng, is appended to the work of Master Meng. Problems of date and authorship are very few; it is the longest and best attested to of the Four Books. Seven parts or books are extant, consisting of a series of conversations between Mencius and various friends, officials, nobles, or disciples. The guiding principle of his counsel about good government was his conviction of the essential goodness of human nature.

THE DOCTRINE OF THE MEAN*

The Chinese name *Clung Yung** combines the notions of "central" and "constant." Hence it is the mean or norm in the sense of keeping constantly in harmony with the universal Way of Heaven and as the avoidance of extremes. The traditional author is Confucius' grandson Tzu-Ssu; it was a chapter in the *Book of Rites* before being singled out by the neo-Confucianists as one of the Four Books.

THE GREAT LEARNING*

Like *The Mean*, the *Ta Hsueh** was taken from the *Book of Rites*. It is a brief statement about self-cultivation as the beginning of a process which reaches out from the person, to the family, the state, and the world. A phrase in the program of self-cultivation, *ko wu*, became the focus of the divergence of the two major schools of neo-Confucianism. One side interpreted it as "to investigate things," and the other as "to rectify the mind."

Tseng Tzu was the traditional author of the *Great Learning*, and of another work which should be mentioned along with the Five Classics and Four Books because of its importance in later Confucian thought as a kind of primer for Confucian students. This is the *Classic of Filial Piety*, or *Hsiao Ching,** in which Confucius expounds to Tseng Tzu the importance and the blessings of the practice of filial piety (duty of a child to parents). It is clearly a late (second or first century B.C.E.) work from the Confucian school.

TENETS OF CONFUCIANISM

In the sections on tenets, ritual, and ethics the most significant religious aspects of Confucianism will be described. As we have pointed out, there are certain traditional elements of the Confucian view which are derived from the past but are interpreted in a distinctive Confucian way. Under tenets the traditional concepts of Heaven or T'ien, goodness or *jen*, and the Way or Tao, are described first, and then Confucian theoretical developments in later centuries are outlined.

In early Confucianism there is less of explicit doctrine or dogma than in any of the other religions we study. (In Taoism there will be no single or simple dogma, but it is quite speculative and dogmatic about explaining why this must be so.)

Traditional Elements

HEAVEN

It is true that these religious or spiritual factors are not always explicitly described in religious terms, and a couple of passages in the *Analects* can be misinterpreted to make Confucius sound almost agnostic. But there are many other statements which imply or entail belief in the existence and reality of Heaven, and Heaven is explicitly invoked by Confucius on many occasions. In Confucius' own thought T'ien is described as a vital and purposive power from which comes the moral law. The Confucian ethic, in short, is based on some kind of supramundane reality, called T'ien or Heaven. This is a simple and fundamental relationship which is characteristic of most religious systems. In the sense that his ethical humanism was based on the profoundest religious ideas of his time, Confucius was a religious man.

The Chinese word for Heaven which is used in the *Analects* is T'ien, not Ti or Shang Ti, the words used to denote the more personal and anthropomorphic ancestral powers in earlier literature. Creel says: "It seems clear that Confucius thought of Heaven as an impersonal ethical force, a cosmic counterpart of the ethical sense in man, a guarantee that somehow there is sympathy with man's sense of right in the very nature of the universe."[11] One time, Confucius said, "The truth is, no one knows me! But the studies of man here below are felt on high, and perhaps after all I am known; not here, but in Heaven" (XIV, 37). Heaven, as the ground of ethics and his own spiritual trust and reliance, was for him a reality; this can be seen throughout the *Analects*. In such passages, the *Analects* breathes the same spirit of the righteous person's implicit trust in the transcendent order as is expressed in more personal terms in the Psalms of the Bible.

Confucius was reluctant, however, to discuss, describe, or speculate about Heaven. It was a fundamental datum, something assumed and necessary in his thinking and his life, and it was real. But he made no effort to describe or define the nature or meaning of Heaven; that did not concern him. What did matter was to be in accord with Heaven; of the three things that a gentleman fears, says the *Analects*, he fears the will of Heaven first of all (XVI, 8). This was consonant with the view in the *Book of History* of the importance of the Mandate of Heaven as the final arbiter of the destiny of kings and peoples. In the "Announcement of T'ang," the Shang king who overthrew the Hsia empire said to the people:

The way of Heaven is to give blessings to the good and misfortunes to evil-doers. Heaven has sent down calamities on the ruler of Hsia in order to make clear his sins. I, the little child, following the Mandate of Heaven which gave me clear power, did not dare to forgive him. The criminal was finally de-graded and subjugated. The Mandate of Heaven is always correct.[12]

We referred to this concept in our description of pre-Confucian ideas, as having been used by the Chou writers to justify their overthrow of the Shang dynasty. These same Chou writers probably wrote the words quoted above, as part of their campaign to promote their use of the concept. In any event, it be-came a fundamental precept of Chinese political theory. If the imperial family becomes corrupt and degraded, ruling selfishly and cruelly, they forfeit the support of the eternal powers—they disqualify themselves. In Mencius the Mandate of Heaven went as far as justification of revolution on moral grounds, in a passage which is often quoted:

King Hsuan of Ch'i asked, "Was it a fact that T'ang banished King Chieh and that King Wen punished King Chou?" Mencius replied, "Yes, according to records." The King said, "Is it all right for a minister to murder his king?" Men-cius said, "He who injures humanity is a bandit. He who injures righteousness is a destructive person. Such a person is a mere fellow. I have heard of killing a mere fellow Chou, but I have not heard of murdering [him as] the ruler."[13]

When a wicked king loses the Mandate of Heaven, revolution against him is justified; Confucianists have always supported this view. As recently as the post–World War II conflict in which the Communists ousted Chiang Kai Shek's Nationalists from China, the doctrine was invoked by both combatants.

JEN*

The second element of Confucianism, which is taken from the pre-Confucian tradition, is also more implicit and assumed than it is explicitly and formally ar-ticulated. *Jen*, the Chinese word for this notion of Confucius' thought, is used because, as with all Chinese words, it is literally impossible to give a single Eng-lish word as a synonym for this complex ideogram, which can be taken to have many meanings. We follow Arthur Waley's analysis and verdict based on actual usage in the *Analects* itself. His conclusion is that to translate *jen* by any other word than "good" in a wide and general sense is inadequate. This is important, because *jen* is the quality or description of Heaven, the nature of God or the ul-timate reality. Confucius' conjunction of *jen* with Heaven answers that ques-tion: Heaven is good. This connection between Heaven and goodness is signifi-cant because good or goodness is the fundamental character of the supreme being in some of the great religions we are studying. In the Western Biblical reli-gions, the goodness of God is explicit and fundamental. In Hinduism and Bud-dhism it is not basic to God's nature in the same way that it is in the Western faiths. Confucianism, then, is like the Biblical religions in this inseparable rela-tionship between the supreme reality or power and the quality of goodness.

Kai Yuan Buddhist Temple, Tainan. Memorial plaques, here found in the Buddhist temple; note Buddha image (Ward J. Fellows).

TAO*

This third chief tenet of Confucianism, which is absorbed from tradition, is another complex Chinese character, but one which is used by Confucius in its ordinary meaning of a road, path, or way, and hence the Way in which things are or should be done. Above all it is the Way of Heaven with which he is concerned. There is a parallel between Confucian Tao in this sense and Hindu *dharma* as the way for all people to go.

Confucius took the basic, simple, practical sense of a way in general, and stressed the Way as the good way of Heaven for individuals, states, and the world. In the *Analects* several passages (VIII, 13; XIV, 1 and 4) express the difference between the Way as an internalized moral norm and merely external laws and practices. Perhaps the Latin motto of the University of Pennsylvania expresses it: "*Leges sine moribus vanae,*" "Laws without morals are useless." The Tao is the Way of the ancients so far as it could be rediscovered from the traditions. By study of Tao and devotion to it, people, kings, and empires live well, precisely because it is the Way of Heaven, the way things are meant to go. The ancient kings, Yao, Shun, and Yu the Great, and especially the Duke of Chou, were to be emulated because they exemplified in their day the Tao as the Way which, when followed by the ruler, made the people happy and the realm secure. The trouble with the degenerate nobility and corrupt officials of his day, Confucius saw, was that they had no reverence for the Tao and hence acted in vicious and destructive fashion. Like Socrates, again, he had a daimon or guiding spirit, who was for Confucius the Duke of Chou as the one who personified the Tao. "The Master said, How utterly have things gone to the bad with me! It is long now indeed since I dreamed that I saw the Duke of Chou" (*Analects*, VII, 5).

Mencius

Mencius elaborated in more detail than did Confucius the operation of goodness or benevolence in a graded pattern, beginning with the family and then reaching out into the state and the world. The most significant, lasting effect of Mencius on Confucian thought was his explicit doctrine of the goodness of human nature, whereas Confucius had at most simply assumed it. In *The Book of Mencius* this innate goodness is made the basis of his far-reaching counsel for the king who would rule wisely. His argument for existence of this innate sense is often quoted:

> Why I say all men have a sense of commiseration is this: Here is a man who suddenly notices a child who is about to fall into a well. Invariably he will feel a sense of alarm and compassion. And this is not for the purpose of gaining the favor of the child's parents, or seeking the approbation of his neighbors and friends, or for fear of blame should he fail to rescue it.[14]

The wise ruler by her policies fosters this quality in the people, for whose benefit she is meant to rule, and thus the natural benevolence of people is enabled to express itself. Likewise, man's innate knowledge is fostered by study, and Mencius advocated study, education, and the scholarly life as strengthening goodness. By *jen*, understood in Mencius as benevolence, and by righteousness (*yi**) in the ruler first of all, the good community can be brought to pass. Mencius defended Confucian filial piety as the true and sensible expression of *jen*.

HAN METAPHYSICS

Confucius and Mencius did not discuss a number of problems, and when during the Han Dynasty Confucianism became supreme among the schools, it moved to broaden its range of doctrines. In particular, metaphysical questions like cosmogony had been left open. During the Han period Confucianism assimilated from the Taoist and the *yin-yang* schools their explanations of the creation and operations of the universe. We take a passage from the *Book of Rites*, which was probably compiled during the same time (second century B.C.E.), as illustrative of what Creel has termed "the eclectics of Han." In this passage can be seen the articulation of a system in which humanity is derived from and related to the same forces and factors which originate and control the world at large. In particular, the *yin* and *yang* are built into the system. They appear in the following passage as "the dual forces of nature," *yang* being "the strong and light force," positive and masculine, and *yin* being "the dark and weaker force," negative and feminine. The traditional "five elements"* are: water, fire, wood, metal, soil. Legge's translation of *The Book of Rites*, Book VII, Section III reads:

1. Man is the product of the attributes of Heaven and Earth, by the interaction of the dual forces of nature, the union of the animal and intelligent souls, and the finest subtile matter of the five elements.

2. Heaven exercises the control of the strong and light force, and hangs out the sun and stars. Earth exercises the control of the dark and weaker force, and gives vent to it in the hills and streams. The five elements are distributed through the four seasons, and it is by their harmonious action that the moon is produced, which therefore keeps waxing for fifteen days and waning for fifteen.

* * * *

7. Therefore man is the heart and mind of Heaven and Earth, and the visible embodiment of the five elements. . . .

* * * *

9. The origin of all things being found in heaven and earth, they could be taken in hand, one after the other. . . .[15]

Later, *The Doctrine of the Mean* said that heaven, earth, and man form a triad, and in Han thought that trinity was a basic idea.

Neo-Confucianism

During the course of Chinese history the classics were several times inscribed on stone tablets, and in the ninth century they were printed from wooden blocks. This signaled the revival of Confucianism after its time of decline when Buddhism was ascendant under the T'ang dynasty. In the Sung dynasty (960–1279) this resurgence took the form of what is now called Neo-Confucianism. One dominant motif was elaboration of metaphysical and cosmological speculations, in order to counteract Buddhist and Taoist doctrines. In the process Confucianism was influenced by the views it opposed. It was during this time and as part of this polemical activity that the *Four Books* became the books of Neo-Confucianism. We follow Wing-Tsit Chan in making Chu Hsi's (1130–1200) synthesis the most important point, and in stressing the religious significance of these developments. Professor Chan says: "By and large, however, it is safe to say that Neo-Confucianism is essentially religious in the best sense of the term."[16]

CHU HSI

Most of the same factors that appeared in the selection from the *Book of Rites* appear again in Chu Hsi's cosmology. In addition, however, are the two basic principles which distinguish his system, *Li** the psychic principle and *ch'i** the material principle. (The Latinized word *Li* is the same as that which means ritual. The *Li* described here is a different Chinese character or ideogram, and therefore a different word and meaning. We use *li** to signify the ritual and *Li* for the psychic principle.)

Although Chu Hsi sometimes made use of a current Confucian cosmological concept called the Supreme Ultimate, the two principles remain distinct and are the basic philosophical concepts of his system. *Li* is the factor of movement and is basic, but it cannot be actualized without *ch'i*, which in some ways is like a primary metaphysical substance. Chu Hsi said: "There is principle [*li*] before there can be material-force [*ch'i*]. But it is only when there is material force that principle finds a place to settle."[17] The two principles work through the *yang* and *yin* as two modes of operation, and the *yin* and *yang* in turn utilize the five elements to form the world. In this system, using elements from the *Book of Mencius* and the *Book of Rites*, Chu Hsi rationalized the creation and operation of the world, and by the same sort of principles or factors explained human nature.

Through *Li* as the psychic principle, people are related to the cosmos and are one humanity, although differences arise among them from their *ch'i*. The moral and religious import of Chu Hsi's views arises from this relation between persons and the world order, for in effect the order has the same moral quality as the explicitly religious Heaven of earlier Confucianism. Speaking of the original nature from Heaven, he says: "How can it be said that the good is not the original nature? . . . Now what is received from Heaven is the same nature as that in accordance with which goodness ensues. . . ."[18] He also reinterpreted another important religious category, *kwei* and *shen*, traditional and ubiquitous earthly and heavenly spirits. In the *Book of Rites* the *kwei* are correlated with *yin* and the *shen* with *yang*. Chu Hsi reinterpreted them as spiritual forces instead of spiritual beings, although this did not prevent their being regarded as personalized forces in popular religion.

In sum, his achievement was to provide a unified and inclusive scheme which offered answers for the basic questions about the nature and operation of the world, including people and the social order. An essentially religious interpretation of humans as moral and spiritual beings who are one with Heaven, it became the dominant Confucian and Chinese philosophy for hundreds of years.

Confucian Temple, Taipei (Ward J. Fellows).

Human Nature

All forms, systems, and schools of Confucianism were first of all doctrines of morality. They were therefore deeply concerned with a prior question or problem: What is the original moral nature of the human being? Is morality a development or a denial of human nature? Confucius did not discuss the morality question but seemed to assume that a good Heaven gave us a good nature. We quoted Mencius' explicit argument to prove people are innately good; this showed, he held, that moral education simply nurtures impulses already in us. In the *Doctrine of the Mean*, Mencius' theory was implied in the first paragraph, which states the initial thesis: "What is God-given is what we call human nature. To fulfill the law of our human nature is what we call the moral law. The cultivation of the moral law is what we call culture."[19]

For a thousand years after that there were differing views among Confucianists. Then Mencius' doctrine was revived by Chu Hsi in a modified form. He and the Neo-Confucianists explained evil as a result of the material principle or *ch'i*. Originally the *ch'i* is good, but when separate physical beings are formed, enmity and strife arise. Yet everyone has the true nature in the psychic principle *Li* and therefore can learn and grow in goodness. In the thirteenth century this became the orthodox teaching in the *Three Character Classic*, which was memorized by all students until 1912.

The United Nations paid tribute to Confucius' wisdom in the UNESCO "Statement on Race" in 1950. Delegates agreed that the essential truth about human nature and racial differences was best expressed by Confucius (*Analects*, XVII, 2): "Confucius said: 'By nature men are pretty much alike; it is learning and practice that set them apart."[20]

RITUAL IN CONFUCIANISM

Ritual and worship in Confucianism is discussed under four headings. The first is the principal traditional concept, *li*, as the theoretical component. The others are the expressions of ritual in three principal areas: ancestor worship, the state cult of Heaven, and the cult around Confucius himself. The first two of these, ancestor worship and the state cult, were traditional elements which long antedated Confucius; the third developed after his death.

Li

Li is another one of the basic Confucian ideas which is derived from tradition. The word is a character of two elements which is usually translated as propriety or code of conduct in the more general sense, and as ceremonies or ritual in a more specific sense. We turn for help to James Legge's comments in the introduction to his translation of the *Book of Rites (Li Chi)*. There are two fundamental ideas which the character *li* was intended to convey. First, it suggested steps or acts in which humans serve spiritual beings, and one of the two elements of the character was the specific symbol for sacrificial vessels. Second, in moral and philosophical discussions it denoted one of the primary constituents of human nature, namely, the proper moral feelings in various circumstances. Legge concludes: "Thus the character li, in the concrete application of it, denotes the manifestations, and in its imperative use, the rules, of

Lung Shan Buddhist temple, Shanghai, on a Sunday in June, 1994; courtyard at entrance. Busy, open to all, no visible problems. (Ward J. Fellows)

propriety. This twofold symbolism of it—the religious and the moral—must be kept in mind in the study of our classic."[21]

From the *Analects* one can gain the main outlines of Confucius' view of *li*. Confucius always insisted on the importance of the motive and of sincerity in ritual, against any attempt to make the ceremony itself, the mere outward performance, significant and effective apart from the heart and purpose of the performer. Among things he could not bear to see were "ritual performed without reverence, the forms of mourning observed without grief" (III, 26). Thus, when Lin Fang asked for the main principles of ritual, Confucius replied that in general it was better to be too sparing rather than too lavish, and in the particular case of mourning rites they should be dictated by grief rather than fear (III, 4). Therefore, only the good man is qualified to deal with ritual and music (III, 3). Confucius said, "If I am not present at the sacrifice, it is as though there were no sacrifice" (III, 12). He meant that unless he was fully present and participating in mind and heart, it was useless.

For the individual, *li* was as important as *jen*—that is, propriety in public or ceremonial conduct was as essential as goodness and benevolence. "The Master said: chun-tzu* bases his character on righteousness, conducts himself according to propriety . . ." (XI, 17).[22] The last saying in the *Analects* (XX, 3) is: "He who does not understand the will of Heaven cannot be regarded as a gentleman. He who does not know the rites cannot take his stand." In *Analects* VIII, 2, Confucius makes "prescriptions of ritual" the necessary condition without which courtesy becomes tiresome, caution becomes timidity, daring becomes turbulence. A sensible observance of the proprieties and amenities of life was for Confucius as essential characteristic of his ideal person, the *chun tzu* or gentleman. Not only was it a balance wheel of conduct for the individual, it was also a method for guiding and facilitating social relations. All people are more at ease in a social or public situation when they know what is expected of them and what to expect of other people. When "the lady" or person of higher social status—found in every social order no matter how theoretically equalitarian it may be—behaves properly, she puts herself and all others at ease.

But it was for the ruler that Confucius most stressed ritual, in the sense of the proper way of conducting affairs or exercising power. Regulations and chastisements do not work, he said. "Govern them by moral force, keep order among them by ritual and they will keep their self-respect and come to you of their own accord" (II, 3). In Confucius' understanding of ritual for the ruler was included the policy of compromising or yielding, rather than trying to conquer and subdue. "The Master said, If it is really possible to govern countries by ritual and yielding, there is no more to be said" (IV, 13). His confidence in this kind of conduct as the most practical wisdom was part of his belief in the true Tao or Way of the ancients. It was because they had followed the good Way of virtue and honor that the good rulers of the past, especially the Duke of Chou and King Wen, the father of the Chou founder, had given the people stable and just government. And their ways of doing things, their rituals and ceremonies, expressed and manifested these good ways. In the *Analects* Confucius says that the proper performance of the most important kingly rituals is effective if it is connected with goodness. "Yen Hui asked about Goodness. The Master said, 'He who can himself submit to ritual is Good.' If (a ruler) could for one day 'himself submit to ritual,' everyone under Heaven would respond to his Goodness . . ." (XII, 1).

Confucius may have been responsible for the theory which operated in later centuries, that the emperor was also high priest of the state cult of Heaven. In any event this was what came to pass.

The Cult of the Ancestors

A glance at the contents of the *Book of Rites* will prove to anyone the central importance of mourning customs and sacrifices to the spirits of deceased ancestors in Chinese religious tradition; a high proportion of the two large volumes in the *SBE* edition describes in meticulous detail the mourning customs and cites Confucius' practices at length. From that day to this, ancestor worship has been the most important single expression of private piety in Chinese religion.

Confucius could not and would not have wanted to deny the importance of these things. Just as he emphasized the primacy of family concerns and relations in his ethical theory, he also saw in honor to ancestors the ritual expression of the proper attitudes. In *The Book of Filial Piety*, "The Master said: . . . even the Son of Heaven . . . sacrifices at the ancestral temple, lest he forget his parents."[23] The evidence in the *Analects* about ancestral rites includes two sayings which both strongly support the traditional "three years"—perhaps meaning 25 months as into a third year—mourning of a son for his father, which enjoined severe limitations on dress, diet, and behavior. Concerning spirits there are several ambiguous and much-debated statements. They add up to counsel that one should take account of spirits and do what is proper, but that, for example, to sacrifice to the ancestors of others is presumptuous. The reverent but reserved attitude of Confucius involved scrupulous and sincere consideration for the feelings of anyone he met who was observing mourning customs. The Confucian intellectuals in later centuries, like Confucius, honored and respected these customs of the people.

From earliest times the ancestors were regarded as part of the family, whose spirits must not be neglected. Mourning, the funeral, and burial or entombment were all elaborate and precise rituals. In more recent times paper and other imitations replaced the sacrificial objects, and were burned. After burial, depending on the social status of the deceased, there were five sacrifices included in the classical pattern, concluding in the twenty-seventh month. A wooden tablet was inscribed with the name of the departed, and a formalized dot over the character *chu* symbolized the abiding place of the spirit. It was consecrated with the formula: "The spirit rests in this wooden tablet, and the tablet is spiritualized by its resting. The spirit and the wood together dwell in ages of unending spring." These tablets were kept in the hall or other special place in the home for several generations, and then they were transferred to the clan or family ancestral temple. On the altar with the tablets in modern times were usually found a Buddha image, an image of a hero of the Three Kingdoms (third century B.C.E.) named Kuan Kung, and a tablet or image of Confucius.

Family or clan worship centered around the altar in the home or at the clan temple, on various occasions of family life: birth, death, anniversaries, marriage, and so on. The officiant was the male head of the household. The actual ceremony was simple. Offerings of food, incense, flowers, and candles were set in front of the tablets, and the officiant, taking three lighted incense sticks, placed incense in the incense bowl and performed ceremonial bows—*kow tows*. The ancestors were invoked, notified of special events, and asked for a blessing. The principal family sacrifice was at the eve of the New Year. Food offerings were usually consumed afterward by the participants. In many ways this family cult resembled Greek and Roman practices.

The State Cult

The imperial sacrifices to Heaven and other major deities and powers were discontinued after the fall of the Ch'ing dynasty (1911). Only the impressive altars at Beijing remain. They were the scene of the supreme ceremonies, for the worship of heaven, earth, the imperial ancestors, and the deities of crops and the land. One of the altars is a three-tiered circular terrace with gleaming marble balustrades and four sets of steps, but no permanent buildings on the central, smallest, and highest flat tier where the sacrifice to Heaven was offered.

It was the supreme act of worship for the whole empire, and only the emperor himself as the Son of Heaven could perform the sacrifice to Shang Ti or Heaven. In December on the longest night of the year the emperor, having purified himself by fasting, was led up the southern steps, lined on both sides by dignitaries and officials. Under the canopy of the winter sky in the night hours before dawn, illuminated only by the light of flaming torches, the emperor was guided in every step of the ceremony by directors of ceremonies. They loudly proclaimed the nature and import of each act. Elaborate ritual paraphernalia, detailed protocol, and many sacrificial elements were involved. A large perpendicular tablet inscribed "Imperial Heaven—Supreme Emperor" was the central object, and the emperor made offerings before it and invited the spirit of heaven to descend into the tablet. It is generally conceded to have been one of the grandest, most imposing, and solemn observances ever performed. In it Shang Ti and the ancestors were thanked for their blessings from above.

In a different part of the same vast altar park on the south side of Beijing is another altar of the same form but smaller, and on this there is a large circular temple with a three-tiered, domed cupola, called the "Temple of the Auspicious Year." There during the first 10 days of the new year, the emperor made prayers to Heaven and his ancestors for a good year, that is, for bountiful harvests. In the first month of summer he also asked for sufficient rains. Comparable sacrifices to the empire of Earth, *Hu-tu*, were conducted in a park north of the city wall of Beijing. The northern park is square, and the altar is a square altar of marble, open to the sky like the altar of Heaven. Sacrifices were offered to Earth and ancestors, usually by the emperor but sometimes by his proxy, on the summer solstice, at the altar to Earth.

At the sacrifices to Heaven and Earth the tablets of the emperor's ancestors were in second place of honor. The royal ancestors thus took precedence over the gods of the principal rivers and mountains, and other divinities related to climate, as well as the spirits of the soil and crops. Supreme sacrifices to these deities were the prerogative only of the emperor, but vassal princes performed sacrifices to lesser spirits and provincial tutelary deities. Each town and village had its own "altar of the land," a mound of earth which earlier had represented the soil as a god and later was the center of local religious activity, at which individual families were represented.

The official pattern of worship was hierarchical although there was no ecclesiastical hierarchy. Officials performed the sacrifices on behalf of the people at every level except the family, and the higher the scope or gravity of the ritual, the higher was the officer or noble who performed it. Clans had their temples for housing ancestral tablets, and finally each family had its private observances for family occasions and sacrifices to their ancestors. But families were otherwise allowed only to worship either the door guardian or the kitchen god of the stove and furnace. In practice, says Professor Overmyer, by the first century C.E. the people "far exceeded what the state supported ritual texts prescribed," and after the spread of Taoism and Buddhism, that was even more the case.[24]

The Cult of Confucius

The state cult was the official, public worship in which the powers of the cosmos were recognized and invoked on behalf of the nation as a whole by the rulers. In it the Confucians functioned as masters of ceremonies but not as priests. This third major area of worship and ritual, the Confucian cult proper, also had official status. In it those who had studied the Confucian classics and become officials had their own special cult and served as ministrants. There was state recognition and support, but it was a ritual of, by, and for Confucian scholars and intellectuals, with its own temples and sacrifices dedicated to Confucius as the great sage and teacher.

In our historical survey the growth of the honors accorded to Confucius was briefly outlined. We saw that the Confucian temple was designated the Hall of Fame for scholars and officials in 647. Thus every district had its temple, in which were tablets or images of Confucius, and other tablets, pictures, and images. The tendency to deify Confucius as the patron of learning and wisdom reached its peak when he was denoted Supreme Saint in 1013. But in the sixteenth century images were removed and replaced by tablets in all but a few temples, and only a brief final attempt at deification was made after the 1906 dissolution of the classics examinations.

As the honors accorded to Confucius were increased, so the sacrifices were magnified. The principal ceremonies were in the spring and fall. They were conducted by the scholars themselves, so there was no priesthood. Because there was no active participation by the masses, there was no need for other cult practices or forms. The content of the faith was simply recognition of the moral order of the universe and belief in the improvement of humanity and society through learning. Thus although the cultic or sacrificial customs were essentially the same as for ancestral worship by the people and in the state cult of heaven and earth, the theoretical content was fitted to the needs and views of the intellectual aristocracy. It served to define and sanctify their place in the total scheme of things in heaven and earth.

In the 1990s tourists may freely visit the restored Confucian Temple, and all the great sacred palaces in Beijing.

ETHICAL AND SOCIAL ASPECTS OF CONFUCIANISM

In this last section we come to the most distinctive aspect of Confucianism, its ethical concern for the welfare of the people. In the beliefs of Confucianism there is little that is explicitly religious, and Confucianists were only indirectly concerned with the rituals of ancestor worship and the state cult. But in its richness and profundity the ethical humanism of Confucianism is moral holiness of a high order.

Innate Principles

You will look in vain for a set of negative moral injunctions like the Ten Commandments in Confucianism. It is not that there is anything wrong with them or that Confucianism would deny them. It is simply that that is not the way the moral or ethical system works. In Confucius and Mencius there are many things which are condemned, and Confucianism shares the basic moral inhibitions of any civilized culture. But it takes them for granted or assumes they are innate. As we have seen, Mencius claimed that benevolence was part of human nature. Fung Yu-lan relates a story about a follower of Wang Yang Ming who caught a thief in his house at night and lectured him about intuitive knowledge. The thief disagreed and wanted to know where was his intuitive knowledge? So the scholar, it being hot weather, invited him to take off his jacket and then his shirt, which he did. He continued: " 'It is still too hot. Why not take off your trousers too?' At this the thief hesitated and replied: 'That does not seem to be quite right.' Thereupon his captor shouted at him: 'There is your intuitive knowledge!' "[25]

The Moral Person

In place of rules Confucianism has the moral person. In terms of the contrast usually applied to political systems, it is a system of people, not laws. The moral person knows the principles and has the character which leads to right action. In the *Analects* the Master described how Yen Hui, the favorite disciple, listened to him without ever disagreeing, so that he seemed stupid. "But if I enquire into his private conduct when he is not with me I find that it fully demonstrates what I have taught him. No, Hui is by no means stupid" (II, 9). It was not an accident that Confucius founded a school and made it his life work to produce disciples who would first of all be moral persons themselves. His intent to produce free moral personalities explains his concern about their entire life, not simply for their theoretical knowledge. Again and again, revealing scenes in the *Analects* show this. His intent also explains his insistence on character first of all in the ruler. "The Master said, If the ruler himself is upright, all will go well even though he does not give orders . . ." (XIII, 6). The basis and the center of Confucian ethics, then, is the moral person. Above the altar of the Confucian temple in Tainan, Taiwan, one of the plaques, referring to Confucius, says: "the great teacher of 10,000 generations."

CHUN-TZU

This Confucian moral person is the *chun-tzu*. The word began as a term for the lord's son, the princely man, and came to mean what has usually been described as the true gentleman in the English sense of the word. It is noteworthy that the Aristotelian ethical man is often interpreted as the gentleman in the same sense, and that Aristotelian ethics are also an ethics of habitual virtue, produced by understanding and applying the moral law as a mean between extremes. One of the Four Books in Confucianism is *The Doctrine of the Mean*, and we will conclude our chapter with a view of Confucius' ethic as a middle way between antinomianism (denial of all moral laws) and fanaticism (excessive rigor). About 40 separate paragraphs of the *Analects* are direct descriptions of the *chun-tzu*. They are nearly all descriptions of what he does or how he acts either toward other people or in his personal life, but some describe his feelings and attitudes. Often the *chun-tzu* is contrasted with his opposite, the *hsiao-jen* or small or common man in the bad sense of a mean and contemptible person. "The Master said, A gentleman takes as much trouble to discover what is right as lesser men take to discover what will pay" (IV, 16). "Tzu-kung asked about the true gentleman. The Master said, He does not preach what he practices till he has practiced what he preaches" (II, 13).

In sum, the *chun-tzu* personifies the Confucian ideal moral personality, and the moral personality is the key to the Confucian ethic. Now it is necessary to give a fuller account of the moral person, using other traditional Chinese terms. The word *te** will describe the power or force of the moral person, and *jen* will appear again as the basis of the power, expressed in the moral attributes of *chung** and *shu*.* To provide the theoretical content and direction of *te* there is *hsueh** or learning. As more specific formal rules or formulae of conduct there are *hsiao** or filial piety and the five relationships (*wu-lun**). The ruler and the state use *wen*, the arts of peace. There are also other aspects of personal character and conduct which will be mentioned. The problem of rewards is raised, and finally the doctrine of the mean is the solution.

TE

This word connotes moral power or force. "The Master said, How transcendent is the moral power of the Middle Use" (VI, 27). Professor Alfred Bloom says: "The major issue confronting Confucius in the *Analects* is the formation of appropriate moral character enabling the individual to wield power without force."[26] This gives us a working definition of *te* in Confucius, in the context of the troubled social and political climate of his day. It gives point and poignancy to his advice to political leaders of his time to rule by this kind of moral authority and not by physical power and armed force. "The Master said, He who rules by moral force (*te*) is like the pole-star, which remains in its place while all the lesser stars do homage to it" (II, 1). This idea was extended to a contrast between the ideal king or *wang*, who ruled by *te*, and the opportunist or *po*, as in *Analects* XIII, 12, the *Mencius*, and later literature. Confucius of course first of all applied *te* to personal relations. The moral person has *te*.

JEN

In the context of ethics *jen* has the meaning which is uppermost in the later literature, especially the *Mencius*, of benevolence, humanity, human-heartedness. The ideogram is a compound character of two elements, "two" and

*Plaques, Confucian Temple, Tainan. The topmost
plaque, referring to Confucius, describes him as "the
great teacher of 10,000 generations." (Ward J. Fellows).*

"man," stressing the ideal relation between persons as love, kindness, and charity. We discussed *jen* as a tenet of Confucianism; *jen* is here the moral expression of the goodness that is the character of the cosmos. It is the ethical or
moral form or manifestation of that high and unattainable *jen* to which Confucius alludes in the *Analects*. Just as *jen* is the fundamental character of the total
universe, so *jen* is the fundamental character of the moral person, the *chun-
tzu*. "The moral man's life is an exemplification of the universal order," said
The Doctrine of the Mean.[27] As such it is the proper attitude or stance of people in their dealings with the world. Their inner nature should be *jen*. "Of the
adage 'Only a Good Man knows how to like people, knows how to dislike
them,' the Master said, He whose heart is in the smallest degree set upon
Goodness will dislike no one" (IV, 3, 4). It is as simple and as profound and difficult as the same notion in any culture: a good person—he or she is good.

Although there is no simple set of rules for *jen* or visible marks that distinguish it, there are two modes or ways in which the inner nature or character
of the *jen* person expresses itself. These are *chung* and *shu*, which have usually been interpreted as two forms of the Confucian Golden Rule. *Chung* is literally loyalty and is the positive form of the rule; *shu* is most often rendered
reciprocity or altruism and is the negative form. There is more than one text
for them; the following are usually cited. From *The Doctrine of the Mean*:

> In the *Tao* of the *chun-tzu* there are four things, none of which I have
> attained to. To serve my father as I would have my son serve me; I am not
> yet able to do that. To serve my sovereign as I would have my minister serve
> me . . . To serve my older brother as I would have my younger brother serve
> me . . . To set an example in behaving to a friend as I would have him behave
> to me; I am not yet able to do that.[28]

The negative form is found in the *Analects*: "Tzu-kung asked saying, Is there any single saying that one can act upon all day and every day? The Master said, Perhaps the saying about consideration: 'Never do to others what you would not like them to do to you' " (XV, 23).

HSUEH

Hsueh is learning as in The Great Learning (*Ta Hsueh*), which gave the Confucian educational, moral, and political programs in a nutshell. Learning is the method by which one discovers the meaning of *jen* in actual practice. Although Confucius evidently considered *jen* in some sense innate in people, he saw the necessity for learning how to express it properly in the world. His devotion to and study of the classics was for the purpose of understanding what was the good way of old. Disclaiming for himself innate knowledge of this practical wisdom, he said: "There may well be those who can do without knowledge; but I for my part am certainly not one of them. To hear much, pick out what is good and follow it, to see much and take due note of it is the lower of the two kinds of knowledge" (VII, 27). His own teaching, as seen in the *Analects*, was directed to that kind of learning. The fruit of such learning, when put into action, is *yi*, righteousness.

Guides and Rules of Action

Although Confucianism is not a system of rules it does have some external forms or guides for moral action. They are of the nature of general or inclusive principles for human relations, not specific laws or rules. This formalization of the ethos is directed to the end of social harmony, the same value which is the point of ritual or ceremony in human relations and which might be called the supreme Confucian value. Regulations concerning family and social relations come as close as one can get to a list of Confucian virtues in the sense of desirable moral qualities or conditions. Once or twice in the *Analects* Confucius lists "four virtues" or "five virtues," and Tung Chung-shu named "five constant virtues:" *jen*, *yi*, *li*, *chih* (wisdom), *hsin** (good faith). But there is no orthodox list. The dictum in *The Book of History* still holds: "There is no invariable model of virtue; a supreme regard to what is good gives the model of it."[29]

HSIAO

Filial piety, the usual translation of *hsiao*, is the nearest thing to a supreme Confucian virtue. It means respect and love for and submission to one's parents. The book, *The Canon of Filial Piety*, was an elementary textbook throughout Chinese history, and the theory and practice of filial piety is a distinctive mark of Chinese culture. It is a correlate of ancestor worship and provides a principle of order and precedence in society, although it has its defects and abuses. In the *Analects* there are a few references to *hsiao* in Books I and II, but it is only in *The Canon of Filial Piety* that one finds statements like: "The Master said: 'Filial piety is the basis of virtue and the source of culture.' "[30] There was a progression in development of the doctrine. It was one of the traditional elements in Chinese culture, and Confucius approved of its practice and of long mourning for parents. In later Confucianism it was magnified through *The Canon of Filial Piety*, and some of the Confucianists took mourning practices to an undue extreme.

THE FIVE RELATIONSHIPS

Filial piety is the model for the five relationships, the Confucian formula for regulating the significant relations in family and society. It is the model in the sense that in each relationship one side is essentially dominant and the other subordinate. Only the full quotation of the key passage in *The Book of Rites* gives the full picture, however, showing that each side has both rights and responsibilities:

> What are "the things which men consider right?" Kindness on the part of the father, and filial duty on that of the son; gentleness on the part of the elder brother, and obedience on that of the younger; righteousness on the part of the husband, and submission on that of the wife; kindness on the part of elders, and deference on that of juniors; with benevolence on the part of the ruler, and loyalty on that of the minister;—these ten are the things which men consider right.[31]

For centuries this formula provided a system of mutual privileges and duties holding together a highly integrated social order. In both *The Doctrine of the Mean* and *The Great Learning* benevolence is extended to the wider world. The Mohists attacked the Confucianists, calling their system of graded or proportionate love "selfishness." In taking account of this criticism, these books said proper conduct and relations should work outwards: the self, the family, the state or society, the world and God.

WEN

A form of moral power which was available to the ruler in the Confucian scheme was *wen*. "In particular," says Waley, "wen denotes the arts of peace (music, dancing, literature) as opposed to those of war."[32] He goes on to show that *wen* in this context connoted the culture of a nation, which brought prestige and attracted support.

Destiny (Ming*)

The problem of human destiny, of the outcome of life, especially of whether or not the virtuous are rewarded, is a vexing question for any religion. In China it took the form of theories about the working of the Mandate of Heaven, or destiny (*ming*). Professor Chan says there were five theories: fatalism, moral determinism, antifatalism, naturalistic fatalism, and Confucius' "waiting for destiny."

> According to this doctrine, man should exert his utmost in moral endeavor and leave whatever is beyond our control to fate. It frankly admits that there are things beyond our control but that is no reason why one should relax in his moral endeavor. The Confucian theory represents the conviction of enlightened Chinese in general.[33]

The Middle Way

To conclude this chapter we pay tribute to Confucius as the practitioner and proponent of a "middle way" of moral action. The term is used by the Chinese scholar Lin Yutang as the heading for the section of his book which includes the *Analects* and *The Doctrine of the Mean*. The middle way which is denoted here is Confucius' rational ethical median between cynical amorality and moral perfectionism. Confucius himself, in *The Doctrine of the Mean*, defined it:

> Confucius remarked: "I know now why the moral life is not practiced. The wise mistake moral law for something higher than what it really is: and the foolish do not know enough what moral law really is. I know now why the moral law is not understood. The noble natures want to live too high, high above their moral ordinary self; and ignoble natures do not live high enough, i.e., not up to their moral ordinary true self. There is no one who does not eat and drink. But few there are who really know flavor."[34]

We read before where he said in the *Analects*, "How transcendent is the moral power of the Middle Use" (VI, 27), and he averred, "If I cannot get men who steer a middle course to associate with me, I would far rather have the impetuous and hasty" (XIII, 21). In our day, as in Confucius' time, the need is for people who have the patience and courage to follow this difficult way. The problem is that it lacks the cold and calculating efficiency of the unscrupulous at one extreme and yet does not have the hot zeal of moral absolutism at the other. Confucius expressed in his life and words the moral courage to live in the world by the Way of Heaven. Surely that is a form of religion.

SUMMARY

Both Confucianism and Taoism are indigenous to China, and share with Buddhism the traditional religious pluralism and cultic variety of China, which for nearly 2,000 years made a "typical Chinese" one who observed some aspects of each of the three. Back of them all lies a long religious history characterized by nature and ancestor worship in general, and by other elements which must be noted for an understanding of both Confucianism and Taoism. Archaeological artifacts like "oracle bones" used for divination and bronze ritual vessels testify to these ancient elements. Literary history gives the idea of some kind of supreme or heavenly reality or force, known as Shang Ti or T'ien that was evident from about 1700 B.C.E. The *yin-yang* theory of complementary forces is not so ancient, but became important in Taoism and in later Confucianism; it postulates *yin* as dark, female, quiet, negative, and *yang* as bright, male, active, positive, forces.

In Western, but not Chinese, terms "Confucianism" is the name of the school of thought which was instituted by the historical figure Confucius, born in 551 B.C.E. He articulated what he considered the good and useful concepts and traditions from the ancient Chinese culture, which were known through various literary documents and historical records. Through a group of student-disciples he promoted the view that good government depends on the good morals which can be learned from the past. After his death his pupils carried on his ideas and probably edited the ancient texts that are known as the Confucian classics. Emerging as one of the major schools of Chinese thought, Confucianism later became the official basis for Chinese government through most of the succeeding centuries, until the end of the Ching dynasty in the early twentieth century. The Four Books of the Confucianists were the substance of Confucian education after about C.E. 1200.

The religious elements of Confucianism are the basis of the ethical humanism which constitutes the substance of Confucianism as a significant factor in Chinese history and culture. Scholars debate whether or not it can properly be called religious. Our position is that these transcendent or supernatural elements, which are the primary side or basis of the humanist-ethical aspect, justify calling it religious in a general sense. There are, moreover, explicitly religious elements in ritual and in family observances. The spiritual factors are found in Confucius' use of Heaven as the basis and support of morals and the moral person, and his description of the essential character of Heaven as *jen*, goodness. He may have been the one who articulated for later Chinese thought the idea from the earlier *Book of History* that any government must be judged by whether or not it has the "Mandate of Heaven," that is, whether it truly governs by and supports moral truth. Another basic Chinese term, Tao, Confucius interpreted as the good Way of Heaven followed by the worthy monarchs of the past, the guide for both rulers and people in a stable and secure society. Mencius, a fourth-century B.C.E. Confucian, stressed the goodness of human nature and further developed the key Confucian emphasis on the proper training of this good human nature.

From Confucius came the emphasis on *li*, propriety or proper conduct, a double Chinese character denoting both proper observance of religious ceremonies and the proper moral attitude in conduct, hence both a religious and a social or moral sense of propriety. Much of Confucius' life and teaching was directed to the importance of this two-sided theory and practice. He also furthered sensible observance of the traditional ancestor worship which was and is central in Chinese culture, so that the memorial tablets to one's ancestors are kept at the Confucian temple. In the Chinese dynasties for hundreds of

years, moreover, Confucian scholar-administrators served as masters of ceremonies for the major Chinese religious observances. Only the emperor, guided
by the scholars, was qualified to perform the ceremonies to the major powers
Heaven and Earth, and to seek auspicious yearly portents for the entire empire.
Lesser nobles sacrificed to provincial mountains and rivers, while town officials honored the city god, leaving only a few personal gods for individual families to worship. The cult of Confucius himself now consists mainly of a birthday sacrifice.

Providing ethical guidance in the Confucian system is the moral person, in
Chinese terms the *chun-tzu*, the "prince's son" or "gentleman." There is no set
of rules, for Confucianism is not a set of rules but the cultivation of moral personality which exemplifies morality in accordance with the way of Heaven.
There are, nevertheless, some traditional norms, such as the set of reciprocal
"five relationships" and, above all, the ancient Chinese ideal of filial piety. The
moral person has *te*, moral power or force, and in relations with others is
guided by *jen* or benevolence expressed in Confucian forms of a negative
(*shu*) and positive (*chung*) Golden Rule. This practical morality has provided a
middle way between excessive moral rigor and amoral license for Chinese society for 2,000 years.

NOTES

1. Julian F. Pas, ed. *The Turning of the Tide* (Oxford: Oxford University Press, 1989),
   pp. 6, 7.
2. *The Analects of Confucius*, Arthur Waley, trans. and ed. (New York: Random
   House Inc., Vintage Books, n.d.; © 1938 by George Allen & Unwin Ltd.) Used by
   permission of Macmillan Publishing Co. Note: In order to eliminate excessive foot-
   notes, most references to the *Analects* will be only by book and stanza
   number in Waley, unless specifically noted otherwise for quotations from other
   sources.
3. Waley, p. 140.
4. Lin Yutang, ed. *The Wisdom of China and India* (New York: Random House,
   Modern Library ed., 1942), p. 816.
5. Lin Yutang, p. 817.
6. Lewis Hodous, "Confucianism," in Edward J. Jurji, ed., *The Great Religions of the
   Modern World* (Princeton: Princeton University Press, 1946), p. 11.
7. *Journal of Professional Activities*, Citizen Ambassador Program, Religion and Philosophy Delegation to People's Republic of China, p. 8.
8. Wm. Theodore de Bary, "The New Confucianism in Beijing," *The American
   Scholar* 64, no. 2 (Spring 1995), p. 188.
9. H. G. Creel, *Chinese Thought* (New York: New American Library, Mentor Book
   ed., n.d.), p. 142.
10. James Legge, trans. *The Sacred Books of China: The Texts of Confucianism*, Part I,
    SBE III (Oxford: Clarendon Press, 1879), p. 352.
11. H. G. Creel, *Confucius: The Man and the Myth* (New York: John Day, 1949), p.
    117.

12. Wing-Tsit Chan et al., *The Great Asian Religions* (London: Macmillan, 1969), p. 100.
13. Wing-Tsit Chan, trans. and comp., *A Source Book in Chinese Philosophy* (Princeton: Princeton University Press, 1963, 1969), p. 62.
14. Wm. Theodore de Bary et al., comps., *Sources of Chinese Tradition*. Vol. 1 (New York: Columbia University Press, 1968), p. 91.
15. James Legge, trans., *Sacred Books of China, Texts of Confucianism*, Part III, *SBE* XXVII (Oxford: Clarendon Press, 1885), pp. 380–383.
16. Chan et al., *Great Asian Religions*, p. 133.
17. de Bary, *Sources*, I, p. 483.
18. Chan, *Source Book*, p. 617.
19. Yutang, p. 845.
20. de Bary, *Sources*, I, p. 23.
21. James Legge, *Sacred Books* Part III, Vol. XXVII, p. 10.
22. Chu Chai and Winberg Chai, eds. and trans., *The Humanist Way in Ancient China: The Texts of Confucianism* (New York: Bantam Books, 1965), p. 32.
23. Chai and Chai, p. 329.
24. Professor Daniel L. Overmyer, *J.A.S* 54, no. 1 (February 1995), p. 128.
25. Fung Yu-Lan, *A Short History of Chinese Philosophy*, ed. Dirk Bodde (New York: The Free Press, Collier-Macmillan, 1948), p. 313.
26. W. Richard Comstock et al., eds., *Religion and Man* (New York: Harper and Row, 1971), p. 275.
27. Yutang, p. 846.
28. Chai and Chai, p. 309.
29. Yutang, p. 727.
30. Chai and Chai, p. 326.
31. Legge, pp. 378–380.
32. Waley, p. 39.
33. Chan, *Source Book*, pp. 78, 79.
34. Yutang, p. 846.

TOPICS AND QUESTIONS FOR STUDY

1. How did Confucius use traditional elements of Chinese culture to frame a school of moral philosophy based on the goodness of Heaven?
2. Why did Confucius work to keep, interpret, and teach the Chinese classics?
3. Explain how Confucianism fits into the total Chinese system, which uses all three religions: Confucianism, Taoism, Buddhism.
4. Why are we justified in calling Confucianism a religion and not just an ethical system?
5. What did Confucius teach about good government? Why was he not himself an important official? How did Confucianism later become the official doctrine of China?
6. Discuss the meaning and importance of ritual in Confucianism, and show how Confucius kept it from being merely formal and external.

7. Why does Chinese religion and morality make so much of ancestors and elders? What did Confucius teach about these things?
8. Explain why "Confucius says" is not a joke, but the focus of Confucian teaching.
9. Compare the "prince's son" or "gentleman" as the key to Confucius' ethical system to the virtuous person in Aristotle's *Nichomachean Ethics*.
10. How was the golden rule used by Confucius to give the structure for social harmony in his heavily populated country?
11. Find parallels between the Confucian form of the idea of the mean between extremes and the "Golden Mean" which is found in Greek thought about the same time.

USEFUL BOOKS

Chinese Religions

General Background and Information

Chan, Wing-Tsit, et al., comp. *The Great Asian Religions: An Anthology.* New York: Macmillan, 1969.

———, trans. and comp. *A Source Book in Chinese Philosophy.* Princeton: Princeton University Press, 1975.

de Bary, Wm. Theodore, comp. *Sources of Chinese Tradition.* Vol. 1. New York: Columbia University Press, 1963.

Joachim, Christian. *Chinese Religions: A Cultural Perspective.* Englewood Cliffs, N.J.: Prentice Hall, 1986.

Pas, Julian F., ed. *The Turning of the Tide: Religion in China Today.* Hong Kong: Royal Asiatic Society; Oxford University Press, 1989.

Thompson, Laurence. *Chinese Religion: An Introduction.* Belmont, Calif.: Wadsworth, 1975.

Wolf, Arthur, ed. *Religion and Ritual in Chinese Society.* Stanford: Stanford University Press, 1974.

Yu, David C. *Guide to Chinese Religion.* Boston, G. K. Hall, 1985.

Confucianism

See Wing-Tsit Chan et al., and de Bary.

Legge, James, trans. *The Texts of Confucianism, in the Original Sacred Books of the East.* Oxford: Oxford University Press, 19th cy. ed.

Waley, Arthur, trans. and annotator. *The Analects of Confucius.* New York: Random House, Vintage Books, n.d.

GLOSSARY

An approximate pronunciation of some words is given in parentheses following the word, using a simple phonetic system without any technical devices, and with no claim to scholarly accuracy.

Analects: the *Lun Yu,* Confucius' sayings, first of the Four Books

Book of Changes: I Ching (ee jing): one of the Five Classics

Book of History: Shu Ching (shu jing): one of the Five Classics

Book of Mencius: Meng Tzu: writings of Mencius; one of the Four Books

Book of Odes or Poetry: Shih Ching (she jing): one of the Five Classics

Book of Rites: Li Chi (lee jee): one of the Five Classics.

ch'i (ch ee): "vital force"; in Neo-Confucianism, matter or natural substance

chia (jhee ah): school of thought, "'ism"

chiao (jhee ow): teaching, cultivation, religion

Chou (jo): dynasty, *ca.* 1100 B.C.E. to 221 B.C.E.

Chu Hsi (jhoo she): Neo-Confucian philosopher, C.E. 1130–1200

chun-tzu (jhun dzoo): lord's son, princely man, true gentleman

Ch'un Ch'iu (chyun chyou): *Spring and Autumn Annals*; one of the Five Classics

chung (jhoong): loyalty, conscientiousness

Chung Yung (jhoong yoong): *Doctrine of the Mean*; one of the Four Books

Doctrine of the Mean: *Chung Yung*; one of the Four Books

Five agents or elements: water, fire, wood, metal, earth

Four Books: *Analects, Doctrine of the Mean, Great Learning, Book of Mencius*

Great Learning: Ta Hsueh: one of the Four Books

hsiao (shee ow): filial, of or fitting a son or daughter

Hsiao Ching (shee ow jing): *Classic of Filial Piety*

hsin (shin): good faith

hsueh (shway): learning, study

I Ching (ee jing): *Book of Changes*; one of the Five Classics

jen (wren): goodness, humanity, benevolence

ju (rue): literati, scholars

Ju Chia: school of literati

Ju Chiao: Confucianism as a religion

K'ung Fu-tzu (koong foo tsu): "Grand Master Kung" or Confucius

kwei (gway): negative, demonic, bad forces or spirits

li (lee): rites, ceremonies, propriety (a different Chinese character from what we designate as *Li*)

Li: principles, laws, psychic factor, complementary to *ch'i*

Li Chi (lee jhee): *Book of Rites*, one of the Five Classics

Mencius (men shus): Confucian thinker, died 289 B.C.E.

ming: fate, destiny, decree

Mohism: system of thought of Mo Tzu

Mo Tzu: died 391 B.C.E.; critic of Confucius

Shang Ti (shang dee): Lord-on-High, Supreme Being

shen: positive, divine, good spirits or forces

Shih Chiao: Buddhism as a religion

Shih Ching (she jing): *Book of Odes or Poetry*, one of the Five Classics

shu: altruism, consideration of others, reciprocity

Shu Ching (shoe jing): *Book of History*; one of the Five Classics

Spring and Autumn Annals, Ch'un Ch'iu: one of the Five Classics

Ta Hsueh (dah shway): *Great Learning*, one of the Four Books

Tao (dow): way, path, principle

Tao Chiao: Taoism as a religion

te (day): virtue, moral force or principle

T'ien (tyen): Heaven, heavenly, in both physical and metaphysical sense

T'ien-ming: Mandate of Heaven

wen: culture, arts of peace

Wu-Ching: Five Classics

wu-lun: five relationships

yang: bright, male, dry, hard, warm; one of two basic forces or factors

yin: dark, female, moist, soft, cold; one of two basic forces or factors

yin-yang: complementary forces or factors

Yin-Yang: *yin-yang* school of thought

yi (yee): righteousness

Chapter 6

TAOISM

Chih Nan Temple at Mu Cha, near Taipei (Ward J. Fellows).

OUTLINE

I. Taoism contrasts with Confucianism:
   A. Confucianism uses reason and learning to structure and guide society by the moral order of Heaven.
   B. Taoism works by intuitive harmony with the Tao, the primal nature of things.

II. Taoism is mysticism, in two distinctive Chinese forms:
   A. A school of philosophical and speculative thought, developing from nature mysticism and playing on opposites like the traditional *yin-yang*. Two leading figures and their books:
      1. Lao Tzu, sixth century B.C.E., the *Tao Te Ching*.
      2. Chuang Tzu, fourth century B.C.E., the *Chuang Tzu*.
   B. Religious and magical practices and organization worked in three ways to assure immortal life.
      1. Physical practices called "hygiene."
      2. Alchemy: drinking or eating an elixir of eternal life.
      3. Finding the blessed isles of immortality.

III. The tenets of philosophical Taoism:
   A. The Tao—what there is, the way, reality, expressed in concrete images:
      1. The "Great Clod" or primal, undifferentiated nature of things, and its human correlate, the "Uncarved Block."
      2. The "Valley Spirit" or "Mysterious Female"—the Tao as spontaneous, alive, proliferating, and ruthless-impartial.
      3. The order of opposites such as *yin-yang*.
      4. The mystic way to the Tao.

IV. The customs of religious and magical Taoism—two divisions:
   A. Orthodox Taoist priests serving traditional gods.
   B. "Folk religion"—popular and magical dealing with spirits.

V. Ethical practices:
   A. Philosophical Taoism calls for people to be humble and to conform to the dialectical ways of the Tao.
   B. Popular religion guides human conduct by traditional rules.

INTRODUCTION

Contrasting with Confucianism, Taoism is the other main element or component of Chinese religious sensibility. Both arose during the decline and dissolution of the Chou dynasty, and both are concerned with humanity and how to
make the social order serve human needs. Confucianism in its broadest sense
can be construed as an attempt to guide, structure, and control human nature
through convention and learning. In contrast, Taoism as a general attitude is
opposed to deliberate attempts to order or guide people by external rules, for
it holds that such methods are useless, artificial restraints. Instead it calls for intuitive harmony with the primal nature of the universe and humanity. In its
treatment of the transcendent order and its view of truth and knowledge, Confucianism is analytical and rationalistic; it believes that analysis and control
yield the best results. Taoism represents the reaction against such planned and
structured life in the name of naturalness, freedom, spontaneity, and intuition.
Another contrast which is generally accepted is between Confucianism's stress
on the collective and social and Taoism's more individualistic and personal
concern.

But we must note at the outset that "Taoism" denotes a collection of
doctrines, practices, and groups and has never been a single or unified
movement. There is, moreover, very little scholarly agreement on what constitutes that oneness or unity of the collection of ideas and practices so denoted. Our usage of "Taoism" will be based on the very name itself, on the
assumption that there must be something in a name. By Taoism, then, we
mean those Chinese schools of thought, traditions, temples which are generally so named by Western scholars, and which are centered on the Tao* as
the ultimate reality and truth. If there is any one term that can be applied to
Taoism, it is mysticism. Taoism is the Chinese expression of mysticism in
the sense of direct experience and intuition of a total and unitary reality,
which is beyond rational analysis and human description or control. In this
Taoism resembles forms of Buddhism with which it is associated after the
rise of that faith in China. Taoism, moreover, makes the ineffability or inde-
scribability of the Tao a central tenet, comparable to the doctrine of Nirguna
Brahman, the Absolute without attributes, in Advaita Hinduism. Note that
for Taoism, mysticism is used in a broad and general sense, and that it is impersonal—it lacks the aspect of individual relation to a personal godhead
which is characteristic of Western mysticism. But in order to have a starting
place, we take mysticism as the closest we can come to a unifying idea for
Taoism as a whole.

Taoism is roughly divisible into the speculative and philosophical forms on
one hand, and the religious and magical on the other; we follow that twofold
division. The theoretical-philosophical side has no organized ritual or cultic expression, while the religious groups have little theoretical content. Therefore
we limit our discussion of the tenets of Taoism to the speculative-philosophical
form, whereas in our section on ritual and worship the religious groups will be

discussed but not the philosophical. In the third category, ethical and social, the ethical aspects of both will be treated.

Origin and Development of Taoism

Philosophical and Speculative Taoism

NATURE MYSTICISM

Everyone has seen Chinese landscape paintings on a scroll, either horizontal (usually showing water) or vertical (usually mountains), depicting mountains, trees, clouds, water, and most always some sign of human presence or habitation. The important thing to note is the feeling or mood of the scroll paintings. The human habitations and beings are small, obscure, inconspicuous, blended into the landscape; but they are not threatened or menaced by the encompassing nature, rather they are secure, established, comfortable, at home in the scene. The attitude toward nature expressed in such paintings is typically Taoist.

The artistic point of view expressed in these romantic landscapes was given theoretical formulation by Taoist artists like Tsung Ping in the fourth century C.E. Tsung Ping wrote:

> Having embraced Tao, the sage responds harmoniously to things. Having puri-
> fied his mind, the worthy man enjoys forms. As to landscapes, they exist in
> material substance and soar into the realm of the spirit. . . . Mountains and
> rivers in their form pay homage to Tao, and the man of humanity delights in
> them. Do not the sage and mountains and rivers have much in common?[1]

Centuries before Tsung Ping, there were actual hermit or recluse sages dwelling in such isolated spots, far from cities, people, and governments. Their nature mysticism is probably the starting point for philosophic and speculative Taoism. At least some of those who lived that life and sought the underlying reality behind the beauties of nature were Quietists, who believed in nurturing the life spirit, ch'i*. Waley sees no reason to doubt that there is a connection between this cultivation of the soul-breath and the practices of later Taoists. He shows that their central conception was Tao. "The Quietists who developed this idea of Tao as the unchanging unity underlying a shifting plurality, and at the same time the impetus giving rise to every form of life and motion, were called Taoists."[2]

The earliest known records of this attitude come from about the time of Confucius. In the fourth century B.C.E. other elements were added to the nature mysticism of the sages. New astronomical ideas and theories about the forces and principles of the universe circulated among six competing schools of thought. These were combined with yin-yang* theory and other elements, and the early Taoists connected the Tao with these forces and principles.

Landscape, *anonymous artist. Yuan dynasty. Thirteenth century C.E. (Courtesy, The Asian Art Museum of San Francisco, The Avery Brundage Collection, San Francisco, California). Copyright © 1972 Asian Art Museum of San Francisco. All rights reserved.*

LAO TZU*

Lao Tzu* is the most important name in Taoism, and his book, the *Lao Tzu** or *Tao Te Ching*,* the chief book, although there are problems about both the man and his book. Yet it is fitting that there are problems, because the teacher is elusive and the teaching enigmatic. The shadowy figure of Lao Tzu and the ambiguous phrases and controverted authorship of the *Tao Te Ching* are appropriate to the doctrine and message of Taoism.

According to the traditional account in *The Historical Records*, Lao Tzu was about 50 years older than Confucius, which would mean that he was born about 600 B.C.E. The name Lao Tzu means "Old Master" or "Old Boy," but in the *Historical Records* Ssu-ma Ch'ien says: "His surname was Li, his given name Erh, and his public name Tan." In his later years he was custodian of the archives of the Chou court. The other principal Taoist book, the *Chuang Tzu*,* describes a visit by Confucius to Lao Tzu, after which Confucius said: "At last I may say that I have seen a dragon." Ssu-ma Ch'ien also reports the interview, and there are four accounts in the *Li Chi* of what Confucius learned about rites from Lao Tzu. Tradition holds that in his declining years, seeing that the Chou empire was disintegrating, Lao Tzu headed west, mounted, according to old paintings, on a water buffalo. At the Western Hanku pass, the keeper asked him to leave a record of his philosophy, and the *Tao Te Ching* was his legacy. After that he rode off into the sunset and was never seen again.

For nearly 1,000 years there have been questions about the authenticity of these accounts, and the existence of Lao Tzu is questioned by many scholars and denied by some. Nevertheless, the weight of tradition should not be disregarded, and there are authorities who can be cited in support of the historicity of Lao Tzu. Professor Chan says: "There is no question that Lao Tzu was a historical person in the sixth century B.C.E. whom Confucius visited."[3] So we shall continue to treat Lao Tzu as the foremost Taoist spokesman and a historical figure.

CHUANG TZU*

Just as Mencius followed Confucius and helped develop Confucianism, Chuang Tzu came after Lao Tzu and developed Taoism; and just as the *Tao Te Ching* is the book of Lao Tzu, so the *Chuang Tzu* is the book of Chuang Tzu. There are differences between the two men and their theories as seen in their books. Whereas Lao Tzu's emphasis is on practical and political use or application of the Tao, and the *Tao Te Ching* is directed to the sage king, the *Chuang Tzu* provides a philosophy for the private individual rather than the public person and is more concerned with speculation about the Tao than with its practical significance. Chuang Tzu lived from 369 to 286 B.C.E. A few facts about him are recorded in *The Historical Documents*: His personal name was Chou; he came from Meng; he was an official in the lacquer garden; and he wrote a book. The *Chuang Tzu* is skeptical yet not cynical, and anarchistic yet not nihilistic; it counsels that the true sage molds himself upon Heaven. It is full of imaginative, witty, and subtle arguments for an ultimate but unknowable reality which is found in all things yet identifiable with none, and it calls for people to find and follow that reality by themselves with untaught wisdom.

NEO-TAOISM

In the following centuries this philosophic and speculative Taoist mysticism found many adherents among both scholars and common people, but it gradually declined as the fortunes of Confucianism rose. After the Han Dynasty a Neo-Taoist revival took place, from about c.e. 200 to 400. Two schools of thinkers reinterpreted Taoist ideas in the light of Confucian teachings. They kept philosophical Taoism alive and influenced later Buddhism and Neo-Confucianism.

Religious and Magical Taoism

Although religious Taoism includes elements of primitive and folk religion, it is a significant, living religious movement that deserves attention. On Taiwan it flourishes among millions of people. In 1994 James D. Seymour and Eugen Wehrli edited a report on religion in the People's Republic of China, quoting various Chinese documents. About "Taoism in Gansu"—a province in south-central China—they first cited the bad treatment of Taoism under the Marxist antireligious policy in the 1950s and during the Cultural Revolution. They then summarized the changes after new policies were established by 1980.

> Gansu reimplemented the party's policy of freedom of religious belief. Temples and monasteries were reopened and normal function resumed. . . . In December 1985, the first Taoist congress of the province was convened which established the Provincial Taoist Association. . . . By the end of 1987 there were 35 sites of Taoist temples and monasteries in function, . . .[4]

According to both official and scholarly accounts, these reforms—such as they were—are now in effect throughout the People's Republic of China. An active group of devoted Asian and Western students of religious beliefs and practices are now at work in both Taiwan and China.

The concern which united early forms of religious Taoism was for personal immortality, so that it can best be described as a cult of immortality, *hsien** Taoism, from the word for an immortal or spiritual being. But it was immortality in the literal sense of one who never experiences death, because earthly existence is prolonged forever. The past tense is used because almost nothing survives of that cult, and the present forms of religious Taoism deal with the question in other terms. There were three chief types of this historic religion; all were directed to attaining immortality. One method for prolonging life was by what has been called "hygiene," meaning elaborate techniques for the regulation of diet, breathing, exercise, and other bodily functions. Another school sought an elixir of life, usually made up of various chemicals, so that it is called a school of alchemy. It was believed that if only the proper concoction could be found, then eating or drinking it would make one immortal. A summary written in the fourth century c.e. said that the most important ingredient was cinnabar, mercury ore. It is therefore not surprising that in the Sung Dynasty (960–1279) at least eight emperors and many high officials died after swallowing elixirs, and there was a trend away from alchemy and toward the internal or hygiene methods. Third was the search for a land of immortals who fed on a food that prevented death. In the fourth century B.C.E. Duke Wei of Chi and others sent ships from the northeast coast searching for these blessed isles.

These movements grew up about the same time as philosophical Taoism, but what their connection was is hard to say. Welch[5] says that in the century from 220 to 120 B.C.E. the different forms of religious Taoism more or less coalesced to form one broad stream. The first four centuries of the Christian era brought more conventional religious methods of prayer, moral practices, and so on, and a different theory of the soul, while a system of heavens and hells was absorbed from Buddhism. Beginning in the second century B.C.E., a system of what might be called churches developed. In the second century C.E. the belief in a supernatural deliverer, a kind of Taoist messiah, motivated two great political-religious rebel movements against the government. Several branches of the Taoist movements arose, operating in different parts of the empire, with varying fortunes, over the next 1,000 years.

Of them the best known are the followers of an early leader named Chang Tao Ling; they succeeded in establishing an enclave on the Dragon and Tiger Mountain in Kiangsi, and in gaining official status for their group in C.E. 1016. Holding the self-conferred title of "Celestial Master," Chang Tao Ling's successors have been called "Taoist Popes," but there is no substance to such a description. In the 1930s Communist troops overran the Dragon and Tiger Mountain retreat and broke the bottles that supposedly held the most potent demons. In the 1950s, after the retreat had been restored, troops looted it again. But the priests have maintained their succession; Kristofer Schipper, a leading scholar, was ordained as a Taoist priest in 1968 by Chang En-pu, the sixty-third Celestial Master in direct descent from Chang Tao Ling.[6]

LITERATURE OF TAOISM

Taoist literature includes the two great works, the *Tao Te Ching* and the *Chuang Tzu*, as well as an extensive collection called the *Tao-tsang*.

The *Tao Te Ching*

The difficult questions of the date and authorship of this fascinating short scripture have been extensively discussed, with no definite resolution. Inasmuch as we treat Lao Tzu as a historical figure, we further assume that there is some basis for the traditional ascription of the *Tao Te Ching* to him. Probably he did begin this collection of sayings about the Way, although many scholars are in favor of a later date for compilation and completion of the full work. It may have been put together in the fourth century B.C.E. by a number of authors or compilers, following a distinctive tradition and point of view. Lao Tzu can, according to some authorities, be considered the originator and formulator of the central teachings and sections.

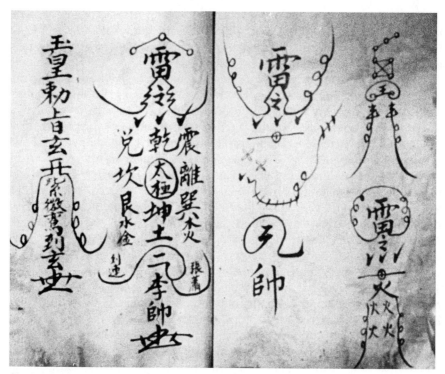

Taoist charms (Courtesy, Sheikh Publications, Inc., New York).

In any event, ancient tradition attached the name of Lao Tzu to the whole book. The earlier and traditional title is *Lao Tzu*, meaning the book attributed to him, in the same way that Mencius' book is called the *Mencius*. During the Han dynasty the new title, the *Tao Te Ching*, was applied to it, which gave it the standing of a classic like the Confucian books. The new title means "The classic of the Tao and the Te,"* or "The classic of the Way and its Power," to use Waley's title. Sometimes it has been called *The Book of Five Thousand Characters*, although there are a few more than that in fact, depending on the Chinese version used. Although in the earlier versions the chapter divisions varied, tradition stabilized the number of chapters at 81. The division into the first or upper and second or lower parts is also traditional, with the dividing line between chapters 37 and 38. The first part is considered the *Tao Ching* and the second the *Te Ching*, or the *Book of the Tao* and the *Book of the Te*, together being the *Tao Te Ching*.

The *Chuang Tzu*

The first seven chapters of the *Chuang Tzu* are considered the best or "inner chapters," and they appear to have been written by one brilliant and imaginative writer. Presumably, therefore, they are the work of Chuang Tzu. Since the rest varies in quality, style, and so on, not all of it is attributed to him, but substantial parts are. There are 33 chapters in all, forming a work of 100,000 words. Chapter 32 includes Chuang Tzu's comments about his funeral preparations, so it may be the end of his work; the final chapter can then be seen as a later, very useful, summary of various doctrines and writers, including Chuang Tzu. Although the work is not so cryptic and ambiguous as the *Lao Tzu*, it is often so playful and fanciful in tone and subject matter that it matches the *Lao Tzu* as the scripture of a way of thought which refuses to be tied down and categorized in any simple formula.

The *Tao Tsang*

Although the *Tao Tsang* is by name the canon (*tsang*) of Taoism, it is so complex a problem and a collection that we can only quote Professor Schipper briefly:

> The *Tao-tsang* . . . is the repository of all Taoist scriptures. The earliest Taoist Canon was compiled in the fifth century C.E. Afterward, all great dynasties reedited the collection and added new materials. The earlier collections are entirely lost. The only surviving Taoist Canon is the last one. It was published during the Ming dynasty, in 1445. A *Supplement* was added in 1606. The collection contains more than 1500 books. Many of these are undated and unsigned, and have not yet been properly studied. Only a very few among them have ever been translated into Western languages.[7]

THE TENETS OF TAOISM AS SEEN IN ITS SPECULATIVE FORMS[8]

One might say that the only tenet of Taoism is that there are no tenets, that there is no such thing as Taoism, and the Tao is beyond, includes, and negates all tenets. But that would be too negative and sophistic a formula. There are some things that can be said about fundamental principles of philosophical Taoism, however vague and elusive it is. They will come mostly from the *Tao Te Ching* and the *Chuang Tzu*, and they will be mostly about the *Tao* and the *te*, the way and its virtue. It must be remembered that Tao was a basic Chinese concept used by others than Taoists, but their special right to it was conferred by common usage, which designated them as the Taoist school or philosophy.

The term *Tao* is complex and difficult even in Chinese and even apart from Taoism; in the *Lao Tzu*, Kaltenmark says, it occurs 76 times with a different connotation each time.[9] Therefore we will use the Chinese word *Tao* and not translate it. Our discussion begins with the nature, meaning, or qualities of the Tao as seen in the *Tao Te Ching* and the *Chuang Tzu*, described under two main subheadings. After that, the other main division of tenets will be the way to the Tao, the fundamentally mystical approach to the supreme reality.

Te, power or virtue, will be discussed under the section on ethical and social aspects; one might call it the way *from* the Way.

The Tao

The Tao is what there is. The most common English translation is "the Way," but it is such a complex Chinese ideogram that the usual practice is to use "Tao." In philosophical terms it is the fundamental metaphysical category, in the traditional sense of metaphysics as ontology or the science of being or existence itself. Whatever Tao is, it is not simply a principle or theory, as it was in Confucianism. Rather it is the ultimate nature of things, what modern nontechnical language calls the "real thing" or basic stuff, as opposed to something merely phenomenal and synthetic. The contrast between the primacy and reality of the Tao and the secondary and derivative nature of all specific things parallels the contrast between the Brahman as the absolute and all else, in Hindu thought. But the Tao is in some way other and separate from the world, more transcendent than the pantheistic Brahman which includes or permeates all ordinary existence. To explicate the meaning of Tao, we turn to Taoist categories which are more metaphoric and poetic than technical or scientific. In doing so we make no claim to define or interpret the original characters, but we follow the translations and interpretations of various scholars.

THE GREAT CLOD

This strange figure for the ultimate reality occurs several times in the *Chuang Tzu*. Its author writes: "The Great Clod burdens me with form, labors me with life, eases me in old age, and rests me in death." The point of the Great Clod as a symbol is the oneness, simplicity, and inclusiveness of the Tao as the one, formless, primal reality underlying all things. Creel says:

> If one could win through to the very center of the universe, and enter the holy of holies, he would find there only a simple clod; utterly simple, because it is essentially like the clod that lies here at my feet; and utterly mysterious because, like everything else, it can never be understood in an absolute sense at all.[10]

In *Lao Tzu* the simplicity and primacy of the Tao is what is stressed. One of the classic expressions is in Chapter 25 of the *Tao Te Ching*:

There was something undifferentiated and yet complete,
Which existed before heaven and earth.
Soundless and formless, it depends on nothing and does not change.
It operates everywhere and is free from danger.
It may be considered the mother of the universe.
I do not know its name; I call it Tao.[11]

There is another figure for the Tao in the *Lao Tzu*, the personal or human correlate of its cosmic function as the Great Clod. That is the "Uncarved Block." Literally, it denotes uncarved wood and figuratively in Taoism stands for simplicity, plainness, genuineness of human nature. Like the Great Clod it is outside human control and yet underlies human nature as the clod does the world as a whole. The sage calls for the people to return, like himself, to the Uncarved Block. Summing up this section on Tao as the one basic reality is this quotation from Arthur Waley:

> For Tao itself is the always-so, the fixed, the unconditional, that which "is of it-self" and for no cause "so." In the individual it is the Uncarved Block, the consciousness on which no impression has been "notched," in the universe it is the primal Unity underlying apparent multiplicity.12

THE VALLEY SPIRIT OR MYSTERIOUS FEMALE

Like Hinduism, Taoism incorporates the female into the ultimate reality. Of course the *yin-yang* combines female-male, but the Mysterious Female is more than one of two correlative forces. In the term used by the Western philosopher Spinoza, it is like Nature, *natura naturans*, "nature naturing," that is, actively expressing itself. So this side of Tao can be thought of as "Mother Nature," although that is not the Taoist term. One of several references to this spirit in *Lao Tzu* occurs in Chapter 6:

The spirit of the valley never dies.
This is called the mysterious female.
The gateway of the mysterious female
Is called the root of heaven and earth.
Dimly visible, it seems as if it were there,
Yet use will never drain it.[13]

Legge says, in part, of this expression: " 'The spirit of the valley' has come to be a name for the activity of the Tao in all the realm of its operation. 'The female mystery' is the Tao with a name from Chapter 1 of the Tao Te Ching, 'the Mother of all Things.' "14 At least three qualities are included in the Valley Spirit. These will be discussed in the sections that follow.

Spontaneity of the Tao   The fundamental quality of Tao as the Valley Spirit or Mysterious Female is spontaneity, the spontaneity of nature: producing, proliferating, alive. Here Taoism counters the rather cold logos (reason) of Confucianism in Chinese temperament and culture with the eros (love) of life and vitality. Life in its natural, spontaneous, irrepressible fullness and vigor is the Taoist's most basic principle, and it accounts for the humor, cheer, gaiety, freedom of Chinese character. Chapter 25 from *Lao Tzu*, which we quoted, refers to the "Mother of the universe." The fundamental figure is clearly of an elemental maternal force, a womb or void whence issues life. Of the qualities entailed by, or at least included under, the spontaneity of nature as the Mother of all, the first is that the Tao is the source, the origin of all things. Another quality or attribute which belongs under spontaneity is the notion of the Tao as inexhaustible. Not only is it the source, but it cannot be depleted; it is unfailing. Although in one sense it is empty, void, yet from it comes an unceasing stream of life, and all things are sustained by it. At least four times the *Lao Tzu* says that the Tao is empty, yet use will not drain it.

Is not the space between heaven and earth like a bellows?
It is empty without being exhausted:
The more it works the more comes out. (Ch. 5)[15]

The Ruthless Impartiality of the Tao   The second quality of Tao as the Valley Spirit is that it is impartial, even ruthless; and it follows that all things are relative before or in the light of it. Producing all, sustaining all, the Tao as nature is impartial toward all mankind; that the rain falls alike on the just and the unjust is an idea with which we are familiar. But Taoism applies this idea more rigorously and carries it farther than Western thought does. This is partly because the Tao is impersonal. Wing-Tsit Chan says flatly that the Tao is not ever personal in the *Chuang Tzu*: "Any personal God or one that directs the movement of things is clearly out of harmony with Chuang Tzu's philosophy."[16] It would be difficult to find any reference in the *Chuang Tzu* to contradict this judgment, and even harder in the *Lao Tzu*. Lao Tzu says the way gives "them" life, but

Virtue rears them;
Things give them shape;
Circumstances bring them to maturity.[17]

Even more harsh are the famous and disputed words of Chapter 5, with their reference to "straw dogs," which were thrown out as trash once they had served their purpose in sacrificial ceremonies:

Heaven and earth are ruthless;
To them the ten thousand things are but as straw dogs.
The Sage too is ruthless;
To him the people are but as straw dogs.[18]

This doctrine can be misused; the sage king can claim that as the follower of the Way he may be ruthless toward the people.

The relativity of all things, as a philosophical and moral doctrine, is found all through the *Chuang Tzu*, although it is usually stated as a simple set of antinomies (opposed principles) and is not worked out systematically. A key and typical passage, from Chapter 2 of the *Chuang Tzu*, which is called "Discussion on Making All Things Equal," is:

> The "this" is also the "that." The "that" is also the "this." The "this" has one standard of right and wrong, and the "that" also has a standard of right and wrong. Is there really a distinction between "that" and "this"? Or is there really no distinction between "that" and "this"? When "this" and "that" have no opposites there is the very axis of Tao.[19]

The amusing fable of "Three in the Morning" is in the same chapter. It says that those who wear out their minds trying to make things one when they actually are one already are like monkeys in the zoo. When the keeper told them they would get three acorns in the morning and four in the afternoon they were furious. But when the keeper said, all right, they could have four in the morning and three in the afternoon they were delighted. The reality of things above the superficial difference was the same, says Chuang Tzu.

The Order of Opposites   Under the concept of the Mysterious Female as the symbol for Tao as nature is a third attribute: The Tao is orderly, and in its total order is unchanging. The order follows from the relativity of all things; it is an order of opposed forces, a dialectical order if you wish, evidently working from *yin-yang* dualism but extending it much farther to apply in all things. (Comparisons with Western "dialectical" systems like Hegel's are tempting but much too difficult and complex to be essayed here.) The order is real, but it is not hierarchical, structured, or logically categorized. It is, rather, the order of cycles, of action and reaction. The Tao works itself out through the waxing and waning of opposed principles or forces. Just as two correlatives are dependent on each other according to the relativist interpretation, so two opposites inevitably counter each other in the world of things. Lao Tzu says:

Being and non-being produce each other;
Difficult and easy complete each other;
Long and short contrast each other;
High and low distinguish each other. (Ch. 2)[20]

Reversion is the action of Tao.
Weakness is the function of Tao.
All things in the world come from being.
And being comes from non-being. (*Lao Tzu*, Ch. 40)[21]

*Principal altar, Chih Nan. The altar is two stories high
(Ward J. Fellows).*

From the working of the Tao through opposites such as *yin** and *yang** comes
the order which sustains all things. When we turn to the ethical norms of Taoism we will see how the sage guides himself and the world according to this
cyclical pattern of correlative forces.

The Mystic Way to the Tao

The way to the Way is the mystic way of vision, not the systematic, structured knowledge of the Confucianist or other schools. This follows from
what the Tao is and what human beings are. For the Tao is the ineffable, the
nameless; people cannot know it by deliberate effort or systematic, piece-
meal construction, but only by intuitive vision of the whole. This is the mys-

ticism of the Tao. The first verse of the *Lao Tzu* says that the Tao is ineffable, indescribable.

The Tao (Way) that can be told of is not the eternal Tao;
The name that can be named is not the eternal name.
The Nameless is the origin of Heaven and Earth;
The Named is the mother of all things. (Ch. 1)[22]

This is a fundamental theme of both the *Lao Tzu* and the *Chuang Tzu*.

The first verse of the *Chuang Tzu* is about a fish named K'un who becomes a bird named P'eng, whose wings are so broad they darken the whole sky like clouds, and about a man named Lieh Tzu who "could ride the wind and go soaring around with cool and breezy skill."[23] They are figures for the mystic way, which is beyond the ken of cautious little birds who can only flutter a few feet in the air and of little men who are blind and deaf. "This man, with this virtue of his, is about to embrace the ten thousand things, and roll them into one." Likewise Lao Tzu rejects all ways to the Tao except the Tao itself: Only by intuitive grasp, not discursive analysis, does his sage know the unknowable. Let us conclude this section with one of the most important chapters in the *Tao Te Ching*, in which these things are suggested.

The all-embracing quality of the great virtue follows alone from the Tao.
The thing that is called Tao is eluding and vague.
    Vague and eluding, there is in it the form.
    Eluding and vague, in it are things.
Deep and obscure, in it is the essence.
The essence is very real; in it are evidences.

From the time of old until now, its name (manifestations) ever remains.
By which we may see the beginnings of all things.
How do I know that the beginnings of all things are so?
Through this (Tao). (*Lao Tzu*, Ch. 21)[24]

Through the Tao one knows Tao. One is reminded of Philo Judaeus, who says that by light we see light.

THE PRACTICES OF RELIGIOUS AND MAGICAL TAOISM

The practices of religious Taoism are mostly expressions of the folk religion, the more primitive and popular faith of the ordinary people. As was previously the case in China, the three religions often blend in actual practice in Taiwan.

The "Temple of Heaven Proper," "The Imperial Vault of Heaven," stands alone in Beijing's Tiantan Park, "the perfection of Ming architecture." For centuries, the most solemn religious ceremony of the Chinese Empire took place there. At the winter solstice the emperor, with an enormous entourage of chosen officials, offered prayers for good harvests on behalf of the nation. Restored in the 1970s, it is handsomely decorated in traditional bright Chinese colors, a central national attraction for natives and tourists. No longer, however, is it the scene of supreme religious ceremonies (Photo, Ward J. Fellows, 1994).

Buddhist temples, for instance, include provision for casting lots at an altar, which is a Taoist custom. The lots are two crescent-shaped pieces of plastic, wood, or bamboo, each having a convex and a concave side. They are used for divination, that is, to decide what course of action to take. After prayer and thought about the alternatives, the worshipper standing at the altar drops the lots on the altar itself. When they fall one heads and one tails—as it were—it is a favorable sign, otherwise unfavorable.

Such practices are common, part of procedure by regular devotees at Taoist, Buddhist, and folk religion temples. The staff from several universities with whom our delegation from the American Academy of Religion met in 1994 deprecated these customs. They approved of properly rational "standard" religions, but disdained such acts as the casting of lots. At East China Normal University in Shanghai, which has 4,000 teachers and 15,000 students, our Journal reports: "We then had an extensive conversation about folk traditions. The Chinese took the position that world religions include systematic or organized religion but exclude 'superstition,' the category into which they put 'folk religion.' " Discussion with academics from the Institute of Religious Studies in the same city is recorded thus:

> On the question of folk religion, we were advised that minority people in Southwest China have such customs and traditions but those of the Han nationality do not belong to folk tradition. In folk religion there are superstitions and customs that are not religious and not appropriate topics of research because superstition is harmful to society. Religions must have a theoretical foundation and scriptures. Superstition is "blind faith."[25]

Worship and Ritual in Taoism and Folk Religion

K. M. Schipper described the Taoist liturgical system on Taiwan, having studied it for five years, three of them as a Taoist priest himself.[26] He found three categories of people in connection with Taoist temples. Those responsible for management of the temple are laymen. The priests to the *shen** or ordinary gods are called *fa-shih*;* they perform exorcisms of demons and manage the temple mediums who communicate with spirits. From their headdresses they are called "Red Heads." The third group—called Black Heads—are the orthodox Taoist priests (*tao-shih**) who supervise or internalize the external ritual acts performed in the main liturgy. They themselves worship higher beings, the Heavenly Honored Ones, who, unlike the *shen*, have never been human. Their sect goes back to Chang Tao Ling in the Han Dynasty, and the senior members claim ordination under the Celestial Master. Their ceremonies are not the ordinary duties of the Red Heads, but special ceremonies like consecration of a temple or periodic services uniting the religious community.

The most significant aspect of the cult on Taiwan is the corresponding division between orthodox Taoism or Tao-Chiao* and folk religion or *Shen Chiao** of the *fa-shih*. The latter is much greater in numbers and represents the basic ancient Chinese religious culture. Tao-Chiao uses the literary language in the liturgy and features spiritual retreats for receiving visions at certain temples like Chih Nan outside Taipei; it is essentially urban and has official government recognition. The priests have a distinctive black headdress, the top of which is silver and shaped like a flame, representing the flame from a figurative incense burner inside the body. The most important object in the temple is the incense burner, which symbolizes union with the Tao. Folk religion is more typically rural, having connections with secret societies and rebellions. The folk religion priesthood is unorganized; members are chosen for aptitude and vocation in their shamanistic and mediumistic practices, in which they use the native language.

Gods and Spirits

It would be impossible to describe or even list the gods and spirits of China or Taoism, which have been developing and changing for thousands of years. In the process of merging many customs, Taoism and Buddhism traded many gods. The spirits in Chinese popular mythology were innumerable, coming from the earlier nature gods, and popular religion sees them all around. When added to the ancestral spirits, they fill the air, are found everywhere. Popular religion tries to deal with these spirits or divinities who influence all of life and must be appeased and courted. To this end most of the ritual of Taoism is directed. In it the divinities are not so much worshipped as manipulated or managed, and thus much of Taoism is essentially magic and the deities are limited in meaning and power. Nevertheless the private or family religious life of most Chinese traditionally included sacrifices at home or in a temple to many such gods on many different occasions.

A catalog of a few among the myriad gods which are the focus of worship in religious Taoism, who often change and trade names and functions, might include the following. The true gods of Taoism are T'ien Tsun,* the superhuman beings whom the Taoist priests of the Tao-Chiao worship. Of them the greatest was Yuan Shih or T'si Shih, Honored Being of the Grand Beginning, creator and ruler of heaven and earth. But after he deputized his power to the Jade Emperor in about the eleventh century C.E., Yuan Shih receded into the background and the Jade Emperor became the supreme deity of the common people. This is an example of a pattern found in many religions: The high or great god withdraws and becomes hidden and inaccessible. Lao Tzu himself was deified and became Tao Chun*, Lord Tao. This is an instance of another familiar religious practice, in which human heroes of the faith become gods. There were Three Pure Ones headed by Yuan Shih, but the identities of the other two differ according to the source and tradition. Another group whose identity varied are the Eight Immortals, eight figures who attained immortality and became a subject for painting and sculpture. Ruler of the Immortals on the Isles of the Blest in the Eastern sea is the queen Hsi Wang Mu, who cultivates the trees that yield the peaches of immortality once each 3,000 years. Most familiar, common, and popular of the domestic gods is the earlier God of the Hearth or Stove, now the Kitchen God, Tsao Chun*. At the New Year, Chinese families sacrifice and feast while he goes to report to the Jade Emperor what he has seen from his place at the center of the household.

THE ETHICAL WAYS OF THE TAO

The Morality of Religious Taoism and Folk Religion

During the Sung Dynasty (960–1279) Buddhist karma was adapted to Taoism in a work called *Book of Rewards and Punishments by the Great Supreme.* Legge's translation says: "In heaven there are spirits that take account of man's transgressions, and, according to the lightness or gravity of their offences, take away from the term of life."[27] Pages of such offenses are listed, ranging from "casts the laws aside and receive bribes" to "spits at a shooting star." This book was widely distributed and used for many centuries, being described by one observer in the nineteenth century as "the most popular religious work in China." As such it inculcated an ordinary standard of morality among the people.

This heavenly accounting of human actions is still carried out in local religious usage on Taiwan. In the Temple of the City God in Tainan, the largest city in the southern part of the island, there are two large abacuses. These are used to count or record the virtue of the people. One to the right of the altar at about shoulder height is horizontal and may be touched and moved by people. The other, high overhead, is taboo and must not be touched, because it is said to move by itself at night; people can hear the sound of the movement when no one is in the temple.

The Ethical Way of Philosophical Taoism

The distinctive ethical temper of philosophical Taoism is found throughout the *Tao Te Ching* and the *Chuang Tzu*.

TE

Te means virtue, in the sense of moral force or power. We need to describe the practice of the *te* which comes from the Tao. The practitioners of *te* are the just or perfect man of the *Chuang Tzu*, and the sage or sage king of the *Tao Te Ching*. They first of all return to the uncarved Block; they are humble like water; the method is *wu-wei*,* nonaction.

The True Man   Just as Confucius had his *chun-tzu*, Chuang Tzu had his just or perfect man of Tao, and Lao Tzu had his sage. But the Taoist sages or just men are not so much embodiments of the Way as channels or instruments for it to operate in its grand simplicity and ineluctable spontaneity. Less by knowing or comprehending Tao than by being absorbed or ruled by it, they are enabled to live and work in the world and yet not be overwhelmed by it. Chuang Tzu's perfect man "works the handles that control the world, but he is not party to the workings."[28] Twice the *Lao Tzu* says that the sage produces things but does not take possession of them. There is a difference between them, however, in how they see themselves and their function. *Chuang Tzu's* just man is always the private individual, and he positively avoids any deliberate attempt to control or direct society. At most he manifests the wisdom, but he does not want any personal publicity; if he becomes known, he has failed. The *Tao Te Ching*, on the other hand, stresses that the sage is not an ordinary individual but a ruler who deliberately uses the Tao as a method of rule. Much of the book describes how the sage rules without overt acts, simply by practicing Tao so as to use its power. It has been suggested by some critics that Taoism is amoral (nonmoral, denying the very idea of moral rules) in this use of the Tao by the sage king to serve his purposes, without regard for some fixed or absolute moral law or judgment. When joined with the ruthlessness of the Tao, the ruler's right to use the Tao does raise questions about the ethical norms of Taoism.

Return to the Uncarved Block   Like Antaeus of Greek mythology, who gained strength from contact with his Mother the Earth, the man of Tao returns to the native simplicity of his nature in the Tao.

Returning to one's roots is known as stillness.
This is what is meant by returning to one's destiny.[29]

We have already seen how the Uncarved Block is the personal aspect of the eternal and primal Tao, to which the sage cleaves. He does this because reversion is the method by which the Way itself works: "Turning back is how the Way moves."[30] This concern for original purity and simplicity helps to explain the anti-Confucianism which is in the *Lao Tzu* and fills the *Chuang Tzu*. Refinement, deliberate cultivation of virtues in the Confucian manner, is not good, because it cuts one off from the primeval simplicity and pristine power and reality of the Uncarved Block.

Humility, Like Water   A frequent symbol for the lowliness of the Way in the *Lao Tzu* is water. Humility is also identified with the female, as in Chapter 28:

Know the male
But keep to the role of the female
And be a ravine to the empire.[31]

Some might decry this alleged "stereotype" of the feminine as the humble and lowly. But Lao Tzu is more realistic and honest, for it can be used as a means, a technique, to gain power.

In the union of the world
The female always gets the better of the male by stillness.
Being still, she takes the lower position.
Hence the large state, by taking the lower position, annexes the small state;
The small state, by taking the lower position, affiliates itself to the large state.[32]

Unlike the *Lao Tzu*, which says that by means of lowliness the sage triumphs, the *Chuang Tzu's* Perfect Man accepts the lowliness of the Way. He does not seek to gain wealth or position, but lives quietly, inconspicuously, simply.

Wu-Wei, NONACTION.

> Act without action.
> Do without ado.[33]

The classic and central method propounded in philosophic Taoism, for which it is known in terms of political philosophy and history, is *wu-wei*. *Wu-wei* can be seen first of all as an analysis of and attitude toward action, activity, and

Temple of the City God, Tainan (Ward J. Fellows).

doing things. Action is seen in the light of Tao, which the activist disregards. But Tao works by return, dialectically, cyclically, with swings of the pendulum, not by action. Hence, "To be overbearing when one has wealth and position/Is to bring calamity upon oneself." This is because "He who tiptoes cannot stand; he who strides cannot walk."[34]

The Taoist theory is not a theory of cycles of time, however, and to that extent the pendulum analogy is misleading. The action and reaction is a law in the sense of the way things are, how they work, in terms of cause and effect. It is more like a social-moral-human third law of motion—"To every force there is an equal and opposite reaction." Therefore all assertion, all actions, but especially pride, dominance, and war, inevitably produce their own antithesis. Only nonaction, precisely because it does not produce a reaction, succeeds. Chapter 39 of the *Tao Te Ching* says that those of old who obtained the One—which means the Tao—became clear or tranquil or divine. "What made them so is the One." For that reason they were exempt from reaction.

If heaven had not thus become clear,
It would soon crack.
If the earth had not thus become tranquil,
It would soon be shaken. . . .

. . .

If kings and barons had not thus become honorable and high in position,
They would soon fall.[35]

Fa-shih *("Red Head") priest, Temple of the City God. He has been performing an exorcism (Ward J. Fellows).*

In the modern idiom the sage is with it, he is cool. By being in accord with Tao, by being open, free, easy, loose, he is able to act without acting and ride with the wave, go with the current. There is a chapter of the *Chuang Tzu* about Confucius at the cataract at Lu-liang, where he was astonished at the old man who safely rode it; the man's secret was, he said, that he accommodated himself to the water, not the water to him.

CONCLUSION

For our conclusion to Taoism let us make a modern application of its position. Taoism expressed reverence toward the ultimate, the Tao; such reverence is the essence of the religious attitude or stance. The *Chuang Tzu* frequently ex-

A Tao-shih, *so-called "Black Head," orthodox Taoist priest. He wears the headdress looking like the flame from an incense burner (Courtesy, Sheikh Publications, Inc., New York).*

presses this sense of human dependence on the Tao as the cosmic order and it opposes all who would interfere in that order. Producing all, sustaining all, the Tao, it says, cannot be coerced or bent by anyone, least of all those who work and fret like the Confucianists or strive and sweat like the activists. Many times the *Chuang Tzu* speaks for and to modern students and others who are concerned with the environment, for nature, and who are disturbed by the way much modern technology has been used in the world. In its pacifism Taoism is also a protest against war and the weapons of terrible destruction which are the fruit of modern technology. With all their benefits, there are dangers and threats in the weapons and tools used so proudly and heedlessly today. Against this pride and blindness all the religions discussed in this book say in effect: humans must adjust themselves to the Tao, and not try to adjust the Tao to themselves.

The *Chuang Tzu*, in a chapter that Lin Yutang, the translator, entitles "Opening Trunks, or a Protest Against Civilization," voices a protest against knowledge. Now that is going too far—we need knowledge and civilization. Taoism includes a doctrine of *wu-ming*, no-knowledge or the nameless. Yet the *Chuang Tzu* does not really protest all knowledge, but only the misdirected knowledge which distorts and destroys the sources of life. Along with knowledge people need mysticism, reverence for and humility before the ultimate and transcendent. That is what all the religions in this book are about—in that they would all agree. With the correction to eliminate irrationalism in the quotation, the *Chuang Tzu* speaks for all religions.

> For all men strive to grasp what they do not know, while none strive to grasp what they already know; and all strive to discredit what they do not excel in, while none strive to discredit what they do excel in. That is why there is chaos. Thus, above, the splendor of the heavenly bodies is dimmed! below, the power of land and water is burned up, while in between the influences of the four seasons is upset. There is not one tiny worm that moves on earth or an insect that flies in the air but has lost its original nature . . . When the rulers desire knowledge and neglect Tao, the empire is overwhelmed in confusion.[36]

SUMMARY

In Chinese terms, if Confucianism is *yang* in its positive and formative activism, then Taoism is *yin* in its humble quietism. But that is really a Taoist way of putting the contrast, because it is Taoism which makes more use of the dialectical model of complementary forces. Although Taoism is not a unified or even clearly defined movement, it has certain general aspects and characteristics. As a whole it is characterized as mysticism in the sense of an intuitive grasp of reality or as religious practices stressing connection with spirit through mediums or shamans. Our description divides it in two parts, a philosophical and speculative tradition of thought and literature, and a magical and religious tradition of popular worship and personal religious practice. Taoism began about the same time as Confucianism and developed both as a philosophical school and a religious movement, but the two aspects are not closely related theoretically or institutionally. As a philosophical school it was one of six major schools of thought, competing and interacting with Buddhism and Confucianism. As a religious movement it was for centuries preoccupied with ways of attaining physical immortality by means of physical practices, or through imbibing an elixir of life made from gold and other minerals, or by discovering certain long-sought islands of immortality. In later centuries it spread over most of China.

The birth of Lao Tzu, the legendary founder of Taoism, is put at about 600 B.C.E. The book ascribed to him at least in part is called either the *Lao Tzu*,* after him, or the *Tao Te Ching*, the classic of the way and its power. Many scholars question the traditions about both the man and the book. The other principal figure, who lived about the fourth century B.C.E., was Chuang Tzu. Both works are cryptic in style, playing on paradox and using figurative language; the *Chuang Tzu* is more speculative and paradoxical, while the *Lao Tzu* tells how the sage king can govern by the Tao.

From the two works one can frame a description of the tenets of philosophical Taoism in Chinese terms as interpreted by various scholars. They center in the Tao itself as the central and supreme reality, which is described in concrete images or metaphors. "The Great Clod" is one, suggesting the simple, formless, unitary reality underlying all things, with its analog in human terms, the "Uncarved Block," or pure, primal human nature. The other principal figure for Tao is the "Valley Spirit" or "Mysterious Female," which is the Tao as spontaneously active and inexhaustible, as impartial and even ruthless, and as an order of opposite or complementary forces. For both Lao Tzu and Chuang Tzu the way to the Tao is by intuition and mysticism.

Officiating in religious and magical Taoism on Taiwan are both the orthodox Taoist priests whose standing goes back to the traditional center in Kiangsi, and the leaders of the folk religion of the common people. The orthodox priests deal with the traditional gods of a Taoist pantheon, while the local priests exorcise demons and are priests to the *shen* or ordinary gods and spirits.

The ethics of popular religion center on the recording of human conduct according to traditional rules. Philosophical Taoism calls for the sage king or perfect man of Tao to return to the Uncarved Block, to be humble like water, and, by always conforming to the dialectical movements of the Tao, to act without action.

NOTES

1. William Theodore de Bary et al., *Sources of Chinese Tradition*, Vol. I, Introduction to Oriental Civilizations Series (New York: Columbia University Press, 1968), p. 253.
2. Arthur Waley, *The Way and Its Power* (New York: © Grove Press, n.d.), p. 48.
3. Wing-Tsit Chan et al., *The Great Asian Religions* (New York: Macmillan, 1969), p. 151.
4. "Religion in China" 1. Taoism in Gansu. *Chinese Sociology and Anthropology* 26, no. 3 (Spring 1994), p. 14.
5. Holmes Welch, *The Parting of the Way* (Boston: Beacon Press, 1957).
6. Kristofer Schipper, *The Taoist Body* (Berkeley: University of California Press, 1993), p. iv.
7. Ibid., p. 249.
8. The gods of religious and magical Taoism will be described under worship and ritual, because their theoretical or doctrinal significance is almost nil and their real import is as the focus of worship and arbiters of personal destiny.
9. Max Kaltenmark, *Lao Tzu and Taoism*, Roger Greaves, trans. (Stanford Calif.: Stanford University Press, 1969), p. 28.
10. Herrlee G. Creel, *What Is Taoism?* (Chicago: University of Chicago Press, 1975), p. 35.
11. Wing-Tsit Chan, ed. and trans., *The Way of Lao Tzu*, Library of Liberal Arts (Indianapolis, Inc.: Bobbs-Merrill Company, Inc., © 1963), p. 144.
12. Waley, p. 55.

13. D. C. Lau, trans., *Lao Tzu: Tao Te Ching*, © D. C. Lau, 1963. Penguin Classic series (London: Penguin Books, Ltd., 1963), p. 62. Reprinted by permission of Penguin Books, Ltd.
14. James Legge, *The Sacred Books of China, The Texts of Taosim*, Part I (Oxford: Clarendon Press, 1891), p. 51.
15. Lau, p. 61.
16. Wing-Tsit Chan, trans. and comp., *A Source Book in Chinese Philosophy* (Princeton, N.J.: Princeton University Press, 1973), p. 681.
17. Lau, p. 112.
18. Waley, p. 147.
19. Chan, *A Source Book*, p. 183.
20. Chan, *Lao Tzu*, p. 101.
21. Chan, *Lao Tzu*, p. 173.
22. Chan, *Lao Tzu*, p. 97.
23. Burton Watson, trans., *The Complete Works of Chuang Tzu* (New York: Columbia University Press, 1968), p. 32.
24. Chan, *Lao Tzu*, p. 137.
25. *Journal of Professional Activities*, pp. 3, 4.
26. Holmes Welch, "The Bellagio Conference on Taoist Studies," in *History of Religions* 9 (203): 107–137.
27. Legge, *The Texts of Taoism*, Part II, pp. 235, 239, 244.
28. Watson, p. 151.
29. Lau, p. 72.
30. Lau, p. 101.
31. Lau, p. 85.
32. Lau, p. 122.
33. Chan, *Lao Tzu*, p. 212.
34. Lau, pp. 65, 81.
35. Chan, *Lao Tzu*, p. 170.
36. Lin Yutang, *The Wisdom of China and India*, The Modern Library (New York: Random House, © 1942), pp. 674–675. Reprinted by permission.

TOPICS AND QUESTIONS FOR STUDY

1. How do Taoist mysticism and individualism contrast with Confucianist rationalism and emphasis on social relations?
2. How did Taoism use elements of ancient Chinese culture, like *yin-yang*, in a different way than Confucius did?
3. What is the difference between the philosophical mysticism of Lao Tzu and Chuang Tzu and the shamanistic mysticism of popular Taoist religion?
4. Explain how the gaiety and spontaneity of Chinese temperament come out of Taoist teaching about the Tao as spontaneous.
5. Why is Taoism essentially religious in its view of the underlying reality and power of life in the Tao?
6. Discuss how individuals relate themselves passively yet creatively to the Tao. Explain why feminists should like Taoism.

7. Consider how the Taoist deals with society and other people, so as to make use of or work with the underlying forces in the world. Why do some commentators consider Taoism amoral in this?

8. Find examples of the difference (in religious Taoism) between the classic and orthodox tradition and what is called "folk religion." Is the latter "superstition"?

9. Why does Taoism appeal to the counterculture ideas opposed to the "destructive" rationalism and technology of modern culture?

USEFUL BOOKS

Taoism
See Chinese Religions: General list, and especially the Chan and de Bary sources, as for Confucianism.

Legge, James, trans. *The Sacred Books of China: The Texts of Taoism.* SBE, Parts I and II. New York: Dover, 1968 *et seq.*

Lao Tzu. *Tao-te Ching.* Translated by D. C. Lau. Baltimore: Penguin Books, Penguin Classics ed., 1963 *et seq.*

Kohn, Livia, ed. *The Taoist Experience: An Anthology.* Albany: The State University of New York Press, 1993.

Schipper, Kristofer. *The Taoist Body.* Translated by Karen C. Duval. Berkeley: University of California Press, 1993.

Watson, Burton, trans. *Chuang Tzu: Basic Writings.* New York: Columbia University Press, 1964.

GLOSSARY

See Confucianism for other Chinese terms.

ch'i: the life spirit

Chuang Tzu (jwung dzoo): Taoist mystic and philosopher, *ca.* 369–286 B.C.E.

the Chuang Tzu*:* his book

fa-shih (fah she): folk religion priests, called Red Heads

hsien (shyen): immortal

Lao Tzu (laow dzoo): legendary founder of Taoism, sixth century B.C.E.

the Lao Tzu: his book

shen: positive, divine good spirits or forces

Shen Chiao (shen jhee ow): folk religion

Tao (dow): way, principle, truth, reality; supreme Taoist concept

Tao Chia (dow jhee ow): Taoism as a school of thought

tao-shih: orthodox Taoist priests in Taiwan; called Black Heads

Tao Te Ching (dow day jing): the book of Lao Tzu; literally, "Classic of the Way and Power"

te (day): virtue, moral force or principle

T'ien Tsun (tyen tsun): Heavenly Honored Ones; higher beings than *shen*

Tsao Chun (tsow jhun): the Kitchen God; God of the Stove

wu-wei (woo way): inactivity, nonaction, nonassertiveness

yang: bright, male, dry, hard, warm, one of two basic forces or factors

yin: dark, female, moist, soft, cold; one of two basic forces or factors

yin-yang: complementary forces or factors

Yin-Yang: *yin-yang* school of thought

PART THREE

Three Western Religions, or Salvation West

As was explained in the Preface to Part 2, the conclusion of this book contrasts an Eastern and a Western version of salvation, the finding of spiritual health through proper relation of humanity to a transcendent spiritual order. This is an underlying, hidden, implicit theme running through these chapters. The hidden agenda or subtitle of Part 3, then, is "Salvation West," the pattern or model of salvation which characterizes all three of what we have called the "Western" faiths. This also justifies including Islam with the Western religions. The mere geographical location of Islam does not make it an "Eastern" faith, because the version of salvation makes it Western and Biblical, or "Semitic," as was suggested in the Preface to Part 2. Christians and Muslims are in this sense spiritual Semites.

In this part we begin with Judaism as the archetype of salvation in Western terms, the historical antecedent of the two others, and the model for revelation in all three. Christianity, comparable to Buddhism in Part 2, comes out of Judaism and becomes the developed and universal paradigm of Western salvation in Part 3. Historically, Islam is the latest, therefore the last; but in terms of Western salvation it stands between the universal community of Christian salvation and the national community of Jewish faith.

Chapter 7

JUDAISM

Open Torah scroll. Part of Genesis 47 and 49. German, nineteenth century (Courtesy, Photographic Archive of the Jewish Theological Seminary of America, New York. Frank J. Darmstaedter, Curator).

OUTLINE

I. Judaism is the religion of a people, coming out of their history and their experience of God as recorded in the Bible. Thus, there are many Judaisms.

   A. According to the Bible everything begins with God; so the Hebrews are chosen by God in the call of Abraham, father of the people, who is promised the blessing, about 1700 B.C.E.

   B. Under Moses the Hebrews were delivered from slavery in Egypt and, before returning to Palestine (now Israel), entered into a covenant with God as their one and only God.

   C. In Israel they later became a kingdom, split into two parts, were captured and exiled, returned, and resumed their worship of God in the temple at Jerusalem.

   D. They had been taught the Law of God, the Torah, and when they were driven out of Jerusalem by the Romans (C.E. 70 and 135) and scattered into the wider world, they lived by the Torah.

   E. Through various vicissitudes in Europe, Asia, and Africa they maintained and developed their religious culture, until after the Holocaust they established the state of Israel as a spiritual and physical homeland in 1948.

II. Hebrew sacred Literature.

   A. The Bible is the record of their experience as God's people; there are three traditional divisions:

      1. The Torah or the Law, especially the first five books.

      2. Nebiim, the prophets, who shaped the faith.

      3. Ketubim or books of wisdom.

   B. Interpretation and application of the basic Torah to specific conditions is in a later collection, the Talmud.

III. Although there is no official doctrine, certain beliefs are shared by almost all Jews.

   A. God is the one and only God.

   B. He is holy, sacred, and separate from the world and people.

   C. By his word he creates, rules, and judges the world and people, and speaks to Israel and all people.

   D. He will bring history to fulfillment in the Messianic age.

IV. Israel responds to the call of God and declares its faith as a people in group worship in the synagogue or temple or at home; the cult centers on their national history.

    A. Important festivals and holy days include:

       1. Passover

       2. Festival of Weeks

       3. New Year and Day of Atonement

       4. Feast of Booths

       5. Hanukkah

    B. The Sabbath, for rest and worship, is most important.

V. Institutional and ethical aspect of Judaism.

    A. Modern Judaism has three main divisions: Orthodox, Conservative, Reform.

    B. Theory and practice of Jewish ethics.

       1. The moral law comes from God; as such it is absolute, universal, revealed, and humane.

       2. The law consists in the commandments of God as interpreted by the rabbis and scholars to be studied and followed by all as a blessing for them and for the world.

INTRODUCTION

James Michener called his book about Judaism *The Source.* This is an accurate commentary, for Judaism is the major source of the religious tradition of the Western world. This is not because the Jewish people and history are the fountain and spring of the many nations, for of course they are not. It is because their experience of God, as known through Christianity, became characteristic of religion in Western thought and culture. From the Jewish religion is derived the Western way of looking at or thinking about the relation between God and the world. God is not part of nature, and nature is apart from God, for God is the creator of everything, the precondition, the prius, before all else. Therefore all things are creatures, and no thing or things can be equated with God. This is not to say that everyone believes in such a God, but that when anyone talks about God some such idea is the core of meaning. Judaism contributed to Western culture this way of thinking, in part directly, but mainly indirectly, by way of Christianity.

ORIGIN AND DEVELOPMENT

Built in 1658, Touro Synagogue in Newport, Rhode Island, was designed by a famous architect of the day, and is now a national landmark. Like many other early American settlers, and many other Jews in later times, those who built Touro Synagogue were refugees, Portuguese-Spanish Jews from Brazil. The presence in colonial America of this and other such buildings was the sign that the Jews were there. For Judaism is the religion of a people, a culture, a civilization; they are the people of the religion, and wherever they go they take their religion with them. The relation between the people and the faith is unique, different from other religions. This is true because in the self-understanding of Hebrew religion, Jews find God revealing himself in history, in the events which happen to them, the Hebrew people. For Jews to know their one Lord means they know that he is their God, they are his people, and their religion is shaped by this historical relation. Thus the study of Judaism requires study of the history of the Hebrew people. This is one of the ways in which Judaism—which claims to be the religion of the Chosen People—is as a matter of fact unique—the centrality of the history of the people in their own religious understanding. Traditional Hinduism and Buddhism, by contrast, are lacking in any concern with history.

The Biblical Age—The People of God

The principal source for our knowledge of Judaism is the Bible itself, but the Bible as studied and interpreted by Jews and others according to scientific methods in the last 200 years. To the Biblical record as so interpreted are added the findings of modern archeology and philology. These studies have mainly strengthened and confirmed the historical accuracy of the Biblical record in its general outline of key events. This combination yields a fairly complete and accurate record of events for the Biblical Age, which is the first major division of this section. Within it there are five subdivisions: the Patriarchs, the Exodus, the Monarchy, the Prophets, and the Exile. In this account the Bible will be treated as a record of the interaction between the Hebrew people and their God. This means that Biblical categories and terms will be used, although that does not entail acceptance of the complete worldview of the Bible. The emphasis is on events which were interpreted by the Jews as having religious significance.

THE PATRIARCHS

Patriarchs, of course, are fathers; the father of the Jewish people is Abraham. (Following the practice of Jewish writers, we will use as temporal designations B.C.E. for "Before Common Era" and C.E. for "Common Era.") He is shadowy and vague, but Biblical scholars say that Abraham has actual historical basis and is not simply a legendary figure. The point of the story for the religion of Israel is that in calling Abraham, God promised to bless him and his descendants, to make them great, and through them to bless all the people of the earth. These are permanent elements in the Jewish faith: the sense of calling or "election" as the people of God, and as such their carrying the promise of divine blessing for all people. Genesis says that in Abraham's life this relation to God was made even more explicit in the first covenant or agreement, the sign of which was the circumcision of all Hebrew males. The promised blessing was not borne by Abraham's first son, Ishmael, whom we will hear of later in Islam, but by Isaac. Isaac's son was Jacob, and late in his lifetime the tribal family journeyed to Egypt to escape famine. The key figure in the migration to Egypt was Joseph, son of Jacob, whose 12 sons are counted the fathers of the 12 tribes. As prime minister of Egypt, Joseph had been able to make them secure there. At first the Hebrews prospered, but their fortunes declined hundreds of years later under a different regime, and a later pharaoh made virtual slave laborers of them.

EXODUS, THE COVENANT, AND AFTER

Although Abraham is only a marginal historical figure, when we reach Moses about 1250 B.C.E. we are dealing with a historical person and era. We follow the account in the book of Exodus. Moses is the hero whom God chose to lead Israel out of Egyptian bondage. One of the great religious figures of all time, he is at once prophet, priest, teacher, statesman, general, and administrator. The Bible, however, counts him above all as prophet, because he spoke with God and for God. Yet when God assigned him to deliver the people from bondage he was reluctant and tried to beg off: "Who am I, that I should go unto Pharaoh, and that I should bring forth the children of Israel out of Egypt?" (Exodus 3:11).[1] Like all slaveholders, Pharaoh was reluctant to let his slave laborers go. Exodus describes the series of calamities that was visited upon Egypt at Moses' word and by divine agency. Finally, in the Passover, the firstborn in every Egyptian household and flock was stricken by the angel of death, which passed by the Hebrew houses marked with the blood of the sacrificial lamb. Then Pharaoh told Moses and Aaron (Moses' brother and spokesman) to leave with their people at once. "And the people took their dough before it was leavened" (Exodus 12:34) and went out from Egypt. That was the Passover, the deliverance from bondage, completed by their miraculous crossing of a body of water. It is pictured in the Bible as a miraculous occurrence, interpreted as a sign of God's care of and purpose for them. A "revelatory event" it is now called, meaning an occurrence which may appear like an ordinary event to others but which is seen by believers as a special sign that shapes and defines their view of the world and history. For the Jews it was God's deliverance and constituted them as the people of God.

A second major revelatory Mosaic event was the covenant* at Mount Sinai. Its importance is in the dual ideas of covenant and election, which can hardly be separated and are both part of the Biblical account. God says: "Now therefore, if ye will hearken unto My voice indeed, and keep My covenant, then ye shall be Mine own treasure from among all peoples; for all the earth is Mine; and ye shall be unto Me a kingdom of priests, and a holy nation" (Exodus 19:5,6). The essential notion is of a binding relation between God and the

Jews, but the specific terms are not stated fully or systematically in any one verse. Exodus 19–24, 34 describes it, and there is a restatement in Deuteronomy. Most people know the covenant for the Ten Commandments (Decalogue*), the code of laws given to Moses for the people. From the Exodus onward the God of Israel is, to use the four letters from the Hebrew, JHWH.* As the "name" of God, this is written as "Yahweh,"* and sometimes as "Jehovah"* in some versions of the Bible. Moses' own view was probably not monotheism (belief in one and only one God) but henotheism (JHWH as supreme among various gods). What is certain is that the exodus and the covenant in effect united God and the Jewish people in an inseparable covenant relation.

After Moses' death the Hebrews under Joshua's leadership moved into the Palestine hill country, where they changed from a nomadic existence to life in settled villages. As in the book of the Bible by that name, it is known as the period of the judges, from the local—rather than familial or tribal—heroes who delivered and ruled the tribes of Israel. For 200 years there was bitter struggle with the native Canaanites, coastal Philistines, and others; moral and religious uncertainty and turmoil prevailed. There was, for example, a tendency to worship the Baal* or "proprietor" god of the natives, because these Baalim (plural) were thought to control fertility of crops and herds. The Bible interprets this period as a time which demonstrated the perils of unfaithfulness to the Lord, and yet his care and protection for the Hebrews. Historically it is important as a time when loyalty to Yahweh as a real, dynamic, present Lord of all Israel began to be forged even before the monarchy emerged.

THE MONARCHY—DIVISION

About 1000 B.C.E., a hero named Saul arose, who united the tribes into one kingdom under his rule as the first king. Saul's successor was David, whose celebrated victory over Goliath, the warrior giant of the Hebrews' traditional enemy, Philistia, began his military career. He was a "mighty man of war" who extended and consolidated the kingdom. David was also the husband of several women, one of whom was Bathsheba; his son by her was Solomon. Solomon is a name for wisdom—tradition ascribes the Proverbs to him. It is a name for magnificence—the Jewish kingdom achieved its greatest extent, power, and wealth under his able administration. He built the temple at Jerusalem, making it into a great and luxurious place of worship with elaborate sacrificial altar and ceremonies. Yet the Bible—including the Christian New Testament—makes David the ideal king and the symbol and ancestor of the eventual God-appointed Messiah or deliverer, for David remained faithful to and feared the Lord above all. Time and again he repented, as when the prophet Nathan reproved him for arranging the death in battle of Uriah, the husband of Bathsheba. From the time when he went out as a stripling shepherd against Goliath, with nothing but his sling and five smooth stones from the creek bed, he said, "the battle is the Lord's, and He will give you into our hand" (I Samuel 17:47).

Following the death of Solomon, his son Rehoboam attempted to continue his policies and to rule all Judea. But in about 900 B.C.E. the 10 northern tribes broke away from the two southern tribes, Judah and Benjamin, which were loyal to Solomon's son Rehoboam. It was civil war, the northern kingdom against Judah the southern. The Biblical record is of a struggle between Yahwism and various forms of idolatry in both kingdoms, with history interpreted in religious terms: When the Hebrews obey God they prosper; when they disobey they suffer. The Bible thus interprets the pattern of history according to faithfulness or unfaithfulness to Yahweh.

About 200 years later, in 721 B.C.E., the Assyrians conquered Samaria (the name used for the territory of the northern kingdom), and exiled 27,000 people of the upper classes. The land and the common people were absorbed into the Assyrian Empire and its successors. Hence arose the tradition of the "ten lost tribes" of Israel. They were lost to the religion and people of Judaism, for the fragments of the faith now remain only among a few hundred modern Samaritan Jews. There is no "mystery" or "disappearance" of all the people. The ten tribes were gradually assimilated into other cultures, lost their separate identity, forsook their ancient religious heritage; only in this sense did they disappear or become lost.

THE PROPHETS AND REFORM

During this time the prophets emerged, who were an essential aspect of Biblical religion. The first prophets were related to bands of ecstatic religious devotees who appeared before the time of the monarchy. A prophet is essentially one who is called to speak or proclaim for God against all unrighteousness and disloyalty to Yahweh. In pursuance of such a task they pronounced judgment against evil and prophesied or announced what was bound to happen in the light of the truths of Yahweh, the one righteous God of all the earth. Not all the prophets were genuine; many served Baal or were merely sycophants of the king. But the genuine Biblical prophets were found in both Israel and Judah, and they proclaimed moral and religious truth without fear or favor.

A great, early prophet was Elijah, who condemned Ahab of Israel and his queen Jezebel for their worship of Baal, and whose dramatic contest with 400 of Baal's prophets on Mt. Carmel is recorded in I Kings. The eighth century B.C.E. saw the first of the written or literary prophets whose messages are preserved in the Bible, beginning with Amos, the shepherd of Tekoa. It has sometimes been the fashion to set prophet against priest, but true prophet and true priest were united against all attempts to subvert the worship of Yahweh. Some prophets were, in fact, priests. Their battle was necessary because in practice it took many centuries for genuine monotheism to prevail. In the period of the judges, before Saul, popular religion considered the local Baalim as having power in their areas, and saw no conflict between them and Yahweh as God of all the Hebrews, their national guide and protector in battle. In the face

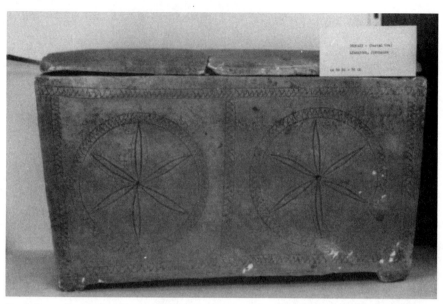

Burial urn, Jerusalem, 50 B.C.E.–70 C.E. (Courtesy, Judah L. Magnes Memorial Museum, Berkeley. Photo, Ward J. Fellows).

of such popular henotheism, prophet and priest were united, although they might conflict at other times.

A ritual of animal and vegetable sacrifice had prevailed among the Jews for hundreds of years, as recorded in the Bible. These practices were quite similar to those of non-Jews who worshipped other gods, and this made it easy for Jews to worship the Baalim and other gods and goddesses, both in north and south. After Samaria fell, Judah itself was besieged repeatedly, and both religious and political conditions deteriorated. Some men of Judah turned back to their Mosaic traditions, seeking to revitalize their society by a recovery of the moral and spiritual power of the past. The search for meaning and guidance brought forth materials which were incorporated in the book of Deuteronomy. The religious and ethical point of view was seventh-century prophetic monotheism, as influenced by Isaiah the prophet and his school. Yahweh's sublime holiness and universal divine justice were emphasized. In 621 B.C.E., King Josiah of Judah proclaimed a reform following the principles enunciated in Deuteronomy, which means literally "second law." One of the chief methods of reform was the requirement that the sacrifices be performed only at the one place which God chose, which meant the temple at Jerusalem. This reform of the cult had profound effects on later Jewish religious practice.

THE EXILE, RETURN, AND THE LAW

But Judah was caught in the web of events involving the greater empires which surrounded it. The capital of the Assyrian Empire, Nineveh, fell in 612, overturned by the Babylonians, who had also defeated the Egyptians at Car-chemish in 605. Little Judah was next. Nebuchadnezzar of Babylon captured the city of David—Zion, Jerusalem, "Ariel, the city where David encamped"—in 587 B.C.E. He razed it as well as every important town in Judah so completely that many of them utterly disappeared. Thirty thousand out of an estimated 200,000 Judeans were forcibly transported into exile, leaving only the poor people in a devastated ruin. The words of a psalm express the anguish then, and the yearning of Jews in all ages, for Palestine and Jerusalem:

How shall we sing the Lord's song in a foreign land?
If I forget thee, O Jerusalem,
Let my right hand forget her cunning.
Let my tongue cleave to the roof of my mouth,
If I remember thee not;
If I set not Jerusalem
Above my chiefest joy. (Psalm 137:4-6)

Yet Israel's sojourn in the land of the two rivers (Mesopotamia) permanently influenced them in important ways. Only 50 years later a new empire arose as the union of Media and Persia, making its emperor "the great king" for hun-dreds of years and bringing to bear on Israel the ideas of Zoroaster. Elements of Zoroastrian dualism perhaps contributed the idea of an evil power, Satan, and added new elements about the final judgment and life after death. Cyrus, king of the Medes and Persians, decided after his conquest of Babylon to repatriate the people; therefore many Jews returned to Jerusalem after 539 B.C.E. Be-tween 520 and 516 they built a new temple.

But they were weak and defenseless until after 445, when a layman named Nehemiah provided leadership to rebuild the wall of Jerusalem. Then Ezra the priest, aided and encouraged by Nehemiah, led the people in a solemn rededi-cation to the Torah* or Law, the center and source of Jewish religion. Strict en-dogamy (marriage of Jews only with Jews), Sabbath observance, and other reg-ulations were instituted. It was the beginning of a new era for Jewish religion. Their sacred writings began to be put together, and these law books of the Torah and other writings became the guide and rule for Jewish religious and moral life. Although himself a priest by birth, Ezra began the process of the transfer of spiritual leadership to the scribes and later the rabbis, leaving to the priesthood the conduct of temple ritual.

The People of the Book

The succeeding centuries saw Judea fight to maintain itself under various em-pires. In 164 B.C.E., under the Maccabees, it gained independence, which it held for 100 years. In 63 B.C.E. Judea came under the Roman Empire, whose heavy rule was all the harder to bear after years free at least of foreign domina-tion. In 70 C.E., revolts by the Zealots culminated in the Roman capture of

Jerusalem and burning of the temple. The Jews remained in Palestine, however, and conditions stayed about the same. In 132 C.E. there was another revolt, by the Zealot Bar Kochba, and in 135 C.E. the Emperor Hadrian resolved to build a temple to Jupiter in place of the Hebrew temple. After a frightful struggle and incredibly heroic measures by the Jewish defenders, Jerusalem was destroyed. The Jews were kept out of Hadrian's new city of Aelia Capitolina. This was another spiritual crisis for the beleaguered people, out of which came a strengthened synagogue and the emergence of rabbinic Judaism, with its distinctive literature in the Talmud. The Talmud is the second great collection of Jewish scripture after the Torah, and the Diaspora* (from the Greek for "dispersion") is the spread or scattering of Jews out from Palestine. They are complementary factors: Talmud is basically interpretation of the Torah for application to new circumstances, and the Diaspora, with its new situation of Jews outside Israel, increased the need of standards for applying the law to novel problems. So a new body of study and interpretation arose to meet the new need of rules for changed situations. Beginning with the exile, Jews had settled in other countries. Their dispersion increased in the following centuries, especially after 135 C.E., to Asia, Africa, and Europe. The loss of the temple accelerated these developments; wherever Jews lived, the synagogue became the center of Jewish life and the rabbis the interpreters of the Torah.

THE MIDDLE AGES—CENTURIES OF PERSECUTION

Although suffering was not extreme all the time, hardships of discrimination, prejudice, and persecution were so pervasive through the Middle Ages that they have indelibly marked Jewish consciousness and religious life and practice. A full recitation of the record is not in order here, but it has to be noted as a relevant fact: In Europe Jews were often persecuted, at times communities were destroyed, and thousands of Jews were murdered in sporadic outbreaks of mob violence. Sometimes they fared better under Islam, which became the dominant power in parts of Asia and North Africa after the seventh century C.E. In Europe, and under Christian rule, the worst problems arose during and after the Crusades, as a result of heightened Christian opposition to unbelievers. The story is too long and harrowing to be told in detail, of how nominally Christian governments imposed increasing restrictions and impossible demands on the Jewish people, not to mention the actual bloodshed. The effect of these circumstances was a very high level of what is now termed ethnocentrism, expressed in Jewish law for all aspects of life. Referring to the pattern of segregation in medieval Europe, Rabbi Joseph L. Blau says: "Yet this *modus vivendi*, which was certainly not developed with the interests of Jewish life in view, had many advantages for the Jews and for Judaism."[2]

In part because of these limiting conditions, a pervasive and intensive moral and religious concern dominated Jewish culture for centuries. It was characterized by study and discussion of the proper law in all circumstances, and meticulous attention to strict observance of that law by all members of the close-knit community. There was considerable variation among different communities, but conformity within each congregation. The synagogue, as a place of worship, study, and assembly, became the center of the Jewish community. The Torah and the Talmud were the source and focus of discussion and interpretation. Form and ritual for festivals, the Sabbath, and all special occasions were standardized in liturgies, although there was no universal liturgical uniformity.

MODERN JUDAISM

In the sixteenth century, after the persecution and expulsion from Spain, the center of gravity of European Jewish life and culture moved eastward. The Ashkenazim, Jews from the north of France and Germany, took over the leadership which had been provided by the Sephardim, Spanish Jews. There was a movement into Poland and Russia for several centuries. In the eighteenth century, for example, they established communities in Poland, called *shtetels* (millions of Americans have seen a shtetel on stage or screen in *Fiddler on the Roof*). From such a community in southeastern Europe came Israel Baal Shem (1700–1760) whose aim was to rescue spiritual religion from rabbis who, he said, "through sheer study of the Law had no time to think about God." He proclaimed a pietistic mysticism, influenced by the cabala,* to foster the indwelling of God in humanity and nature, and held that the favor of God is channelled through the perfectly righteous person, the Zaddik. Not a large group now, they influenced Jewish life in the direction of personal piety and mystical joy in the Lord. They are called Hasidim.*

The larger movement of Judaism, beginning in the eighteenth century, was toward freedom from old disabilities and to full participation in the life of the wider world. It is ironic that freedom came in the form of a movement which was in part opposed to organized religion. That is to say, the secular philosophic movement of European intellectuals called "the Enlightenment," centered in France and Germany in the eighteenth century, was generally opposed to religion, or at least to clerical control over education and science. The spread of Enlightenment ideas by the French Revolution and Napoleon led to removal of restrictions on the Jews in the French dominions. In the eighteenth century, Moses Mendelssohn had already led the Jewish community in Germany into the wider intellectual world, and the nineteenth-century revolutions in Germany and elsewhere furthered Jewish freedom. In the American colonies and, later, the United States, the Jews were free from formal legal restraints and disabilities and were able to take advantage of the opportunities there.

Thus the eighteenth and nineteenth centuries were a time of transition for Jewish culture—out of the ghetto and into the mainstream of modern life. Modern Judaism took its present form as a result of liberation from ancient restrictions that had also served to unify the Jews. Once free of the restrictions, they were also free to change the religious customs and practices of the old life. For centuries Judaism had been a total way of life by which the behavior

Israelites Worshipping the Golden Calf, *Poussin, 1594–1665 (Courtesy, M. H. de Young Memorial Museum, San Francisco).*

of people in the community was regulated in all its aspects. Judaism as a comprehensive program of living in a homogeneous community changed to the compartmentalized religious scheme of personal piety and participation in the synagogue and home ritual and worship. Moreover Judaism as a faith had to come to terms with modern secular culture, and there were different solutions found for this problem. The three major divisions of Judaism reflect different ways of meeting contemporary secularism.

For all Jews the twentieth century has been marked by the tragic and indescribable holocaust of 6,000,000 European Jews exterminated by Hitler and the Nazis before and during World War II. This latest and most terrible and traumatic campaign of extermination has had incalculable effects on Jewish consciousness and attitudes. After the war came the triumphant emergence of the State of Israel, the realization of a hope that was nurtured through the centuries and furthered by the modern Zionist movement. The Jewish nation-sate is now an actual home for 4,000,00 Jews and the focus of loyalty and devotion for nearly all Jews everywhere. Its emotional and practical importance and significance for both the communal and personal life of Jews cannot be overestimated. Nor can the problems generated for Jewish self-identity and unity by the establishment of "Eretz Israel."

JEWISH SACRED BOOKS

The basic Jewish literature is a series of separate booklets that comprise the Hebrew Bible. The Jewish word for the Hebrew Bible, Tanakh, is defined as: "an acronym in Hebrew, referring to what is commonly known as the 'Old Testament,' reflecting the division of scripture into three levels of revelation-based sanctity."[3] We will head the first part of our discussion of Jewish literature "The Bible." The second part will then cover the Talmud, the later oral tradition that has been collected in many volumes.

The Bible

A controversy exists over the question of the authorship or source of the Bible—whether it is to be taken as the literal, direct word of God or not. This is a problem for all three Biblical religions. For hundreds of years the view of complete divine verbal inspiration was accepted without question. But for more than 200 years the Bible has been studied scientifically, on the assumption that specific human authors, places, times, and events can be identified to explain its origin and contents. Actually, this sort of analysis was implicit in the traditional division into separate books by different authors. An enormous amount of information has been gathered as the fruit of these scientific studies, and the most significant effect has been to make the Bible more rather than less meaningful to the modern mind. Jewish, Protestant, and Catholic study has made it a cooperative or even joint venture, with conservative or literalist scholars often sharing their efforts. The literalist position, which holds that the Bible as divinely inspired must be accepted word for word as it has come down to us, is held by millions of people and is strongly defended by able interpreters. The result of these labors by scholars of different points of view has been to preserve the significance and integrity, and to establish the essential reliability of the Biblical record.

In the brief description of the contents of the Bible and its significance, for our purposes the traditional Jewish classification is followed: Torah or the Law, Nebiim* or the Prophets, and Ketubim* or the Writings.

THE LAW (TORAH)

The first five books of the Bible—Genesis, Exodus, Leviticus, Numbers, and Deuteronomy—are denoted as the Pentateuch,* or the five. Traditionally, Moses was considered the author; hence, they are the five books of Moses. They are The Law or Torah because they are the most basic and fundamental for Judaism's understanding of itself. The identity—to use the modern word—of Israel is established by the mixture of myth, history, ethical precepts, ceremonial rules, social and criminal statutes, and religious wisdom contained in the Torah. They constitute the heart of the written law on which the oral law, which interprets and expands it, is based. The five books are therefore the basis for all Jewish law in a special sense. That is, the truths and principles which they enunciate have fundamental force and legal sanction. Although other books of the Bible are equally important as scripture, they are secondary to the Torah as the primary source or basis for later elaboration and interpretation of Jewish law.

Included in Genesis are: myths of the creation of the world and humanity, and of the beginning of evil and strife; the story of Abraham and his descendants; and the account of the move to Egypt. Exodus is the story of deliverance from Egypt and of the covenant, a mixture of history of past events and explanation of religious ceremony at the time of writing. Leviticus is literally laws. Numbers describes the wilderness sojourn. Deuteronomy has been referred to as the second law book, dating from the time of Josiah. Scholars have analyzed the different strands of authorship and editing, and their findings are available in many sources.

THE PROPHETS (NEBIIM)

Listed under this heading are some books of the Bible that contain mostly history of the Hebrews' entrance into Palestine after leaving Egypt: the settlement, the monarchy, the division, the fall of Jerusalem, and the exile. Joshua, Judges, I and II Samuel, and I and II Kings are listed as Early Prophets. The Latter Prophets are three long prophetic books: Isaiah, Jeremiah, and Ezekiel. The Twelve Minor Prophets are not all of minor importance, but are shorter in length than the Latter Prophets. They include: Hosea, Joel, Amos, Obadiah, Jonah, Micah, Nahum, Habakkuk, Zephaniah, Haggai, Zechariah, and Malachi. Amos, the earliest great literary prophet, was a shepherd from Tekoa near Bethlehem; in about 750 B.C.E. he proclaimed that Israel would fall because of its sins. In 721 B.C.E. Samaria was captured by Sargon, King of Assyria. A short while after the time of Amos, Hosea in Israel compared the Israelites to a wife who was faithless, yet loved by Yahweh her husband. Isaiah exalted God in holiness, magnificence, and universality, and he foresaw the downfall of Jerusalem, yet said God still would save his people. The prophet of the capture of Jerusalem was Jeremiah, who agonized over the impending doom but would not soften his message unless Judah would repent and return to Yahweh. From among the first hostages to Babylon in 597 B.C.E., Ezekiel was made a prophet by his vision of the glory of Yahweh. He foresaw not only the final destruction of Jerusalem, which came in 586, but her restoration. He proclaimed a new covenant of individual faith and a new order of righteousness. The spiritual vision and moral force of the prophets was the major factor in the transformation of Judaism into a religion of universal moral law and righteousness.

THE WRITINGS (KETUBIM)

Many of these books are designated "wisdom literature" by commentators, because they are about personal events or general religious truth, or of devotional nature like the Psalms. The first eight fall into such a group: Psalms, Proverbs, Job, Songs of Sons, Ruth, Lamentations, Ecclesiastes, and Esther. The last five are: Daniel, Ezra, Nehemiah, and I and II Chronicles. The importance of these books is not perhaps so readily apparent as the other sections: They are less dramatic and more personal—important in a different way. But in the long run they have contributed just as much to Jewish faith and life. For they articulate wisdom in the sense of knowledge for the conduct of life, enabling people to live well. They are based on perennial themes; they discuss and illuminate the basic human emotions and problems. A variety of moods and points of view are represented, ranging from the earthy prudence of the Proverbs to the high moral devotion of the Psalms, from the erotic symbolism of the Song of Solomon to the world-weariness of Koheleth in Ecclesiastes. Above all, the soul before God is comforted and strengthened, and perhaps that is the ultimate function of religion.

Talmud

"Talmud" means study, but it is the fruits of study that are collected in the Talmud.* All of the Hebrew Bible is dated well before the destruction of the second temple and the major Diaspora. After that Judaism is based on the Torah as studied, discussed, interpreted, and applied in the Talmud. At first the Talmud was Oral Law; the Talmud interpreted the Written Law and applied it to changing circumstances. Later this Oral Law was written down, but the name stayed the same. The Talmud is a large collection compared to the smaller corpus of the Bible; it includes the oral-literary material of centuries of legend and law, moral precepts, and Biblical interpretations.

Sorting out the various collections of Jewish literature is only for experts. A short outline of the Talmud will be essayed here. Let us state the conclusion first: There are two Talmuds, two collections. *Talmud Babli* is the Babylonian Talmud, later, larger, and more authoritative than the other; when "Talmud" is used without the descriptive "Babylonian" or "Palestinian," it is taken to mean the Babylonian Talmud. The other is the Palestinian, and usually its full name is used—Palestinian Talmud, or the literal name in Hebrew, Jerusalem Talmud.

MISHNAH*

Mishnah is the basic component of the Talmud. The word means repetition in the sense of restatement of the Law. The Talmud is not a systematic exposition or codification, being rather a heterogeneous collection of recorded discussions about the meaning and application of the Law. Nor is it authoritative or final, being more like an opinion or a consensus about what a sincere Jew ought to do—in the sense of moral obligation—in a particular situation. The method employed during the early centuries of this long process of interpretation was called midrash,* or interpretation in the sense of investigation or search. But, as time went on and precedent and information increased, there was a great accumulation of these opinions that had been preserved in the various Jewish communities. The method became cumbersome and had to be abandoned in favor of a simpler process than accumulation of *all* opinions. This was found in the method, and corresponding statements of formulations, of halakhah* as legal precedents or decisions. Halakhah comes from the Hebrew meaning "walk," hence the proper way to go or proceed. Not all the opinions had to be preserved and consulted, but only those considered binding as Halakah. This greatly reduced the amount of material and simplified the task of reading authoritative or definitive opinions. By the end of the second century c.e. the rabbinical center in Palestine undertook to compile these accumulated traditions. The names of Rabbis Akiba and Meir are identified with it, although about 150 scholars did the work. All those who had a part in it are known as the Tannaim. In about 200 c.e., therefore, the Mishnah was put in writing, compiled by Rabbi Judah the Prince.

The whole collection is arranged under six "Orders": Seeds, Festival, Women, Damages, Holy Things, and Purities. Each Order is in turn divided into tractates, chapters, and clauses.

GEMARA*

The other principal collection included in the total Talmud is Gemara, a second strand or layer of interpretation and elaboration, this time directed to the Oral Law. Gemara is study in the sense of completion or conclusion; the Gemara completes the Mishnah. Now, most of the Mishnah was composed of Halakhah, but there were also traditions of all kinds known as haggada* or "telling," being folklore, sayings, medicine, biography, and, above all, legends of every description. Both Halakhah and Haggada entered into Gemara. About four fifths of the Talmud can be classified as Halakhah, the one-fifth Haggada being scattered through it.

Two chief collections of Gemara were made, Babylonian and Palestinian. Some time after 300 c.e., the Palestinian Gemara was compiled and written, and in about 500 the Babylonian. With the Mishnah they comprise the Talmud. The Palestinian Gemara comments on 39 tractates of Mishnah, and the Babylonian on 37. For various reasons, the Babylonian proved more useful and is much more important.

The complexities of the process of Judaic study and interpretation of various canonical materials are beyond us here, but mention of the genius of the overall method and achievement should be made. The double task for any religious organization in dealing with its sacred texts is to preserve significant fundamental principles while allowing for necessary changes. It is comparable to the duty of the U.S. Supreme Court to keep the Constitution intact, yet make it applicable to modern conditions. In Judaism the two poles are revelation as fixed and permanent, and decisions for circumstances in a changing world. Jewish scholars deal with the dichotomy in terms too sophisticated and intricate for our general survey. But, taken together, they are a remarkable solution that should be noted, especially in the light of religious pluralism, for all major religions face a similar issue.

TENETS: THE FAITH OF THE PEOPLE OF GOD

Most people explain or interpret religious differences in terms of belief or doctrine. Because of the divisions of Christianity and the nature of Christian faith, the key or clue to marking or identifying different Christian groups is the creed or statement of faith. But that is not necessary for understanding Judaism, nor is it adequate. It is inadequate in the first place because there is no single, simple Jewish "creed" or "dogma"; that is not the way Judaism is constituted. Nor is it the way in which a Jew thinks of herself as being a Jew. According to Jacob Neusner's "Table of Dates" for 1986: "Established law regards only the child of a Jewish mother as a Jew by birth. Now Reform and Reconstructionist Judaisims also accept as Jewish the child of a Jewish father and a non-Jewish mother."[4] This formula, however, is still disputed. A headline in the *San Francisco Chronicle* for December 13, 1995, said: " 'Who Is a Jew' returns as Israeli

Sabbath menorah (Courtesy of Judah L. Magnes Memorial Museum, Berkeley. Photo, Ward J. Fellows).

flashpoint." The religious parties wanted to subject conversions to Orthodox standards. In Jewish understanding, Jews are Jews by birth, and they affirm their religious identity by various actions involving participation of some sort in Jewish religious life.

But Jews disagree over the place of belief and doctrine and the content of such religious dogma, and there is no authoritative statement or summary to which we can appeal. In any event, certain fundamental notions, whether they be called dogmas, beliefs, concepts, or theories, have held a relatively fixed position in Judaism, and we treat them under the headings: the Source, God, Humanity, the Messiah and the Future, and Maimonides.

The Source

There have been Jewish theologians, Philo and Maimonides above all, but they cannot be considered the source of Jewish beliefs. The prophets proclaimed fundamental truths about God, but they were not official. One must turn again to the Jewish people as a whole in order to uncover the sources of Jewish faith and doctrine. For it was in and through the living experience of the people of God that the fundamental truths—which *are* there in Judaism—were manifested. Thus the ritual, worship, prayer, and practice of the Jew imply or entail certain truths or beliefs.

God

If the Bible is the source of information—the record—then there can be no question about the first and most important tenet of Judaism. The whole Bible is religiously meaningless without God: Indeed, the Bible is incomprehensible without God as the central reality and principal actor.

ONE: שמע ישראל יהוה אלהינו יהוה אחד

> *Shema Yisroel Adonoy Elohaynu Adonoy echod.*
> Hear, O Israel, the Lord our God, the Lord is One.

These words from Deuteronomy 6:4 are the most important words in Judaism, "the Shema," from the first words in Hebrew. They resound in the synagogue at all times of prayer; they are on the lips of the faithful many times a day; they are the last words a devout Jew utters in this life. The philosophical concept here is monotheism, but the basis of Biblical monotheism is not an intellectual concept. For it does not come from such abstract ideas as "absolute" or "universal," or any physical or metaphysical premises. "Thus says the Lord, the King of Israel and his Redeemer, the Lord of hosts: 'I am the first and I am the last; and beside Me there is no God' " (Isaiah 44:6). So Isaiah asks: "To whom then will ye liken God, or what likeness will ye compare unto him?" (40:18). God is the incomparable One. The earlier Biblical writers spoke of other gods as weaker and lesser deities, but they were competing powers; at the high places in Canaan many Jews for centuries made offerings to Baalim. Five hundred years later, Isaiah refers to other gods as idols made by men. The people of Israel gradually learned that the other gods were nothing in comparison with Yahweh who is unique, the only one. Taught by the prophets, they also learned that their one God is inherently righteous or moral and calls for righteousness in his people. If we need a theological term, "ethical monotheism" is used to describe Jewish monotheism. The moral aspect of God is primary and constitutive, an essential element of him in Jewish, and hence Christian and Islamic, doctrine. Goodness and God cannot be separated—they go together.

HOLY

Another fundamental characteristic of the Biblical God is holiness; it is synonymous with the Godhead from early Biblical times, so that no additional information or description was conveyed by it except that it denoted or applied to God, "The Holy One of Israel." Certain ideas or elements of meaning did gather around the term, above all that of separateness, unapproachableness, absolute transcendence, which then became more specific as greatness, power, and majesty. The modern word is "numinous," for the divine force or potency which inheres in God and flows from him. Yahweh in the Exodus was always enveloped by the cloud, so he would not overwhelm the people. Isaiah saw the Lord "high and lifted up," and before him the attendant seraphim covered their faces with two of their wings. Elijah's God answered by fire at Carmel. Job at last was answered from out of the whirlwind. All this is an aspect of the separateness, sacredness, or holiness of God in the Biblical tradition. It is also the explanation for the wariness of Judaism and much of Protestant, especially Calvinist, Christianity about mysticism, which tends to put aside the numinous in order to unite with God in the mystic trance. (Eastern mysticism does not usually have this problem, because it does not so stress the power and majesty of God, although there is a theophany of Krishna in the *Bhagavad Gita*, and there is a terrible aspect of Shiva.)

CREATOR AND RULER

This is the most familiar and obvious of the characteristics of God which Judaism explicitly affirms. Genesis begins: "In the beginning God created the heavens and the earth." Although Biblical literalists have some problems with the creation story taken as a scientific or historical report, most Jews and Christians are able to see this as a Biblical myth—the ultimate origin of the cosmos is in the creative word of God. What is not always recognized is that it is a double truth: The world is a created, dependent order, not self-caused and self-sufficient, because God is creator of all. In the Eastern religions the gods are secondary to being or existence, which precedes them. Nothing precedes the God of the Bible; the technical term in later thought for this teaching is

Qumran Cave No. 4, Dead Sea, Israel. One of the caves where ancient Biblical scrolls were found (Ward J. Fellows).

"creation out of nothing," although it is not put that way in the Bible. The obvious corollary of creation is that God is not only creator but also ruler, sovereign, and judge. He rules nature, humanity, and history. That is to say, he makes laws for them and enforces those laws. Biblical theism, both Jewish and Christian, holds that the physical realm follows God's laws—it is a realm of order. God's authority is also over the world of persons and events, of history. This was the final truth which the Psalmist took as his basic datum: "God reigneth over the nations; God sitteth up on his holy throne" (Psalms 47:9). But people do not obey as nature does, and the laws and operations of history are not so clear as in nature—hence arise the problems of the world of human events. People are punished if they disobey, and Israel itself is judged and punished, for God's judgment is sure.

GOD SPEAKS

The cornerstone of the structure of Jewish doctrine is the conviction that God is a God who makes himself known, first of all to Israel. God speaks; he is not always silent or hidden. He came unbidden to Abraham and to Moses and spoke to them. From out of Ur of the Chaldees Abraham was called by God to go to Haran and Canaan. From out of the burning bush God called, and spoke face to face with Moses. (The cornerstone of the Jewish Theological Seminary [Conservative] in New York shows the flames of the burning bush and the words: "The bush was not consumed.") The primary credential of a prophet is that God speaks to him, so that he speaks for God. God reveals himself to Israel and declares his will for the life of mankind. The idea of revealed religion is fundamental and pervasive in Judaism; in the Written Law and the Oral Law are declared, directly or indirectly, the duty of humanity.

Speech between two parties is communication. The Bible does not need to say that there is communication between man and God, because it is full of human speech to God in reply to God's word to humankind. Sometimes God is addressed as the king who is far above, but Israel also rejoices that God is near to them. He can be spoken to as an understanding and compassionate Father, full of love and pity for his children. A significant aspect of the divine–human dialogue as it developed in the Bible is Judaism's later reluctance to use the name of God. In place of it the Bible uses "the Lord," the "Holy One," the "Almighty," or other adjectives made into substantives. The motive for this was reverence for God's holiness.

Humanity

Into the framework of the world humanity fits as the head of the created order, a child of God. Each person is a unity of body and spirit, made to live in and enjoy the world. The very presence of the law implies that people are capable of obedience to it. For Israel minimizes human sinfulness and stresses human capability of obedience and faithfulness; people are free to obey. As unified organisms, living souls, people have the power to live in the world as free spirits following the laws of God, for God's providential care is over all.

The Messiah and the Future

An important difference, often noted, between Eastern and Western religions is in their views of history: The Eastern is cyclical; time goes, as it were, in a circle so that ages repeat themselves. The Western Biblical doctrine of history sees it as moving from a beginning at Creation to an end, a fulfillment. Eschatology,* the doctrine of last things, expresses these ideas, and the Messiah is part of this teaching in Biblical religion. Israel not only looks backward to all that God did, but forward to what he is doing and wills to do for humankind. At first that end was thought of as only for Israel, and the special place of the land and the people remain as part of the Messianic hope. But it was broadened and universalized by the prophets to include all people. This was a corollary of an ethical monotheism which was implicitly and necessarily universal. Just as all peoples—including Jews—are under the rule or law of God, so all peoples share in the final fruition of God's holy will and purpose. The dream is not for Israel alone, but through them it is extended to all the world.

The Messiah is a Hebrew notion that has entered into world culture through Jewish faith. Literally, the Messiah is the Anointed Messiah or Kingly Champion of Israel, "Mashiah." More generally the Messiah is one who brings in a new era of peace, righteousness, and justice for the world. Messianic symbolism and ideas enter at many points into Jewish thought, ritual, and ethics, but the content and form of the Messianic hope has varied considerably and there is no standard theory for it now. During the Hitler extermination program, for example, Polish Jewish partisans, and prisoners en route to concentration camps and death, chanted *"ani me'emon,"* "I believe" the Messiah will come, the twelfth article of Maimonides' creed. At first the Messiah was a future scion of the house of David, a good king on whom rested the spirit of law and the fear of the Lord, who would bring in a reign of peace. The Davidic descent is a fixed feature of that doctrine. Under the pressure of persecution and suffering, the coming of a superhuman divine deliverer has sometimes been the form of the Messianic hope, but many modern Jews would make the ideal king an ordinary human being or even eliminate the idea of any specific individual deliverer.

The complement of the Messiah is the Messianic Age. Modern Jewish prayer books speak of the "Kingdom of God." Traditional terminology refers to the World to Come, and the Garden of Eden stands for Paradise or Heaven, in which the righteous are occupied with the study of Torah under God's guidance, so that they gain perfect understanding of it. Resurrection of the dead, a doctrine based on Biblical passages, is expressed in the traditional morning prayer. Maimonides included God's rewards and punishments, the resurrection of the dead, and the sure coming of the Messiah in his 13 articles of faith. Some Jews accept the doctrine of immortality but deny the resurrection of the body, and many modern Jews are skeptical about both. In the Seder* at the Passover a door is left open for Elijah, who is the Biblical messenger or announcer of the approach of the Messiah and coming of the Messianic Age. The Age is preceded by necessary suffering and sacrifice, and in the Bible Isaiah speaks of the Suffering Servant. Three specific characteristics of the final consummation are generally agreed to be: the assembly of all Israel in the Holy Land; triumph over all the forces of evil which oppose them; and a new age of peace, justice, and righteousness. For many modern Reform Jews the Messianic hope is in a gradual amelioration of conditions to produce a peaceful and just world order. For all Jews, the Messiah is still to come, because the proof that he is the Messiah will be the end of evil in the world and the establishment of the new age. The most significant modern form of Judaism's ancient hope is the focus on the geographical factor, the Holy Land itself. In the late nineteenth century the idea of the promised land, which had persevered through the centuries in the Jew's yearning for Zion (the spiritual synonym for Jerusalem), was renewed in the Zionist movement for the reclamation of the very land of Israel. This Zionist dream was realized in the establishment of Eretz Israel in 1948. Since then it has been the intellectual and spiritual homeland of the Jewish people. (A few Jews do not accept Zionism and Israel, because they represent a break with the ancient tradition that not until the actual end of the age will the Jews return to Israel.)

Maimonides' Articles of Faith

In the age of scholasticism, it was Maimonides, the supreme Jewish scholastic, who produced the best known statement of Jewish faith or dogma, Thirteen Articles of Faith. As written in the prayer books, it is in the form of a creed, with each article prefaced by "I believe," but that was not the original form. The creed, any creed, in Judaism is unusual. A summary of Maimonides' articles of faith is given by a modern scholar:

> Maimonides provided a definition of Judaism, a list of articles of faith he thought obligatory for every faithful Jew. These are as follows: (1) God's existence, (2) his unity, (3) his incorporeality, (4) his eternity, (5) the obligation to worship him alone, (6) prophecy, (7) Moses as the greatest of the prophets, (8) the divine origin of Torah, (9) the eternal validity of Torah, (10) God's knowledge of man's deeds, (11) his punishment of evil and rewarding of goodness, (12) his promise to send a Messiah, and (13) his promise to resurrect the dead. Though these philosophical principles were hotly debated and much criticized, ironically they achieved a place in the life of Judaic piety. In the end they were sung as a prayer in a hymn, Yigdal, which is always sung at the conclusion of synagogue prayer.[5]

WORSHIP: THE PEOPLE OF GOD RESPOND TO GOD

Like so much else in the Western Biblical religions, the central importance of public communal worship comes from the mother faith, Judaism. It is a natural expression of the spirit and heart of Biblical religion. For that religion is one of revelation and response: God speaks, calls, summons, and the people of faith respond. They are called to respond in many different ways, and about any religion it has often been pointed out that a merely verbal or outward response is not enough. With that comment any religious leader would agree. But the leader of a Biblical religion would have to add that in such a religion, where God has uttered an explicit and direct word to a specific group of people, it is incumbent on them to make an explicit, verbal response to God in return.

It is, moreover, a communal response because the revelation from God is directed to a community, not simply to individuals. This communal element of Judaism has been stressed in our account, because it is in fact a key aspect of the religion: They are the *people* of Israel. Nowhere is this ethnic aspect of

Hanukkah lamp (Courtesy, Judah L. Magnes Memorial Museum, Berkeley. Photo, Ward J. Fellows).

Judaism more apparent than in its worship and ritual. For the ritual comes out of the history of the people, and most of the Biblical festivals arise from some actual event in the history of the nation. The cult of Judaism is in this sense nationalistic or parochial in its origin and core. We shall see that the ethic, like the religion as a whole, is universalistic in intent. But the historic, specific, Jewish nature and content of the festivals are unquestionably particularistic. It is the Jewish people, to whom God spoke and who experienced the events, who respond to God in their worship.

In that communal response are blended many voices, each one adding his or her word to the collective response. The unity is meant to be in heart and purpose, not simply in the unanimous voice. The Talmud describes this worship as *avodah sheh bah-lev*, "the service of the heart." Each one adds a particular voice, expresses personal praise, voices individual needs as part of the common response to God's word, in the synagogue—or the church or mosque, for that matter. Traditionally, Jewish worship is not cold, staid, formal, but warm, emotional, impulsive, enthusiastic, allowing scope for the expression of personal joy in the Lord.

How Israel Learned to Worship God

To tell the full story of how Israel learned to worship God would require telling the full story of the Jews, because their worship—like their beliefs—

comes out of their history, their experience. Only a few central historical and Biblical factors can be mentioned here.

Anyone who reads the Bible knows that the formal worship of God by the Hebrews from the age of the Patriarchs on centered in sacrifices of plants and animals on altars, and that during the centuries of the temple at Jerusalem it was the central place of such sacrifices. The Deuteronomic reform under King Josiah of Judah was intended to purify the cult of foreign and pagan elements, and centralization of the sacrifices at Jerusalem was the chief method for control of the purity of the sacrifice. Josiah led the people in a solemn acceptance of the new law book, and it was therefore with Deuteronomy that the movement began by which Judaism changed from a religion of sacrifice to the religion of a book. The local synagogue as the place of worship for Jews outside Jerusalem became more important, and the synagogue puts the book in the central place once occupied by the altar of sacrifice. That is the case both figuratively and literally: The Ark is central in the synagogue, and there is no altar.

During the time before and after the exile, a complex of events—as was suggested in our section on the development of the religion—radically altered the character of Jewish religion. The political and social upheavals of the fall of Jerusalem, the exile, and the return profoundly affected Jewish consciousness. Prophets like Jeremiah and Ezekial reinterpreted the relation between God and the Jews to put more stress on the inward personal or individual response and responsibility, and less on the nation as an undivided whole, a collectivity in which the individual did not matter. Thus Jeremiah spoke of a new covenant "in their inward parts," and Ezekiel said that the way to exalt the holiness of God was for individuals to observe the rules of worship according to the strict requirements of the law. This trend toward personal piety is also reflected in such books as the Psalms and Proverbs, and was stressed in the renewal of the covenant by Ezra and Nehemiah. Rabbinic Judaism, study and observance of the Law, became the religion of Israel. In effect, it replaced the sacrificial cult in which the priest served on behalf of or instead of all the people, although, of course, the temple sacrifices continued until 70 C.E. One of the sayings of Rabbi Nathan illustrates the movement from temple cult to acts of mercy in Judaism:

> Once Rabban Johanan ben Zakkai was going out of Jerusalem, with Rabbi Joshua walking behind him. When he (Joshua) saw the ruins of the Sanctuary, he said, "Woe for us, for the destruction of this place in which the transgressions of (the people) Israel are atoned!" He (ben Zakkai) said to him: "my son, do not grieve yourself; we have another equally efficacious atonement." And what is it? Deeds of lovingkindness, as Scripture states: "for I have desired lovingkindness, and not sacrifices."[6]

The last formative external factor was the series of events under Roman rule, culminating in the destruction of city and temple in 135 C.E. After that Judaism learned to live and worship by synagogue and Torah, not by temple and altar, for they were no more.

Times and Places

A nineteenth-century German rabbi, Sampson Hirsch, said, "The catechism of
the Jew is his calendar." The Jewish New Year falls in September or October,
and the old Jewish civil year began then. But the liturgical calendar for religious festivals begins in the spring of the year. That is why the New Year is
counted as the first day of the seventh month; it is the liturgical calendar, following a lunar cycle computed at 29½ days, which is followed. (Seven years
out of 19 an extra month is added, to make up the total days of a sidereal
year.) The round of Jewish holidays and holy days begins with Passover in the
spring, and continues throughout the yearly cycle. These festivals and fasts
make up the full round of Jewish observances, and these observances constitute the faith of a Jew. That is what Rabbi Hirsch meant by his statement.

A list follows, showing the name, Jewish calendar date, and approximate
secular calendar months for the major festivals followed by many Jews. (Calendar dates are complicated by the fact that the Jewish day begins at sunset or
evening, hence the festival begins at the evening hour when the previous day
ends.)

Jewish month (approximate secular month)

   Nisan (March or April)
      14—Passover Eve
      15–21—Passover (Pesach*)
   Iyyar (April or May)
      5—Israel Independence Day
   Sivan (May or June)
      6, 7—Shabuoth* (Festival of Weeks; Pentecost)
   Tishri (September or October)
      1—Rosh Hashanah* (New Year Day) "Days of Awe" (Orthodox:
      Tishri 1 and 2)
      10—Yom Kippur* (Day of Atonement)
      15—Sukkoth* (Feast of Tabernacles) begins
      21—Hashanah Rabbah (seventh day)
      22—Shemini Atzeret (eighth day)
      23—Simchat Torah (Rejoicing in Torah) (ninth day)
   Kislev (November or December)
      25—Hanukkah* begins (eight days), to the second of Tebet (De-
      cember or January)
   Adar (February or March)
      14—Purim (Feast of Esther)

In the above list Passover, Shabuoth, Rosh Hashanah, Yom Kippur, and
Sukkoth are the traditional holy days. Hanukkah in recent times has had increased emphasis as the Jewish holiday near Christmas. The importance of Israel justifies the inclusion of Independence Day as a major modern date, and its
inclusion is consonant with the national character of several other Jewish holy

Boy and girl dressed for Purim. Safad, Israel, 1974 (Ward J. Fellows).

days. Likewise Purim, although not technically a holy day, is of major importance to many Jews; in Israel, for example, small boys and girls dress in costume for the day.

Synagogues—or "temples" as they are usually called—look much like Christian churches from the outside. Inside, the platform is occupied by one or two lecterns and several chairs, and is dominated by the Ark containing the scrolls of the Torah. A curtain hangs in front of the Ark, and a perpetual light hangs overhead. Although the seven-branched candlestick or menorah is frequently used in Jewish symbolism or decoration, it is not used in the synagogue as an actual candelabrum, because it is forbidden to have in the synagogue an exact replica of the equipment used in the original Temple. Other types of candelabra may be used. On the walls will be tablets for the names of those who are being remembered after their death.

The Sabbath

The Roman writer Seneca sneered at the Jews for their day of rest and worship, but modern psychology gives a different verdict on the practical helpfulness of rest. The Sabbath was not intended simply as a useful expedient, but also as a duty to make the day holy because God is holy; because even God rested after his labors, people should rest. From this arises the strictness of the injunctions against all work on the Sabbath, which have sometimes seemed excessive to outsiders and which are not always observed nowadays even by the orthodox. Nevertheless, the force of the custom remains, with many Jews marking the day by contemplation, prayer, and recreation. Through its adoption by Christians in a modified form, the idea of a Sabbath rest has entered into modern culture, with salutary effects for everyone. Many Jewish writers consider this institution of the Sabbath the most significant Jewish contribution to the pattern of modern life. Some would also say that Sabbath observance is the most important single way in which a Jew expresses his or her belief and follows the Law. A renowned mystic in Poland, the Gerer Rabbi, is said to have asked only one question of a young Reform rabbi in 1925: "Do you observe the Sabbath?"

The scriptural authority for Sabbath is the fourth of the Ten Commandments, equaling the second (against graven images) in the length of the explanatory passage. "Remember the sabbath day, to keep it holy" (Exodus 20:8) is the bare command. Beyond the scriptural injunction there is no uniform rule binding for all Jews, and therefore the following description has to ignore many differences in actual practice.

In the home, Sabbath begins, like all festivals, at sunset or a little before. The lighting of the "Sabbath Lights," as the candles are called, is one of the traditional duties of the Jewish wife. Holding her hands before her eyes so that she may not behold the light until she has pronounced the blessing, she recites: "Blessed art Thou, O Lord our God, King of the Universe, Who has sanctified us with Thy commandments, and commanded us to kindle the Sabbath lights." Theoretically the Sabbath Eve service is at dusk, and the family returns home afterward for the Sabbath meal. In actual practice nowadays that is not possible for most people; generally Sabbath Eve services are after the meal, in the evening. The meal is preceded by a special blessing, the *kiddush** or "sanctification" of the Sabbath. Those who attend the longer Sabbath and festival morning services are expected not to eat until afterward. Sabbath ends about half an hour after sunset with *havdalah*, a blessing of farewell to the Sabbath. As literature, history, and the experience of millions of Jews testify, the Sabbath blesses them.

The principal occasions for common worship in the synagogue are: (1) daily services of prayer, especially in the morning but including forms for afternoon and evening; (2) Sabbath Eve and Day; (3) the festivals as seen in the list already given; and (4) Day of Atonement.

The typical Sabbath Eve service includes prayers, hymns, chants, and readings from the prayer book, which are led by the cantor in ecclesiastical vestments, who is assisted by a choir and organ in Reform and some Conservative congregations. The rabbi delivers a sermon and discusses congregational matters, and the lay president of the congregation may discuss some business. Any Jewish layman may lead in worship if there is a quorum of 10 adult males, and women are now included in the quorum (*minyan*), except in Orthodox usage. On Sabbath morning (Saturday) in addition to the prayers, hymns, psalms, and other elements, rabbis may explain the Biblical readings. On special days there are different liturgical materials befitting the occasion, but the general pattern is the same. The *Kaddish*,* from Aramaic for "holy," is a doxology recited with congregational responses at the close of the service and its sections. Portions of the Torah are read by special functionaries or selected readers at Sabbath morning and festivals, new moons, and fast days. Hebrew and English are both used in the service; in general, the more orthodox the congregation the more Hebrew is used.

The Holy Days

Two of the holy days carry more solemn themes of judgment and repentance than the other three, and are sometimes called the High Holy Days.

DAYS OF AWE—YAMIN NORAIM

"The Solemn or Awe-Inspiring Days" is the descriptive term for Rosh Hashanah (New Year) and Yom Kippur (Day of Atonement), stressing judgment before God. Although there are specific Biblical origins for both, most of the liturgy is post-Biblical. Whereas the other festival days are closely associated with particular national events or eras in Jewish history, these two are more general in their challenge to a spiritual accounting. The period is one of repentance and return to God, spiritual renewal.

The New Year, for various reasons related to the calendar, is observed for two days, the first and second of Tishri, at least in Orthodox and Conservative congregations. The observance is characterized by soul-searching, penitence, and the theme of judgment, with both synagogue services and a home observance of the New Year. The sounding of the ram's horn during the month preceding Rosh Hashanah at the synagogue service each morning has prepared the congregation for the day. Then on Rosh Hashanah itself three blasts of the ram's horn or *shofar* are the most dramatic and meaningful parts of the ceremony. The theme of God as King of the Universe is emphasized both in the prayers of the day and in the trumpet blasts before, during, and after the prayer. Breaking the hush after the reading of the Torah portion, the sound of the *shofar* is heavy with associations from Israel's history and with each person's thoughts of the year past and the one to come. The day also includes other special occasions of prayer, and sometimes, in the afternoon of the first day, an ancient ceremony interpreted as casting one's sins into a river. Special foods are eaten on the evening of the two days, and greeting cards may be sent to friends. The day immediately after Rosh Hashanah is a day of fasting.

The 10 days following are Days of Penitence, during which the people are expected to consider their conduct and how they may better live a life of obedience to the Law and blessing for others. On the ninth of Tishri, the day preceding Yom Kippur, traditional meals are eaten, and an oral prayer of confession is made in the afternoon prayer. The Day of Atonement itself is marked by fasting and special prayers at the synagogue, with time for meditation; confession is mostly personal and unspoken, but there are oral unison prayers. Before the day itself, for wrongs done to other people one is expected to seek forgiveness from the person wronged. A framework is provided for this by custom on the eve of Atonement, and a general prayer of forgiveness of others is included in the service.

The service on the eve of Yom Kippur includes the *Kol Nidre* prayer of absolution and remission of ceremonial vows, with its distinctive plaintive melody. Services at the synagogue continue all day; at each one there is a confession of sin and prayer for forgiveness. At one point the members, or some elders, ceremonially kneel, something which is not done during the rest of the year. An important feature is the Yizkor, a great Memorial Service in which departed family, friends, and martyrs are remembered. Frequently the Ark is opened at the time of special prayers and hymns. The *Neilah* (closing) service ends the day with the note of hope and assurance in God's mercy, whose gates have been open all the day.

MOSAIC FESTIVALS

The three other great festivals are Biblical or Mosaic in origin, being from the Pentateuch. Passover in the spring still includes agricultural features; it is the great festival looking back to the deliverance from Egypt. From the story in Exodus the unleavened bread has now become the chief ceremonial and symbolic feature, so that the Feast of Unleavened Bread is the other name for what has become one continuous festival, and the matzoh or unleavened bread is to be eaten for the entire week. Extreme measures are taken by the pious to avoid any ritual contamination by leavened bread, and a ceremonial "search" for any leaven (yeast) or leavened (raised) bread is made in the house before the Seder. The Seder is the home ceremonial meal service on Passover Eve, and has become the main observance, so that synagogues usually have a communal Seder for those unable to observe it at home, and families often get together for the meal. All aspects of the meal carry symbolic significance, which is brought out by questions from children that the father answers with the story of their bondage and redemption, in order to enhance the joys of liberty. Unleavened bread (affliction), bitter herbs (slavery), and other dishes carry specific associations. Wine, songs, and hymns enliven the occasion. Synagogue services are also conducted on the first and seventh days of Passover, which lasts for seven days.

Shabuoth or Pentecost is tied in time to Passover. In ancient Palestine the second night of Passover was observed with the sacrifice of the first sheaf of

Torah cover (Courtesy of Judah L. Magnes Memorial Museum, Berkeley. Photo, Ward J. Fellows).

barley, marking the beginning of barley harvest. Some Jews continue the practice. Pentecost was originally the festival of wheat harvest, 50 days (Greek *pentekostos* means "fiftieth") or seven weeks after the beginning of harvest during Passover. It is therefore also called "The Feast of Weeks." Its spiritual significance now centers on the giving of the Law to Moses, the Ten Commandments. Freedom for the Jews after Egypt did not mean the absence of law, but rather the God-given Law for the free soul, in place of slavery to

Pharaoh. A further significance has been given to the day by making it (as in Christianity) a day for Confirmation of boys and girls, in Reform and Conservative Judaism.

Sukkoth is from *sukkah*, "booth," in which according to tradition Jews lived, or at least ate their meals, in remembrance of Israel's sojourn in "booths" while in the wilderness. Hence it is the Feast of Booths. The harvest festival theme is the other note of the occasion, seen in the fruits and vegetables that may hang in the booth, and in the name "Festival of Ingathering." The booth itself is a rude shelter of poles and branches, and the family may build one in the yard. The synagogue will surely have one somewhere, since many families, especially in the city, cannot have their own. The symbolism is meant to recall Jews to their dependence on God and his mercy and care, like Israel in the wilderness. The *lulab*, a cluster of a palm branch, three myrtle twigs, and two willow branches, is waved, along with a citron, in the morning service, to show that God, the giver of gifts, is everywhere. The seventh day includes special prayers for rain, and the "eighth day of solemn assembly" is the climax of the season of thanks for harvest. A ninth day is set aside for "Rejoicing in the Law," a reminder that more than material things come from God, and the completion of the cycle of readings from the Pentateuch is celebrated by carrying the scrolls from the Ark in a procession through the synagogue.

Hanukkah, Purim, Israel Independence

Three festival days look back to triumphs of Israel. The victory of conscience against Antiochus Epiphanes' attempt to impose pagan rites, in 168–165 B.C.E., is celebrated at Hanukkah. The record of these events is found in the books of Maccabees in the *Apocrypha*. The Maccabean triumph was marked by rededication of the Temple, which is reflected in the name Hanukkah, an Aramaic word meaning "rededication." The Temple lights were rekindled then, from which comes the central symbolism of the Feast—the lighting of candles in an eight-branched candelabrum during the eight days of the holiday. The giving of gifts has become popular among many Jews at this time; songs are sung and games played.

Purim is a joyful celebration of Queen Esther's vindication and the victory over Haman, as recounted in the book of Esther.

Israel Independence Day is contemporary and relevant, and many Jews identify with Israel by observing it.

Home and Personal Occasions

Like most other religions, Judaism marks special occasions in the life of families and individuals by prayer and gratitude to God for his blessings. A male child is circumcised on the eighth day, and a girl is named at the temple service on the Sabbath or some other day after her birth. Both are instructed in home and synagogue, and on the Sabbath after his thirteenth birthday a boy

becomes *bar mitsvah*,* son of the commandment. He is now mature enough
to obey the law and answer for himself. A similar *bat mitsvah** for girls takes
place in many congregations. In other communities a confirmation ceremony
for boys and girls from 14 to 16 is conducted, in place of *bar* or *bat mitsvah*.
Marriage and funeral ceremonies are conducted by the rabbi.

Kosher Laws

Many Orthodox and Conservative Jews observe the dietary rules known as
Kosher laws. Various other considerations such as health and cleanliness may
have operated in the institution of the laws, but their fundamental meaning is
religious: God's special rules for his special people. By the original prescriptions in Leviticus and Deuteronomy certain foods are prohibited, such as pork
and rabbit meat, as well as some birds and shellfish. There are also restrictive
conditions on the permitted foods, and only approved or kosher methods of
slaughter and preparation of animal food may be used. There are further rules
about utensils and dishes. Jews vary widely in their attitude toward and observance of Kosher laws; in general, the more conservative groups tend to be
more careful and strict about them. To them they are significant and meaningful practices which further link the observant Jew in body as well as soul to
God who gives the laws.

ETHICAL AND SOCIAL ASPECTS OF JUDAISM

In moving from cult to ethics is there a conflict? Do they stand in opposition to
each other? It has been alleged that there is, that the demands of ritual observance conflict with ethical norms of conduct. This view sets the priest against
the prophet, and finds the former lacking. It is true that some of the prophets
denounced meaningless ritual and animal sacrifices, as Amos did, proclaiming
the Word of the Lord:

I hate, I despise your feasts, and I will take no delight in your solemn assem-
blies. . . .
Take thou away from Me the noise of thy songs;
    And let me not hear the melody of thy psalteries.
But let justice well up as waters, and righteousness as a mighty stream.
(Amos 5:21, 23, 24)

But there were specific reasons and occasions for his denunciations, and the
prophetic protest was not a complete condemnation of all ritual. It is true, as
we have seen, that the forms and practices of the Jewish cult are associated
with the life and experience of Israel, and in this sense are nationalistic.
Yet the moral and spiritual truths of God are implicitly universal. This is a

characteristic of Jewish religion. From the unique people comes the law of God for mankind. Rabbi Abraham A. Newman writes:

> Judaism therefore appears under two aspects: the universal and the national. As a system of religious thought it is transcendent and universal. As a religious cult it is characterized by historic associations and even geographic coloring. Its ethical principles embrace all mankind; its religious discipline binds only its own adherents.[7]

Divisions of Judaism

Before dealing with the ethics of Judaism we should say something about the different forms of institutionalized Judaism, particularly as seen in the United States. With nearly 6 million Jews in over 4,000 congregations, the United States has the largest Jewish population in the world. Judaism has adapted itself to modern secular culture and American religious pluralism by following the pattern of compartmentalized religion.

There are three main divisions of organized American Judaism: Orthodox, Conservative, and Reform in order from most traditional to most liberal. Reconstructionism is now recognized as a fourth division. They have their differences, but these are rarely seen by the world at large. History and blood make them one, and they share the same Torah, observe the same festivals, and, of course, pray to the same God. Whence, then, arose the divisions? The answer seems to be that the divisions embody different answers to the problem of living as a religious Jew in the modern world. That problem is basically the same for the Jew as for the person of any other faith. The modern individual goes to school or work, buys or sells, attends a play or a movie, drives the car across the country, votes, serves in public office, simply as an individual citizen, not as a member of a particular religion. For the Jew, however, that is a comparatively new situation, and the old patterns of religious institutions have had to change. The question was, how much of the old traditions and rules to keep and how much to change? These groups began in Europe, because more Jews were there in the nineteenth century; but now their main strength is in the United States.

REFORM

Reform Judaism began in Germany in the early nineteenth century, when about 50 young men in Berlin formed a society for scientific study of Judaism. Abraham Geiger (1810–1874) had most to do with starting it. This group began the ferment and movement toward modernization. After 1850 the movement centered in the United States, under the leadership of Rabbi Isaac M. Wise. Another early leader expressed the reformist tendency this way: "Not that man will ever be able to dispense altogether with visible signs, but the expression and form of these must necessarily change with different stages of

Jews Crying near the Wall of Solomon, Verestchagin, 1842–1904. (Courtesy of Judah L. Magnes Memorial Museum, Berkeley. Photo, Ward J. Fellows).

culture, national customs, industrial, social, and civil conditions."[8] The movement came of age with the founding of Hebrew Union College in Cincinnati in
1875. The national reform organization is the Union of American Hebrew Congregations.

ORTHODOX

German Jews who recognized the need for coming to terms with new conditions but wanted to adhere to the Torah as closely as possible were the Neo-
Traditionalists or Neo-Orthodox. Their first major spokesman, Sampson
Raphael Hirsch (1808–1888), "felt that it was necessary to save as much of
Jewish tradition as possible by discovering a way of giving meaning to the old
tradition in the new situation."[9] His achievement was in working out a formula
that justified traditionalism and yet was consistent with modern intellectual
and social conditions. Although American Orthodoxy has not succeeded in
agreeing on just what should be in such a formula, they are a strong party,
working together in the Union of Orthodox Jewish Congregations.

CONSERVATIVE

A group of American rabbis called the Historical School represented a middle
position; they saw the need for change but wanted to keep it as much as possible within the historical traditions of the Jewish people. Once organized as the
Conservative movement, it grew rapidly after about 1890, the Jewish Theological Seminary of America having begun work in 1887. The union of Conservative
Congregations is known as the United Synagogue of America, established in
1913. The Conservative movement agreed with the Reform in wanting to reject
the dominance of the *Shulhan Arukh*. This was a detailed codification of Jewish laws for every moment of the day for the ordinary person, printed in 1565.

THE JEWISH COMMUNITY IN AMERICA

All three of these groups, but especially the Reform and Conservative, have
built many large synagogues, especially during the post–World War II years.
They provide for the traditional triple function of the synagogue—a sanctuary
for prayer, classrooms and library for study, and a social hall for assembly.
Many of them maintain their own daily as well as weekly schools. Of course, it
is the people and the living faith that matter. In these terms, the synagogue has
proved itself in the American scene. Any city that has a Jewish congregation
feels their collective and individual influence for good in social issues and charity, in educational, cultural, and civil life.

The tradition of learning is upheld in the American rabbinate, each of the
three major groups having its own seminary where rabbis study for five years.
Acceptance, training, and ordination of candidates for the rabbinate is conducted by the seminary. Obviously, this serves as a guide and control in re-

cruitment, training, and indoctrination of Jewish spiritual leadership. The rabbi is an interpreter of the Torah and a spiritual counselor, not a priest with sacred powers and status. He is a layman who is learned in the Bible, the Talmud, and the later literature based on them. As head of an organization, he or she is also an administrator and organizer in the American pattern of denominational religions. Most synagogues also employ a cantor or reader, who may wear vestments during the service, and who leads the music, chants, and prayers. The cantor is professionally trained for this function, and so takes a more active role in formal worship than the rabbi.

The Basis of Jewish Ethics

Biblical monotheism is ethical monotheism; therefore, Biblical ethics are theistic ethics. God's moral righteousness is definitive both of his power and of the law for human beings. The spiritual meaning and expression of the divine for persons is seen in the moral and ethical laws that God provides. The meaning and implications of this fundamental truth will be worked out in the rest of this section and in the two following sections, The Content of Biblical Ethics, and The Motive and Fulfillment of Jewish Ethics. There are four characteristics of the Law, which follow from its basis in ethical monotheism: The Law is Absolute, the Law is Universal, the Law is Revealed, and the Law is Humane.

THE LAW IS ABSOLUTE

This claim flies in the face of all speculative, relativistic, and secular ethical theories, but it is the starting point of Jewish ethics. It is seen or symbolized in a masterpiece of Genesis legend that has been a stumbling block for many commentators—the "binding" of Isaac. It is billed as a "test" of Abraham, in which he is called to sacrifice his "only" son—there are other children, but Isaac is the child of promise by Sarah—as a burnt offering on Mt. Moriah.

> And Abraham took the wood of the burnt offering, and laid it upon Isaac his son; and he took in his hand the fire and the knife; and they went both of them together. And Isaac spoke unto Abraham his father, and said "My father." And he said, "Here am I, my son." And he said, "Behold the fire and the wood; but where is the lamb for a burnt offering?" And Abraham said: "God will provide Himself the lamb for a burnt offering, my son." So they went both of them together (Genesis 22:6-8).

But when Abraham lifted his hand to slay his son, God stopped him and provided a ram in Isaac's stead, and promised that he would indeed bless Abraham. There are many meanings and lessons in this story, but the central point is that God's command is the ultimate basis of the Law, and the sole and ultimate source of the Law in God's word. No prior empirical, human, axiological (values), or deontological (rules) considerations determine God's commands. He speaks, and before him there is no other, *no* other. Theistic ethics of all

*Torah cases and curtain, and Eternal Light. (Courtesy of
Judah L. Magnes Memorial Museum, Berkeley. Photo, Ward
J. Fellows).*

three Western faiths agree: What God says is holy or just; by his word he constitutes it.

> These laws are just simply the inscrutable and mysterious will of the perfect God.
>
> It is written, "This is an ordinance of the Law" (Num. xix, 2). Who has made it? Who has ordered it? Who has decreed it? Is it not the Unique Only One of the world? And he has said, "I have enjoined an ordinance; I have decreed a decree: it is not permitted to you to transgress my decree." (Num. R., Hukkat, xix, 1)[10]

THE LAW IS UNIVERSAL

The prophets articulated for Israel this truth, which came out of the people of Israel itself, in spite of their slowness to see it and reluctance to accept it. The entire prophetic tradition, including such an unpretentious book as Jonah, proclaims that the Law is not only for Israel—because God's love and care is over all people. Isaiah says, "The Lord will whistle for the fly which is at the sources of the streams of Egypt, and for the bee which is in the land of Assyria" (Isaiah 7:18) to come up on the land of Israel as his instruments of judgment. In Jeremiah 25, the prophet says that the Lord has an indictment against the nations; "He is entering into judgment with all flesh." The Law is the blessing Israel carries for all the world; its destiny is to proclaim that Law to all peoples. "And many peoples shall come, and say: 'Come, let us go up to the mountain of the Lord, to the house of the God of Jacob; that he may teach us his ways and that we walk in his paths.' For out of Zion shall go forth law, and the word of the Lord from Jerusalem" (Isaiah 2:3). By all the logic of the call of Abraham, the long travail of the people, the message of the prophets, and the teachings of the rabbis, the one God's one Law is for one world. In the full faith of Israel nothing could be more certain than this.

THE LAW IS REVEALED

Again the point is comparatively simple and familiar, but its implications are not always realized. The Torah is, in the first place, not a human construction, in spite of the centuries of study and discussion and the uncountable words spent on it. For the point of mishnah is to repeat or restate, and the point of midrash is to interpret; neither is primary or original legislation. Torah is not a committee report, or legislation by a human agency, or theoretical and academic construction. It is not discovered or found or intuited by spiritual geniuses. It is given, pronounced, uttered by the mouth of the Lord before it is interpreted by human beings. The first creative word of God in Genesis was, "Let there be light." It is by light that we see and know what to do, in the moral realm as in all others, and the light, says the Bible, comes from God.

THE LAW IS HUMANE

The divine lawgiver is the great and terrible judge, but he is also loving and merciful. At first, in the Bible, his mercy was shown only toward Israel and those who obeyed his laws, but ultimately it was seen as toward all humanity, indeed all creation. This too is a necessary corollary of his nature; his love and mercy must be not only for his people Israel but for all people. So said the prophets. The reason in human circumstances for the humanity of the Law is the frailty and imperfection of all persons. God sees that human beings are limited, weak, sinful creatures, and has mercy on them. Therefore people should show the same consideration to other people. One Biblical paradigm (ideal

Shofar. European, nineteenth century (Courtesy, Judah L. Magnes Memorial Museum, Berkeley. Photo, Ward J. Fellows).

example) for this is in the prophet Hosea, where God is like a forgiving husband of an unfaithful wife: "Go yet, love a woman beloved of her friend and an adulteress, even as the Lord loveth the children of Israel . . ." (Hos. 3:1). The psalmists many times declare to the soul that the Lord "encompasseth thee with loving kindness and tender mercies" (Psalm 103:4).

The Talmud develops this same theme:

> *Middat ha-Rahamim* (Measure of Mercy). God tried mercy in the rule of the universe. This failed as did strict justice. He then applied the rule of justice tempered by mercy. This proved to be effective. This *Midrashic* moral is intended to guide human behavior—to teach that mercy is indispensable to justice.[11]

In the chapter of the book on Jewish words from which the preceding passage is quoted, there are at least 10 such key terms from Jewish moral wisdom, directed to this motif of forbearance, mercy, and compassion in moral judgment and the application of the Torah.

The Content of Biblical Ethics

The Law of God is the will of God for the world. He says what he wants people to do, how people should behave; the explanation or justification for the Law is that God wants it that way. This is another instance of the way the Judaeo-Christian Bible provides the substance of our culture: For the ordinary person, the basis of morality is the word of God; moral laws are God's laws. For that reason our culture at large is not concerned about ethical theories. (At least it was not formerly; things may be changing in this regard.) Philosophical ethics treats the religious sanction as only one among many possible justifications of morality, but for most people it is still an adequate explanation.

THE DIVINE COMMANDMENTS

The Ten Commandments and a few other sections of the Pentateuch have been called "apodictic" laws, meaning absolutely certain and necessary. They are bare positive and negative commands, unqualified and categorical statements of God's will, according to this understanding and description. "Thou shalt" and "Thou shalt not" are the older and more vivid terms, as in the Ten Commandments of Exodus 20. These laws, being unquestioned, fundamental, a priori propositions as it were, are the basis of the fuller development of the Talmud. The rabbinic tradition sets the number of commands at 613. "R. Simlai said: Six hundred and thirteen commandments were given to Moses, 365 negative commandments, answering to the number of the days of the year, and 248 positive commandments, answering to the number of a man's members" [archaic for bodily parts, limbs, or organs.][12] Many virtues, in the sense of more general moral practices, wider than specific commandments, are important in Jewish ethics. Among them are justice and righteousness. Justice (*mishpat*) is what God demands of humanity: "Hate evil, and love good, and establish justice (*mishpat*) in the gate" (Amos 5:15). The reference to the gate where judges sat suggests the context of *mishpat* as a formal decision, final and binding. It is the basis of the prophetic Hebraic demand for justice in the social order, as part of God's fundamental and unquestionable Law. Righteousness (*sedeq*) is the conduct enjoined by God which brings good results in the life of the world. "And it shall be righteousness unto us, if we observe to do all this commandment before the Lord our God, as He hath commanded us" (Deuteronomy 6:25). We will discuss righteousness later, as part of the motive and fulfillment of the Torah.

THE HUMAN INTERPRETATION AND APPLICATION OF THE TORAH

The details of the meaning and application of the Torah are the great preoccupation and achievement of Jewish religion. The form of conditional law is, "If someone commits a certain crime, then he or she is liable to such and such a punishment"; or, "When someone does this or that, then you shall find out what the circumstances were and decide the application of the law accordingly." It involved endless discussion about the application or interpretation of the Law in particular or specific terms; for the Law by its nature is general or universal, while, as a popular saying has it," circumstances alter cases." The results of this vast body of elaboration, discussion, clarification, and interpretation are in the Talmud. The continuing duty of the rabbi, the scribe in modern form, is to interpret and explain the Torah in these terms for his or her people.

Thereby arises the body of tradition, which becomes a second vehicle of revelation. The entire opening scene of the musical and movie *Fiddler on the Roof* is on the theme of tradition. The people of Anatefka are like a fiddler on the roof, who is trying to play a pleasant tune without breaking his neck, and what enables them to keep their balance is: Tradition! It guides all their lives, gives each one his or her place, dress, and duties. Tradition—the very life of the community of faith itself, the established institutions and practices—constitutes ethical guidance and support. Of course, this is true of all religious groups; the unique feature in Judaism is the method for institutionalization of tradition.

The Motive and Fulfillment of Jewish Ethics

A central and important part of Jewish piety is the system of blessings. In all circumstances of life the Jew is to bless God for his goodness and love: upon arising, before eating, when viewing the stars or the ocean, in undertaking a journey, at all times. The basis for this is the love and pity of God for us. The only possible attitude for a person to show in response to God is love and trust. Inasmuch as God wants all to be happy and blessed, he gives his laws for the way to find blessedness. Human response is, therefore, love and trust, and our concern is to find out what God wants us to do, because that is what is best for us. "Oh, how love I thy law!" says the Psalmist. Not only that, the child of God wants to please and delight the Father of mankind, and this she does by obedience above all. The Bible and the later portions of the Torah are permeated by this theme; it is the key to understanding the Jews' intense concern for the Law. Study of, knowledge of, the Law is therefore both a first and last joy of the devout Jew.

The debate has never been settled as to which is more important, study or action, although there are references to support each side. Let us quote:

> Famous and familiar is the following, which attempts to solve the problem as to the relative merits of study and practice.
>
> > Once R. Tarfon and the elders sat in the upper chamber of the house of Nitzah in Lydda, and the question was raised, "Is study greater, or doing?" R. Tarfon said, "Doing was greater." Akiba said, "Study was greater." Then they all said that study was greater, for it led to doing. (Kid. 40b)[13]

Nevertheless, there is no question about the importance of action. Righteousness as conduct in accordance with God's laws for the ordering of human life is a prime requirement of the one to whom God speaks. But there is a problem here in the discrepancy between divine expectation and human performance. The problem and the solution have been so well stated for Judaism by Rabbi Bamberger that we quote him at some length. (The "Paul" referred to is the Christian apostle Paul.)

> Their sane and tolerant outlook enabled the Rabbis to solve in their own way the contradiction between God's demands and human performance. No mortal man can fulfill completely and perfectly all the commandments of the Torah. This realization had plunged Paul into despair, until he concluded that the whole purpose of the Torah was to reveal to man his hopeless plight and so rouse him to seek salvation through divine grace.

The Rabbis meet the difficulty through their teaching of repentance, or to use their own word, return (*t'shuvo*). Both the idea and the word are Biblical, but are more fully developed in rabbinic thought. God expects us to obey His law; but when we fail—as fail we must sometimes—we should recognize our shortcomings, confess them with honest regret, and return to God and His Torah. Sincere repentance will not be rejected by God, the loving Father of mankind. If the sinner has even the smallest impulse to do better, God's grace will strengthen that weak effort at improvement.[14]

What the religious person wants above all is to maintain this relationship with God. Each one shows and does this by acceptance of the belief in the will and purpose of God, and by doing God's will. But if he does break a law he has not thereby destroyed the relationship. He may go to the synagogue in order to say that he is sorry to have disobeyed and that the relationship is still there. The sincere religious person often goes to service precisely because she is not perfect, in order to reaffirm her basic relationship of loyalty to the total will and command of God.

But of course the righteous person obeys the commandments of God as far as she can. She is expected to follow and not to flout the law. Deliberate, ostentatious, and consistent lawbreaking makes one a lawbreaker before both God and others. Whereas keeping the Law—righteousness in the sense that we have been describing—makes one part of God's order and brings beneficial results for the person and the society. The typical, actual, practical attitude of Jewish morality is that of the book of Proverbs, where the righteous person is the one who conforms to the order of the world which God has provided in his laws. Proverbs says that in a sense it pays to keep the Law, because in the long run it is better for the individual himself, as well as society. This doctrine is consistent with the Biblical picture of the world as God's world, ruled by his laws.

Some problems remain, for the Jew and any moral person, in a naughty world, because that world does not always follow God's laws. Hence even in the Proverbs occasionally, and in the Psalms throughout, the righteous may and do suffer, while the wicked often flourish like the green bay tree. This conflict is never fully resolved, and it is a problem for the religionist of any faith. It is impossible to demonstrate a 100 percent correlation between virtue and happiness. If it were, religion would not be necessary. The most honest and searching depiction of this dilemma in the Bible is in the book of Job. Job, a righteous man, is forced to face the fact that he cannot call God to account for his own sufferings. (This is the problem of theodicy—how to "justify God's ways to man," as Milton put it.) The final solution in Job, obscured by the later happy ending, is that Job can only humble himself before the superior power and wisdom of God: "Wherefore I abhor my words, and repent, seeing I am dust and ashes" (Job 42:6). Yet, even so, the Jew is to delight in the Law of God and to bless God at all times.

The righteous Jew rejoices in the Law and delights to praise the Lord who gives it. Some Jews believe that finally there will be the fulfillment—the

Messiah and the Messianic Age. Then the loose ends will be gathered up and righteousness will fully prevail. In the meantime, Judaism considers itself the custodian of the Torah, striving to know and follow it in all things. It looks on Christianity and Islam as outgrowths of Judaism and of the Law. Insofar as they proclaim the Law and point the way to the truth, they are good. But Judaism holds itself to be the chosen messenger of the moral laws of God, and of the principles and practices of the Jewish faith.

CONCLUSION

It has often been remarked that the preservation through history of the Jewish people is a standing miracle. In any event, the Jewish people of the Law is a fact, a specific, tangible, visible reality. Yet at the same time this people is a witness to moral reality, to spiritual laws from God. Thus in a new way Judaism itself serves as a religious purpose: As a people and a cult it is visible and real to the most skeptical unbeliever who accepts only verifiable perceptual evidence. But there is an indissoluble connection between the visible people and cult, and the invisible universal spiritual reality, for it is the same God back of both. Hence Judaism itself is a symbol of and witness to eternal and universal moral Law. Like a great bell, the Torah calls and recalls mankind to God's laws. Judaism sounds that bell, keeps it echoing down the corridors of time.

SUMMARY

The line of Western religion is set by Judaism, for the Jewish experience of God as recorded in the Bible and extended in Christianity became characteristic of Western religion and culture. Judaism is the religion of the people or culture, the Jews, and is not understandable apart from them: They count themselves the people of God, and Judaism is simply the religion of these people. The relation between the people and the faith is unique, in that the faith unfolds as a process of interaction between God and the people. For this reason their own history is at the same time the history of the religion, and its beliefs and practices come out of their experience, and thus their history. The Bible as the record of this relation between God and the Jews is, therefore, not simply a record of past events but gives the substance and meaning of the present faith.

The story begins with God, because in Western Biblical religions (including Islam in that list because of its Biblical roots, although it has its own Qur'an), nothing comes before God. When God speaks, things happen, creation and other prehistoric events first. After that, God spoke to Abraham, the progenitor, for the call or word of God is always primary at every crucial epoch of Israel's history. Certain other recurrent themes also appear at the outset. God promised to bless Abraham and through him all people—"promise" is

a key word. Abraham entered into a covenant or agreement with God—
"covenant" is another central Biblical category. Abraham led the tribe into
Canaan, and after him came Isaac and his son Jacob (renamed Israel), whose
sons were progenitors of the 12 tribes. When famine came they were saved by
Joseph, another son, who ruled under the Pharaoh in Egypt, where they mi-
grated. Centuries passed, and they were saved again, under the leadership of
Moses, who led them out of slavery in Egypt. Moses received for them God's
covenant, binding them to serve him as their one and only God, and, in return,
promising them blessings as his chosen people. Back in their "promised land,"
they nevertheless had to fight for it, while spiritually the Jewish people struggled to learn and practice the way of faith in one God and his Law.

Organized as a kingdom, their greatest king was David, who ever after was
looked back to as the ideal king and the model of the future king, the Messiah,
who will come to unite all the world under one God. Then the kingdom was
divided. First the northern, then the southern divisions were conquered, the
holy city of Jerusalem was lost, and the Jews were exiled. But later they returned, rebuilt their temple and city wall, and reestablished their laws and
ways. Their prophets taught them deeper truths and meaning of the Law and
showed them that one God meant one Law for all the world. The Jews were
obliged to teach that one Law to all people, thus making one the divided
world. When the Roman Empire conquered them they rebelled; Jerusalem and
the temple were again destroyed, and henceforth they lived by the Torah—the
Law and the book—and not by temple and altar. Most of them were scattered
into Asia, Africa, and Europe where they often suffered from prejudice and
persecution, so that they turned inward into their own communities. Only in
the eighteenth and nineteenth centuries did they finally gain a measure of freedom and merge with other peoples in Europe and America. Modern times have
seen the most traumatic event of all, the Holocaust or death of 6,000,000 Jews
under Hitler and the Nazis, and the dramatic reestablishment and military victories of the state of Israel. Out of this great saga came the sacred books of the
Jews and their beliefs and practices. The Bible is the one great book, but there
are also interpretations of and commentaries on the Torah, as well as philosophical works.

The beliefs of Judaism came out of the Jews' encounters with God and
thus center in their God as the one, almighty Creator and Lord of all things and
beings; the world and all in it are, therefore, creatures, limited and dependent
on God, and subject to his laws. As the sovereign Lord he is sacred and unap-
proachable, "awful" in the proper meaning of that word, and as Lawgiver he is
righteous. Yet he speaks, to Israel first of all, and through them to all people,
giving them his law for guidance. He leads them toward the fulfillment of his
purposes and promises for Israel in a truly holy order, under the Messiah in the
Messianic Age.

The people of Israel respond to the call for God in group or communal
worship, which sets the pattern for the group or public worship characteristic
of Western religion. A famous rabbi said, "The catechism of the Jew is in his

calendar." He meant that it is in observance of the festivals and holy days, which follow a liturgical calendar, that the Jew finds and expresses his or her faith. Three such festivals, two in the spring and one in the fall, are based on commemorations of Jewish victories, while the two most solemn observances, in the early autumn, are New Year and Day of Atonement. But it is the Sabbath, the regular weekly day of rest and prayer in the home and temple on Sabbath Eve (Friday night) and Day, which is the heart of Jewish piety. Special occasions such as weddings, funerals, and so on, have, of course, their distinctive Jewish observances.

Modern institutionalized Judaism in Western countries is divided into three principal groups, ranging in order from the most conservative to liberal: Orthodox, Conservative, and Reform Judaism. Although they differ in their views of the forms that should be followed in the modern world, they all follow the same basic calendar of worship and share the same fundamental beliefs. Thus all Jews believe that the Torah or Law gives the basic commandments, which have been explained in the Talmud, and are interpreted for the modern age by the rabbi in the synagogue or temple. But all Jews can and should themselves study the Torah in order to know how to observe it. For the Law is the good way of God for all people, and those who practice it will be blessed, as God promised Abraham long ago. Above all, it is through the Torah that the people of God are joined to God, and their relationship to God is the most important thing for the people of the Jews who collectively and individually constitute Judaism. Through them and their Bible the Law of God is proclaimed to all human beings.

NOTES

1. All quotations from the Bible in this chapter are from The Holy Scriptures, according to the Masoretic Text (Philadelphia: Jewish Publication Society of America, 5719-1958 © 1917). Used by permission of the Jewish Publication Society of America.
2. Joseph L. Blau, *Modern Varieties of Judaism* (New York: Columbia University Press, 1966), p. 5.
3. Harvey E. Goldberg, ed., *Judaism Viewed from Within and Without* (Albany: State University of New York Press, 1982), p. 420.
4. Jacob Neusner, *The Way of Torah* (Belmont: Wadsworth, 1982), p. xxxv.
5. Ibid., p. 93.
6. Avot deRabbi Nathan 20a (4:5). Translated by Rabbi Mark W. Gross.
7. In Edward J. Jurji, ed., *The Great Religions of the Modern World* (Princeton, N.J.: Princeton University Press, 1967), p. 226.
8. Blau, p. 53.
9. Blau, p. 65.
10. C. G. Montefiore and H. Loewe, *A Rabbinic Anthology* (New York: © Schocken Books, Inc.). Used by permission of Raphael Loewe, and Schocken Books, Inc.
11. Abraham M. Heller, *The Vocabulary of Jewish Life*, rev. ed. (New York: Hebrew Publishing Co., 1967), p. 198.

12. Montefiore and Loewe, p. 199.
13. Ibid., p. 183.
14. Bernard J. Bamberger, *The Story of Judaism* (New York: Union of American Hebrew Congregations, 1964), p. 126.

TOPICS AND QUESTIONS FOR STUDY

1. How and why is the Jewish idea of God the commonly accepted conception of the divine in Western culture? How does that concept affect our view of the world and people?
2. What is the place of the Hebrew people themselves, their long history, and, since 1948, the state of Israel, in Jewish self-understanding and religion?
3. Explain how our culture gets its ideas of the right and duty to speak out on an issue of conscience and right, and why so many Jews are active in movements for peace and justice, as well as charitable agencies.
4. What does it mean to be an active religious Jew? Why is "the catechism of the Jew his calendar" of religious holidays?
5. Discuss why Jews are sensitive about anti-Jewish sentiment, and why they feel justified in physically defending themselves and their land as essential to Judaism's survival.
6. Where does Western culture get the idea of a Sabbath rest one day a week? Why are many Jews very careful about observing it?
7. Describe how the modern divisions of Judaism developed over the past 200 years out of the gradual emergence of the Jewish people from isolation in the ghetto.
8. Where does our culture get its characteristic ethical model of moral laws based on the command of God? How does Judaism develop this ethical system?
9. The Torah, as well as the Talmud for many, are the most meaningful Jewish writings. Explain their significance and use, and tell why Jews consider it important to study them.
10. The Jews are known as "the chosen people." Discuss the basis for this name and its significance.
11. Discuss the relation between the nationalistic cult or worship and the universal ethical norms of Judaism.

USEFUL BOOKS

Blau, Joseph L. *Modern Varieties of Judaism.* New York: Columbia University Press, 1966.
Cohn-Sherbrook, Dan. *Issues in Contemporary Judaism.* New York: St. Martin's Press, 1991.
de Lange, Nicholas. *Judaism.* New York: Oxford University Press, 1986.

Goldberg, Harvey E., ed. and trans. *Judaism Viewed from Within and Without*. Albany: State University of New York Press, 1987.

Gordis, Robert. *The Dynamics of Judaism: A Study in Jewish Laws*. Bloomington: Indiana University Press, 1990.

Katz, Steven T., ed. *Interpreters of Judaism in the Late Twentieth Century*. Washington: B'nai B'rith Books, 1993.

Neusner, Jacob. *A Short History of Judaism*. Minneapolis: Fortress Press, 1992.

———. *The Way of Torah*, 4th ed. Belmont, Calif.: Wadsworth, 1988.

———, ed. and trans. *Scriptures of the Oral Torah*. San Francisco: Harper and Row, 1987.

——— et al., eds. *Understanding Seeking Faith*. Vol. 4, *Judaism Then and Now*. Atlanta: Scholar's Press, 1995.

The Union Prayerbook for Jewish Worship. The Central Conference of American Rabbis. Cincinnati: 1954 *et seq.*

GLOSSARY

Baal (bay uhl): "proprietor," fertility deity

bar mitsvah: "son of the Commandment"; religious ceremony for boys' coming-of-age; *bat mitsvah* for girls

cabala (kab uh luh): Jewish mystical tradition and writings

Covenant: the agreement between God and the Jews received by Moses on Mt. Sinai, including the Ten Commandments

Decalogue: Ten Commandments

Diaspora: literally, "dispersion"; dispersion of the Jews out from Palestine after the exile

eschatology: doctrine of the last things, end of the world

Gemara (guh mah rah): the commentary of the Talmud, the second strand

Haggada (hah gah dah): the non-legal part of Mizhnah; *haggada:* a story or legend

Halakah (hah lah kah): oral law tradition of Misnah; *halakah:* usage or custom

Hanukkah (hah noo kuh): "rededication" festival, commemorating rededication of the altar in the temple, 165 B.C.E.

Hasidim (haas ih dim): plural, term meaning "pious or godly ones"; Jewish sect

Jehovah: combining form of "JHVH" and "aDoNaY"

JHVH: the "Tetragrammaton" or four Hebrew letters, the holy name of God

Kaddish (kah dish): a prayer of praise and invocation in daily synagogue service and for mourners

Ketubim: "the writings," devotional and wisdom books of the Bible

kiddush (kid ossh): a benediction before the evening meal

Midrash: literally, "explanation"; Midrashim, plural, a collection of expositions of the scriptures

Mishnah: teaching or learning, in the later sense; traditional doctrine, basis of Talmud

Nebiim (neb ih eem): the prophetic books of the Bible

Pentateuch: first five books of the Bible

Pesach (pay sockh): Passover

Purim (poor im): feast commemorating victory over Haman, celebrating Esther in the Bible

Rosh hashanah (rosh huh shah nuh): New Year

Seder (say der): family or communal meal, center of Passover

Shabuoth (sha voo oath): Festival of Weeks or Pentecost

Sukkoth (sook oath): Feast of Tabernacles or Booths

Talmud: the body of civil and canonical law, at first oral, later written

Torah: literally—law or teaching. The will of God as revealed in Mosaic law.

Yahweh (yah way): English form of Hebrew "JHVH"; also spelled "Jahweh"

Yom Kippur (yom kipper): Day of Atonement

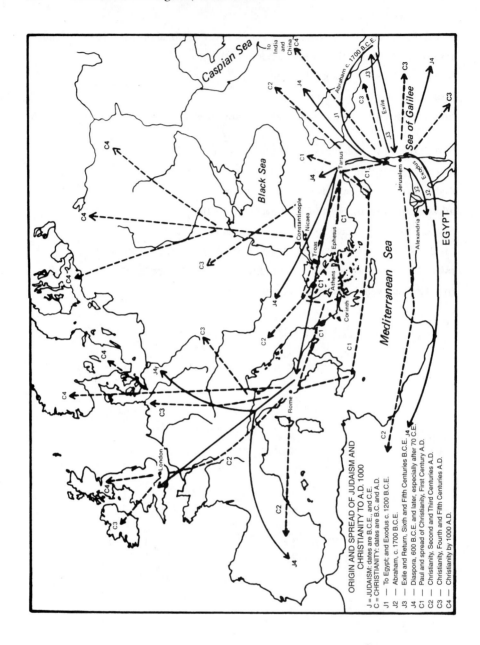

ORIGIN AND SPREAD OF JUDAISM AND
CHRISTIANITY TO A.D. 1000

J = JUDAISM: dates are B.C.E., and C.E.
C = CHRISTIANITY: dates are B.C. and A.D.

J1 — To Egypt; and Exodus c. 1200 B.C.E.
J2 — Abraham, c. 1700 B.C.E.
J3 — Exile and Return, Sixth and Fifth Centuries B.C.E.
J4 — Diaspora, 600 B.C.E. and later, especially after 70 C.E.
C1 — Paul and spread of Christianity, First Century A.D.
C2 — Christianity, Second and Third Centuries A.D.
C3 — Christianity, Fourth and Fifth Centuries A.D.
C4 — Christianity by 1000 A.D.

Chapter 8

CHRISTIANITY

Virgin and Child, *Dieric Bouts, d. 1475 (Courtesy, M. H. de Young Memorial Museum, San Francisco).*

OUTLINE

I. Christianity began within Judaism, growing into the largest and most universal religion of more than one billion adherents.

   A. Jesus of Nazareth.

      1. Life. Born about 6 B.C.E. in Judaea, he first appeared as a preacher announcing the kingdom of God, teaching and healing, and gathering many followers. The Jewish religious leaders opposed him, and he was finally crucified by the Romans at Jerusalem when he was about 30 years old. According to the four Gospels of the New Testament, which tell the story, he was then seen again, having risen from the dead.

      2. Teaching. Combining Jewish (Old Testament) materials with new emphases in a unique mixture, Jesus proclaimed that God's kingdom was a present reality and that people should live—as he did—in the light of God's love for them, in complete love, trust, and obedience.

   B. The Christian church.

      1. It began shortly after Jesus' death and Resurrection; the apostles, those who had seen the risen Lord, proclaimed the gospel (good news) in him and led the organization and spread of the church.

      2. By the fourth century Christianity was first legitimized and then established under the Roman Empire. Divided into two major parts, Eastern and Western, it grew in spite of doctrinal differences, which were settled at general or ecumenical councils. It became the dominant moral, spiritual, and cultural force in both East and West.

      3. The Protestant Reformation in the sixteenth century split the church in Europe, but missionary expansion brought worldwide growth to the present three main divisions: Catholic, Orthodox, Protestant.

II. The Christian Bible includes 39 books of Hebrew scriptures which Christians call the Old Testament (covenant), and 27 Christian books, such as the Gospels, called the New Testament.

III. Christianity's central belief is in the Trinity: God as Father, Son, and Holy Spirit.

   A. God the Father. The Hebraic-Biblical view of God is taken over in Christianity, and God is known as "the God and Father of our Lord Jesus Christ."

B. God the Son: Jesus Christ.

   1. The church both affirms and proclaims that Jesus is the Christ, God's chosen Savior of humankind, and it interprets and defends this in creeds and doctrines.

   2. These doctrines say that Jesus is both divine and human, and that he suffered, died, and rose again in order to save the world.

C. The third person of the Trinity, the Holy Spirit, works in the world now to effectuate salvation.

IV. Christian worship is of great variety and richness.

A. Various ideas and truths, such as thanksgiving to God and forgiveness from him, are the meaning or content of worship.

B. Many different ways or methods, such as music and prayers, are used to express the meanings.

C. The sacraments of Baptism and Communion convey the grace of God in Jesus Christ to the faithful.

V. The organization and ethical life of Christianity.

A. The church, in three major divisions, is the community of faith of those who acknowledge Jesus Christ; it ministers in different ways to the world.

B. The Christian life is to live by the gospel in the world, sustained by the help of God in Jesus Christ.

INTRODUCTION

Christianity is the religion that is based on Jesus Christ. It is not only named for him, it is centered on him as its actual content and substance. Christianity did not simply originate with Christ; it also lives only in and through him as its indwelling essence and vitality. In geographic terms Christianity is the most nearly universal faith, and in demographic terms it is the largest religion, having approximately two billion followers, although the members are concentrated in Europe and America and are a minority in Asia and Africa. There are many differences and divisions among Christians, which they themselves often seem to emphasize and exacerbate, but nevertheless there is an inescapable oneness in their allegiance to Jesus Christ as Lord and Savior. As the nominal religious culture of the West, it has played a key part in the history of Western civilization, and as such it feels the present problems and changes of that culture as it faces the uncertain future.

In this book we will stress the similarities of and unity among the Christians, but it is necessary to recognize important differences. The three major divisions which are usually recognized will be noted at many points, but we will not divide the study into three independent sections. In alphabetical order the three divisions are: Catholic, Orthodox, and Protestant. Sometimes the adjective "Roman" is prefixed to "Catholic"; it serves to identify that branch as comprised of approximately one billion Christians who acknowledge the See of Rome as head of the Christian church. The word "catholic" means "universal" and adherents of the church claim universality and prefer that title. Other communions claim catholicity and sometimes use the term "catholic," as in "Orthodox Catholic," but "Catholic" denotes Rome in this book. The Orthodox are sometimes called Greek or Eastern Orthodox, but "the Greek Church" is too narrow, and "Eastern" is too broad. "Orthodox" literally means "right belief," but to about 220 million Orthodox it also connotes "right praise," and to them belief and praise are essential characteristics of their faith. "Protestant" derives from the protest in favor of their religious freedom by the German states at the second Diet of Speyer in 1529. Here it denotes nearly 450 million members of many constituent Protestant denominations.

ORIGIN AND DEVELOPMENT

Christianity is based on a historical event, not on theoretical or abstract doctrine but a concrete, empirical occurrence in the world. That event is the life, death, and Resurrection* of Jesus Christ. Jesus was a Jew, born in Palestine during the reign of Herod the Great, and the first Christians were Jews. Christianity, therefore, comes out of Judaism and its origins can only be understood against the background of Jewish history, life, and religion.

The Jewish Background

In the chapter on Judaism we saw that at the time of the birth of Jesus Israel was under Roman domination, although the immediate rulers were the Herodian kings. Herod the Great died about when Jesus was born, and 10 years later his son Archelaus was deposed and the part of Palestine he ruled was put directly under a Roman procurator. Roman rule weighed heavily on the Jews, and there was much national discontent. Three groups were active in political and religious life. The Sadducees were the party of the high priest of the temple. The were mostly from the wealthier portion of the population, adhered to traditional written forms of the Pentateuch, held conservative social views, and supported efforts to keep peace with Rome. Adhering scrupulously to the Torah and its commandments were the Pharisees or "Separated Ones," who urged devotion to God and performance of duties to God and man as the way of deliverance for Israel. Open revolt against Rome was advocated by a direct action party centered in the hills, the Zealots. A fourth group, smaller than the others, were the Essenes; nonpolitical and nonviolent, they were essentially religious quietists.

The Lord Reprimanding Adam and Eve, *fourteenth century (Courtesy, M. H. de Young Memorial Museum, San Francisco).*

Jesus of Nazareth

SOURCES

For the life of Jesus and the early years of the Christian faith the New Testament is almost the only source of direct information, references to Christianity in other records being very few. Modern Biblical study has clarified the nature of the four Gospels,* meaning "good news," which tell the life of Jesus. They are not biographies or scientific factual accounts, but neither are they forgeries or fairy tales. There is a nucleus of reliable historical facts, and a fairly clear outline of the basic picture emerges from scientific study, comparison, and evaluation of the records. We take Grillmeier's statement as our assumption for dealing with the literary sources of our outline of Jesus' life: "So today . . . a synthesis is being sought between the extremes (pure Jesus of history—pure Christ of faith); the Jesus of history is taken as a presupposition of the Christ of faith. There is a recognition that the primitive [Christian] community itself already achieved this conjunction."[1]

LIFE

Inasmuch as Christian faith and worship alike are based on events in the life of Jesus Christ, it would be illogical to omit them from an account of Christianity, however familiar they may be to many Christians. The story of Jesus' life is found in the four Gospels—Matthew, Mark, Luke, and John—and the account given here is accordingly derived from them.

Two of the Gospels, Matthew and Luke, describe the conception by the Holy Spirit (the Virgin Birth) and the birth of Jesus. This event is dated usually about 6 B.C.E., because of a mistake in basing the calendar supposedly on his birth, as in A.D., *Anno Domini* or "year of the Lord." He was born in Bethlehem, near Jerusalem, to pious Jews, Joseph and Mary. Reared in Nazareth, in the province of Galilee, only one incident from his youth is recorded, in Luke. The fact that he was sometimes addressed as "teacher," and other evidence, indicates that he may have received training in the Torah and its interpretation. Both Mark and John begin their gospels with the appearance of Jesus among the adherents of a preacher of repentance, John the Baptist, and John's baptism of Jesus in the river Jordan near Jerusalem, which was accompanied by the appearance of the Holy Spirit declaring Jesus' sonship to God. Following a 40-day period of fasting and prayer in the desert, in which his temptation to and rejection of misuse of his powers took place, he began his actual ministry.

Mark says: "Now after John was arrested, Jesus came into Galilee, preaching the gospel of God, and saying, 'The time is fulfilled, and the kingdom of God is at hand; repent, and believe in the gospel' " (Mark 1:14, 15).[2] Making his headquarters at Capernaum, a small but strategic city on the Sea of Galilee, Jesus assembled a group of 12 men chosen from among his disciples or followers to assist in the proclamation of the Kingdom. The Galilean ministry was essentially an itinerant (traveling) operation, in which he visited numerous towns and both taught and preached in them, as well as outside in the open country. A more spectacular activity was his healing of the sick and crippled as recorded in the Gospels, the accounts of which are so circumstantial that, says Goguel, "it is impossible to doubt that Jesus did work cures."[3] Most miraculous of all was his raising people from the dead. All this brought great public interest and popularity, so that crowds of people began to follow him about.

Many of these people saw in Jesus a national and political deliverer, and many saw him as a holy man, so the traditional leaders—Scribes, Pharisees, Sadducees—were fearful that he would use his power in ways they did not like. Jesus actually repudiated the attempt to make him into such a political or military leader. Some schools of thought interpret Jesus as an antiestablishment or revolutionary figure, but the New Testament does not use these modern sociological categories. The Gospels make essentially spiritual and moral questions and issues the focus of the conflict and the drama of Jesus' life. It should be noted, however, that moral questions include social and not simply personal issues. In any event, there was hostility to him from without, and—presumably—personal turmoil within him, which moved Jesus to leave Galilee.

Probably on Mt. Tabor or Mt. Hermon, in the company of three disciples, Jesus experienced a vision which is known as the Transfiguration. "And after six days Jesus took with him Peter and James and John his brother, and led them up a high mountain apart. And he was transfigured before them, and his face shone like the sun, and his garments became white as light" (Matthew 17:1, 2). It was undoubtedly a crucial event, probably signalizing his own spiritual and psychological decision to proceed to Jerusalem to work and face the risks there. But the problems raised by the nature of the Gospels as embodying tradition and interpretation after the fact complicate the picture here as they do throughout. The journey to Jerusalem on the east or Perean side of the Jordan is dominated by foreshadowings and predictions of the sufferings to take place there.

The events at Jerusalem are the climax of Jesus' life and the center of Christian faith, and the accounts in the four Gospels are the fullest, most complex, and most varied part of the story. Christian tradition treats the events as compressed in the one "Passion Week." It is probable that Jesus actually spent more time in Jerusalem than the Synoptic Gospels report; the story emphasizes the significant events by concentrating attention on the last week of Jesus' life. Many aspects of the Gospel narrative, however, are more understandable if a longer Jerusalem ministry is assumed. We summarize the traditional account. A few days before the Passover, in about the year 30, Jesus was hailed by crowds of people as he entered Jerusalem riding on an ass. He visited the temple and in the precincts of the temple he disrupted the traffic in exchange of money and for purchase of sacrificial animals. One or two other minor events are usually located early in the week, before the decisive last 24 hours of his life.

On the eve before the Sabbath of the Passover, Jesus had a meal with the 12 disciples, which is known as the Last Supper, in an upper room of a house in Jerusalem. Although the exact time and the nature of the occasion within the Jewish liturgical or religious customs of that time are not clear, the Gospels substantially agree in their interpretation of it. They all see it as a solemn and deliberate farewell meal of fellowship and dedication, for it is an etiological narrative, that is, it is intended to explain or account for a ritual custom. (In this it resembles the Old Testament account in Exodus of the origin of Passover, which likewise combined present ritual and past history.) The Gospels agree that the center of the occasion was Jesus' act of breaking and distributing bread to the 12 saying, "Take; this is my body," and likewise distributing wine, saying, "This is my blood of the covenant, which is poured out for many" (Mark 14:22, 24). Following the meal, they went together to a spot on the Mount of Olives called the Garden of Gethsemane, where Jesus, after praying for deliverance if possible, was arrested by the temple authorities. The Gospels say he was taken before the high priest and the Jewish Sanhedrin or council and interrogated by them. When he was asked the crucial question whether he was the Messiah, he answered equivocally according to all the Gospel writers except Mark, who reports he said flatly, "I am." What the group who examined him decided to do with Jesus is not clear, because the records differ. They do agree that thereafter he was handed over by them to the Roman procurator, Pontius Pilate, and charged with offenses against the peace and safety of the state. After some maneuvering, in the course of which Pilate sought to release Jesus while the accusers and the crowd called for his crucifixion, Pilate ordered his crucifixion. On exactly what grounds the judgment was made is not clear from the records; they do say that the inscription above the cross (INRI *Jesus Nazarenus Rex Iudaeorum*, Jesus of Nazareth, King of the Jews), put there by the Romans, included the key words "The King of the Jews." The sentence was carried out by Roman soldiers as usual in the execution of criminals, at a spot called Golgotha, "the place of the skull." The crucifixion took place on the Friday when Passover was to begin, evidently starting at 9:00 A.M., with death occurring at 3:00 P.M. Various incidents, and words spoken by Jesus, constitute important parts of Christian worship and devotion. The body was removed before evening and deposited in a tomb belonging to Joseph of Arimethea. On the day following the Sabbath, or Sunday, certain disciples discovered that the tomb was empty, and others reported that they had seen Jesus himself. The year is uncertain; most scholars put it before the year 30.

One important observation about the character of the "Christ event," as the life of Jesus is termed in this context, is relevant. That is, although Jesus was a Jew in a specific time and place, a universally human, personal, flesh-and-blood story is told in the Christian gospel. The events that are the focus of Christian faith and life are never parochial, limited, or national in any way: the birth of a child, human compassion and suffering, human evil and death, heroism and faith, are the stuff of the story, and they might have happened anywhere on earth. Thus Jesus finally stands forth as representative of all humanity, the New Adam as Paul called him, in the New Testament as well as in Christian faith and doctrine.

TEACHING

It is impossible to separate the teaching of Jesus from its context in his life and from the events of his career. Christianity insists on this against any attempt, whether polemical from without or doctrinal from within, to isolate the message or teaching of Jesus from his life. The distinction has been stated by the Christian scholar Harnack and others as a contrast between the gospel* *of* Jesus and the gospel *about* Jesus. It has then, by still others, been urged that the religion of Jesus and the religion about Jesus are unrelated to each other and even inconsistent with each other. But this is, as the church has always recognized, a veiled polemic against its very life, for the heart of Christianity is Jesus Christ himself. On the contrary, the teaching can neither be properly understood theoretically nor applied in actual life by people without invoking the teacher himself. It is true that many segments of Jesus' teaching are familiar Jewish ideas; but the total unity and force of his doctrine are not understandable apart from his whole personality and the events of his life. This is why the

Christian message is called the "gospel," the good news; it is not simply a set of principles, but the record of a life. There are, however, specific elements which can be isolated and described in the teachings of Jesus.

The Old Testament Basis of Jesus' Teaching   Many items of his teaching come directly out of the Old Testament (as Christians denote the Jewish Bible) and the whole stance and form of the teaching reflects the Jewish matrix out of which Jesus literally, and Christianity figuratively, came. Perhaps the most striking brief formulation of Christian teaching is what is called the Great Commandment. In answer to a scribe, Jesus quoted the Torah, with which of course the scribe was familiar.

> And one of the scribes came up and heard them disputing with one another, and seeing that he answered them well, asked him, "Which commandment is the first of all?" Jesus answered, "The first is, 'Hear, O Israel: the Lord our God, the Lord is one; and you shall love the Lord your God with all your heart, and with all your soul, and with all your mind, and with all your strength.' The second is this, 'You shall love your neighbor as yourself.' There is no other commandment greater than these" (Mark 12:28-31).

The first command is from Deuteronomy 6:4, 5, the Shema, and the second is Leviticus 19:18. Throughout his message Jesus appeals to Old Testament teaching and uses Jewish forms and especially prophetic insights. But he combined them in his own new way and reshaped them to fit his distinctive message.

The Eschatological Character of Jesus' Teaching   The Kingdom of God has been mentioned in the chapter on Judaism, for it comes out of the Old Testament and Jewish religion; in Jesus' message and teaching it played an important part. The Kingdom of God, under various names, is the focus of the eschatological element which underlies Jesus' teaching and ethics. (Eschatology* is the doctrine of the last things, the end of time.) Mark's statement has been quoted, that Jesus began his ministry with the proclamation that the Kingdom of God was at hand, and all the Gospels reiterate this theme. Luke, least eschatological of the evangelists, says: "Soon after he went on through cities and villages, preaching and bringing the good news of the Kingdom of God" (Luke 8:1). Examples could be multiplied to show that Jesus took as a fundamental datum the sure and soon coming of the age when God would rule not simply in heaven and by moral authority, but in fact, as all people obeyed and served him. Furthermore, in some way he identified himself with that kingdom, and he held that in a sense it had already come, or begun, or was partly realized. His own Messianic function and claim, about which there are many problems, were related to the kingdom. He reinterpreted both conceptions and used them in his own way.

In effect, Jesus invited people to start living their lives on the same basis he did, that is, on the assumption that the Kingdom of God is a partial reality now and that the time of God's full realization of his kingdom is in the near future. That this eschatological or future reference and framework underlies his ethical teaching is now recognized, but the exact form and significance of it are still disputed. There was tension, in both his Messiahship and the kingdom, between the present and the future. It may be that he himself changed his own views as he saw that the end was not coming in his lifetime, and certainly the Christian church had to shift its time scheme during the early centuries.

The basic point and emphasis of Jesus' eschatological ethic is not, however, dependent on an exact timetable. The main idea was quite simple: To respond to his call and to follow him was to live a new kind of life dominated by expectation of God's fulfillment of the kingdom. It is coming; the ship will arrive; the promise will be kept; God will fulfill his word. This mood of confident expectation is one of the elements necessary to make sense of Jesus' ethical standards. Part of the moral preeminence of Jesus was that he saw the world for what it is now and yet saw the kingdom as equally real and utterly, absolutely certain of complete fulfillment. In calling people to follow him, therefore, it was not simply commitment to him that he asked, but to him as God's representative for God's Kingdom, which is coming now.

God and Persons in Jesus' Teachings   The Judaic stamp of Jesus' teaching is also evident in the dual or double doctrine of God as the one who is to be both feared and trusted, both obeyed and loved. This paradoxical combination was pointed out in the chapter on Judaism, and Jesus, in all his teaching, built on the fundamental truth and meaning of the Law. First of all, the individual person is a child and creature of God. Jesus took this essential Hebraic-Biblical notion seriously, and for that reason he called for believers to act like children in offering God their obedience, trust, and love even while they were to be mature, sophisticated, and self-reliant in their dealings with the world. Both others and oneself were to be treated as children of God: "Thou salt love they neighbor as thyself," that is, as a human being with human hopes, fears, loves, joys, sorrows, powers, limits before God. This simple yet profound formula accounts for the way Jesus dealt with all people, whoever they were and whatever their relation to him. Through their and his common relation to God, he found the basis of a human relationship, which took account of individual differences and yet affirmed their shared humanity.

The Sermon on the Mount, comprising chapters five, six, and seven of the Gospel of Matthew, is the most famous single compendium of Jesus' teaching. It is a description of the righteousness of the Kingdom of Heaven (one of several terms used by Jesus in place of "Kingdom of God"). As a conservative Jewish Christian, the writer sets forth in Jesus' words the new law of the church, in contrast with the Torah of Moses. It is true that Jesus himself frequently characterized his sayings as new forms, differing from the old law, and he did, on occasion, contradict and denounce the scribes and Pharisees as champions and authors of a narrow legalism. Thus the greatest contrast with the old law, and the most striking characteristic of the Sermon, is its drastic and absolute demand for purity of soul and motive which issues in a higher righteousness than any mere outward compliance with conventional and prudential morality. At the same time, the moral strictness of the code is so heightened that its demands are absolute, and people were either delighted or scandalized by it.

The clue to at least an understanding of it, if not observance, is the eschatological context to which we have referred. As the ethic of a new order, it calls on those who believe in that order to behave as if they lived in it now. There is no question that it stands as the most exalted such code ever proclaimed, and that it would long since have been erased and forgotten if it were not for the speaker. While it remains the Sermon on the Mount is at once a conscience for humanity as it is, and a promise and hope of what the world might be. But, again, the basis for this is the double aspect of Jesus' own life and the dual character of the ethic he enunciated. God's law is absolute and total and calls for complete and utter obedience, in defiance of the world's way; at the same time God's mercy and love—the church will call it his "grace"—are equally unlimited and complete, unlike the grudging, and unsatisfying rewards of the world.

The Beginning and Growth of the Church

His death seemed to have destroyed the group centered around Jesus of Nazareth, but the Resurrection reconstituted it, and the event, recorded in the Acts of the Apostles, called "Pentecost," transformed it into a dynamic and expansive fellowship. As we have seen, Pentecost was the Jewish Feast of Weeks, Shabuoth, 50 days after the beginning of Passover.

> When the day of Pentecost had come, they were all together in one place. And suddenly a sound came from heaven like the rush of a mighty wind, and it filled all the house where they were sitting. And there appeared to them tongues as of fire, distributed and resting on each one of them. And they were all filled with the Holy Spirit and began to speak in other tongues, as the Spirit gave them utterance. (Acts 2:1-4).

Then—as seen in the rest of the account in Acts—and now, public interest has fastened on the physical manifestations of the Holy Spirit: the tongues of flame and "speaking with tongues." But the significant historical effect of the Holy Spirit was in the gifts of unity and power which were displayed by the church beginning at Pentecost. For the fact is that the New Testament records a steady growth in the number of Christians, which is confirmed by historical data.

THE APOSTOLIC AGE

The earliest phase of the development of Christianity was led by the apostles and marked by conflict with and eventual separation from Judaism. The apostles were "ambassadors" for Christ in the formation of the first Christian groups, called *ekklesia* in Greek, meaning "assembly" (in English the word is "church" for "*ecclesia*"). The first duty of an apostle was to witness to the

Resurrection, and the qualification for this was to have seen the risen Lord. They were specially called, like the 12 disciples, who are often called the "Twelve Apostles," although not all of them are among the "apostles" mentioned in the New Testament outside of the Gospels. Further qualified by gifts and powers, they were like traveling salesmen and organizers for the infant church, often moving into new territory, seldom settling down in one place. Most of them were Jews, as were the first Christians, but the first conflicts were with Judaism. Some persecution was directed at them, as recorded in the Acts of the Apostles. The best known, and most influential for later Christianity, because of the incorporation of his letters into the New Testament, was the Apostle Paul. Born Saul the Jew, as a "Pharisee of the Pharisees" he records that he first persecuted Christians, but then was converted and made an apostle. Jesus appeared to him, according to Acts, in a vision: "And he said, 'Who are you, Lord?' And he said, 'I am Jesus, whom you are persecuting; but rise and enter the city, and you will be told what you are to do' " (Acts 9:5, 6). What he did was to carry the message to the Gentile world and to articulate it in such a way that it was open to all people. He and other apostles carried Christianity beyond Palestine and transformed it from a Jewish sect to a separate faith.

Before the conquest of Jerusalem by Titus in 70, there were small but vital Christian churches outside Palestine. The first was at Antioch, where Jesus' followers were first called "Christians," then in other places in Syria, and in cities of Asia Minor, Greece, and Italy. The problems of Jewish dietary laws and circumcision for Gentile converts were settled by abandoning Jewish laws for non-Jews, in all except the original Jerusalem community. The Acts reports that council. The Christian Jews, interpreting the conquest of Jerusalem as fulfillment of Jesus' prophecy, escaped Jerusalem by flight before its fall; Christians gradually abandoned Jewish ceremonial law after that. Coupled with the early proclamation of Jesus as the Messiah and Paul's successful polemic against legalism, this solidified the division between Judaism and Christianity. The center of Christian strength and influence shifted from Palestine to major cities of the Roman Empire. At the same time the dominant factor in their environment ceased to be Judaism and became the Greco-Roman culture of the wider world. When opposition and persecution came, for example, it was no longer Jewish or Herodian but Roman. In historical perspective, the preeminent apostles are Peter and Paul. Both of them are thought to have been martyred at Rome under the Emperor Nero in 64, during the first great Roman persecution. The *Pax Romana* (Roman peace) and Roman roads facilitated the geographical spread of Christianity, and Hellenistic culture became the vehicle for Christian thought.

ANTE-NICENE ERA

A council of all the churches at Nicaea in 325 is used to mark the division between the early and later centuries of the church. Unfortunately, the sources of information about the first two centuries are limited to some of the later

The Adoration of the Magi, Osona the Younger,
*c. 1600 (Courtesy, M. H. de Young Memorial Museum,
San Francisco).*

books of the New Testament and similar writings, and full documentation is
impossible, especially for the period 70 to 110 or later. Books were being written and the New Testament was being put together, but this tells us little about
church organization and doctrine. Of course the basic sacraments* of baptism
and communion had taken shape quite early, and organizational forms became
more complex as membership increased in numbers and diversity. It was Gentile Christianity, still mainly in the eastern part of the Empire except for Rome.
Quite simple in belief, it was centered on Jesus as bringer of a new covenant
(testament) and the church as the new Israel; the life of believers was prevail-
ingly quiet and sober, shaped by the new Christian rules then being set. A
number of writers who were active about 100 are called "Apostolic Fathers,"

because it was long assumed they were instructed by the apostles. They expressed the primitive and simple doctrine of Jesus Christ as the victor over sin and death.

Paul in his letters saw the gifts of the spirit exercised by three kinds of leaders: prophets, teachers, apostles. During the early years this charismatic (spiritual, divinely inspired) leadership of the spirit sufficed; for example, it at first produced a primitive and free communism in the Jerusalem church (Acts 2:43–47). With the passage of years, growth in numbers and diversity, increasing wealth and sophistication inevitably came institutionalization of organization, ritual, and belief. Instead of free, unstructured cooperation there were organized patterns of behavior and stabilized roles and offices. By the time of Paul's later letters, his salutation includes bishops and deacons; "To all the saints in Christ Jesus who are at Philippi, with the bishops and deacons" (Philippians 1:1). He took a last journey to Jerusalem, "And from Miletus he sent to Ephesus and called to him the elders of the church" (Acts 20:17). The Greek for "elders" is $\pi\rho\epsilon\sigma\beta\acute{\upsilon}\tau\epsilon\rho\omicron\iota$, presbyters, whence by long derivation "priest." This threefold ministry—bishops, presbyters, deacons—was evidently, to judge from other sources, the developing pattern of church administration. What the actual division of functions was at first is now disputed, but probably each local unit had a group of presbyters and bishops assisted by deacons at its head. Soon after, the "monarchical" bishop in the modern sense of head of a group of churches appeared. The idea of apostolic succession was joined to the bishopric by the middle of the second century, and some time later came its expansion beyond the local congregation to a larger area or diocese.

Elaboration and systematization of doctrine, as distinct from proclamation of the basic message, began with the Apologists in the middle of the second century, whose concern was to explain and justify Christianity against Judaism and paganism. About this time an early form of the Apostles' Creed was in use as a baptismal formula. By the third and fourth centuries, controversies arose within the church over differing interpretation of doctrine, and doctrinal disagreement has troubled Christianity ever since.

By about 200 the church was strongly established in many cities and provinces of the Empire, both East and West. The relative decline of Asia Minor left Rome the strongest and most prestigious center of Christianity, as well as the church of the imperial city, presaging the preeminence of the bishop of Rome in the Western Church. Persecution was a fact of the Christian life for much of the time before 200; the faith was illegal and might come under active persecution at any time, bringing martyrdom for many. In the first half of the third century, however, Christians seemed quite secure, despite local persecutions, in prestige and numbers. At the same time the Empire began its long decline, and in 250 the Emperor Decius made a general and systematic attempt to force Christians to sacrifice to the Roman gods. Many endured and were martyred. Many lapsed from the faith and later sought readmission; this set off a controversy which lasted for centuries and resulted in a clear statement of doctrine that all sins were forgivable. Intermittent persecution continued until 260, then virtually ended until the last great trial under Diocletian, from 303 to 311.

CONSTANTINE AND NICAEA

Legend explains how Emperor Constantine's policy of freedom for all religions including Christianity was occasioned by a vision. He saw in the sky the cross with the words "In this sign you will conquer" before he won a decisive battle in 312. In any event, he changed the situation of Christianity from a struggling illicit sect to a legal religion with increasing imperial support. As such it grew rapidly. Yet there were still problems of division, and now the dominant group, which used the term "Catholic," had government support in its opposition to others. When splits and quarrels even among the Catholics threatened the unity of the church, Constantine used his power to summon councils of bishops to settle the issues. The first General Council of all the church was in 325 at Nicaea, near Constantinople, which Constantine had made the new capitol of the Empire. It made the first attempt at settlement of the Arian controversy, and under pressure from the Emperor adopted the first Nicene Creed. In 337 Constantine died, having received baptism shortly before his death.

Theodosius I, emperor from 379 to 396, decreed that Christianity was the official religion:

> It is our desire that all the various nations which are subject to our Clemency and Moderation should continue in the profession of that religion which was delivered to the Romans by the divine Apostle Peter, as it hath been preserved by faithful tradition; . . . According to the apostolic teaching and the doctrine of the Gospel, let us believe the one deity of the Father, the Son, and the Holy Spirit, in equal majesty and in a Holy Trinity. We authorize the followers of this law to assume the title of Catholic Christians; but as for the others, since, in our judgment, they are foolish madmen, we decree that they shall be branded with the ignominious name of heretics. . . . They will suffer in the first place the chastisement of the divine condemnation, and in the second the punishment which our authority, in accordance with the will of Heaven, shall decide to inflict.[4]

In the context and in the event, setting it alongside the New Testament, it is in some ways a curious document. There are those who say that not because of, but in spite of, such documents, the gospel survives. Whatever the forces at work, Christianity was on its way to become the "substance of culture" (Tillich) of the Western world.

EAST AND WEST

At Nicaea, only about six out of 300 bishops were from the West; the language of the Council was Greek; in 250 Novatian had been the first scholar in the Roman Christian community to write in Latin rather than Greek. Christianity had begun in the East, had first grown there, was still in some ways stronger there and was under imperial patronage. For many reasons there were differences and rivalry between East and West, which were subsequently exacerbated by events, so that this is a schism (split) which goes back to the beginning, was made deeper by history, and now appears to be a permanent breach. Constantine's removal of the seat of empire to Constantinople meant that the East had to learn to live under an absolute monarch, and subsequent history continued that condition, permanently marking its character. On the other hand, the removal of the imperial power permitted the assumption by the Bishop of Rome of much of the power of the state.

For nearly a thousand years, however, East and West collaborated, and the first seven general or ecumenical (worldwide) councils, which began with Nicaea and included both Eastern and Western bishops, are recognized by the Catholics and Orthodox as legitimate ecumenical councils. The first six general councils, through the Third Council of Constantinople, were concerned with questions about the nature of Christ. Second Nicaea in 787 defined veneration due to images; this was part of the iconoclastic controversy, which helped to produce the final split. All the councils reflect controversy, because the occasion for them was to solve some unresolved conflict, and the doctrinal content of the six, all being Christological questions, reveals the problems of the church over interpretation of the nature of Jesus Christ. In local churches, however, the ordinary Christian was not concerned with such theoretical problems. Baptism, communion, and other sacraments developed as the content of the religious life of the faithful, both East and West.

In the West the bishop of Rome had from the first claimed primacy as the successor of Peter by direct line of spiritual authority, and time and events strengthened his position. Cyprian, bishop of Carthage in the third century, and Augustine, bishop of Hippo (also in North Africa) in the fourth, defined and defended the Western idea of the church. In 445 a weak emperor, Valentinian III, dependent on the Western church for support against the Huns who were threatening Rome, decreed, "by a perpetual edict, that nothing shall be attempted by the Gallican bishops, or by those of any other province, contrary to the ancient custom, without the authority of the venerable pope of the Eternal City."[5] Later in the fifth century, Pope Gelasius I developed the doctrine of the two powers, temporal and spiritual, the latter greater as more fundamental, although spiritual leaders must obey laws required for public order. This was the basis for later expansion of the power of the Western church, culminating in the claim to supreme power in the doctrine of papal infallibility in 1870.

The Eastern position, in brief, is that the bishop of Rome is first among equals and entitled to the seat of honor in an ecumenical council, but that he does not have juridical authority over all the church. When the pope attempted to extend his authority over the East, conflict deepened and led finally to complete rupture. The first specific occasion was a dispute between Pope Nicholas I and the patriarch of Constantinople, Photius, in 865. A doctrinal question became another focus of disagreement—the *filioque* clause. *Filioque* is Latin for "and the Son." At the Third Council of Toledo in 589 it was inserted into the words of the Nicene Creed about the "procession" of the Holy Spirit, thus: "that proceedeth from the Father *and the Son. . . .*" The Latin church used this formula, but the East did not. As most commentators agree, nowadays it does not seem so important. Even then, it was more a focus of struggle for power than an irreconcilable doctrinal disagreement. But there was a difference of interpretation, and to the East it was a falsification of an ecumenical creed. In the Gospels the Spirit proceeds only from the Father, and the Son is begotten of the Father; this helps to preserve the unity of the Trinity, said the Greeks, and should not be changed. The Latin response is to quote Jesus in John 14:16 and 26, about sending the Comforter, the Holy Spirit.

Although the Photian and *filioque* controversies of the ninth century were publicly healed, no real reconciliation was achieved. Beginning in 1009 Rome officially adopted the *filioque* clause, and the pope's name was omitted from the official list at Constantinople of Orthodox patriarchs. An attempt at reconciliation in 1054 ended with mutual excommunications exchanged by Cerularius, patriarch of Constantinople, and Pope Leo IX, and this is the conventional date for the break between East and West. The most bitter memories for the Orthodox Church come from the Crusades, which deepened and hardened the division. During the Fourth Crusade, in 1204, Constantinople was sacked by the Crusaders and churches were desecrated and despoiled. Byzantine Christians have never forgotten this. In recent years, however, conciliatory moves have taken place between the Catholics and Orthodox.

GEOGRAPHICAL EXPANSION

In spite of these quarrels and divisions, the life of the Christian church and people continued and developed. As the Roman imperial administration in Europe broke down, the church often filled the gap, so that the Western church grew in power and influence. Through the Dark Ages of the sixth through eighth centuries, learning as well as piety were preserved and nurtured by the church. Missionaries carried the faith to the boundaries of the empire while it lasted, aided by Roman roads and administration. When the empire disintegrated, the church turned to conversion of the Germans, as the various tribes and peoples of northern Europe are usually denominated. The zeal of missionaries even in the face of martyrdom, piety and devotion by ordinary believers, constructive service and work by parish clergy, and astute management and collaboration with secular authority by bishops brought the gradual expansion of the church. Its growth is almost synonymous, for hundreds of years, with the development of Western civilization. The first great kingdom to be Christianized was that of the Franks, which had already included many Christian cities, about 500 and after. Various Germanic tribes had become "Arian" Christians, the unorthodox losers in the great contest over the doctrine of Christ, but they were subsequently brought under Catholic doctrine. In Britain the early Christian movement almost disappeared when the empire collapsed, but

The Tribute Money, *Rubens, 1577–1640 (Courtesy, M. H. de Young Memorial Museum, San Francisco).*

was revived by Patrick in Ireland during the fifth century, and in England about 600 by the missionary Augustine. Germany was evangelized in the eighth century, Boniface being the leader. Later the Scandinavian countries followed. Slavic missions were begun for the Eastern Church by the brothers and missionaries, Cyril and Methodius, late in the ninth century; but Russia itself was only gradually evangelized, by the Eastern church, after the year 1000.

MEDIEVAL CHRISTENDOM

The church was by no means always strong and pure even in the centuries of hardship and growth, but outward pressures and inward revitalization kept it alive and growing. Beginning in the middle of the seventh century, Islam literally overwhelmed the Eastern church in an astonishing, lightning spread out of Arabia after the death of the Prophet in 632. The Caliphs subjugated the resplendent Byzantine culture and church in Asia in all but the margins of Asia Minor and around Constantinople, where a battle in 714 saved the city. While the church continued there and in the Eastern part of Europe, Islam overshadowed the Eastern church in Asia so that Christians lived there only quietly and inconspicuously. Islam's control of the Holy Land was later to be the occasion for the Crusades. Europe itself escaped Islamic conquest only through the victory of Charles Martell over the Islamic host at the battle of Poitiers in the Loire valley of France, in 732.

Another Frankish king, Charlemagne, was crowned by the Western pope on Christmas Day, 800, as Holy Roman Emperor, and his support of learning and of the Western church helped revive both. After his death division of the empire and growth of the feudal order left room for the church to expand its claims and power, while pope and emperor struggled indecisively for two centuries. Monasticism had begun earlier and now became more important.

MONASTICISM

Christian monasticism developed from asceticism. As early as the third century in Egypt it was customary for men and women in search of holiness to live in solitary retirement outside settled towns, abstaining from sex, meat, and intoxicants, and living with a minimum of comforts, devoted to prayer and meditation, and sometimes to works of charity. Traditionally, St. Anthony at the end of the third century was the first Christian hermit, and as such has figured prominently in later Christian and non-Christian iconography as the paradigm of the tempted ascetic. A different type of asceticism was begun in 323 by Pachomius in southern Egypt. This is called "cenobitic" monasticism to indicate its community nature as contrasted with the solitary life of the hermit. In the monastery, asceticism (fasting, and so on) is part of the larger total rule and discipline under which all members of the community engage in common meals, worship, prayer, meditation, study, and manual work, in proportions depending on the specific order. Although individual hermits have continued to be found in the East to this day, cenobitic monasticism has been the typical form in both East and West. Both men's and women's orders were found from the first, and convents for nuns developed at the same time as the monasteries.

St. Basil first adapted monasticism to both Eastern and Western ideas and conditions, and his pattern has become typical of Eastern monasticism. In about 500, St. Benedict of Nursia adapted monasticism to Western Christian thought and conditions, and established the monastery at Monte Cassino whence the order spread. Benedict's rule was less austere than others', but placed more emphasis on manual work and a stable community in which all served the same rule. His type of monasticism became characteristic of most Western religious orders, both for men and for women.

One Roman Catholic historian calls the period from 880 to 1046 the "dark age" of the papacy, so low did the spiritual quality of the church sink. The revival in the following three centuries was sparked by vigorous new monastic orders and rejuvenation of the old monastic houses. The Cluniacs, starting from Cluny in Burgundy, flourished in thousands of affiliated houses through the twelfth and thirteenth centuries. In the eleventh century the Cistercian order under Bernard of Clairvaux was the center of reform. The thirteenth century saw the rise of what are called mendicant orders, meaning that they embrace poverty and therefore live by begging or mendicancy. Dominic founded an order devoted to preaching and scholarship. The black-robed friars were nicknamed *Domini canes,* "dogs of the Lord," because among other tasks they sought to bring heretics back into the fold and often served as inquisitors in the Inquisition. A rather different sort of saint and order were St. Francis and the Franciscans, dedicated to works of charity and service, who came to symbolize joy in nature and the Lord. Nearly all these orders, with their affiliated convents of nuns, continue to this day, and there are many newer ones, especially women's orders.

SCHOLASTICISM

Another fruit of the monastic orders was the learning that was fostered in the monasteries and by members of the orders. Scholasticism is a complex movement, the specifically intellectual activity most characteristic of the medieval age. In the broadest sense, it was the application of study and thought to the doctrines and faith of Christianity in the light of the rediscovered literature and ideas of Greek philosophers. Out of it came such subtle minds as that of Thomas Aquinas in the thirteenth century, whose great achievement was to Christianize the philosopher Aristotle and philosophize Christian theology in Aristotelian terms. So important and complete was his systematization of Christian doctrine, that in the nineteenth century his thought was declared to be the norm for Catholic theological formulation.

MYSTICISM

Complementary to scholasticism was mysticism, which in its Christian form naturally focused on mystical communion with Jesus. Bernard of Clairvaux expressed his preference for the mystical approach over the subtleties of Abelard, the most brilliant theologian of the time, whom Bernard disputed. Meister Eckhart (died 1327) in Germany, and Jan van Ruysbroick in the Netherlands at that time, articulated a mysticism which was practiced by many laymen in societies of the Friends of God. Some mysticism, like that of Eckhart, was condemned and is regarded as a forerunner of Protestantism. But people like Thomas à Kempis, St. Catherine of Siena, St. Teresa of Avila, and St. John of the Cross, whose writings are classics of mystical devotion, were orthodox Catholics.

THE CRUSADES

In the twelfth and thirteenth centuries, the Crusades appealed to the piety and devotion of the common people and nobility, and many joined them out of genuine desire to "deliver the Holy Land from the hands of the infidel," as the preachers phrased it. It is true that Seljuk Turks had threatened to stop Christian pilgrims from visiting Jerusalem, and the Orthodox Church, threatened by Turkish pressure and supporting the Byzantine state, joined in the call for a crusade. The results, however, did not contribute anything of lasting value to

Christianity proper, while their cost in lives and the hatred they generated was clearly evident. A rise in anti-Semitic policies was one evil fruit of the Crusades. In the end, they probably contributed to the decadence of the Western church which presaged the Reformation. Of course in other ways they did affect the development of Europe and the Middle East.

THE WESTERN CHURCH BEFORE THE REFORMATION

After the achievements of the thirteenth century came problems of too much power and prosperity. An expression of such problems was the "Avignon Captivity" in the fourteenth and early fifteenth centuries, referring to the removal of the papacy to Avignon in France. For a time there were two and even three claimants to the papal throne, before the Council of Constance in 1414 elected Martin V and returned the seat to Rome. The secularism and corruption of some of the later popes is acknowledged by Roman Catholic scholars. The Inquisition, motivated by zeal for orthodox doctrine, was primarily directed against Christian heretics, but in practice Jews and others also suffered. Measured discussion of the Inquisition is difficult, and we do not have an accurate count of the thousands of victims of imprisonment, often torture, and death. The term "Inquisition" is now a byword for religious persecution, and no one would defend it.

It has been necessary to emphasize the problems and shortcomings of the Western church in order to explain the background of the Reformation. But that is a partial and one-sided picture. Medieval Christendom was a great achievement, and in many ways it was a golden age of faith. Through their support of the arts, popes and bishops subsidized most of the great artists of the Italian Renaissance. Fund-raising for St. Peter's in Rome helped to precipitate the Reformation, but that basilica and the cathedrals of many styles stand as perhaps the greatest architectural triumph of the ages. For centuries the church provided a stable, unified, and satisfying spiritual home which enabled the faithful, ordinary people of Europe to live a basically secure and confident daily life. The humane works and attitudes which modern Western culture takes for granted—schools and learning, hospitals, asylums, and social agencies of all kinds—owe their origins, at least, to medieval Christian charity, above all by the religious orders. Not because it was so bad, but because in spite of everything it was so good, the church called for reform.

THE PROTESTANT REFORMATION

Historians discuss the Reformation in its wider political, economic, and social context, emphasizing such factors as the rise of nationalism, economic changes, Renaissance culture, and the invention of printing. No doubt those were related factors in the genesis and spread of the Reformation. Our limited purview restricts us to the more specifically religious aspects, on the assumption that they are the genuine and significant issues.

The Religious Issue—Martin Luther and Justification by Faith

There were reformers before him, but it was Martin Luther (1483-1546) in Germany who carried through his convictions to the point where the Western church was irrevocably split. His original intention was reform, but the logic of his position led inevitably to the division, because there are differences between Catholicism and Protestantism. These differences did not appear all at once, and they cannot be described in full in this brief history section, but will emerge in the discussions that follow. The central issue was the basic question of Christianity: What must one do to be saved? In modern terms it is the Christian form of the "existential" question, and it was where Martin Luther began. For all his faults, he was a giant; he turned his whole personality to that question, and out of his quest came a reshaping of Christianity.

Luther's own religious experience was—as in the case of all religious innovators—formative for the Protestant tradition. Having joined the Augustinian order, Luther was a learned doctor and professor at Wittenberg and an almost fanatically devoted monk when his decisive personal experience started him on his way. People believed, as many still do, in a realistic heaven and hell, and the church dramatized the battle of the soul. For evidence, look at the tympanum (over the door) of almost any Romanesque or Gothic cathedral and see the Judgment scene—Christ receiving the saved on his right and rejecting the damned on his left. Despite the fact that he had climbed to the top in the monastic system, Luther's thirst for spiritual assurance was not satisfied. Having undertaken what the church counted as counsels of perfection, he wanted the reward reserved for those who fulfilled the demands—spiritual assurance of salvation.

The importance of the Bible in Protestantism is foreshadowed in the fact that it was from his Bible study and lectures that Luther finally found the answer he sought. Although the Gospels were read during the mass, Luther evidently never saw a Bible until 1503, after he had earned the baccalaureate, when he read one in the university library. But he did not really study the Bible until he began to prepare to lecture on the Psalms and Paul's letters. The penitential system had only made him more conscious of his sins, and the mystic way of devotion was closed because his God was too terrible to unite with such unholy sinners. Protestantism's rejection of the authority of the pope is the basic negative factor in its constitution. But the rejection—as seen in Luther's experience—is spiritual and soteriological* (relating to salvation). The church and the clergy cannot save us: Only God can. And because the Bible is the story of and guide to that salvation, the Bible replaced the church as the ground of assurance and the source of authority for Protestantism.

In Paul's letter to the Romans, Luther found the answer. The letter reads:

> For I am not ashamed of the gospel; it is the power of God for salvation to every one who has faith, to the Jew first and also to the Greek. For in it the righteousness of God is revealed through faith for faith; as it is written, "He who through faith is righteous shall live" (Romans 1:16, 17).

St. Francis Receiving the Stigmata, *Patinier. St. Francis is hon-*
ored by all branches of Christianity (Courtesy of M. H. de
Young Memorial Museum, San Francisco).

Luther's own words are:

> Night and Day I pondered until I saw the connection between the justice of
> God and the statement that "the just shall live by his faith." Then I grasped
> that the justice of God is that righteousness by which through grace and sheer
> mercy God justifies us through faith.[6]

Faith in Jesus Christ, said Luther, enables the believer to trust the gracious and
loving God and receive salvation.

Over the next few years, Luther worked out the implications of these ideas
in his own mind and through his experience. Gradually, the practical significance of his own position became clear and led to questioning the whole system of the church for meeting people's spiritual needs. In this confrontation
between a German monk and the mightiest religious organization in the world,

logic and conscience, both of which had been nurtured by the church, drove Luther to refuse to compromise.

The occasion for the open break was Luther's attack in 1517 on the misuse and selling of indulgences, remission of temporal penalties for sins. The indulgence question was important as the first occasion of open controversy and as a focus of larger issues.

For two main reasons controversy did not stop. One was that Luther's theses were reprinted—using a new invention, the printing press—and in a week they were spread all through Germany, where they became a sensation. He was propelled into the position of a spokesman for widespread popular resentment against the Roman church; his action set off a conflagration, his words caught fire among the German people. The other reason was that Luther continued to follow the logic of his position and the urging of his conscience in his fundamental Christian concern about the nature and means of salvation. Between outward events and inward decision he moved inexorably forward.

The rest of the story is simply action and reaction between Luther and the church authorities; two sides formed, the argument and conflict widened and deepened, and the end was a breach in the Western church. In the partisan Catholic view it was willful disobedience by schismatics and heretics who rent the body of Christ; in partisan Protestant terms it was the inevitable, God-directed reform and restoration of a church that had become totally corrupt and was led by anti-Christ. In any terms the controversy was often a sad spectacle; it brought strife on a wide scale, and it left a divided Western Christendom. It is impossible to say whether or not it was historically necessary or justified. But it is a fact that there was and is a difference between the views; indeed there are a number of significant differences.

The fundamental soteriological issue is posed in oversimplified form as faith versus works: Can and do people effect anything for their own salvation, or does God do it all? Luther was Augustinian and Pauline, Rome was Thomistic and Petrine. The trouble is that in religion there always are loose ends, inconsistencies, imperfect resolution of conflicting ideas. The two sides stressed contrasting factors in Christian salvation: divine grace and human effort. Although Luther did not want to say that the Christian life does not matter, he insisted that only God can actually effect salvation and humans can do nothing in the crucial operation except have faith. The pope said, in effect, that human responsibility in the process of salvation must be maintained along with divine grace in order not to weaken morality.

Never did Luther and the pope confront each other face to face, but each adhered to his position and denounced his opponent, and their irreconcilable views collided. The pope first sent his legate to demand Luther's retraction, but Luther refused to retract his views unless the pope refuted him by using scripture. Luther appealed first to the pope and then to a council. The Diet (formal assembly of German councilors) at Worms in 1521 is taken as the final round, when Luther again refused to recant, in words that are often quoted:

> Unless I am convinced by Scripture and evident reason—for I do not accept the authority of popes and councils, which have often erred and contradicted each other—my conscience is taken captive by God's word, and I neither can nor will recant anything, for it is neither safe nor right to go against conscience. God help me. Amen.

Under Luther's leadership Protestantism developed and expanded in Germany during the remaining 25 often turbulent years of his life.

John Calvin: Reformer and Scholar   Luther, the son of a miner, was earthy, affectionate, brash, and even vulgar sometimes, yet his religious experience shaped Protestantism. John Calvin, his French counterpart, was aristocratic, polished, severe, extremely scholarly; his writing articulated the Protestant spirit and his theories of church government set the lines for what are called the Reformed churches. An outstanding student who at first started on an ecclesiastical career, he turned to the law in 1528, when he was 19. His own conversion to the reformed ideas, which were still new to France, came in 1532 and 1533. Although Calvin was always the complete scholar, he was also a religious enthusiast deeply committed to the evangelical faith, and he described his as a "sudden conversion" brought about by divine agency. His brilliance and devotion soon made him the leader of the French Protestants, but after being forced to flee France, he settled in Geneva, Switzerland, by 1536, and spent most of the rest of his life there. Calvin at first shared direction of the reform movement in Geneva with the man who had started it, Farel, but after 1541 was the sole leader of the Genevan church. In church administration his achievement was the form of organization which later, somewhat modified, is known as Presbyterianism. But it was his writing that provided the first great systematic formulation of the Reformation faith. This work, known in English as the *Institutes of the Christian Religion*, started from the ideas of Luther but made the sovereignty of God the dominant theme. From that key idea came the Biblically based system of redemption through Christ and the doctrine of God's election or choice of souls to salvation or damnation. His work helped Protestantism to grow beyond Germany in a form which enabled it to adapt to different cultures.

EXPANSION OF THE REFORMATION, AND THE COUNTER REFORMATION

Many of the German states embraced the Reformation after Luther's break with Rome, and religious and political conflict went on until the Peace of Augsburg in 1555. In Switzerland the movement had begun in 1520, before Calvin came to Geneva, under Ulrich Zwingli, a younger and more liberal reformer than the basically conservative Luther. Calvin's Reformed Church movement spread to Scotland under the dynamic John Knox, while in England political and dynastic issues contributed to the break with Rome by Henry VIII and establishment of a state church which developed its distinctive Anglican character. In the Netherlands both Lutheran and Reformed doctrines found a permanent place, and in Scandinavia all the state churches became Lutheran. Protestantism never succeeded in establishing itself strongly in the Latin countries, for various reasons. There is a vigorous but not large Reformed minority in France, dating from Calvin's time but having experienced many vicissitudes since then.

Meanwhile strong internal forces for reform of Catholicism resulted in the Council of Trent, 1545 through 1563, the principal organ of the Catholic Counter Reformation. Protestants decided not to participate in the Council, and its task became not reconciliation but definition of the difference between Catholic and Protestant doctrine, and extensive reform in church discipline and order. No fundamental changes in doctrine were enunciated, but many specific abuses and problems were dealt with, marking a new era in the life and administration of the church. The Nicene Creed was reaffirmed, although that was not an issue with the Protestants. On the question of the Bible, the Council affirmed the equal authority of the Scriptures themselves and the traditions of the church, and asserted the church's right and duty to interpret the Scriptures for all their public uses. It dealt most carefully with justification. Perhaps the most significant formulation was its explicit affirmation of doctrine about the sacraments, which had been implicit before but not formally articulated. Trent said that all grace is given through sacraments and that all righteousness starts, is nourished by, and is restored through the sacraments. It followed logically that outside the church there is no salvation. The implementation of the reforms and decisions of Trent strengthened Catholicism and enabled it to combat Protestantism effectively in many places, which further solidified the split in Western Christianity. The most dramatic and effective single force against Protestantism and in renewing and spreading Catholicism was the Society of Jesus, the Jesuits. The Spanish nobleman and soldier, Ignatius de Loyola, who founded the order, impressed on it his spirit of soldierly discipline, obedience, and militance in spiritual devotion and warfare. Among other things, the Jesuits revived Catholic education and began the modern Christian missionary movement.

THE ORTHODOX CHURCH IN LATER CENTURIES

The Eastern church had suffered a traumatic blow in 1453, when Constantinople was captured by the Turks of the Ottoman Empire. This was the greatest of all Islamic victories over the Christian world, and in the sixteenth century their expansion on the European continent put much more of the Orthodox Church under their dominion. The Eastern church existed under the emperor for cen-

*St. Sophia's Cathedral in Kiev was begun in the eleventh century. The
Virgin Mary is on the viewer's left and Christ on the right of the eighteenth century iconostasis (icon stand). Mary is enthroned in the dome,
rather than the more usual Christ as Pantocrator (ruler of all). The
priest can be seen at the central altar, and we can look into the sanctuary beyond it. (Photo, Ward J. Fellows, 1993).*

turies, then under Islamic caliphs, Russian czars, Mongols, and finally Soviet commissars. It has been marked by the necessity to adjust to oppressive secular authority in order to exist. At the same time it has provided spiritual life and unity to the people and nurtured their hearts to survive through dark days. After the fall of Constantinople, Russia finally threw off the oppressive Tartars who had followed the Mongols. There arose the legend of "Moscow, the Third Rome" as an expression of Russian hopes and aspirations, and in fact the primate of Russia became Patriarch of the fifth Patriarchate in the Eastern church. These often oppressive conditions helped to nurture the moving solemnity of Orthodox liturgy, the mysticism of the Hesychasts (Quietists) with the Jesus prayer, "Lord Jesus Christ, Son of God, have mercy on me," and the mystical piety of monks and peasants. The Russian Revolution decimated the ranks of Orthodox clergy in Russia; thousands of them were murdered. Concerted campaigns failed, however, to destroy the faith, and in World War II the unseen power of the church was called on to help unite the people. After that, although still under severe limits, the Orthodox Church established a stable *modus vivendi* with the state and fought to survive. In 1985 the situation of the Russian Orthodox Church changed.

CATHOLICISM AND PROTESTANTISM IN THE MODERN ERA

In Europe religion tended to follow the national lines and divisions inherited from the post-Reformation wars. Geographical expansion from Europe to North and South America followed a pattern of national exploration and settlement. Thus the divisions of Christianity have to a large degree been perpetuated in the Americas. In the United States, for nearly 200 years the pattern of religious and national derivation was clearly discernible along the geographical lines of European settlement. Freedom of religion under the First Amendment of the Constitution permitted the development of American religious pluralism.

Jesuit missionary work has been mentioned as the start of modern Christian missions, and Catholics were in the field for 200 years or more before the major Protestant effort began. The nineteenth century witnessed a prodigious Christian missionary effort, above all by Protestants from the United States. As a result of centuries of such work, Christianity by the twentieth century became the most universal of all religions in the geographical, national, racial, and ethnic distribution and diversity of its adherents. Despite many valid criticisms of missionaries, they were (and are) devoted people who brought with the gospel modern education, science, medicine, and social service to the Orient and Africa.

As the predominant religious tradition of the Western world, Christianity has felt the shocks and suffered from the spiritual unrest of the twentieth century. If, as was suggested earlier, the preeminent gifts of the Holy Spirit at Pentecost were unity and power, those are what the church lacks now. Vast in numbers, staff, buildings, traditions, wealth, influence, and all such marks of institutional maturity, it undoubtedly exercises enormous influence for good in many ways. Christian teaching has used the terms "Church Militant" to describe Christianity fighting evil in the present world, as contrasted with the "Church Triumphant," the faithful in Heaven. In the present time of troubles, the promise, the hope, and the expectation of the future sustain the faithful.

The most significant modern movements are: Vatican II, the Council called by Pope John XXIII, which met for three sessions between October 1962 and November 1964; and the continuing ecumenical (worldwide) and other efforts of Protestantism to unify and strengthen Christianity, notably through the World Council of Churches. At Rome the informal theme of Vatican II was *aggiornamento*, modernization, and there was also a significant reconciliation when Paul, Pope John's successor, embraced Athenagoras, the chief Orthodox Patriarch of the East in January of 1964. Less spectacular but pervasive and continuing are the ideas and influences from the ecumenical movement, which continue to inspire and direct significant new trends in Protestantism. Perhaps the force which Christians see in the third person of the Trinity, the Holy spirit, will be the real source of the revival that is sought. Christianity is founded on, and has always looked for and found its help in, the divine power and action.

CHRISTIAN SCRIPTURES AND OTHER LITERATURE

Is the Old Testament a Christian book? The title "Old Testament" is a Christian term, although "testament" was first used in the Septuagint, the Greek version of the Old Testament. The Christian Bible includes the Old Testament of 39 books and the New Testament, 27. "Old Testament" means "Old Covenant," and thus the new is the "New Covenant"; this designation of the two covenants is obviously Christian. The old describes the relations of God and the Jews under the Mosaic covenant, and the new describes the covenant in Jesus Christ between God and all people who acknowledge Jesus as the revelation of God. When Christians read the Old Testament they find Christ foreshadowed there, and they regard the New Testament as the fulfillment of the Old. In all these ways, then, the Old Testament is read or interpreted by Christianity in a different way than by Judaism.

The New Testament

As was noted in discussion of the Hebrew scriptures, modern study of the Bible has applied scientific methods to the entire Bible in what is called Biblical criticism. These investigations have given us much knowledge about individual books and the collection and editing of the New Testament as a whole, by experts in various parts of the science of Biblical criticism. These studies are used in modern translations of the New Testament, and they serve as helps for understanding it. Many books make such information available to the non-expert, in what are called Introductions and Commentaries. The few statements which follow here about the New Testament are very broad and general and make no claim to expert finality.

Out of the faith and needs of the early Christian church came the 27 books, which were selected from many more, to be included in what is called the canon.* The books were written for readers of that time and addressed to minds and problems of that time; to understand them fully the modern readers need to try to put themselves in the situation of the early Christians. None were written as purely objective history or reportorial accounts, but none were forgeries or complete fabrications from whole cloth.

The New Testament writings were in Greek. Paul's letters were written first, coming out of his later journeys and imprisonment at Rome, in 50 and after. The first three Gospels are called the "synoptic Gospels" because they follow the same outline ("synopsis") of Jesus' life. Mark wrote the first Gospel, which was used by Matthew a little later, and by Luke, who also wrote Acts, before the end of the century. Matthew is the most didactic (formal teaching) of the Gospels, and Luke is apologetic in purpose—that is, he wrote to prove that Christianity was not subversive. Some of the so-called "pastoral epistles," namely I and II Timothy and Titus, are dated well into the second century. It has generally been agreed that the latest, most complex, and most theological of the Gospels is John. In the synoptic Gospels Jesus' miracles are done to meet human need and are deliberately minimized by Jesus himself; but in John the miracles serve the theological idea of the divine Logos (Word), whose miracles demonstrate and prove his power.

CANON

By a gradual process of discussion within the church, certain works were selected from among many others as worthy of inclusion in the list or canon of inspired and authoritative books. Before 150, the four Gospels had been singled out, and probably Paul's letters had been assembled earlier. The canon was not completed or agreed upon until the fourth or fifth century; in Athanasius' Easter epistle of 367 the list first appeared as it is now in the New Testament.

The earliest extant (now existing) manuscripts or copies of the New Testament date from the first half of the second century and the third century, while the important Greek uncial (capital-letter) manuscripts are from the fourth and fifth centuries. These are supplemented by later manuscripts, used by the scholars who do the modern translations. The most famous English translation of the Bible is the "King James" version, so called from the English king under whose orders it was completed in 1611.

Apostolic Fathers

The writings of the Apostolic Fathers overlap the New Testament in their dates and character. Many of them are letters from typical leaders of the early churches, such as the unknown writer from Rome to Corinth known as I Clement, about 95. The Shepherd of Hermas, about 140 or earlier, a mixture of vision and instruction, is the longest work. The most important material for theological study is in the letters of Ignatius, Bishop of Antioch, on his way to martyrdom at Rome, in 115.

Apologists

In the face of persecution, first Jewish or Herodian and then pagan or Roman, Christians composed defenses of Christianity. Justin Martyr's *Dialogue with Trypho* is a friendly statement of the case for Christianity in dialogue form to a Jewish questioner. His two other works, to Gentiles, are more polemical and attack paganism. About half a dozen writers are listed under this heading, all from the second and third centuries.

TENETS

Of all the major religions, Christianity has the fullest, most explicit formal statements of faith. The practice of using a creed is so familiar and universal in Christianity that most Christians think of the creed as the most important and distinctive thing about a religion. This tells much about Christianity: The faith is explicit, declared, defined, and affirmed in statements, creeds, and formulas.

The threefold nature of God as Father, Son, and Holy Spirit (the Trinity) is fundamental in all branches of Christianity except a few unitarian and humanistic Protestant denominations. Although Trinitarian doctrine proper has never been adequately formulated, it is accepted as meaning "One God in Three Persons." This Triune God is the focus of doctrine and worship. Our statement of Christian tenets is therefore divided: God the Father, Jesus Christ, the Holy Spirit.

God the Father

The Biblical view of God is not lost in Christianity, but is affirmed in the first sentence of both the Apostles' and Nicene creeds. God the Father is the one ultimate ground of all existence, just as in Judaism; all else is second to him. The created order is good and it is real, but it is not divine. The Biblical doctrine of God, which was described under Judaism, is taken over by Christianity and must be presupposed here. In addition, Christianity has its own description of God as "the God and Father of our Lord Jesus Christ." God is the ultimate reality for Christianity, but God as seen and known through Jesus Christ. Therefore our discussion of Christian tenets must treat at length the doctrine concerning Jesus Christ.

Jesus Christ the Son

The doctrine about Jesus Christ is the meaning that Christians find in the life, death, and resurrection of Jesus Christ—what is called the "Christ event" to

Corpus from a crucifix, thirteenth century (Courtesy of M. H. de Young Memorial Museum, San Francisco).

stress that Jesus' life was a concrete happening in the world. Because this was a historical process of development, we will deal with it chronologically, but our concern is the content of the doctrine, not the process. After a preliminary statement about the existential crux of the issue, there will be three sections: Affirmation, Proclamation, and Explanation and Definition of the Christ event.

THE IMPORTANCE OF THE QUESTION: SALVATION OR DAMNATION

Any religion can be thought of a cure for a spiritual sickness, comparable to a medical doctor's cure for a physical illness. Just as the doctor diagnoses the disease and prescribes the way to health, so a religion says "you are ailing here and here" from such-and-such spiritual ill and you must do thus-and-so to be saved from it. All the religions described in this book could be analyzed—necessary changes being made—according to this model of spiritual sickness and cure. It may be that the Biblical view has been strongly influenced here by Zoroastrian dualism and the corresponding choice between good and evil, but at any rate all three of the Western religions define the issue in the form of decision and commitment. They say: Avoid spiritual death and choose spiritual life by committing yourself to God. Judaism says: Follow the God of Abraham, Isaac, and Jacob and join your Hebrew compatriots. Islam says: Submit to Allah and acknowledge his prophet Muhammad. Christianity says: Accept Jesus Christ as your Lord and Savior and receive the salvation of God.

Christianity, and above all Christian doctrine, cannot be understood except in the light of this dichotomy: On the one side are the Devil or Satan, evil, damnation, spiritual death, hell, and the legions of the damned; on the other side are God and Christ, goodness, salvation, spiritual life, heaven, and the communion of the saints. Nowadays, of course, many churches and Christians would not put it that baldly or literally. But it must be said that historically and theologically Christianity cannot be understood except in the light of this fundamental division. This is what lent urgency to the Arian controversy and the basic religious question in the Reformation. The choice is usually presented by the preacher as between the ways that lead to heaven or to hell—for instance: Jonathan Edwards's mid-eighteenth-century American Protestant sermon, "Sinners in the Hand of an Angry God"; Father Arnall's four sermons on the Last Things to Stephen Dedalus and others at a retreat, in James Joyce's *Portrait of the Artist as a Young Man*. To accept Christ leads to heaven, to reject him leads to hell—hence the emphasis on Jesus Christ.

AFFIRMATION OF THE EVENT

Many churches preserve in their Easter customs and liturgy the first Christian affirmation. "He is risen," one says, and another replies, "He is risen indeed." That is what they said, in love and wonder, on the first Easter Day, and it is affirmed in all the churches of Christendom every Easter Day. Likewise with all the key events of Jesus' life; they constitute the basic content of Christian faith. The story of Jesus Christ, then, is the core of Christian doctrine. It is called "the gospel," meaning "the good news," which is the basis and center of Christian faith and life. For all Christians in all places and all times Christian faith first means the story of Jesus Christ. The basic statement of this is in the four Gospels, which tell the story as a fact, a series of connected events in the world. They were written to preserve the account of the facts. The prologue of Luke's Gospel says in part: "It seemed good to me also, having followed all things closely for some time past, to write an orderly account for you, most excellent Theophilus, that you may know the truth concerning the things of which you have been informed" (Luke 1:3, 4).

The primacy of affirmation in Christian doctrine is most clearly expressed in the words with which such affirmations always begin, and from which their generic name is derived: *Credo*, I believe. A person who says that is solemnly declaring that the event did take place in that way, that it is true; and the essential content of a Christian creed is a recital of the events of the life of Jesus Christ. The creed first affirms that the event happened, and then also affirms, in effect, that the story, the facts, are normative and determinative. That is why the Gospels have such importance: They are the first statement of what happened, of the event that is determinative and normative for Christian faith. The nature of Christian doctrine as affirmation is also seen in the fact that when it is used in worship, the creed is usually spoken in unison; it is a common as well as a personal affirmation of the Christian event. The first Christians said *Credamus*, "we believe."

PROCLAMATION OF THE SIGNIFICANCE OF THE EVENT

But it is not enough to affirm the event for oneself and as part of the Christian community. The church from the first also proclaimed the Christian faith to all the world. Proclamation is therefore a second essential aspect of Christian faith—it is a proclamation to the world. But it is more than a proclamation of the bare event, and affirmation affirms more than the bare fact. Christians affirm and proclaim the significance, or impact of the facts, the event. This was clear from the first and is true now. Some modern Christians in the United States proclaim Christ with stickers on their cars. Others put up signs and pay for outdoor advertising billboards to proclaim that Jesus is the answer. The wisdom of such methods is debatable, but it is all part of Christian proclamation. The New Testament quickly moves from affirmation to proclamation; the Book of Acts continues the Christ story after the resurrection, beginning with Pentecost. Pentecost was witnessed by many Jews from other nations who, according to Acts 2:5 following, heard the Christians speaking in tongues intelligible to them, although they spoke different languages. They asked what was happening, and Peter replied in the first sermon to the world: "Men of Israel, hear these words. . . ." He affirmed the facts, and then he proclaimed their significance, concluding with the summary statement: "Let all the house of Israel therefore know assuredly that God has made him both Lord and Christ, this Jesus whom you crucified" (Acts 2:36). When Peter's listeners asked what to do, he told them to repent and be baptized in the name of Jesus Christ for the forgiveness of sins. The last formula may have been read back into Luke's account of the event, for it carries the Christian doctrine and program farther.

Modern New Testament studies use the Greek word κήρυγμα (Eng., kerygma), which means "proclamation by a herald" or "public notice," to denote the early proclamation of the Gospel. The New Testament writers did not simply report the events, they affirmed and proclaimed them, because that is what the early Christians did. The Apostle Paul's importance in the New Testament comes in part from his constant proclamation of the gospel: "The gospel

Knight, Death and Devil, *Durer, 1513 (Courtesy, Achenbach Foundation for Graphic Arts, California Palace of the Legion of Honor, San Francisco).*

concerning his Son, who was descended from David according to the flesh and designated Son of God in power according to the Spirit of Holiness by his resurrection from the dead . . ." (Romans 1:4). In its simplest form, the kerygma was "Jesus Christ is Lord"; in other words Jesus Christ was not just another crucified criminal, but the divine deliverer.

The Apostolic Fathers and the Apologists were essentially proclaimers of the gospel. To determine their place in the history of Christian doctrine, we will outline the differences in their views. The Apostolic Fathers resemble New Testament writers in that their writings are directed to a specific occasion and topic. They were not trying to write formal theology, but they were concerned to speak about Christ in theological terms. As Clement of Rome says: "Brothers, so we must think about Jesus Christ as about God. . . . The absoluteness of salvation requires an absolute Divine Savior." The Fathers proclaim that Jesus Christ is the Lord who brings salvation; but they do not explain him or his work beyond that essential proclamation.

The Apologists were the first Christian philosophers, who proclaimed a more specific philosophic defense against the accusations that Christianity was politically subversive and philosophically nonsense. The most important was Justin Martyr, who in about 150 called Jesus not only the Son of God but also the Logos. This was perhaps the most important single apologetic idea: Jesus Christ is the Logos. λόγος is the central Greek philosophical term, denoting reason, thought, mind, rationality, and also speech or word in the abstract sense of what is spoken or meant by words. It had been used by many philosophers in many ways long before the Christian era. The crucial Christian move is the combination of Hebrew concrete religious categories with Greek abstract philosophical terms in application to Jesus Christ. Some genius, perhaps the author of the fourth Gospel, inasmuch as it appears there earliest, first made this identification of the Hebrew Messiah (χριστος or "annointed one" in Greek) or Christ with the Greek Logos. Although the later doctrine added much to this, the combination of Hebrew and Greek ideas in Christ as Logos is central to the development of Christianity. It marked the beginning of interpretation of the Christian Biblical affirmation and proclamation in terms of philosophical concepts.

EXLANATION AND DEFINITION OF THE EVENT

With the passage of time, disagreements about the meaning of Christ and the proclamation emerged. These are the doctrinal differences which have troubled Christianity. As soon as the church was institutionally stabilized under Constantine, it became necessary to adjudicate these long-standing differences. Within a period of 450 years the seven ecumenical councils were devoted chiefly to this task, and they formulated some basic principles that are still generally accepted. The general term "dogma" means the doctrine systematized in creeds and articles for acceptance and use by the church. The principal legacies of the councils are the creeds that they formulated in the endeavor to state and define dogma. These became decisive for the thought content of the church. (Every religion has such a thought content or substance; in Christianity it was carefully and fully formulated.) There is another function of dogma; it serves as protection against distortions of doctrine, called "heresy," especially in the later stages of development. Once formulated, creeds become the central dogma of the Christian community and are used in worship. Therefore they are quoted here as expressions of Christian doctrines used in churches.

THE APOSTLES' CREED

This is the earliest and simplest of the major creeds, although, because it was not promulgated by a council, it lacks full authority in the East. Known as "the Old Roman Creed," it was probably not actually from Jerusalem or the apostles. The Roman baptismal confession from which the modern creed is derived was known from the fourth century; and a later form was composed in the eighth century. Both Protestants and Catholics recognize this creed. Notice that it has the Trinitarian form, and that the Christ-doctrine center of it is a recital of facts or events, using simple direct verbs of physical action:

THE APOSTLES' CREED

I believe in God the Father Almighty, maker of heaven and earth; and in Jesus Christ his only Son our Lord, who was conceived by the Holy Spirit, born of the Virgin Mary, suffered under Pontius Pilate, was crucified, dead, and buried. He descended into hell; the third day he rose again from the dead. He ascended into heaven, and sitteth on the right hand of God the Father Almighty. From thence he shall come to judge the quick and the dead.

I believe in the Holy Spirit, the holy Catholic Church, the communion of saints, the forgiveness of sins, the resurrection of the body, and the life everlasting. Amen.

THE NICENE CREED

This most famous and universal of Christian creeds also has the most complex evolution. Although the Nicene Creed takes its name from the First General Council, its wording and the doctrinal issues it encompassed were not settled until later. Behind it lies the first great doctrinal struggle of Christianity. Often this dispute is described as being over the Trinity, because by implication it does pertain to Trinitarian dogma. In simpler terms it is over the question of the divinity of Christ, because the full or complete divinity of Christ as really God was and still is at issue. In that sense it was about the Trinity, the question in effect being whether Christ was truly part of the Godhead. For our purposes, the question was whether or not Christ is God; in the outcome it was decided that he *is* divine. (Later it had to be decided *how* the divine and human are related or joined in him.) Technically, these are Christological (doctrine of Christ) questions about the person of Christ.

The loser in the contest was a priest in Alexandria named Arius, whence came the name "Arian" Christians. The great theoretical problem for Christianity from the first had been how to reconcile the divinity of Christ with monotheism. If Christ is divine, does that make a second God and deny the oneness? The orthodox outcome of this and other controversies was the eternal equality of the Three Persons of the Trinity. Arius' view jeopardized this equality because he taught that the Son had a beginning: ἦν ποτε ὅτε οὐκ ἦν, "there was once when he was not." But the philosophical difference was not the real issue, which was salvation itself in real and personal terms. In about 175, Irenaeus, bishop of Lyons in Gaul, made the first systematic exposition of Christian faith. He taught that in Christ "God became man that man might become God," and that the Incarnation* (God in human flesh) and the Resurrection brought salvation to man from death and sin. Athanasius, Bishop of Alexandria, saw the fundamental soteriological importance of the issue and became the champion of the orthodox view. Arius' view threatened this crucial personal Christian faith that Jesus Christ *as God* had done the work. It was essential that his full deity be maintained, because only God can pay the price to redeem man, "for the wages of sin is death" (Romans 6:23). This was a matter of spiritual life and death to the contenders, not simply a theoretical issue.

At Nicaea it was affirmed that Christ is "of the substance of the Father" and "begotten not made, of one substance with the Father." The key phrase for "one substance with the Father" in Greek is ὁμοούσιον τῷ πατρί. Other questions were involved in the issue, however, and because of that there was continued debate over ὁμοούσιον, the same substance. After Nicaea another party wanted to use ὁμοιούσιον, meaning like or of similar substance with the Father. After years of controversy, a council at Constantinople in 381, which became known as the Second General Council and the author of the creed, finally rejected the ὁμοιούσιον or "like substance" view in favor of the "same substance," ὁμοούσιον. The form of the Nicene Creed in general use in churches now was not actually read and approved until the Council of Chalcedon in 451, although the main verdict was made at Constantinople. The effect of this series of controversies was essentially to confirm, by 381, the equality in essence or substance of the three Persons of the Trinity, the Father, the Son and the Holy Spirit.

THE NICENE CREED

I believe in one God the Father Almighty, maker of heaven and earth, and of all things visible and invisible.

And in one Lord Jesus Christ, the only-begotten Son of God, begotten of his Father before all worlds, God of God, light of light, very God of very God. Begotten, not made, being of one substance with the Father; by whom all things were made. Who for us men and for our salvation came down from heaven, and was made man, and was crucified also for us under Pontius Pilate. He suffered and was buried, and the third day he rose again according to the scriptures. And ascended into heaven, and sitteth on the right hand of the Father. And he shall come again, with glory, to judge both the quick and the dead, whose kingdom shall have no end.

And I believe in the Holy Spirit, the lord and giver of life, who proceedeth from the Father and the Son, who with the Father and the Son together is worshipped and glorified, who spake by the Prophets. And I believe one catholic and apostolic church. I acknowledge one baptism for the remission of sins, and I look for the resurrection of the dead, and the life of the world to come. Amen.

The Crucifixion, *Matteo de Giovanni (Courtesy, M. H. de Young Memorial Museum, San Francisco).*

CHALCEDON

Not only the Arian controversy was finally resolved at Chalcedon; other basic Christological decisions were affirmed there. The most important was the second problem of the person of Christ—that is, the nature of the combination or union of the divine and human in Jesus Christ. The defeat of Arius answered the question whether or not Christ was divine, by affirming his full divinity. The other side of his nature, the humanity, was affirmed in various decisions. The point was that just as Jesus must be divine to effect salvation, so must he be fully human. Unless he truly lived, suffered, and died as a human being, like other human beings, his death and resurrection were just a trick and not the guarantee that humanity has been reborn in Christ as the God-man, the new Adam. The theological problems were: What kind of being was Christ, and how was it possible to be both divine and human? This double question is what we call the second problem. In the final Chalcedonian definition (451), the full humanity and full deity are both flatly affirmed. No really adequate theological explanation has ever been worked out for this doctrine. Chalcedon formulated a "definition," not a creed, to make its central affirmation that Christ is "recognized in two natures, without confusion, without change, without division, without separation."[7] Thus the dual nature is reiterated so as to make it clear that Jesus is both like God in divinity and yet like people in humanity.

THE DOCTRINE OF THE WORK OF CHRIST

In traditional theological terms, the next question after answering the issue of the person or nature of Christ is about the work of Christ—what he does. All

Christians agree that his work is salvation—he saves people from sin and death. But there is disagreement about how to define the human problem, what people need to be saved from, and the way Jesus as Savior effects salvation—how he works it. The central work of Christ is the Atonement*: Jesus Christ suffered and died for our sins. The important thing is that all Christians in all times and all places agree to that as a general formula. But it has been subject to such a long history of change and such a wide spectrum of differing explanations and interpretations, particularly in the past 200 years, that a summary or outline is not feasible in such a book as this. What must be reiterated is the importance of this facet of Christian belief to the individual Christian: *Christians of all persuasions regard Jesus Christ as in some unique way their personal Savior.* This is the heart of doctrine, worship, devotion, meaning, and life for the Christian: Jesus Christ is Lord and Savior. He saves them now in the world, but at best that is a partial victory. The fulfillment of Christian faith is the Resurrection of all Christians after death to share in the complete and eternal victory of the risen Christ.

The Holy Spirit

The third Person of the Trinity denotes the invisible reality of God working in the world, by which the Christian church was formed and is sustained. It is from or by the Spirit that the church, the ministry, the sacraments, and the Christian life derive their spiritual substance and power.

CURRENT DEVELOPMENTS

Beyond our Trinitarian survey of Christian doctrines there are significant contemporary trends that transcend those categories and affect them all. These trends reflect Christian concerns about contemporary issues and problems, but with different approaches and theories about how to deal with them. Here, all we can do is to note one theme that has appeared in various contexts and forms. It is the "blessed word" of much contemporary philosophy and theology: hermeneutics. The basic singular word meaning is simple—interpretation; but the plural complicates it—*theories* of interpretation. They go far back in religions, because from the beginning of the modern study of sacred texts, scholars realized they had to be aware of their own way—their theory—for doing such work.

Christian theology is now full of new, alternative methods for doing theology, thinking about God in relation to a concrete problem, in a new way free from old, unquestioned presuppositions. These various approaches are alike in two ways: they question traditional presuppositions and methods; and they embrace certain political/social causes and concerns, to be espoused and supported by the churches. Juan Segundo, theologian of Latin American liberation, has refined it to the "hermeneutic of suspicion." In it, people become *suspicious* that the dominant culture and system are misleading their thinking, so they generate a new hermeneutic for their scriptures. Segundo goes on to develop the necessity for the Catholic Church, because that is his base, to change its whole viewpoint. There must, he says, be "an option for the poor" on the part of the hierarchy and in Catholic theology itself.

James Cone, whose seminar I once attended, relates his "black theology" to Martin Luther King Jr.'s struggle for civil rights in a Christian context. Referring to the origin of the term, Cone gives a brief definition: "What is clear is that the idea of black theology (i.e., an interpretation of the faith in the light of black history and culture and completely separate from white religion) was present . . . in 1968."[8] The other pioneer we note is the redoubtable Rosemary Radford Reuther, a feminist theologian. Her blast against "patriarchal theology" in *Sexism and God Talk: Toward a Feminist Theology* was given a new Introduction in the 20th anniversary edition, 1993. Over the years she has carried the battle to the basic assumption of traditional, and especially "patristic," theology. Born a Roman Catholic, she accuses the fathers of the church, and the hierarchy, of blatant sexism not simply in their views of women and their place in the Roman church, but of twisted ideas of God and the nature of the church itself. She has also developed an ecological-feminist theology, a rethinking of doctrine for the earth and the very cosmos.

RITUAL AND WORSHIP

The contrast between the individualism of the Hindu or Buddhist in his or her worship, even while participating in the great mass festivals, and the corporate character of worship in the Western faiths has been noted. Like Judaism, Christianity calls for the response of the Christian community to God in worship; worship is important in Christianity because spiritual life is nourished thereby, and only with God's help can the Christian life be lived. As a result, public communal worship is characteristic of and deemed essential to Christianity, and the formal ceremonies of Christianity are varied and complex. It was to a worshipping congregation of disciples that the Holy Spirit came at Pentecost. Historically, Christian worship at first was like the Hebrew synagogue service. To it was added Holy Communion or the Eucharist, and the whole ceremony was part of a love feast or agape (from Greek ἀγάπη) in which all shared food and drink. When the church grew larger some disorders arose in connection with the agape, and it was separated from worship.

The explanation for Christian worship coming on the first day of the week, not the last or seventh as in Judaism, was given by Justin Martyr in his Apology, about 150.

> We hold our common assembly on the day of the sun, because it is the first day, on which God put to flight darkness and chaos [*literally* matter] and

made the world, and on the same day Jesus Christ our Savior rose from the dead; for on the day before that of Saturn they crucified him; and on the day after Saturn's day, the day of the sun, he appeared to his Apostles and disciples and taught them these things, which we have also handed on to you for your consideration.[9]

It would be impossible to list and describe the ritual practice of all churches. We follow a simple theoretical division which permits us to summarize the types and varieties of Christian worship. The division is between the essentially inward content, meaning, idea, or mood of Christian worship on one hand, and the essentially outward form, method, way, or mode of Christian ritual on the other; in philosophical terms the content and form of Christian worship.

The Content, Meaning, Idea, or Mood of Christian Worship (What Is Expressed)

The Christian voices or expresses many things in and through the different forms of worship. Here we list some of the principal ideas or meanings that are the content, substance, or thought which is expressed.

PRAISE AND ADORATION

The first element in Christian response to God is praise and adoration of him as God, simply for his glory, his being God, apart from any specific thing which one enjoys or receives from him. The Westminster Catechism says, "The first duty of man is to glorify God and enjoy him forever." Most Christian services begin with a hymn of praise, and the *Gloria* ("Glory be to the Father"). Praise affirms the Christian conviction that in spite of appearances God yet rules the cosmos, is God.

THANKSGIVING

The note of thanksgiving is in some ways the most persistent or pervasive element of Christian worship. As Paul said, Christians are "always and for everything giving thanks" (Ephesians 5:20). For specific and personal, for general and universal blessings, the church thanks and blesses God. At all times, even in suffering and adversity, one is to give thanks. But especially and above all, as the prayer book says, for the gift of the grace of God in Jesus Christ. Therefore the ancient name for Communion, the Eucharist, is from the Greek for "thanksgiving."

CONFESSION, PENITENCE

Any complete service or mass includes the note of repentance. Before the glory of God, the Christian feels his or her unworthiness and makes confession in one form or another. Penance is one of the Catholic sacraments. The inescapable moral concern of Christianity, in which sin is first of all offense against God, is thus voiced in worship.

PETITION

There is no rule against asking or seeking help, mercy, gifts, blessings from God in worship. Some Christians are diffident about this, and some critics are scornful of it. No doubt pure selfish materialism should not be the only kind of "asking," but tradition sanctions the idea of asking, for oneself and others (intercession), in the service.

FORGIVENESS, ABSOLUTION

First of all as forgiveness of sin, the mercy of God is celebrated in worship for all the gifts of grace that minister to the need of the soul for reassurance in spiritual terms. Liturgically, this is pronounced in different ways, but the note or meaning is always the same—the peace and comfort of God is freely given to all who ask it. Jesus Christ is the seal or guarantee of this.

EXHORTATION AND ENCOURAGEMENT

Inasmuch as the Christian life is "wayfaring and warfaring" in the world, public worship includes the call to action, perseverance, courage, and steadfastness. This may be in a sermon by the clergyperson, but it is also expressed through such means as scripture reading and hymns.

INSTRUCTION, EDUCATION

Christian worship may include specific teaching about God and holy things. In a sense, the entire service is education or conditioning. But some formal instruction is often included, especially when many are new to the faith.

COMMITMENT, DEDICATION

Psychologically, this note fits best near the end or close of worship. The formal "offering" of money symbolizes and expresses dedication, which may also be expressed in other liturgical elements. In all of them, the idea is that just as God has given of himself in Jesus Christ, so Christians are to fulfill their Christian covenant by dedication and commitment of their lives to God.

The Form, Method, Way, or Mode of Worship (How It Is Expressed)

Any theme or idea (the *content* as listed above) may be expressed in any *form* or mode, and many themes may be carried by one mode or many modes may carry the same theme. For example, the words of the hymn "Faith of our Fathers" (mode of music) express the themes of praise, thanks, and commitment. The different ways or forms in which the ideas of the Christian are expressed in worship include:

1. Music, including hymns, solos, organ, choir anthems;
2. Prayers of confession, petition, thanks; collects and invocations—spoken and silent, clerical or congregational;
3. Readings from scripture and other devotional material;
4. Antiphonal (responsive) readings, chants;
5. Sermons or addresses, announcements, instructions;
6. Congregational or unison readings, declarations, chants, creeds, affirmations, prayers;
7. Physical actions such as bowing, kneeling, crossing oneself, shouting; ecstatic phenomena such as shaking or jumping.

As another example, the idea or mood of confession is most commonly expressed either by the direct, personal act of confession, or in common as part of the service, but may be carried by music, readings, antiphons, and other methods. Almost any service can be analyzed by using combinations of the foregoing ideas and forms.

The actual forms and formulas or orders of worship and ritual vary enormously. Probably the paradigm of formal liturgical order is a Catholic high mass, and the least structured is a Quaker silent meeting in which anyone or no one may be moved by the Spirit to speak aloud. In between is the usual Protestant service with a simple, more or less fixed order of service. Significant is the Pentecostal type of worship, in which free and frequent expression of joy in the Lord as manifestation of the Spirit is encouraged. Many black churches and others fit this pattern, but some liturgical churches are experimenting in this direction.

Church architecture reflects the type of worship conducted in it. Protestant churches are customarily simple or plain, with only a few symbols. The amount of decoration is greater in Catholic churches, and they use statues and images, as do some Lutheran churches. In Orthodox churches the most important symbols are two-dimensional, painted sacred icons of Christ, the Virgin Mary, and other figures.

The Christian liturgical year begins with Advent, a month before the Christmas celebration of the birth of Jesus. The most important day is Easter,* which commemorates the Resurrection of Jesus and is preceded by Lent. Pentecost and Trinity Sunday follow Easter after several weeks. Other special days depend on the particular tradition.

Sacraments

The sacraments are distinctive ritual observances of Christianity, more or less separated from the regular service as a whole. In Protestantism they are outward and visible signs of inward and spiritual grace; and Catholic and Anglican theory concur, adding that the sacraments are "instituted by Christ." Orthodoxy describes them as external vehicles of the unfathomable presence of the Holy Spirit. The seven sacraments of the Catholic Church are: Baptism, Confirmation, Eucharist,* Penance, Anointing of the Sick, Holy Orders, and Matri-

View from the ancient Pecherskaya Laura (monastery), Kiev. The scene suggests a historical fact about Russian Orthodoxy: always having to live under the shadow of the rulers. For the (at least) five golden church domes on the left are dominated by the huge statue of Mother Russia in the distance at extreme right. The monastery is thronged with visitors. (Photo, Ward J. Fellows, 1993).

mony. Orthodoxy includes all these, but combines Baptism and Confirmation, and adds other related "sacramentalia." In Protestantism there are only two: Baptism and Communion. Ceremonies similar to some of the other Catholic sacraments are observed in Protestantism, but not as sacraments.

BAPTISM

The rite of Baptism is the sign of spiritual cleansing by the grace of Christ, and constitutes inclusion in the community of faith. The Nicene Creed says, "I acknowledge one Baptism for the remission of sins." Because of this, even the Catholic Church recognizes other baptisms as valid, provided they are according to the universal formula: "I baptize thee in the name of the Father, and the Son, and the Holy Spirit. Amen." The element used is water (except in emergency), and the manner varies, from complete immersion to pouring water three times or gently placing a few drops on the head.

The model of a sacrament, as seen in Baptism, is that certain visible things are done and words are spoken, following the example of things done and spoken by Jesus. These words and actions correspond to certain intangible spiritual meanings or events. For Baptism the original event was baptism of Jesus in the river Jordan by John the Baptist, with the appearance of the Holy Spirit in the form of a dove, and the voice from heaven saying, "This is my beloved Son." Jesus specifically instituted the sacrament of baptism when he said: "Go therefore and make disciples of all nations baptizing them in the name of the Father, and of the Son, and of the Holy Spirit" (Matthew 28:19). God's work, as symbolized and celebrated by the sacrament, effectuates spiritual regeneration from evil, and applies an indelible spiritual mark. When Martin Luther was in the depths of his spiritual struggles he consoled himself with the reminder, "*Baptizatus sum*," "I am baptized."

COMMUNION

The other chief or universal Christian sacrament is Communion, which is also the center of Catholic mass and is part of the Orthodox and some Protestant regular Sunday liturgies. In Protestant churches of the Reformed and other traditions it is performed less frequently, only on "Communion Sunday." Communion proper may be shortened to the bare essentials and performed separately. The Greek term for it is the Eucharist, and it is often called the Lord's Supper.

Following the same model that was used for Baptism, Communion has a specific New Testament basis. The occasion was the last supper of Jesus and his disciples, the night before Passover, in "an upper room," after which he went out to his betrayal, arrest, and crucifixion. This institution of the sacrament is described in all four Gospels and by Paul. Jesus took a loaf of bread and blessed and broke it apart before giving each disciple a piece, saying, "This is my body, eat of it in remembrance of me." Likewise he passed the wine cup, telling each of them to drink, and saying, "This is my blood." Although the exact words of the four Gospels and Paul differ slightly, these outward actions and spoken words are the fundamentals of the Biblical institution by Jesus. They constitute the essentials of any Eucharist. Within Christendom there is wide variety of customs for Communion, with Catholic mass, Orthodox liturgy, and some Protestant liturgies being very long and formal; at the other extreme some Protestant services are completely free and unstructured. The elements are always bread in some form, often a special wafer, and grape juice or wine, mixed with a little water. Methods of distribution and reception of the elements vary. In all, the spiritual meaning and effect is the point and purpose of communion. This purpose also varies and calls for comment, because as the most solemn and important of the sacraments Communion reveals much about the nature of Christianity.

Theories of Worship

ORTHODOX

The Orthodox Church finds its center and meaning in the worshipping church, in the liturgy itself. The ancient Greek word *lietourgia* meant a public service or public duty, and the Orthodox interpret it by dividing the word into two component words, as the work or service of the people. Whether this etymology is correct or not, it is true that in the liturgy of the faithful Orthodoxy finds the presence of the risen Christ. In the Orthodox tradition, as in Protestantism, the Eucharist cannot be performed by the priest alone, but only when people are present, because they do the "work" (the second half of the word in Greek). According to the *Russian Primary Chronicle*, Prince Vladimir of Kiev (980–1015), who made Orthodoxy the state religion of Russia, sent emissaries to seek the true religion; they were unimpressed by Muslim, Jewish, and Western Christian worship. But when they stood in Hagia Sophia in Constantinople with the Holy Liturgy filling its vastness, they said:

> Whether we were in heaven or on earth we knew not. Surely there is no such splendor or beauty anywhere upon earth, and we are at a loss how to describe it to you. Only this we know, that God dwells there among men, and that their service is fairer than the worship of other nations. For we cannot forget that beauty.

The central affirmation of the Orthodox liturgy is the Incarnation and Resurrection of Christ the God-man, and his sacramental and mystical presence is the core of the service. The Incarnation is affirmed as the answer to the separation of God and man, which Orthodoxy sees as the fruit of the Fall. Although in some ways Orthodoxy does not stress sin so much as Augustine did in the Western tradition, it teaches that human nature itself was corrupted by Adam's sin. By the Incarnation God so entered into the world as to overcome the separation, reestablish the unity of creator and creation, and restore human nature. This transformation of the world, of the very cosmos, is guaranteed by the Resurrection, which is central not only on Easter but at all times in the Orthodox liturgy. By participation in the liturgy the believer shares in the life-giving power and grace of God bestowed in Christ and manifested by the Holy Spirit. There is no such special communion doctrine in Orthodoxy as in Catholicism, because the life and meaning of Jesus Christ are mystically present in any congregation where the liturgy is "worked."

CATHOLIC

According to Catholic teaching, the church is the exclusive channel or vehicle of God's grace in Jesus Christ, and the two principal means for transmission of this grace are prayer and the sacraments. The principal function of the church is to disperse, through the duly ordained clergy, the sacramental grace of which it is custodian. The mass is a complex whole, a ritual developed over the centuries, each major part having its rationalized place and meaning. Rich in color, movement, sound, scent, and symbolical elements and acts, it nourishes the spiritual life of Catholicism. If Jesus Christ is the heart of the church, the mass is the blood which carries life to all parts of the Body of Christ, as the church is often called. The mass is the reenactment of the sacrifice of Christ on the cross, and this is the inclusive meaning and drama of the sacrament as a whole. According to the doctrine of transubstantiation the elements are changed into the body and blood of Christ.

Outwardly or in form they remain the same wafer and wine, but their substance or inward matter is changed to the body and blood of Christ. In the "consecration," the priest holds the elements and recites the scriptures: "This is my body. . . . This is my blood," when transubstantiation occurs. Following that, the "elevation" is the priest's raising overhead the wafer and the chalice, for adoration by the faithful.

When the mass is celebrated by a Catholic priest according to the canons (laws) of the church, the miracle takes place *ex opere operato* (by the work or action performed); that is, it is not dependent on the moral or spiritual condition or attitude of the priest. The Catholic Church thus in effect guarantees the faithful that the veritable sacramental grace of Christ is brought to them. Now this is a tremendous claim. To the true Catholic this assures one's salvation and is the basis of faith and life. It is the spiritual center of a church of a billion souls.

PROTESTANT

In Protestant Communion (the term they prefer), the celebration as a memorial of the Lord, a remembrance of all that Christ did and does, is the central idea. There is no claim that the Communion is "an unbloody sacrifice," a veritable reenactment of the crucifixion and Resurrection in Christ himself, as there is in Catholic theory. For Protestants believe that the one original, historical, atoning death of Christ on the cross is effectual for all time and all believers. The term "Communion" is preferred, because it emphasizes the sharing or relation "in common" of the believer in Christ and of believers in fellowship together. There are Protestant doctrines about the "real presence"* of Christ in the elements, which in effect resemble the Catholic doctrine. Although some Lutheran scholars reject the term, "consubstantiation" is used to describe the doctrine that the substance of Christ's body and blood veritably are present together with or in the elements. Although it is not closely defined by them, Anglicans and Orthodox each in effect hold to a doctrine of the real presence. Calvinists believe in the "spiritual presence" of Christ in the bread and wine. The many Protestant denominations which follow Ulrich Zwingli treat the Lord's Supper as a memorial of the fellowship with and in Christ, and they affirm its spiritual efficacy to the believer.

This discussion of worship and the sacraments should show that the keynote of worship for all Christians is set by its character as glad affirmation of God's victory over evil, sin, and death by the crucifixion and Resurrection of Jesus Christ. All believers share the fruits of that victory. Any description that gives only Christianity's serious view of sin and of the reality of evil and death, without countering that with the affirmation of the atoning and redeeming love and mercy of God in Christ—any such view is a polemical caricature. The abiding note or mood of Christian worship and life is praise, thanks, gladness, rejoicing, celebration of what God did, does, and will do. The corresponding personal attitude is trust, and expectation, because Christ's victory is eternal and will finally be fully manifested

Pope Clement, 1730-1740. Bouchardon, 1731 (Courtesy, M. H. de Young Memorial Museum, San Francisco).

in his coming again in glory to establish the kingdom of God. His final victory, moreover, includes all believers, who will share in the resurrection of the dead. Something of this is expressed in the best-known and loved, most widely used, uniquely Christian prayer taught by Jesus to his disciples and known as the Lord's Prayer or Our Father. As given in Matthew 6:10-13 it is:

Our Father who art in heaven,
Hallowed be thy name.
Thy kingdom come,
They will be done,
　On earth as it is in heaven.
Give us this day our daily bread;
And forgive us our debts.
　As we also have forgiven our debtors;
And lead us not into temptation,
　But deliver us from evil.

THE INSTITUTIONAL AND ETHICAL ASPECTS OF CHRISTIANITY

The public and visible institutions of Christianity in the United States are so familiar to many readers of this book that the need is more for analysis, classification, and explanation of data than for description. This is especially true of the church as a pervasive and accepted factor in the community: The buildings are identified as this or that church, with so-and-so as clergy, where they have certain customs, and to which such-and-such persons belong. But in these circumstances the deeper meaning of the faith and more significant differences among churches may easily be lost. Therefore we need to bring out and to summarize some of these significant factors. Two major divisions of this section are the church and the Christian life.

Catholic, Orthodox, and Protestant Churches Today

The Christian church, whatever name or description it may bear in its fragmented state in the world, is the Christian community of faith. Following the Biblical-Jewish model of revelation and response, the word or call of God in Jesus Christ is answered by those who acknowledge and accept that revelation. In the sociological sense of an identifiable group constituted by its common espousal of a set of myths and symbols, the church is like any other institutionalized religion. More specifically, like the two other Biblical religions, it is constituted by its response to a specific divine revelation. We have seen the Hebrew form of this revelation and response, and we will see the Islamic in our next chapter. Christianity differs from them in that Jesus Christ is the content and focus of that revelation, and the essential response, therefore, is in the affirmation and acceptance of Jesus Christ as the distinctive and final revelation of God. In that fundamental affirmation that Jesus is the unique revelation of God, all churches are one. The question in the twentieth century is whether the church can survive in its divided state. Much oversimplified, the Catholic-Protestant dilemma can be stated thus: Catholicism has unity but not freedom; Protestantism has freedom but not unity.

CATHOLIC

Catholics base their claim to Petrine authority on Matthew 16:18–20, Jesus' reply to Peter's declaration that Jesus is the Christ:

> And I tell you, you are Peter, and on this rock I will build my church, and the powers of death shall not prevail against it. I will give you the keys of the kingdom of heaven, and whatever you bind on earth shall be bound in heaven, and whatever you loose on earth shall be loosed in heaven.

Their claim of apostolic succession (line of bishops back to the apostles and Christ) is based on traditions about the death of Peter at Rome and the founding of the church there. The outcome is the vast hierarchical ecclesiastical structure headed by the pope. The pope sometimes speaks of himself as the "servant of the servants of God." He appears to the world as head of the hierarchy and spokesman for the Catholic Church. In 1870 the doctrine of papal infallibility was defined; according to this dogma, when the pope speaks officially (*ex cathedra*) on matters of faith and morals he cannot err. Only once has the pope exercised this authority, to proclaim the dogma of the Assumption to heaven of the Virgin Mary. In actual practice his direct and immediate legislative, executive, and judicial power over all clergy and laity is more pervasive and significant. Catholic clergy, whose function is to minister the sacramental grace of Christ, are ordained into this hierarchical system, and gain their status through it. Vatican II laid increased emphasis on the place and function of the laity and relaxed the church's claim to exclusive control of Christian grace. Despite much discussion and unrest on the questions, the pope has reaffirmed the rule of priestly celibacy and the ban on women in any priestly role. By any empirical standard, the churches, schools, orders, clergy, and adherents included in the Catholic Church comprise the greatest ecclesiastical organization ever known.

ORTHODOX

Orthodoxy sees the unity of the church in the oneness of God and persons, Creator and creation, in Christ; and that unity is nurtured and manifested in the liturgy of the faithful. For the church, as the living Christ in the present world, is itself—says Orthodoxy—the reality and the source of the redemptive power, and no external or visible authority is possible. This essentially mystical doctrine has given Orthodoxy its power to survive for centuries under oppression and persecution. Perhaps its emphasis on the Holy Spirit, which like the wind "bloweth where it listeth" will help to strengthen all Christianity.

My description of the Russian Orthodox Church after perestroika and Gorbachev (1985) is based on my participation in, and the Journal record of, the Citizen Ambassador Program, Religious Education Delegation from the American Academy of Religion to Ukraine and Russia in June 1993.

Comments on our meetings and quotes from the Journal are revealing, but must be limited. There is no question that people attend the liturgy; the cathedrals were crowded with the (standing) worshippers. In Kiev, at old St. Vladimir's, I was reminded of the words of the prince's emissaries, quoted earlier in the section titled Theories of Worship, on the choice of Orthodoxy. The male voices in the responses by the congregation filled and reverberated through the vaulted cathedral, and I stood near one of the "old women" like those referred to by a monk at St. Petersburg's Lavra (monastery), quoted in our Journal: "In response to a question about the 'heartbeat' of orthodoxy during the time of stagnation, our host stressed that many believers went underground, giving part allegiance to the state and part to the church. The 'deepest' believers (mainly old women) went to church even in the worst time, . . ." The woman I observed in St. Vladimir's knew every word and gesture of the liturgy. It was very moving. At our visit with professors in the T. G. Shevtchenko University in Kiev, according to our Journal: "An interesting dialogue between the professors developed as to whether atheism rules the people in Ukraine or whether feelings for God still prevail and need to be uncloaked. Those professors who confessed atheism still conceded to attending Orthodox services occasionally and even to lighting candles."

At the Alexander Nevsky lavra in St. Petersburg these comments were made by teachers in the seminary:

> The distinctive character of Russian orthodoxy includes its emphasis on contemplation, its ability to absorb the life of the believer and lead him/her to disregard economic or political affairs (leaving them in the hands of atheists), and the mystical emphasis. The vice rector was concerned to unite the traditional mystical quality of orthodoxy with concrete social life. The students also spoke in favor of this goal, noting that religion should permeate all of life and that the divorce of church from social life by the revolution of 1917 was an aberration in the tradition of orthodoxy that must now be overcome.

PROTESTANT

The Protestant doctrine of the church and of the ministry places primary emphasis on faith in Christ as the constitutive factor for both. A church is first of all a worshipping and serving community of people who have faith in Jesus Christ, and a minister is first of all a believing Christian. Sincere belief being a spiritual and intangible factor, it cannot be directly measured and controlled, so various expedients and methods are adopted to institutionalize the church and the ministry. The two marks of the church for Protestants are the preaching of the Word of God and administration of the sacraments. The diversity and the division of Protestant institutional forms reflect the differences of belief which gave rise to the separate communions of Protestantism. If the world pictures Catholicism as being a rigid, authoritarian hierarchy, it pictures Protestantism as being a confusing array of many sects, divided and competing. Protestants accept the divisions as a necessary condition for freedom of belief, for personal faith in Jesus Christ as Savior, for the ability to relate to him in that role. One might say that the Catholic finds salvation through the assurance and direction of a divine and infallible church ministering the grace of God, whereas the Protestant finds salvation within a human and fallible church of those who personally and directly know the grace of God in Jesus Christ.

Conscious of the practical and spiritual disadvantages of so many and deep divisions among them, Protestants in the twentieth century have reduced the number of denominations through many unions or mergers. The vast majority of Protestants are members of about 15 major denominations; the nearly 200 other denominations are mostly quite small. However, in saying this one has to ignore the national divisions which persist, although these have been mini-mized by international groupings of the same system, and through the World Council of Churches. Yet there is nothing to compare with the international unity of Catholicism.

Among Protestants, divisions occurred over what were originally signifi-cant doctrinal differences. In the course of time the original disagreements often became less important, but the divisions remained as matters of custom, organization, and structure. Meanwhile new differences and divisions have emerged, but often these cut across denominational lines and do not follow the historic divisions. As a result, an adequate typology of Protestantism is al-most impossible to devise. The classification used here makes no claim to theo-retical adequacy; it is simply a convenient way to include as wide a spectrum as possible of Protestant denominations under a few headings.

Deriving from the two major reformers are the Lutheran and the Re-formed or Presbyterian branches of Protestantism, found in Europe and Amer-ica, and propagated by emigration and missionaries. Luther was conservative in his changes in liturgy and other practices, and the Lutheran liturgy was not at first greatly changed from the Roman. German and Scandinavian Lutherans are numerous in the United States, still retaining their distinct national affilia-tion in some cases, and varying in doctrinal rigor. The Reformed churches are "presbyterial" in government, that is, governed by the presbytery of el-ders from the churches in a certain vicinity. Their Calvinist double predesti-narianism is sometimes relaxed, but still preserves the corresponding empha-sis on the sovereignty of God. Arising out of a larger political struggle, but not finally determined by it, the established church in England claims to be a bridge between Catholicism and Protestantism. "Anglo-Catholics" they are sometimes called, or "Anglicans," and the Episcopal Church of the United States and the churches in former British colonies are affiliated with them through the See of Canterbury. Their prayer book, *The Book of Common Prayer*, is a classic of Elizabethan English, certainly the masterpiece of liturgi-cal literature in English.

A large group, including the Baptists of several varieties as the largest American Protestant denomination, comprise a main stream of traditional, mid-dle-of-the-road, historic American denominations. Although no single charac-teristic can be applied to all, they share several distinctive marks. These de-nominations are "evangelical" in that they propagate the faith simply as the gospel or good news, εὐαγγέλιον being Greek for proclamation of good news. They are formed or "gathered" solely on the basis of the gospel, not by any earthly distinction. Their worship is "free" in the sense of not being deter-mined by a higher authority. They often, but not always, have a measure of doctrinal flexibility and the individual congregations are more or less au-tonomous. Some of the first churches in colonial America, Congregationalists and Baptists, originated thus. Others are the Disciples, Christian, Mennonites, Methodists, Nazarene, Church of God, various Evangelical groups, United Brethren, Moravians, and others.

The Resurrection of Christ, *French, fifteenth century (Courtesy, M. H. de Young Memorial Museum, San Francisco).*

Pentocostal churches are a large and significant, distinctive group within Protestantism. Many black churches are Pentecostal. As the name implies, they emphasize the guidance of the Holy Spirit in worship and church government. They sometimes cultivate visible physical manifestations of the Holy Spirit, such as speaking with tongues, jumping, rolling, shouting, or other "charismatic" (spiritual grace) gifts. In fact, a strong charismatic movement is developing which includes Christians from many different churches, and even some non-Christians.

The Protestant churches constitute a significant body of self-governing and responsible churches which are centers of Christian life, devotion, and service.

OTHER GROUPS

Several groups are, for one or another reason, outside the mainstream of classic Protestant Christianity. Christian Science and the Latter Day Saints or Mormons can be classified together, because each has its own special scripture which supplements the Bible and serves as the basis of their distinctive faith and practice. For Christian Science the book is Mary Baker Eddy's *Science and Health, A Key to the Scriptures*, and for the Latter Day Saints it is the *Book of Mormon*. The Mormons now claim over 10 million members worldwide, and some commentators predict they will be the largest church organization in the world some day. Two other variant forms of Protestantism are the Seventh Day Adventists and Jehovah's Witnesses, both of which espouse a literal or realistic Second Advent or second coming of Christ. Many if not most churches include the Second Advent in their eschatology, but it is usually interpreted more symbolically than in the completely literal, graphic, and precise terms of these sects. In the near future, they say, Jesus will come to inaugurate the Millennium, his 1,000-year reign at the end of history.

The Christian Life: Living in Two Worlds

Augustine of Hippo considered *The City of God* his masterpiece. In it he set forth a theology of history. He describes the world as the place of conflict between a good city of God and an evil city of the world. The two cities are constituted by the two loves of mankind—the love of God and the love of the world. Without ascribing the Augustinian view to modern Christians, we can use it as a figure for the Christian in the world: In life good and evil are inextricably mixed, and the Christian has to live in this naughty world but love God and good. This ancient metaphor of the two cities describes the problem of the Christian life—to live by eternal truth in a fallen and perishing world.

This explains the exalted and absolute standards Jesus set in the Sermon on the Mount, as well as the perfection of act and purity of motive he spoke of as being required from his disciples. These are the ethics of the kingdom that he brought in his person—the kingdom that he proclaimed was to come. This eschatological framework of the Christian ethic has already been discussed in our section on Jesus' teachings. At first, the church believed literally that Jesus would soon come, and they lived in expectation of his imminent return in glory. When this hope faded, adjustments were required to reconcile the exigencies of the world and the demands of the gospel. There are different solutions to this problem.

The Catholic solution has been twofold. A distinction is made between the "religious," who live by the strict demands of the gospel and fulfill a higher righteousness, and the laity who are not expected to be perfect but to be obedient. Thus the monks, nuns, priests and all "clerics" (from the Greek κλῆρος for "inheritance") satisfy the higher standard and receive honor for giving up some of the world's goods, while the laity (from the Greek for "people," λαός) are permitted to enjoy the satisfactions of the world if they live in accordance with the guidance of the church. The principal focus of the high standard for the religious is the requirement of celibacy, the abnegation of sexual life, while the rule of poverty is observed only in some monastic orders. The other part of the Catholic solution is a complete set of moral rules and directives for every possible situation. In terms of modern philosophical ethics, this is a "deontological" system, in which right and wrong are matters of the rules. In the light of eternal Christian principles, the church knows and lays down the rules. Like the driver of a car, one is to go when the traffic light is green, and stop when it is red. Catholic moral theology and canon law are the most systematic and comprehensive system of moral rules ever devised; they have or can find an answer for every possible ethical situation. (There is a remarkable and little-noticed resemblance between Judaism and Catholicism in the importance of casuistry—application of general moral rules to particular cases—in both, although the systems of interpretation are different.)

In Protestantism the solution to the problem of living the Christian life is for each one to make her or his way through this dark world by the light of the gospel. The literary example is that Protestant classic, *Pilgrim's Progress*, written by John Bunyan in the seventeenth century. It depicts Christian as a pilgrim bound for the eternal city "whose builder and maker is God" (Hebrews 11:10). Christian's life on earth is, therefore, wayfaring and warfaring. The pilgrims are part of a great company, and they strengthen and encourage one another on the way; but each one must fight the good fight. An artistic symbol for this classic view is Durer's "Knight, Death, and the Devil," which shows the Christian warrior riding calmly past his ancient enemies. This is the individualism of Protestantism. In terms of philosophical ethics, Protestantism is a "teleological" system. That is, the final goal, the purpose or "telos," is used to determine what is right as applied to a particular situation. In the light of the final goal and the eternal principles of the gospel, Christians are to guide themselves in this world. The fellowship and teaching of the church helps in this. The Christian's responsibility is to believe and trust in Christ as the standard of moral excellence, and to make decisions and live in the light of his transcendent truth. This puts a heavy burden on the individual conscience; the Protestant's conscience is her sense of moral responsibility before God and in Christ. Individual ethical responsibility entails the right and duty to read and interpret the Bible for oneself, because it is the final source of the truths and principles of the Christian life. Many churches and church people espouse and practice "social gospel" activism in social, economic, and political issues as working on earth toward the kingdom of God.

The Content of Christian Ethical Norms

The Ten Commandments, the wisdom of Psalms and Proverbs, the truths of the prophets, the stories and history in the Old Testament, and above all the Gospels and the rest of the New Testament all find their place as guidance for

Christian life. These are interpreted by the church and clergy and supplemented by a rich literature of guidance and inspiration for the Christian life. If there is one single value and motive which is central in Christian ethics, it is love. God's love for his world is constant and is manifested in Jesus Christ: It is the ultimate spiritual reliance of the Christian in all circumstances. Therefore it is also the Christian's chief guide. Jesus' Great Commandment combining two Old Testament passages made love of God and man the first law; Jesus' own life, death, and resurrection made love the fulfillment of the law. As Augustine said: "Love, and do what you will."

The Positive Basis of Christian Morality

The Christian ethic is not legalism, which is to make the keeping of the letter of the law the method of winning God's favor. The legalism issue was Paul's quarrel with Judaism, which led to his polemical contrast between law and gospel. In Christianity, the ethical life begins with the grace of God, that is, with what God has done in Jesus Christ. In Christ God made available to humanity his free, open, and unconditional mercy and love. The redemption promised in the Old Testament, says Christianity, has been brought and fulfilled in Jesus Christ. God has shown that he cares for and helps human beings as they are in the world, by coming into the world under the limitations and conditions which people know. This means that people do not have to buy or earn their spiritual freedom—it has been freely given to them. But then the Christian life begins with, starts from, is based on the gospel; when people set out on the Christian pilgrimage, they find Christ going with them. This has been the Christian experience. If enough people discover it anew, the Christian faith, some say, will be renewed by the gifts of the Holy Spirit bestowed at Pentecost: unity and power.

SUMMARY

Like Judaism from which it came, Christianity is grounded in history, not of a people over thousands of years, but in the life, death, and Resurrection of one man, Jesus Christ. From that event issued the Christian church in three branches—Orthodox, Protestant, and Roman Catholic—more than 2,000,000,000 souls over all the world. Although separated and divided, they are one in their allegiance to Jesus Christ as Lord and Savior, and the world's calendar is fixed by his birth, *Anno Domini*, "year of the Lord."

Jesus' life, as recounted in the four Gospels of the New Testament, is here summarized. He was born to Mary and Joseph, devout Jews in ancient Israel, then under Roman domination. At about the age of 30, after baptism by the prophetic figure, John the Baptist, he began to preach a message of encouragement in the light of the coming of the Kingdom of God. With a group of disciples he conducted a ministry of preaching and healing in Galilee, which brought him great popularity from the crowds and increasing hostility from the religious leaders. During a brief withdrawal to a northeastern area of the country he accepted for himself and shared with his disciples the probability of his own death as the Messiah from God, and they made their way to Jerusalem. There he was hailed as a spiritual deliverer. He made an even greater call for repentance and commitment to himself, and he proclaimed the new age of righteousness which he somehow represented. This brought him into open conflict with the religious authorities of the Jews. After a final fellowship meal with his disciples Jesus went to pray in the Garden of Gethsemane. There he was seized by agents of the religious leaders and taken to a hearing before the high priest and a council of elders. The nature of their condemnation of him is not clear, but they handed him over to the Roman officials. The Roman procurator Pilate condemned Jesus to be crucified, Roman soldiers carried out the sentence, and he died after a few hours on the cross. He was given a hasty burial before the Passover Eve, but on the third day, the day after the Sabbath, the tomb was found empty. Some of the disciples saw him and talked with him.

The Christian faith is centered on Jesus and these events of his life, above all the Resurrection from the dead. His followers reassembled, and, after a charismatic group experience on Pentecost, began to proclaim Jesus as Lord and Savior, to baptize people in his name, and to celebrate a service of communion based on his example. Coming out of these experiences, the Christian church, faced with persecution, grew very slowly at first. But after 100 years, the basic doctrinal, scriptural, and institutional forms of the faith had been established. After enduring extreme persecution for another hundred years, the church won Roman recognition and shortly became the official religion. As the western Roman Empire disintegrated, the church grew in influence. Two main branches—the Eastern, centered in the new capital of the empire at Constantinople, and the Western under the bishop of Rome, who became the Roman Catholic pope—developed in different ways. Between them they provided the religious substance of culture for Europe and parts of Asia. The growth of Islam reduced the extent of the Orthodox Church, and in the West the Reformation in the sixteenth century split the church and produced the Protestant churches. These are the three major, traditional, institutional divisions of the Christian church, although there are many groups which are hard to classify or which fall outside them.

Christian scriptures include the Jewish Bible as the Old Testament, the record of the covenant between God and the Hebrews; and the New Testament, the record of the covenant between God and all who accept Jesus as Christ (Anointed) Lord and Savior.

Christian beliefs center on the life and teachings of Jesus, and have traditionally been expressed in creeds (from *credo*, "I believe") affirming the facts and the significance of Jesus' life and teachings. Disagreement over aspects of these basic doctrines has produced the separate organizations and differing practices of the major divisions of Christianity. The central and classic tradition, largely adhered to by all branches, holds that Jesus as the Son of God is both divine and human, that he suffered and died for the sins of humanity, and saved them by his death and Resurrection. Anyone who accepts him as Lord and Savior and is baptized in the name of the Father, the Son, and the Holy Spirit will be saved, that is, freed from the hold of sin and death. The formula of God as Father, Son, and Holy Spirit is known as the Trinity. The doctrine is the basic Christian belief in God as almighty and eternal Creator, whose son Jesus came as Savior, and whose Holy Spirit is active power of God in the world. The three divisions differ about the exact meaning of salvation: precisely what the need is, just how Jesus Christ effects salvation, and the way in which the believer gains or receives it. But they agree that there is a spiritual need in all humanity as somehow corrupted by sin, that the deliverance in Jesus Christ is only by the free grace or gift or mercy of God, and that anyone who confesses Christ and is baptized and incorporated into the church is redeemed.

Christian worship, accordingly, focuses on these things. Thankfulness and praise to God for all his gifts and goodness pervade regular, corporate worship on Sunday as the Lord's Day on which Christ was raised from the dead. Many different ideas or aspects of Christian faith are expressed in different ways. Special days of the liturgical calendar celebrate occasions in the life of Christ, from Christmas for his birth to Easter for his Resurrection. The sacraments, sacred ceremonies in which physical acts and words symbolize invisible spiritual truths, include baptism once for each believer, and regular communion for all.

The Roman Catholic Church is headed by the pope at Rome, who exercises supreme spiritual and juridical authority over all clergy and laity in the church of about a billion members. The celibate clergy are priests, custodians of the sacramental grace dispensed in the mass, who also direct the affairs of the churches. Protestant churches are constituted first of all by the laity or believers, who maintain final control, although the forms of organization vary and some groups, Anglicans and others, have bishops. Protestant clergy are essentially ministers to the people in the name of Christ. Orthodox churches have an episcopal (bishop) structure, and find the spiritual life of Christ manifested through the worshipping congregation of the faithful. In all branches of Christendom the ethical ideal of Christians is set by the example of Jesus. Christians are called to live like him, with faith in God, hope in the victory of God's goodness over evil and death, and love for others because of God's love for them.

NOTES

1. Aloys Grillmeier, S. J., *Christ in Christian Tradition*, vol. 1 (Atlanta: John Knox Press, 1975), p. 4.
2. The Scripture quotations in this chapter are from the Revised Standard Version of the Bible, copyright 1946, 1952, and 1972, 1973 by the Division of Christian

Education of the National Council of Churches of Christ in the U.S.A., and used by permission.

3. Maurice Goguel, *The Life of Jesus* (New York: Macmillan, 1933), p. 330.
4. *Cunctos populos*, 380 Cod. Theod. XVI, 1, 2, in Henry Bettenson, ed., *Documents of the Christian Church* (New York: Oxford University Press, 1957), pp. 31, 32.
5. Bettenson, *Documents*, p. 33.
6. Roland H. Bainton, *Here I Stand: A Life of Martin Luther* (Nashville: Abingdon Press, 1950), pp. 49, 50.
7. Bettenson, *Documents*, p. 72.
8. James Cone, *For My People, Black Theology and the Black Church* (Maryknoll: Orbis Books, 1984), p. 19.
9. Bettenson, *Documents*, p. 95.

TOPICS AND QUESTIONS FOR STUDY

1. Why does Christianity call the Jewish scriptures the Old Testament and their own the New Testament, and put the two together in their Bible?
2. Explain the importance of revelation in Western religions, as seen in Christianity, and how and why Christianity claims that Jesus Christ is the supreme and unique revelation of God.
3. In what sense is Christianity based on an historic event? How does it happen that the Western (and now the world) calendar is dated A.D., *Anno Domini* ("Year of the Lord")?
4. Discuss why Christianity talks a lot about "sin" and "judgment," although that is not the main point, which is the "grace" of God.
5. What are the source and the significance of the divisions and differences among Christians, especially Catholic-Protestant?
6. Do you agree with the book that Jesus is the paradigmatic (ideal example) Western religious savior figure? Why is the religion named for him?
7. Explain the importance of doctrine or creed in Christianity. Why, and in what way, are the main parts of the creeds about Jesus Christ? Does this explain why Christians (justifiably) resent jokes about him?
8. Why is worship so important in Christianity? Why is it communal and public? Why is it above all thanksgiving and celebration? Why do Christians worship on Sunday?
9. Show how the ethical system starts from what God has done in Jesus Christ, rather than with human effort and goodness in keeping God's laws.
10. How did it come about that although Jesus was a Jew, Christianity says that he is a universal spiritual figure, not limited to one people or culture?
11. Why does Christianity talk about the future, the afterlife, the Kingdom of God?
12. Discuss why the Christian need not and may not ever use force or violence to defend Christ or essential Christianity.

USEFUL BOOKS

Bettenson, Henry, sel. and ed., *Documents of the Christian Church*. New York: Oxford University Press, 1957.

Carmody, Denise and John. *Christianity: An Introduction*. Belmont, Calif.: Wadsworth, 1983.

Clebsch, William A. *American Religious Thought*. Chicago: University of Chicago Press, 1973.

Frankiel, Sandra S. *Christianity: A Way of Salvation*. San Francisco: Harper and Row, 1985.

Lohse, Bernard. *A Short History of Christian Doctrine*. Translated by F. Ernest Stoeffler. Philadelphia: Fortress Press, 1963.

Pelikan, Jaroslav. *Jesus Through the Centuries: His Place in the History of Culture*. New Haven: Yale University Press, 1985. Reprint, New York: Harper and Row, 1987.

Perrin, Norman, and Dennis Duling. *The New Testament: An Introduction*. New York: Harcourt Brace Jovanovich, 1982.

Reynolds, Stephen. *The Christian Religious Tradition*. Belmont, Calif.: Wadsworth, 1977.

Spitz, Lewis W., ed. *The Protestant Reformation*. Englewood Cliffs, N.J.: Prentice Hall, 1966.

Tillich, Paul. *The Shaking of the Foundations*. New York: Charles Scribner's Sons, 1948 (or any book of Tillich's sermons).

Waddell, Helen. *The Desert Fathers*. Ann Arbor: University of Michigan Press, 1981.

Wiggins, James B., and Robert S. Ellwood. *Christianity: A Cultural Perspective*. Englewood Cliffs, N.J.: Prentice Hall, 1988.

GLOSSARY

Apocrypha: "hidden" or "secret" books included in some canons of the Old Testament

atonement: doctrine of the work of Christ as making God and humanity one, by paying the penalty of sin for all people

canon: official list of inspired or authoritative books worthy to be included in the New Testament

Easter: central Christian celebration, commemorating the resurrection of Christ; movable date between March 21 and April 24, which determines the dates of all other movable festivals and observances

eschatology: doctrine of the "last things" at the end of the world

Eucharist: Communion; the Lord's Supper; principal Christian sacrament

gospel: the "good news" of salvation in Jesus Christ

Gospel: one of the four Gospels in the New Testament: Matthew, Mark, Luke, and John. Records of Jesus' life

Incarnation: doctrine of the embodiment of Christ as divine in human form

real presence: doctrine that Christ's body and blood are veritably present in the communion elements

resurrection: the raising of Christ from the dead, and, through him, the future raising of all believers; as a formal doctrine, the Resurrection

sacrament: most solemn Christian ceremony, combining outward acts, physical objects, and spoken words, with inward and spiritual meaning, its origin being ascribed to Christ

soteriology: theory of salvation

Vulgate: early Christian Latin text of the Old Testament

Chapter 9

ISLAM

The Taj Mahal, the tomb built 1632-1650 for his wife, Mumtaz Mahal, by Shah Jahan, fifth ruler of the Islamic regime in India known as the Mughal Empire (Courtesy, Har Bans Singh).

OUTLINE

I. The religion of submission to the one God is the latest of these religions, and it grew very rapidly to over 900,000,000 adherents today.

    A. The Prophet Muhammad, born about c.e. 570 in Arabia, was called to preach belief in Allah, *the* God, to the Arabs. He organized a community of faith at Medina, later taking over Mecca and making it the holy city. By the time of his death, 632, the conquest or conversion of all Arabia was almost complete.

    B. Under the caliphs the militant faith in Allah and in Muhammad as the Prophet spread rapidly into Africa, Asia, and Europe, often enjoying much prosperity and developing a rich culture, frequently divided by strife, but developing a unifying religious center of sacred law and lore.

II. Islamic literature

    A. The Qur'an, God-given to Muhammad by an angel and "recited" by Muhammad, later written down by others, the very word of God to Muslims, their fundamental revelation.

    B. The Hadith or Traditions, records of the *sunnah*, the custom or practice of Muhammad, as remembered and recorded by the Islamic community.

    C. Four books of *fiqh* or wisdom of the schools of interpretation of Islamic law.

III. Beliefs.

    A. Allah, the one and only God, undivided, supreme ruler and judge.

    B. Angels and prophets, and above all Muhammad, are messengers of God.

    C. Allah will judge all souls at the end of time.

    D. Various schools of thought and movements interpreted these things in different ways.

IV. The five Pillars of Islam constitute its religious practice.

    A. The creed: "There is no God but Allah, and Muhammad is his Prophet."

    B. Prayer, both public and private, the heart of worship.

    C. Giving alms to the poor brethren.

    D. Fasting in the month of Ramadan.

    E. Making a pilgrimage (*hajj*) to Mecca if possible.

V. Islam as a system of religious moral law.

    A. The body of Islamic moral laws is the Shariah, and the more specific legal principles; and applications are the *fiqh*.

    B. Divisions of Islam.

        1. The major group, about 80 percent, are the Sunni, those who follow the *sunnah* or custom of Muhammad as in the Hadith and Shariah.

2. The principal minority is the Shiah ("partisans" of Ali) who look back to Ali's son Husayn as a martyr at Karbala.

3. Other groups are the Wahhabis and the Amidiyya.

━━━━━━━

INTRODUCTION

James A. Michener, author of many books about many countries and cultures, wrote for the *Reader's Digest* of May 1955 an article entitled "Islam: The Misunderstood Religion." That description is now more true than ever; past errors have been compounded by present hostility to and disinformation about Islam caused by the Middle East conflict and by suspicion about the alleged role of Muslims in terrorism. Although our picture of the religion will try to avoid these political and cultural conflicts, they are an inescapable part of the background. Currently Islam is the fastest growing religion in North America, and by the end of the century, Muslims will outnumber Jews in the United States.

Its Arabian origin and character mark Islam with the starkness, clarity, and intensity of the desert. Although the Prophet Muhammad[†] founded it and impressed its fundamental character upon it, he was simply a human being, pointing humankind to God. For that reason the religion is not named for him but for the fundamental attitude of humanity before the one God who rules all: the desert, the sky, the sun, people, and history. Islam, "submission" (the infinitive form means "to resign oneself"), is the name of this religion: submission to God. "The true religion with God is Islam" (S. 3:17)[1] says the Qur'an. One who "submits" is a *muslim*, hence a Muslim is an adherent of the faith. Only in a secondary sense does the Muslim accept the faith or the order; the essential submission is to the reality and the rule of the one God, Allah.* As a total culture Islam is much more than simply a religion in the narrower sense. It is a culture that still keeps the central faith and practice which we shall describe.

ORIGIN AND DEVELOPMENT

Beginning in one of the most barren lands in the world, Islam spread with astonishing speed and vigor. According to Islam's own time scheme, the year C.E.

[†]To express the Arabic character of some key Islamic terms we will spell the founder's name as "Muhammad," the book as the "Qur'an," the tribe as "Quraysh," etc. The article "al," as being part of the surname, will be kept where it is customary, separated by the usual hyphen from the rest of the name. In general, Arabic names and terms will be written without diacritical marks.

622 is designated as the year 1 A.H. (*anno Hegirae**) year of the hegira (*hijra**), that is, the "migration" of Muhammad to Medina. (Because the Islamic calendar is based on lunar months, and correlation with the solar calendar (C.E.) is complicated, we will not use A.H. but will use dates as they occur in the solar calendar.) A few thousand Arabs in the Arabian peninsula were the only Muslims when Muhammad died in 632. One hundred years later Islamic forces were finally turned back at Tours in central France, which kept Europe from being conquered by them. Today Muslims number over 900,000,000 in a broad belt extending from the Arabian heartland westward into Africa and eastward into Asia. We consider first the life and career of Muhammad and then the expansion and development of the complex total culture which is Islam.

Muhammad

Muhammad is the Prophet. This is his official designation and is the best word to describe him. Never does he make any claim for himself except to be the spokesman of Allah, but that claim is absolute. The Qur'an says:

> Say: "O mankind, I am the Messenger of God to you all, of Him to whom belongs the kingdom of the heavens and of the earth.
> There is no God but He.
> He gives life, and makes to die.
> Believe then in God, and in His Messenger,
> The Prophet of the common folk, who believes in God
> and His words, and follow him" (S. 7:158).

In some versions of the Qur'an* the word *ummi*, translated by Arberry as "of the common folk" is taken to mean "unlettered" or "illiterate"—Muhammad was "of the common folk." Muslim tradition so treats it. But *ummi* can mean other things, as Arberry's translation shows; the word probably signifies simply that he was a layperson, not instructed in scriptural questions. The motive for suggesting that Muhammad was illiterate is to exalt the wonder of his recitation of the Qur'an, but that is a questionable tribute. It does not derogate from his achievement to assume that he was literate. At the end of his career his duties, in addition to being the spokesman for God, included chief administrator, religious leader, general, and head of a family. But the source of his power and influence then and now was his office as messenger of Allah for the people of Islam.

THE ARABIAN BACKGROUND OF MUHAMMAD

We know a little about Arabian society at the time of Muhammad, and by modern Western standards the life was harsh and primitive. Yet there was a developed civilization in southern Arabia before the Christian era, and extensive trade and commerce were carried on along the caravan routes, especially the spice traffic. Mecca and other urban centers benefited from the commercial

The Kaaba and the Great Mosque, Mecca (Courtesy, Arabian American Oil Company).

life that came to them as a result of their location on the caravan routes. Mecca was at the center of the route along the Arabian peninsula on the east side of the Red Sea. In spite of its forbidding climate, in which almost nothing grows because there is virtually no rain, Mecca was a comparatively prosperous and sophisticated commercial and religious center. Muhammad was not a Bedouin; he came from the urban culture of Arabia.

The Arabs, and especially the Bedouins of the more remote desert regions, were—from the point of view of Jews and Christians—mostly pagans. Their animism or spirit worship was directed to the gods who were believed to inhabit stones, tress, rocks, and wells. These objects were stroked and kissed, and the spirit invoked, and sometimes the Arabs observed communal sacrificial feasts. Among early goddesses were the "daughters of Allah": Al-Lat* ("the Goddess"), Al-Uzza* ("the Mighty One"), and Al-Manat,* representing the Sun, the planet Venus, and Fortune. In the north this Arabian paganism had been influenced by Christianity; however, both Jewish and Christian ideas were familiar to people in the more prosperous south, and some Arabian tribes had been converted to Judaism or Christianity. Under these and other influences there were various tendencies toward monotheism among the Arabians, and some informal groups of worshippers of God. Both northern and southern Arabs claimed descent from Ishmael, the son of Abraham and Hagar as told in Genesis, chapter 21. At Mecca is the Kaaba* (*Kaʿbah*), a cubic stone structure, in one outside corner of which is set the sacred black stone which had probably originated as a meteorite centuries before, but which has always been considered a supernatural object. The Kaaba was the center of pilgrimage rites for Arabs who came to Mecca every year. At different times, inside the Kaaba were images of the "daughters of Allah" and various other deities. The name for the Semitic god known and worshipped for centuries in the Middle East was "Il" to the Babylonians, to the Hebrews "El," "Ilh" to South Arabians, and "Al-Ilah" to Bedouins. The name "Allah" was brought into Arabic from Aramaic before the time of Muhammad. Properly speaking it is "Al-lah" or *the* God, but customary spelling makes it "Allah" in English. Others besides Muhammad preached monotheism in Arabia, but it was he who succeeded in converting Arabia from pagan deities to Allah, the God to be identified with the one God of Judaism and Christianity.

THE EARLY LIFE AND THE CALL OF MUHAMMAD

Muhammad was born in about 570, to Abdullah and his wife Aminah, after his father's death. His mother died soon after. "Did He not find thee an orphan, and shelter thee?" (S. 93:6) asks the Qur'an. For a short while he enjoyed the care of his wealthy grandfather, but after that his guardian was his uncle, *Abu** Talib, who was poor. But Abu Talib, so long as he lived, gave love and help to Muhammad. Arab society was structured by tribes; Muhammad was born into the Quraysh* tribe, and his clan was the banu-Hashim. It is uncertain what was his given name; "Muhammad" means "highly praised." Muhammad became a caravan driver and manager or steward. The next event for which there is firm evidence was his marriage at the age of 25 to his employer Khadijah,* a wealthy widow of 40. This was a turning point in his life, for it gave him some leisure and status. The marriage was a stable and happy one and produced six children, of whom four daughters survived. Until Khadijah's death in 619 Muhammad took no other wife, but after the *hijra* to Medina he instituted a harem and had several wives, which was comfortable with custom and law.

Beyond these general factors and circumstances there are only conjectures about more specific personal developments in Muhammad's own life. It is generally conceded that the moral and ethical life of the culture was essentially brutal and often inhumane. The Qur'an reveals Muhammad's sensitivity to such practices as death by exposure of unwanted female infants. On his journeys Muhammad undoubtedly met and talked with Jewish and Christian merchants, camel drivers, priests, and other travelers, from whom he could have learned some things about their religions and contrasted them with Arabic customs. Many times in the Qur'an Muhammad speaks of the "books" of Judaism and Christianity, expressing his wish that there were a book for his people; he referred to the Jews as "the people of the book." At some time he evidently began the practice of prayer and meditation in the desert or caves in hills near Mecca.

These prosaic facts and circumstances are not sufficient to account for the amazing insight and courage of the Prophet of Allah, who all alone received the vision and proclaimed it to his unbelieving and uncomprehending tribesmen. Indeed, the relationship between their own religious personality and the divine inspiration and call is part of the mystery of all the great leaders whom we meet at the outset of these movements. A fruitful subject for comparison is the founders of the several religions described in this book. In no case are the sociological and historical data sufficient to account for the phenomenon of leadership they provided; personal and spiritual factors must be adduced in order to explain them. But the nature of these factors and how they combined to produce a spiritual leader is not easy to determine.

Muhammad's career as Prophet began with his call, which tradition says is described in what is considered the earliest sura* of the Qur'an. In a cave on Mt. Hira above Mecca, the 40-year-old man was meditating when the revelation came.

Recite: In the Name of the Lord who created,
     created Man of a blood-clot.
Recite: And thy Lord is the Most Generous,
     who taught by the Pen,
   taught Man that he knew not. (S. 96:1-5)

In the literature called the Traditions (Hadith*) this experience is enlarged on to describe Muhammad's awe and consternation at the vision. Another visitation described in the Qur'an is assigned to Gabriel or even Allah himself.

By the star when it plunges,
your comrade is not astray, neither errs.
   nor speaks he out of caprice.
This is naught but a revelation revealed,
   taught him by one terrible in power,
     very strong; he stood poised,
     being on the higher horizon,
   Then drew near and suspended hung,
   two bows'-length away, or nearer,
then revealed to his servant that he revealed.
   His heart lies not of what he saw;
what, will you dispute with him what he sees? (S. 53:1-12)

A reading of the Qur'an leaves one completely convinced of the sincerity and truth of Muhammad's reports of his call and commission. He found himself appointed by Allah to proclaim the truth of the one God to the people of Arabia and to call them to acknowledge and obey God.

The traditional date of the "night of power" is in the month of Ramadan* in the year 610. There seems to have been an interval of a year or two after that, during which Muhammad had no other visions and thought that he might have been deceived by an evil spirit or be going mad. Khadijah believed in him and supported him from the beginning; she was his first convert. The second was the 10-year-old boy Ali, Muhammad's first cousin and the son of Abu Talib; Muhammad had taken Ali into his own household because of his uncle's age and straitened circumstances. (Later, Ali became the fourth caliph.) The third convert was a Christian slave boy, Zayd. During the first 3 years Muhammad's communications were only with his relatives. The fourth convert, Abu Bakr, marked the transition to public proclamation, Abu Bakr being a prosperous merchant who himself became an active proselytizer. Popular tradition makes the first four caliphs* the first converts, beginning with Abu Bakr. Scholars say the other converts at this time were mostly young and either poor or slaves, and that Muhammad only reluctantly began to make public pronouncements under the direction of his angelic mentor Gabriel.

MECCAN PREACHING

At first Muhammad had to contend chiefly with indifference and scorn, and his own uncertainty. But when his public preaching of judgment and wrath to come touched on the ancestors of the people, and his denunciations of idols endangered the pilgrimage business, his Quraysh fellow-tribesmen threatened him and his uncle. In Mecca there were extremes of poverty and luxury, and the Prophet sympathized with the poor and unfortunate. Although he did not preach a social gospel, his call to repentance and mindfulness of the judgment had overtones of prophetic demands for justice, and this aroused resentment. Slowly the number of adherents increased, but so did opposition. The Qur'an reflects the charges of his enemies and the divine reassurance given the Prophet as he steadfastly reiterated his proclamation of the necessity to submit to God. About 100 of his followers took refuge among Christians in Abyssinia, and Muhammad began to look for escape from Mecca. In these difficult years Muhammad's sense of mission, his uncompromising message of the greatness of Allah, and his ability to win and hold the loyalty of steadfast characters like Omar were the chief factors in the success of what appeared a hopeless enterprise. The early believers in Mecca are called "Companions";* "Exiles"* were those who went with him to Medina; and those at Medina who turned to him were "Helpers."*

THE HIJRA TO MEDINA

About then Khadijah and Abu Talib died, and Muhammad was left alone in his grief and desperation at the loss of his two dearest and most faithful supporters. He was forced to look elsewhere for converts and for peace from his enemies. After an unsuccessful venture in Taif, he was invited to Medina, called Yathrib at that time, about 200 miles north. Gradually all the believers who wanted to leave Mecca, except Muhammad, Abu Bakr, and Ali, emigrated to Medina. Finally they too left Mecca, and the Islamic era began. The traditional date is celebrated as the new year, July 16, 622. Muhammad and his companions just escaped assassination, were forced to hide, and reached the outskirts of Yathrib on September 24. Legend says that to solve the question of whom he would honor by staying with them, Muhammad gave his camel its head and let it make the choice. Already there were 100 or more Helpers at Medina, and although there were great problems and obstacles still to be overcome, the career of the Prophet of Islam was one of almost unbroken success from then on, such that even defeats turned into victories.

The details of Muhammad's battles and accomplishments in the triumphant last 10 years of life, the first 10 of the Islamic era, cannot be recited here, but the shape he gave to the total movement which began then is important for understanding Islam. In consolidating his position in Medina he made the brotherhood of the faithful, a concept similar to the familiar Arab rule of tribal loyalty, the fundamental principle of their human relations. This is seen in "The Covenant of Medina," an agreement between the Exiles and the Helpers that included provisions for the safety of the Jews, of whom there were many in Medina. The Covenant says: "The bond of God being one and the believers being bonded in brotherhood to one another in contradistinction to other men, any protection given by the least of them shall be honored by all."[2] As his Meccan opponents perhaps saw more accurately than others, Muhammad's claim to be God's spokesman implied autocracy for him, and at Medina he was able to put this into effect. This entailed a common source for religious and social or civil law, and this essentially theocratic model was characteristic of Islam for centuries. In a few years he built up a self-contained religious community having its own structure of laws, government, and institutions.

TRIUMPH—MECCA

From the first the Prophet envisaged his message as reaching all people, as can be seen in the Qur'an. Muhammad in the Qur'an is the spokesman calling all idolators, which in effect meant non-Jews and non-Christians, to acknowledge Allah. Once he had consolidated the movement in Medina he moved to gain control of Mecca. A series of three minor engagements, none being very bloody, were sufficient, over a period of years, to bring him back in triumph to Mecca. Muhammad's personal courage and leadership were displayed in these battles, but even more important were the diplomatic maneuvers and adroit conciliatory policy which brought final, almost bloodless, capitulation of the Meccan community.

In the course of these operations Muhammad had to articulate a motive and policy for his troops to attack the enemy, who were often their own kinsmen, always an abhorrent idea to Arabs and Bedouins. This was set forth in the concept of holy war (*jihad**) in the Qur'an. For this doctrine the chief text is the "Verse of the Sword," the most extreme adjuration to war:

Then, when the sacred months are drawn away,
slay the idolaters wherever you find them,
and take them, and confine them, and lie in wait
for them at every place of ambush. But if they
repent, and perform the prayer, and pay the alms, then
  let them go their way. (S. 9:5)

But the Qur'an is full of other sentiments, and the proponents of literal holy war, or others who would use this verse, must disregard at least 124 other verses that stress peace and toleration toward non-Muslims, especially Christians and Jews as theists. There are many such verses as this one: "And fight in the way of God with those who fight with you, but aggress not: God loves not the aggressors" (S. 2:187). For the time and circumstances, this policy was if not commendable, at least understandable, and modern apologists point out that it could now only be invoked as defense against physical attacks on Islam, which has no organized political form.

Muhammad was not a religious innovator or original thinker, and he made no claim to be. The Qur'an is full of restatements of Jewish and Christian Biblical materials, and he claimed that his revelation confirmed them. He acknowledged the Jews as chosen by God, and Jesus as a prophet, although not the Son of God. He was not interested in denying or exterminating either faith so long as the members did not denigrate or attack Islam. His policy toward Arabic polytheism and primitive moral concepts was likewise adaptive and reformative rather than totally destructive. This policy was displayed in the beginnings of the cult at Medina, and above all at the victory over Mecca and the expansion of Islam throughout Arabia.

In the eighth year of the *hijra*, 630, a pivotal year, the city was his, almost without a struggle at the end. Except for a few fanatical defenders killed while fighting, only four people were executed. True to his zeal for Allah, the Prophet's first act after entering Mecca in triumph was to destroy the images of gods and to pray in the Kaaba, which he established as the center of Islam. As we shall see, the Muslim pilgrimage preserved most of the pre-Islamic pilgrimage customs, although purged of idolatry. The leading Meccans embraced Islam, and after a year all Arabs in the vicinity were converted either voluntarily or under duress. Armies were mobilized to convert the outlying areas of Arabia, and when Muhammad died in 632 the conquest of the Arabian peninsula was being conducted.

In addition to the many pious legends there are traditions and memories which testify to Muhammad's personal charm and winning character. An overzealous inquirer once grasped the reins of his camel and demanded to know what would save him from Hell and assure him of Heaven. Another leader might have struck or killed the man, but Muhammad patiently told him what to do to gain Paradise, ending with "and let go the neck-rein of my riding beast." Other stories tell of his simplicity, helpfulness, and affection with his family, and all sources stress the personal love and loyalty which his conduct

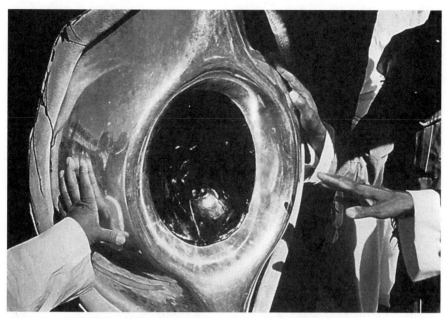

The Black Stone in the Kaaba (Courtesy, Sheikh Publications, Inc.).

and character brought to him. In the crowded and difficult last years, with the final decisions always left to him, he never lost his humility and willingness to take counsel with advisors. He seems to have been almost unfailingly thoughtful of others. To the end it was his sense of mission as God's envoy to "warn a people whose fathers were never warned" (S. 36:5) which guided and strengthened him. Undoubtedly he changed and his utterances recorded in the Qur'an changed in the later years, but he was still first of all the Prophet. As such, he was one of those who change lives and shape history in the name of God—"and Muhammad is his Prophet."

Expansion of Islam

THE FIRST CALIPHS

After a short time of confusion and uncertainty following the Apostle's death, Abu Bakr as the first caliph ("successor" to Muhammad) led the forces of Islam through north and east Arabia and against the Byzantine and Persian boundary states. Within 10 years Syria, Iraq, and Egypt were tributaries to Medina, the people often being glad to throw off their Eastern Christian or Persian rule and accept Islamic domination. By the payment of a tax Jews and Christians, as members of tolerated religions, came under Muslim protection, while thousands of them converted to the dominant religion. Having succeeded Abu Bakr upon the latter's death in 634, Omar was the real organizer of the empire, which, at the time of his assassination 10 years later, extended from the borders of India on the east to Cyrene (in Libya) on the west. A model ruler, austere and resolute, the first to be called *amir al-muminin* (commander of the faithful), history counts Omar the greatest of the first caliphs and second only to Muhammad himself. The third caliph, Othman (644–656), is regarded as in some ways a lesser personage, under whom the old Meccan aristocracy consolidated their control against the Helpers and other veteran and devoted Muslims of Medina. After Othman's murder, Ali ibn abi Talib, to give him his full name, son of Abu Talib and thus Muhammad's cousin, was elected caliph, the fourth of the so-called "rightly-guided caliphs." Ali had married Muhammad's daughter, Fatima; thus Ali was Muhammad's son-in-law, and his sons were grandsons of the Prophet. These facts are important for understanding the Shiah,* to be described shortly. Ali in turn was murdered by a fanatical Kharijite* or "seceder" in 661, and the Umayyad* dynasty began under Muawiya, with its seat at Damascus.

The religious significance of these power struggles within Islam and against other peoples is first of all the sheer geographical spread and vast growth in numbers of an essentially theocratic culture. But the beginnings of permanent divisions within Islam also date from these events. The most important division is between the majority Sunnis* and the permanent dissenting Shiite minority sect, the Shiah, "the partisans or adherents of Ali." Ali's is a name honored by both Sunnites and Shiites, but his son Husayn is the great martyr figure of the Shiah. Ali's older son Hasan resigned his claim to the caliphate and died a few years later; the Shiah say he was poisoned by Muawiya's agents. Husayn, having lived quietly at Medina during Muawiya's reign, proclaimed rebellion when Muawiya died and was succeeded by Yazid in 680. At the invitation of the Iraqis Husayn set out for the north to claim the caliphate, with a mere 200 followers. They refused to surrender when surrounded and completely outnumbered at Karbala by Yazid's forces, and were slaughtered. Husayn's head was taken to Damascus, but was later buried with the body at Karbala, now a great Shiah shrine. The heroic but pathetically hopeless stand of Husayn, the grandson of the Prophet himself, is annually commemorated by Shiites. They beat and cut their naked upper bodies on the tenth of Muharram,* the climax of 10 days' lamentation, punishing themselves because they did not rally to support Husayn the martyr.

UMAYYAD AND ABBASID* CALIPHATES

Despite its defects, the Umayyad dynasty maintained and extended the faith of Islam in its original form. During it the universalism of Sunnite Islamism was forged in the Islamic heartland of the Near East and North Africa. Its principal architectural monument is the Dome of the Rock in Jerusalem. When he conquered Jerusalem in 638, Omar was shocked to find the site of the temple was then the city dump, and he began cleaning and restoration. The Mosque of Omar was built there, over the rock which was the traditional sacrificial center of the Jewish Solomonic and Herodian temples. During the Crusades the mosque served as a church, and a great iron grill was built around the rock itself. (The grill was replaced by a wooden fence in about 1958.) The Dome of the Rock still stands, the principal building on the raised area of the old temple, and it is still a mosque. The Dome of the Rock is not far from the Western Wall portion of the massive foundations of Herod's temple at the southwest side. This wall, formerly known as the "Wailing Wall," has been a place of Jewish prayer for centuries. Islamic associations with Abraham, and other traditions, make the Dome sacred to all Muslims, and thus Jerusalem is a sacred city to all three of the faiths which originated in the Near East.

The separation of the capital at Damascus from the old center of religious learning at Medina meant a division between secular and religious institutions. At the same time, the grievances of the non-Arab peoples, who were culturally more sophisticated but suffered under social and economic discrimination, moved them to unite with the Shiah in opposition to the Umayyad dynasty. The Umayyad caliphs contributed to their own downfall by excessive luxury and corruption, especially after the death of Caliph Walid in 715. When Abu-al-Abbas arose as a leader of the dissidents, they united under him and overthrew the Umayyad Caliphate in 750 to form the Abbasid Caliphate. This dynasty held power for 200 years and its capital at Baghdad became a name for luxury and sophistication. A remnant of the Umayyads ruled in Spain until 1031. The ninth and tenth centuries were the great era of Islamic civilization; religious sciences, philosophy, and literature richly expanded; minor decorative arts and architecture flourished; commerce and industry were strong. The Umayyad Caliph in Cordova, Spain, and the Abbasid at Baghdad lived in cultivated ease, and their subjects enjoyed a high level of economic prosperity, while the people and rulers of Europe were still struggling out of the Dark Ages into the sunshine of medieval times. Not all aspects and leaders of the Abbasids made positive contributions to religious life, for religion was to them only a useful element of a well-organized society. They encouraged the Islamization of the great empire, but a cleavage developed between religious and secular institutions and authority. Yet Islamic law maintained the religious center of culture, and provided the unity for the vast and diversified empire.

LATER CENTURIES: ISLAMIC RELIGIOUS CULTURE

The complex political history of Islamic nations after the decay of the two caliphates, and the virtual end of that office by the six hundredth year of the *hijra* (1222), is not directly pertinent to our story. The caliphate remains only as a central issue in Sunnite–Shiite controversy: Sunni orthodox Islamic theory considers it an elective office of a political leader; to the Shiites, the caliph as *imam** (guide) has spiritual authority from on high and should be a descendant of Ali. The significant fact is that no one leader or empire ever again united Islam as a political unit, and the religious faith alone has provided a measure of cultural homogeneity. There were great Islamic empires, however, and they

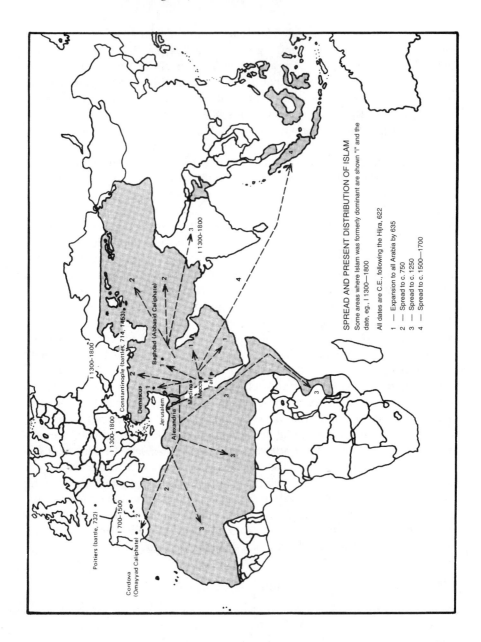

SPREAD AND PRESENT DISTRIBUTION OF ISLAM

Some areas where Islam was formerly dominant are shown "I" and the date, eg., I 1300—1800

All dates are C.E., following the Hijra, 622

1 — Expansion to all Arabia by 635
2 — Spread to c. 750
3 — Spread to c. 1250
4 — Spread to c. 1500—1700

carried with them the faith of the Prophet, thus extending Islam to millions of people in India and what are now Pakistan and Afghanistan. For centuries there was warfare between Islamic and Christian nations in Europe and the Mediterranean area. The warfare that set Islam against Christianity was the sort of struggle that unites a people or a faith against the enemy. The real struggle of Islamic faith has always been within Islamic society itself, between the faith as a subservient tool of national policy and as independent and genuine religion.

The governments supported Islamic orthodoxy and the sacred law, and these did provide spiritual content and guidance for the society. The great mosques of Istanbul, for example, testify to the support by the sultans of the Ottoman Empire for Islam after they conquered the city in the fifteenth century. In some form this problem faces all great institutionalized religions. The modern definition of the issue is that religion always has to fight against being simply a subordinate aspect of the total culture, a "culture religion" instead of a faith which maintains some autonomy and transcendence and has a core of independent spiritual vitality. In Islam it has been intensified by the theory and claim of Islam to be a total way of life for the entire Islamic society, while the government claims that it upholds the religion of the Prophet. Modern Turkey was the first to break the pattern and declare itself a secular state. For 76 years, Turkey maintained a secular state. But in July 1996, the Turkish parliament elected an Islamist, Necmettin Erbakan, as the new prime minister. His Welfare Party controls hundreds of municipalities. "Few have shown any sign of advocating a purely Islamic agenda or pushing such measures as head scarves for women."[3] The event serves as an example of similar current issues in Islamic nations.

There have been various answers to this problem, several ways in which Islamic religion has sought to establish and maintain the spiritual substance of faith. The way of the predominant Sunni majority is adherence to the *sunnah*,* the tradition or practice of Muhammad, as their guide. This Sunnite faith is what will be described in most of the rest of this chapter—the traditional *sunnah* or custom followed by the majority of Muslims. The Shiite minority, perhaps 20 percent of Muslims, reject the *sunnah*, honor different leaders, and have some distinctive observances as well as their own saints. But they agree with the majority on such things as the Five Pillars of religious obligation.

Another important group, which is not so much a separate division as a minority found scattered throughout Islam, are the Sufis.* They were originally the ascetics and mystics of Islam, and when rigidity and formalism have threatened to smother Muslim piety, they have helped keep alive the vital personal relation to God which was the core of Muhammad's religion. (However, Allah is not described as a "personal" God by Muslims.) Because of tension between them and the orthodox leaders, the Sufis tended to migrate in search of freedom to the farther reaches of the Islamic realm. There they provided the religious substance for many peoples who had never really been assimilated into Islam as a religious movement. Through their travels they also helped in the gradual missionary expansion of Islam to places like Indonesia. Professor Faruqi describes the Sufis as "a movement that dominated the whole Muslim world for a millennium."[4]

ISLAM AND THE MODERN WORLD

Islam is having a difficult time coming to terms with the modern world. Nevertheless, it is still a living religious tradition in most of the places where it is found. Not so long ago we could have cited an internal problem as the focal point for Islamic concern about its place in the world: coming to terms with

The Kaaba (Courtesy, Sheikh Publications, Inc.).

postmodern culture, science, mores. And today many people would say that is their problem—adjusting their religious ideas to contemporary opinions. But a glance at the morning paper will show that the most problematic aspect of Islamic existence is its position or status among the great universal religions of our time—not as a theoretical or abstract situation, but in the messy give-and-take of immediate human concerns. For Islam is considered the wild card, the obstreperous problem child, of global religious pluralism. A year or so ago a *New Yorker* cover depicted the Arab child in a summer beach scene as a crazy kid jumping around messing up the sand castles.

The focus in the news media and popular opinion is "fundamentalism," not in general or abstractly, but Islamic fundamentalism demonized as the causal factor in Middle Eastern and other venues of conflict. For a brief summary of a few relevant points on this fractious topic I will draw heavily on a journal article by Martin Van Bruinessen, "Muslim Fundamentalism: Something to Be Understood or Explained Away?" (Page numbers for quotations will be in the text, to eliminate multiple notes.)

Definition of "fundamentalism" is elusive, because there are so many differences among the groups so labeled and "the term as it is used nowadays commonly has judgmental overtones" (p. 157). But "fundamentalism, if the term is to have any empirical validity, should not be equated with resistance to modernity" (p. 159). "Fundamentalists wish to place the Sharia, God's law, above human-made law. The striving for implementation of the Sharia constitutes perhaps the most apt criterion for distinguishing fundamentalism, a minimum definition" (p. 161). Discussing "Fundamentalism and the West," Van Bruinessen notes that past history and present tensions produce a tendency for fundamentalists to blame their problems on and to demonize the West, so that is a two-way street (pp. 162, 163). A study did conclude that "the militants were relatively highly educated" (p. 164). Yet "it is obvious that relative deprivation as such does not automatically lead to militancy" (p. 165). The article's conclusion noted that the emphasis had been on fundamentalist movements, not thought, but that "one of the hallmarks of Christian sects and Islamicists alike is their religious intensity."[5]

Our conclusion for this sociological excursus into a genuine problem in modern life is that there is hidden strength in the refusal of Muslims to forsake their faith in the face of massive secular forces against it. They may be able to preserve the spiritual integrity and unity of Islamic thought from the disintegrative effects of modern skepticism.

ISLAMIC LITERATURE

To associate any other book with the Qur'an is almost as impious as to associate any other thing or god with Allah, which is *shirk*,* the unforgivable sin. There are, nevertheless, two other major bodies of Muslim literature: the Traditions or Hadith and the four basic texts of jurisprudence (*fiqh**) or specific laws covering all aspects of life. Three divisions of this section will be, therefore: the Qur'an, Traditions, and the four schools of law.

The Qur'an

Muhammad's recitation of the Qur'an is the only miraculous exploit ascribed to him, if one counts the Night Journey (from Jerusalem to heaven) as mythological or legendary, as most educated Muslims do. This is conformable with the orthodox insistence on his complete humanity, but it is a fundamental dogma for all Islam. For all Muslims the Qur'an is *the* book, a divinely dictated scripture, unique and incomparable. For Muslims, God's revelation is the *book* itself, in contrast to Judaism which sees it in events such as the Exodus, or Christianity which sees it in a person, or Taoism which sees it in nature and mystic experience. This produces an attitude of reverence and awe toward the Qur'an and its words, which pervades all Islam. A critical but sympathetic, modern, non-Muslim reader can readily acknowledge the spiritual power and depth of the book.

*Qur'an stand (Courtesy of The Metropolitan
Museum of Art, Rogers Fund, 1910).*

This impression arises from two aspects of the Qur'an which come through even in an English translation. One is the sincerity, conviction, and intensity of Muhammad's call to submit, to yield to God; the other is—in spite of its unsystematic character as directed to specific occasions and circumstances—the cumulative vision of the glory, majesty, power, judgment, love, and mercy of God.

THE TRADITIONAL VIEW OF THE QUR'AN

All scriptures suffer from translation, and none more so than the Qur'an, according to all authorities. When read aloud in the original it has a power over the hearers which confirms for them their view that the Glorious Qur'an is the very word of God given to Muhammad. God's words were mediated to Muhammad by "the spirit" according to several references in the book itself, and tradition has identified this spirit with the angel Gabriel. The Sunni theory is that the full text of the book as it now exists in Arabic is contained in a "Heavenly Book," "the uncreated Qur'an." This was revealed by Gabriel to Muhammad in longer or shorter sections according to his times and circumstances. (Shiites deny the doctrine of the Uncreated Qur'an.) It was written down by scribes and other hearers as it was recited; the Arabic word *qur'an* is from a verb "read, repeat aloud." Hence, Muhammad did not "write" the Qur'an; taught by the spirit, he "recited" it.

Various passages in the Qur'an itself and the books of tradition recognize that Muhammad was in some kind of ecstatic state when he uttered the words. Such states were a recognized phenomenon associated with the general prophetic tradition of the *nabi** in Semitic culture. In this state, then, Muhammad received revelations which always say or imply that they are what "God has said." Uttering them in the form of rhymed prose, which resembled that of the Arabian oracular soothsayers called *kahins*, Muhammad was derided as just another *kahin*, and he himself feared that perhaps he was. Later, his style of utterance became less oracular. It became part of the received doctrine that his style is inimitable, and the Qur'an includes a challenge for anyone else to produce comparable inspired verses. From among numerous passages in the Qur'an which state and defend the doctrine of revelation is this passage:

This Koran could not have been forged
apart from God; but it is a confirmation
of what is before it, and a distinguishing
of the Book, wherein is no doubt, from
    the Lord of all Being.
Or do they say, "Why, he has forged it"?
Say: "Then produce a sura like it, and
call on whom you can, apart from God,
    if you speak truly." (S. 10:38, 39)

SOURCES, COMPOSITION, AND CONTENTS

Although scholars raise a number of questions about specific parts, modern study has not raised serious question of the Qur'an's authenticity. As for the actual process of the recording of the Prophet's words and the preparation of the official text, however, there is much disagreement. There were professional reciters who had much of it by heart at the time Muhammad died. (Memorization

and recitation of the book is still a recognized art and a method of education.)
Large parts of it had also been written down, but this was unsystematic. Verses
had been inscribed on any available material—clay shards, stones, palm leaves,
bones. Before the time of Othman there were four collections of Qur'anic material in various places, but none of these has survived. Differences and disputes over the text led Othman to commission Zayd, who had been secretary
to Muhammad, to direct the revision and comparison of texts and produce an
authorized version. Bell says:

> This revision under 'Othman, which may be dated somewhere between the
> year XXX and 'Othman's death in XXXV, or about twenty years after Muham-
> mad's death, is the cardinal point in the formation of what we may call the
> canon of the Qur'ān. Whatever may have been the form of the Qur'ān before
> that time, and as to that Tradition is by no means clear, we can be fairly cer-
> tain that the book retains still the form then established.[6]

The traditional arrangement of the Qur'an was purely mechanical: the
longest chapters first and the shortest last. Many suras can be assigned as earlier or later, and therefore some translators arrange them according to the supposed chronological order of the 114 suras.

INTERPRETATION OF THE QUR'AN

Aids to understanding and interpretation of the Qur'an soon appeared, especially in connection with the rise of schools of theology and jurisprudence
which appealed to it. The first great systematic study and collection of these
commentary materials was done by al-Tabari about the year 900. His 30 volumes were the source for later, more specialized studies, and are still valuable.
The most authoritative and useful for modern scholars is the commentary of al-
Badawi (922).

There are two principal methods of interpretation applied to the Qur'an,
representing the Sunnite–Shiite division. The Sunni line is that interpretation
should be simple exegesis (critical and analytical study) based on human intelligence and understanding, using the Qur'an itself plus the tradition of the
Prophet's own practice. The Shiah advocate the use of allegory, to get more ultimate meanings, and the right to personal interpretation, independent reasoning, or original thinking (*ijtihad**) by learned commentators.

Tradition and Custom, or Hadith and Sunnah

HADITH

When the words are not what God said, but what "The Prophet said," the saying is a tradition, *hadith** in the narrower sense, which literally denotes a nar-
ration, statement, or story. In the broader sense tradition includes both the actual traditional practice or custom of the Prophet and the written record of

that traditional way of action. This double meaning of "tradition" is confusing, and the confusion reflects the complex development. The key to understanding that development is to realize the importance of tradition in Islamic religion. Like any society, pre-Islamic Arab culture proudly followed its own customs (*sunnah*) or traditional way, and Islam likewise was concerned to act in accordance with accepted moral and religious practices. What we are really talking about are what sociologists call mores, customs with ethical meaning and sanction. For Muslims the sanction or source of Islamic custom is what Muhammad either recited in the Qur'an or is reported to have said according to the written traditions, the Hadith. We will use the word "Hadith" for these written records of traditions. A *hadith* is a statement or story telling what Muhammad is reported to have done or said about something. The collection of these reports is called the Hadith.

SUNNAH

The Hadith preserve in written form the customs, as we said above. These customs or mores are called *sunnah*, and as they developed the meaning of the word changed. The first or simplest meaning was of ancient custom, pre-Islamic, revered as the practice of the ancestors. Then the actual ways of doing things in the Islamic community, and especially in the Medina group and among the Companions, were considered normative. But then in time different kinds of *sunnah* developed in different areas, so there was need to decide which customs were really according to Muhammad's usage. The Hadith served to define the true *sunnah*. The Hadith is therefore the vehicle of Muslim custom or *sunnah*. Guillaume's summary is: "Thus *sunnah* was first ancient custom, then contemporary, immediate past practice, and finally the ideal behavior of the prophet as enshrined in tradition."[7]

COLLECTIONS

As Muslim writers themselves admit, the Hadith included many nonauthentic, manufactured traditions. Nevertheless, it is now generally reliable and serves its purpose, because a method of control and verification was adopted; and the best-known collections followed the criteria in sifting hundreds of thousands of *hadith* for the comparatively few chosen as genuine. Any accepted tradition included two parts which must both be valid: (1) the chain (*isnad**) of narrators, including the one who heard the saying from Muhammad or an associate; (2) the statement as delivered (*matn**). Traditions were graded "genuine," "good," and "weak." The greatest early collection, called "The Genuine" (*sahih**), is that of al-Bukhari (d. 870), and the other "genuine" collection, from the same era, is that of Muslim ibn al-Hajjaj. Four later collections are considered canonical, but do not rate so highly as the two "genuine." There are, therefore, six major collections of the Hadith. Each *hadith* begins like this (showing the *isnad* leading to the *matn*): "Muhammad b. Bashshār has related to us on the authority of Yahyā, from 'Ubaidallah, on the authority of Sa'īd b. Abī Sa'īd, from his father, from Abu Huraira, that the Apostle of Allah . . . said:"[8]

Law and Laws, or Shariah* and *Fiqh*

Just as there is a relation between *sunnah* and the Hadith, so is there between Shariah and the four books of jurisprudence or law. The relation of Shariah and jurisprudence (*fiqh*) is likewise very complex, and we limit our discussion to a few simple points. Shariah is the most comprehensive and important term for the functioning system of divinely ordered, Islamic social structure and law. As in Judaism, its ultimate basis and justification is the divine command, although mediated through tradition and usage; it is divine law. Shariah includes both religious law or duty proper and social or secular conduct. We will consider its application in those two areas under "Ritual" and "Ethical and Social Aspects of Islam." The process of formulating these practices was long and complex. It was finally effected through slightly different schools or systems for stating the content and character of this divine legislation. All the major Islamic group, the Sunni, accept the general approach to the Shariah embodied in the first four schools. They are, therefore, not to be construed as separate or dissenting sects, but four variant schools of one basic system. The Arabic expression is "ways," *madhhahib*.* Each one is dominant in certain geographical areas. They are listed here.

SHAFITE*

Al-Shafi (d. 820) was the founder of the classical theory of Islamic law, and his system of jurisprudence combined insistence on the importance of proper prophetic tradition with the use of analogy to reason to new applications.

HANAFITE*

This was the first school to arise, in Iran in the eighth century, originated by Abu Hanifah and developed by two disciples. It is characterized by much freedom for personal interpretation, hence in this sense is more liberal than others.

MALIKITE*

The school of Medina was under Malik ibn Anas (d. 795), who relied on "living tradition" of Medina as vindicated by Hadith.

HANBALITE*

The latest school, and also the most conservative, is now dominant in Arabia through Wahhabi espousal of its principles. It is extremely literalistic

and legalistic and is antagonistic toward the other three. The founder was
Ahmad ibn Hanbal (d. 855).

IMAMIYYAH*

This fifth school serves the minority Shiah fellowship; since the sixteenth century it has been the official school in Iran. Their concern being more political
than for jurisprudence proper, followers include the idea of individual interpretation called *ijtihad*. Professor Faruqi writes: "Because their theology grants
to their *imams* ('leaders') unlimited authority, ascribing it to the charisma they
inherited directly from the Prophet, the *imam* for them is himself a living
source of law almost as much as the Prophet had been."[9] This comment enables us to understand the power of the Ayotollah Khomeini in the overthrow
of the Shah of Iran and establishment of the oppressive regime that has out-
lived him in Iran.

TENETS

Although the formal creed is short and appears only as the first of the five pillars of Islam, there is a set of fundamental beliefs. But the fact that there is no
organized priestly group or machinery for Islam means that exactly what
should go into such a list is not determined except by informal consensus.
Islam falls between the elaborate creedal and doctrinal nature of Christianity
and the minimal doctrinal character of Judaism. The topic will be divided thus:
a list of traditional explicit doctrines, and philosophical and theological formulations.

A List of Muslim Doctrines

This list is more or less traditional. There are Islamic formulations of the faith
to be found in the literature, like the Forty Traditions of Salman, but no one of
them can be taken as authoritative for all Muslims. In each doctrine cited here
Muhammad used materials from his own time and culture, transmuting them
as necessary. Later generations then expanded his ideas.

ALLAH

The most comprehensive explication of the Prophet's doctrine of Allah would
be to outline the teaching of the Qur'an, but it is too rich and varied. The
Qur'an, nevertheless, is the source that will be used here, because it is the one
source which all later theologians used to develop the doctrine of God.

The uniqueness of God is the first article of the *Shahadah*,* which can be
called the creed or confession of faith. Although it is not found as a single statement in the Qur'an, the first phrase occurs in many places in slightly differing
forms. "He is God; there is no God but He" (S. 59:22). He is one in being

Mount Arafat and Mina, pilgrimage time (Courtesy, Arabian American Oil Company).

unique and incomparable; nothing else can be compared to him: *shirk*, "association" of any other with Allah, is the worst sin. The denial of his oneness by division is likewise forbidden, with explicit mention of the Christian Trinity (in a form Christians would not accept).

They are unbelievers
who say, "God is the Third of Three."
No God is there but
One God (S. 5:77).

God's complete transcendence is the distinctive emphasis of Islamic monotheism in comparison with Judaic and Christian monotheism, in which God's immanence (indwelling) is stressed as well as his transcendence. Allah's absolute transcendence is seen in and guarded by the rigid prohibition against depiction of living things in the decoration of mosques. In the Qur'an the infinite spiritual character of God is expressed in metaphorical terms rather than the abstractions of omniscience and omnipotence: "He knows the treachery of the eyes and what the breasts conceal" (S. 40:20). A famous litany to be used with the rosary of 33 beads lists the 99 "most beautiful names" of God. All of them are specific, concrete, descriptive terms from the Qur'an, the most abstract being such as "the Wise," "the Eternal," "the Knowing One"—"He has knowledge of everything" (S. 2:27).

But it is as maker, ruler, and judge with complete power over all things past, present, and future that the Qur'an most exalts and glorifies Allah. Nearly every page calls upon the believer to acknowledge God as such, to remember that Allah creates all, is above all, and rules all, and that people and things are utterly dependent upon him.

JUDGMENT

It is from this work of God as ruler and judge that the other central doctrine of Islam comes: the judgment of all souls at the end of time. With consistent logic and persistent denunciation the Prophet warned that there is no escape from the final moral decision of God over humankind. It was as a preacher of righteousness and judgment that Muhammad first broke in upon the astonished Meccan merchants and townspeople. The two doctrines at which his hearers scoffed most disdainfully were the resurrection and concomitant judgment; but both of them followed from his doctrine of God, and to deny them was to reject God. Allah is active will; he doesn't just stand by—he is forever working out his purposes. To Muhammad, therefore, it was axiomatic that the righteous God must demand an accounting of, and must reward or punish, his creatures at the end of this world. For this there must be resurrection, judgment, and an afterlife. The Prophet's responsibility, his task from God, was to warn—and he did. In the Qur'an there are dozens of passages like this:

By the mount
and a Book inscribed
in a parchment unrolled,
by the House inhabited
    and the roof uplifted
    and the sea swarming,
surely thy Lord's chastisement is about to fall;
    there is none to avert it.
Upon the day when heaven spins dizzily
    and the mountains are in motion,
Woe that day unto those that cry lies,
    such as play at plunging,
the day when they shall be pitched into the fire of Gehenna:
    "This is the fire that you cried lies to!
    What, is this magic, or is it you that do not see?
Roast in it! And bear you patiently, or bear not patiently,
    equal it is to you; you are only being recompensed for
        that you were working."

Yet the picture is incomplete and Islam is misunderstood if we stop here. Muhammad is not only a messenger of judgment, he is also the messenger of mercy. There is no Christ in Islam. But in "Books and Prophets" we shall see that the Uncreated Qur'an is like the Word or Logos in Christianity, and Muhammad "recites" the word. The forgiveness and mercy which are seen in Christ, in Islam are found in Allah at the time of judgment. Every sura of the Qur'an begins with the invocation, "In the name of Allah, the Compassionate, the Merciful." God's mercy (*rahman**) is central to his nature, is recited in the Qur'an, and is manifested to the faithful at the end. Hence the coda of the above sura:

> Surely the godfearing shall be in gardens and bliss,
>> rejoicing in that their Lord has given them;
> and their Lord shall guard them against the chastisement of Hell.
> (S. 52:1–17)

ANGELS

Belief in spiritual beings of various kinds is found in the Qur'an and was systematized in later Islamic thought. In the Qur'an angels are usually presented as God's messengers, and later believers identified the chief as Gabriel. Jinn* are created of fire and are either good or bad, the leader of the evil ones being the evil one, or Iblis.*

BOOKS AND PROPHETS

Just as other faiths have their books in which God speaks to them, so God speaks to Islam through their sacred book. Thus the doctrine of the Uncreated Qur'an in heaven has been compared to the Word of God in the Torah and Wisdom, and to Christ as the eternal (uncreated) Logos or Word with God from eternity. Judaism knows the Word through its history; and Christianity beholds it in Christ. But inasmuch as Allah is never a father and has no son, the book must serve alone as the revelation for Islam. The importance of the Qur'an to Islam cannot be overstated. Associated with the books are the prophets. In the creed the prophethood of Muhammad ranks with the Unity of God as central doctrine; the second phrase of the *shahadah* is: "And Muhammad is his prophet." Books come from God and prophets are sent by him to proclaim God's oneness and warn of his judgment. Twenty-eight prophets are mentioned in the Qur'an, including 18 from the Old Testament, as well as John the Baptist and Jesus. Muhammad is the "seal," that is, the last of the prophetic line. Others before him had claimed this title, putting themselves in the line of the prophets. Somehow Muhammad's spiritual power prevailed upon his followers, so that they now hold that 1,300 years of history and 900,000,000 adherents vindicate his claim to be the Seal of the Prophets. Although Muhammad claimed only to be the Prophet, some of his followers have exalted him to a position little short of a deity. They have attributed miracles to him, and they regard him as the most excellent of all created beings. In popular folk belief he is sinless and works miracles.[10] His intercession at the day of resurrection for some believers is received doctrine for all Muslims.

PREDESTINATION

Predestination is a problem in any theistic religion which takes seriously both morality and judgment, as Islam does. In Christianity it is Calvinism which has most fully articulated double predestination (God's prior judgment of an individual to heaven or hell), based on Paul's letters. Islamic orthodoxy has used the more extreme statements of the Qur'an to support a doctrine of predestination of both the saved and the damned. These verses are from a key passage used to support double predestination:

Whomsoever God guides,
    he is rightly guided;
and whom He leads astray—
    They are the losers.
. . . .
Whomsoever God leads astray,
    no guide he has;
He leaves them in their insolence
    blindly wandering. (S. 7:177, 185)

The words suggest sheep or goats that willfully wander and are allowed to go astray. Of course, there are other suras used to support other views. Efforts to soften the doctrine involve making a distinction between God's unsearchable decree (*qada*), which determines all things in general, and his predestination (*qadar*) of specific occurrences, for which the individual by his or her own acts becomes responsible. In the *Summa Theologica* Thomas Aquinas argues, in a similar vein, that God's knowledge and will do not impose necessity on human beings in such a way as to deny human responsibility.

PHILOSOPHICAL AND THEOLOGICAL FORMULATIONS

The beginning of Muslim theology was in the emergence of an Arabian type of orthodoxy which developed at Medina during the first Islamic century. This central orthodoxy has continued to this day, but other movements influenced Islamic faith and doctrine. One school of thought promulgated a rationalistic metaphysics that set abstract doctrines and essences above the personal and absolute divinity of the one God as seen through the scriptures themselves. Against them, orthodoxy upheld the insight in the faith and message of the Prophet: Nothing may impugn the uniqueness of the Godhead. A brilliant scholar, Al-Ashari (C.E. 873–935), having previously been aligned with the rationalists, changed his mind.

Interior, Great Mosque, Mecca (Courtesy, Arabian American Oil Company).

Al-Ashari   Beginning as a Mutazilite,* al-Ashari (d. 935) used the methods he learned from the Mutazila to help defeat them. He evidently became convinced that revelation was superior to reason as a guide in religion, and so he joined the orthodox party.

According to stories that go back to his own reports, al-Ashari had a dream-vision in which Muhammad told him to devote himself to the Hadith and commentaries on the Qur'an. This the thinker did, abandoning his rationalistic methods entirely. But then the Prophet appeared to him again and told him: "I did not tell you to give up rational arguments, but to support the true traditions." Al-Ashari got the message—his method became the support of revelation by reason.

Al-Ashari's differences from the Mutazilites and his contribution to a restored or moderately rationalized orthodoxy have been summarized by Watt under four headings.[11] (1) He agreed with Sunnite orthodox theory that the Qur'an was uncreated and the actual Speech of God, but in a subtle way distinct from God's essence. (2) The anthropomorphisms of the Qur'an, such as references to the hand of God, must not be interpreted completely as metaphors, but accepted "without specifying how." (3) The eschatology of the Qur'an must likewise not be reduced to metaphor but left as it stands. (4) The Mutazilite doctrine of free will was opposed by al-Ashari's statement of a modified theory of "acquisition." This theory holds that in his own actions a person "acquires" responsibility for his act, even though God's omnipotence is not denied. Al-Ashari's view gave the human will only the power to "accept as his" what God does through him. In all his writing al-Ashari's primary concern was to uphold the fundamental dogma of the omnipotence and omniscience of God.

The Doctrines of Sufism   Sufism essentially is Islamic mysticism, although its origins are complex and its forms diverse. At the outset it stood for a protest against an arid theoretical scholasticism, divorced from popular understanding and empty of religious feeling. It began as asceticism, which had existed in Islam from the beginning. The mark of adherents was blue wool (*suf*). In the beginning the mystical element was subordinate, but by 800 the woman saint Rabia al-Adawiya articulated the mystic's motive: "O God! If I worship Thee in fear of Hell, burn me in Hell; and if I worship Thee in hope of Paradise exclude me from Paradise; but if I worship Thee for Thine own sake, withhold not Thine everlasting Beauty!"[12] As Sufism grew it became more and more unorthodox in the elevation of personal mystical ecstasy to the chief good and central meaning of religion. A leading proponent of this mystical way to truth and loving union with God was Mansur al-Hallaj, a wool carder. His claim, "I am the Reality," was interpreted as identification of himself with God, and he was executed by crucifixion in 922 as an example for other enthusiasts. Such repressive measures failed, however, because the instinct for religious sustenance was not being met by the Sunni orthodox leadership. These leaders believed that their theological system and authority were necessary to preserve the substance of Islamic doctrine, but they were actually in danger of losing the substance of religious devotion, which the Sufis—despite their errors and excesses—maintained. Because of this struggle more and more sincere believers were forced into the Sufi school. The man who, like al-Ashari 2 centuries before, effected a reconciliation between orthodoxy and mysticism was Al-Ghazzali.

Al-Ghazzali   Al-Ghazzali (d. 1111) gave to Islamic theology and ethics the form which it has essentially kept ever since; he is the Thomas Aquinas of Muslim theory. Becoming a student of theology for lack—as he said—of any better career, he studied at several of the Islamic schools, and became a professor at a new one in Baghdad, where he was enormously popular. In the midst of this success he suffered a breakdown as the result of his own doubts and uncertainty, from which he was delivered by personal experience of God in the tradition of Sufi mysticism. After this he made the pilgrimage to Mecca and remained in semiretirement most of the rest of his life except for a few years teaching at another school. During these years he wrote several books, including *The Revivification of the Religious Sciences*, which did serve to revive and restore them.

Al-Ghazzali's central conviction was that religious certainty is to be discovered only in religious experience; this made a place for religious feeling and thus for Sufism in the accepted doctrine of Islam. At the same time he practiced and promoted a moderate form of mysticism in which the love of God is the central conception and motive. He wrote:

> Whoever loves another than God for other than God's sake does so from ignorance . . . (though to love the Messenger of God is praiseworthy, for it is really loving God) . . . for among men of insight (basā'ir) there is no true beloved save God most High, and none deserving of love save Him. In order to explain this we shall turn to the five causes of love which we have mentioned, and we shall show that all of them unite in the truth of God.[13]

Emphasis on the love of God did not prevent Al-Ghazzali from also stressing the importance of fear of judgment. His own reaction against philosophical speculation meant that he called for a return to the living word of the Qur'an and the traditions. Theologically, however, he maintained above all the supremacy of God, who, he said, "knows the very tread of the blackbird in the dark night on the hard stone."

RITUAL AND WORSHIP

The great majority of Muslims are Sunni, the central and traditional line of Islamic faith whose intellectual formulations we have just outlined. Only about a fifth of Muslims belong to the minority sects which will be mentioned later. For most of the great Sunni majority, Islam is a total way of life which governs all aspects of their existence under the heading of Islamic law, the Shariah. Out of the history, literature, and doctrine we have analyzed so far, there emerged a more or less coherent body of custom, tradition, law, usage, which is theoretically binding on all the faithful. They submit (*islam*) to this combination of traditions and of principles with specific prescriptions for worship and conduct.

The Shariah was mentioned in connection with the four books of jurisprudence, as their total content or meaning which they embody. One of the four authors, Al-Shafi, formulated what became the Sunni doctrine of the Shariah. Al-Shafi's theory was that the law is founded on four sources or principles: the Qur'an custom or *sunnah* from Muhammad's words and actions, the consensus (*ijma**) of the community itself, and the use of analogy (*qiyas*). The product of these various sources is the set of divinely revealed principles and laws for Muslims to follow in all actions relating to society and God. In practice, the Shariah is divided into two major sections: the worship of God (*ibadat**), and "dealings" among people, regulation for human relations (*mua-malat**). Religious laws, *ibadat*, give us the content of this section on ritual and worship.

The Five Pillars

"The Five Pillars" is the usual designation for the fundamental religious ritual laws or practices that are binding on all Muslims. They come from the Qur'an only in part and were established early in the life of Islam. So familiar and basic are they that no extended explanation or analysis is necessary. They are: creed, prayer, alms, fast, and pilgrimage.

CREED

"There is no God but Allah, and Muhammad is his Prophet." (*La illaha illah Allah, Muhammad rasul** Allah.*) This formula, the *Shahadah*, becomes a profession of faith when preceded by, "I bear witness that. . . ." Solemn recitation of the first clause constitutes one as a *muslim*, submitter to God, and of the second makes one a Muslim, an adherent of the faith. It is understood and stated in religious instruction that reciting the creed implies belief in the Qur'an, in traditions, and in traditional teachings about angels, prophets, saints, the scriptures, and judgment. Any educated Muslim would be expected to understand and accept a rational explanation and description of these teachings. The brief, formal creed, therefore, actually entails a larger body of belief, such as was described in our section on tenets.

The celebration of the birthday of Muhammad is the most important expression of reverence for him, and perhaps the most universal Islamic festival except for the feast at the end of Ramadan.* It falls on the twelfth of the month Rabi, which of course is a movable date. The actual celebration is often on the eve of the feast, observed with a parade and other public celebrations.

PRAYER

It was because Muhammad was outraged by intoxicated persons causing disorder at the time of prayer in the mosque that wine was restricted and later prohibited. *Salat*,* ritual prayer, has a wider meaning than the more personal communion with God connoted by the word *du'a*, because *salat* refers primarily to public and ritual prayers. There is no doubt that prayer was the core of Muhammad's personal devotional life and the source of his power, and it is the most important element in Islamic public and private piety. The canonical rule is for prayer five times a day, wherever one may be, at dawn, noon, before sunset, just after sunset, and after dark. Ritual purity calls for washing, if possible, before liturgical prayer, and thus there is a pool in front of a mosque; and for purification of the place where one prays, the prayer rug is used.

Prayer rug (Courtesy, The Metropolitan Museum of Art, The James F. Ballard Collection, Gift of James F. Ballard, 1922).

There is a simple basic formula for prayer: praise to God, petitions, and recitation from the Qur'an, accompanied by kneeling and prostration. "The Opening" (Fatihah*), or first sura from the Qur'an, is so named because it is used to begin the prayer ritual:

Praise belongs to God, the Lord of all Being,
the All-merciful, and All-compassionate
    The Master of the Day of Doom.
Thee only we serve; to Thee alone we pray for succour.
    Guide us in the straight path,
the path of those whom Thou hast blessed,
not of those against whom Thou art wrathful,
    nor of those who are astray. (S. 1:1–6)

Although Friday is not a sabbath day, men are expected to convene in the mosque at noon for common recitation of prayers, usually under the direction of an *imam* or leader. Any devout layman may lead public prayer—there are no priests in Islam.

Muhammad helped construct the first mosque in Medina. The mosque is a place of prayer, and is frequented by the faithful at all times for their study and devotions. In the Middle East the floor of a mosque is usually covered with carpets, on which one kneels and prostrates oneself during the prayers. No images or representation of any living creature are permitted in a mosque, only geometrical patterns and script from the Qur'an. The central spot of the mosque is the *mihrab*,* a small niche in the wall which indicates the direction (*qibla**) of Mecca, toward which all turn for prayer. There is also a pulpit (*mimbar**), usually raised on steps.

ALMS

The duty to give alms for the poorer brethren was at first voluntary but was later made into a system of taxation for other purposes. In modern times the payment of alms in the proper sense is again mostly a voluntary matter. Benevolence toward the needy is the prime social responsibility of a Muslim.

FAST

During the liturgical month of Ramadan all pious Muslims must fast during each day from the time in the morning when one can tell a white thread from a black until sunset. No food or water is allowed and sex is prohibited during those hours. Meals are allowed before and after the daytime, but the spirit of the fast is supposed to govern the whole month. In Islamic countries the daytime Ramadan fast is generally observed by the faithful.

PILGRIMAGE

Among the pre-Islamic elements which Muhammad preserved and adapted were the central stone (Kaaba) at Mecca and the pilgrimage rites connected with it. Tradition identified Islam as derived from Abraham through Ishmael, the son of Abraham by Hagar, as recounted in Genesis 16, 17, and 21. Abraham is said to have built the Kaaba, and one of the structures near it houses the stone on which he stood. The well Zam Zam is described as the one which saved Ishmael's and Hagar's life, Genesis 21:19.

The pilgrimage to Mecca (*hajj*,* literally "setting out") is supposed to be performed by every Muslim who can afford it, in obedience to numerous injunctions in the Qur'an. Although it is not observed by all, the *hajj* has served to unify Islam and to relate and unite Muslims who are scattered across the world. Those who do make the pilgrimage are considered representatives of all Muslims. They gain forgiveness of sins and assurance of salvation; afterward they are called *hajj* or *hajji* (Turkish). Gathering at the sacred city in the month of pilgrimage, they all wear identical, white pilgrimage robes, observe the rules, and perform the ceremonies which take nearly two weeks. The physical and spiritual center of Mecca is the Great Mosque, a large open square surrounded by wide covered corridors opening on the square, with the minarets that are the mark of a mosque throughout Islam towering overhead. The center of the mosque is the Kaaba or cube—a square, empty, windowless, stone structure covered by a great black brocade richly embroidered in gold thread with Qur'anic texts in Arabic script. Set in the southeast corner is the holiest object, the sacred stone from earlier times, now much worn and enclosed with a silver collar or frame.

The three duties absolutely required of pilgrims are: to wear the white garment (*ihram**); to "stand before God" from noon to sunset on Arafat, the Mount of Mercy where Muhammad delivered his farewell sermon, on the ninth day; and the *tawaf*,* seven ceremonial counterclockwise circuits of the Kaaba, kissing or touching the stone each time if possible (the crowd may be too great). There are five less strict duties; one of these is running between two low hills in remembrance of Hagar's frantic search for water for her child Ishmael. Another is the vigil at Muzadalifa before the great feast at Mina on the tenth day, which is the joyous end of the major parts of the pilgrimage.

Saints

A number of primitive customs survive in large areas of Islam. While the mosque itself has been kept free of any kind of saint worship, the tombs or shrines of holy men and women are the most popular places of worship in most countries. The tombs of great scholars and heroes, Shiite figures, and Sufi holy men are shrines. Such places are often packed with devotees clinging to the central tomb as they circle it, all the while murmuring prayers. Muslim theory authorizes prayer only for the intercession of the saints, but in practice they are treated as local deities to whom prayers are addressed for all manner of direct blessings.

ETHICAL AND SOCIAL ASPECTS OF ISLAM

The traditional structure and content of Islamic ethics are the Shariah and books of jurisprudence. Islamic books set out in systematic fashion the traditional Qur'anic law texts under a few major headings, but that is hardly an adequate description of the working system. We can only indicate the general theory and structure of Islamic ethics. Several factors in the complex total picture can be identified: the doctrine of consensus and the place of the ulema,* personal interpretation, the Shariah, and social dealings or relations. We will discuss the major sectarian division between Sunni and Shiah, and conclude with stress on submission as the key to the mood or attitude of the Muslim toward God and the world.

Consensus, and the Ulema

Sunnah,* tradition, the books of jurisprudence, and Shariah are not understandable without the doctrine of consensus (*ijma*). Islam has no priesthood, for the Friday worship at the mosque can be led by any layman, although usually it is done by the local religious leader, called the *imam*,* or in Shiite Iran the *mullah*.* But there did develop a class of learned doctors of Islamic law, the ulema (*ulama*), corresponding to Christian clergy or Judaic rabbis as religious authorities. As the religious leaders of Islam, their agreement constitutes the consensus of the community. A tradition of the Prophet is adduced as basis for the idea that a consensus among them validates a decision or verdict: "My religious community will never be unanimous in error." While the ulema are not an official group, in effect their consensus makes and unmakes the body of Islamic principles in any field, so far as there is any such unified body of opinion.

Ijtihad

In former times *ijtihad* or personal interpretation by individual scholars was recognized in some schools of jurisprudence as authoritative teaching. But now an individual's interpretation is personal and not binding upon anyone else. *Ijtihad* amounts to a recognition of the right of individual conscience, although, of course, shaped by tradition and consensus.

Shariah and "Dealings" (*Muamalat*)

The second major portion of Shariah, after *ibadat* or religious laws, are the regulations for human relations known by the general name of *muamalat* or "dealings." According to Islamic theory the actual content of *muamalat* is contained in Qur'anic regulations as interpreted and applied by tradition and in the books of the four schools of jurisprudence. It is very much a bookish and theoretical body of regulations, and how much direct, practical bearing they have is questionable.

MARRIAGE, SEX, THE FAMILY

By far the largest body of regulations are in this area. For the most part, Islam found customs regarding men, women, and marriage already established, and it is true that the position of women is quite low. Marriage is a simple agreement between the two parties. The man can divorce his wife at any time by pronouncing three times, "I have divorced you." Until recently women had no such right, but conditions have begun to change in some Islamic countries. The theoretical right of an intelligent, upright, and financially able man to have four wives is not often exercised now. In religious matters women are not discriminated against, except for the pilgrimage, which must be made accompanied by a man and under his guardianship. In some countries women now go to the mosque at the time of prayer, but are usually sequestered behind a curtain. Religious obligations are equally binding on women, and both men and women who submit go to Paradise.

THE FORMAL AND EXTERNAL CHARACTER OF ISLAMIC ETHICS

Islam developed as an elaborate system of rules and customs for the worldwide Islamic community, in some ways comparable to Judaism as a total way of life for Jews during earlier centuries. In Islam this system has produced an ethic in which the stress is on external compliance with the rules. But the rules or customs of Shariah are so numerous and varied that the Muslim has to have some way of establishing priority. Various terms and grades are used for this purpose, but one general formula developed by the *fiqh* scholars in the later centuries is fairly well accepted. It classifies behavior into five categories of things enjoined, forbidden, or neutral:

1. obligatory
2. desirable or recommended, but not obligatory
3. indifferent
4. disapproved, but not prohibited
5. forbidden

Because the personal conscience is not stressed, the tribal or communal aspect of Islamic mores is very strong, as seen in this system of gradations of social or community opinion, from obligatory to forbidden. Although ultimately God enjoins, forbids, and finally judges, it is Islamic public opinion which provides sanctions in this world. The peer group gives Islamic customs their strength and makes change, for example, in the position of women, so difficult. Thus Muslims have the custom of "bidding to Good," under which they enjoin their fellow-believers to do what is required and shun what is forbidden. Muslims in an Islamic community will exhort even strangers to observe rules for the Ramadan fast, for example, in a way which would be considered rude and offensive by a Western autonomous individual. The canonical daily prayers and the Ramadan fast are obligatory for all Muslims except the sick and the traveling. Some of the pilgrimage customs are obligatory, and others are "desirable but not obligatory." Gambling, the eating of pork, and the use of alcohol are supposedly in the category of "forbidden," but the actual practice in regard to drinking alcohol has practically changed it to "disapproved but not prohibited" in some parts of the Islamic world.

Prayer in the Mosque, Gérôme, d. 1904 (Courtesy, The Metropolitan Museum of Art, Bequest of Catherine Lorillard Wolfe, 1887).

Islamic Divisions and Sects

The majority of Muslims adhere to the *sunnah* as tradition of the community as a whole and hence are known as Sunnites, in distinction to the minority Shiah. Their views are the classic and central system of Islamic faith and practice developed from Muhammad's teaching and example as found in the Qur'an and Hadith. Other minority movements, however, are accepted parts of Islam. There are religious leaders in Islam, but as we have said, no priests in these various groups or divisions.

THE SHIAH SECT, OR THE SHIITES

The history of Ali and is sons has been outlined. The further history of the Shiites is a record of beliefs and doctrines that center on Ali and his descendants in relation to the leadership of Islam. Although the original and continuing issue between Sunni and Shiah Muslims is the caliphate, Shiite doctrine has taken it much farther. To them, the caliph as "successor" to Muhammad was not simply a political leader. He was also the religious leader, Imam,* qualified by birth as a descendant of the Prophet and by God-given nature as a sinless and infallible guide. All Shiites came to believe in the return or second coming of the Imam. This was possible because it was claimed that Ali and a son named Muhammad had not actually died but had retired or withdrawn to a secret place to await God's call. The doctrine of the concealed Imam was easily expanded to include belief in the return or second coming. This expectation combined with a general Muslim belief in the coming of the Mahdi* or "rightly guided one," a kind of Messiah, based on a tradition ascribed to Muhammad. They combined these ideas by saying that when the concealed Imam emerges he will be the Mahdi.

The two principal Shiite subsects both invoke these ideas, but in slightly different forms. The Imamites or "Twelvers" acknowledge a succession of twelve Imams. The twelfth, who vanished from earth, Muhammad ibn Hasan, is the concealed Imam who will return as Mahdi. Since 1502 their faith has been the religion of what is now Iran. The other group are known as "Seveners" or "Ismailis" because they acknowledge only seven visible Imams, ending with Ismail ibn Jafar. Among Ismaili subsects are the Druzes of Lebanon, who combine teachings from the Qur'an with Jewish and Christian ideas.

ISLAMIC SUBSECTS

Among many more narrowly sectarian movements, the most important are Wahhabism and the Ahmadiyya. The Wahhabis were begun by Muhammad ibn Abd al-Wahhab (1703–1792). He promulgated a puritanical and antimystical revival directed against the alleged laxity of the broad, catholic tradition of Islam, claiming that all Muslims must return to pure, primitive Islam. Because the Kingdom of Saudi Arabia adopted the Wahhabi movement, it is important now. It represents the revival of the Arab influence as opposed to Persian and Sufi trends.

Mirza Ghulam Ahmad proclaimed himself the Mahdi in India about 100 years ago. His teachings, however, were more orthodox Muslim. He stressed peaceful missionary work as the modern form of holy war, and the Ah-

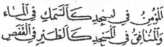

"Within the house of God,
The believer is like a fish in water,
The hypocrite like a caged bird."

This medallion is an Arabic proverb copied from the wall of the Mosque of Rustem Pasha in Istanbul, Turkey. It is possibly the work of the great 16th century calligraphist Ahmet Shemsettin Karahisari. It has been printed by The Redhouse Press in Istanbul.

madiyya missionary movement is strong and active in northern Africa and other areas.

CONCLUSION: SUBMISSION AND PEACE

"To designate the voluntary self-surrender of a believer to the Divine will Muhammad coined the term 'Islam.' "[14] Muslims are often reluctant to press this simple formula, because it can be misunderstood and misused. But we will use "submission" to conclude the chapter, because it holds the essential meaning of the religion. Submission is not simply the name of Islam, but the clue to understanding it.

Whomsoever God guides
   he is rightly guided;
and whom He leads astray—
   thou wilt not find for them
   protectors, apart from Him. (S. 17:98)

But who are the "rightly guided"? They are *those who submit*. "And say to those who have been given the Book and to the common folk: 'Have you surrendered?' If they have surrendered, they are right guided" (S. 3:17). At the same time those who submit are right guided in the ethical sense. Submission provides the basis for ethical life, because the one who submits to God is guided in this life, which means he is given moral guidance on earth. What, then, of the afterlife?

Submission qualifies one for God's mercy at judgment and for eternity. The stanza which precedes every sura in the Qur'an describes God as "the Merciful, the Compassionate." *Rahman*, the mercy of God, is fundamental to his nature. Yet the Qur'an is full of verses which proclaim judgment, and picture God as awful and terrible. How does one reconcile these two images of God? "Submission" again supplies the answer. To whom is Allah compassionate and merciful, now and at the end of time? Throughout the Qur'an God is always merciful to the faithful, to those who submit.

The other side of surrender is peace. Scholars have pointed out how the pre-Islamic experience of the Arabs' dependence on powers and forces beyond their control shaped their view of the cosmos, and the Qur'an is insistent on our dependence on forces beyond ourselves. Moreover, the Qur'an repeatedly says that those who accept the power of God over them gain peace, assurance, and security thereby. Another key Islamic word is *iman*,* faith. The second meaning of *iman* is submission and obedience; it connotes a feeling of security, rightness, or being established. This is the experiential core of Islam for the individual believer: a calm and relaxed sense of assurance, peace of mind. In writing about predestination, Guillaume recognized that it can go too far, like having the text "Place your reliance on God" on the windshield of a bus careening around curves on a dangerous mountain road. He concludes: "But the attitude of the local population is characteristic of Islam, the religion of complete and absolute resignation to what is believed to be the will of Allah."[15] The Muslim gains from this what one always gains from submitting, giving up, yielding, giving in to the One who is stronger: peace, assurance, security, calmness, relaxation. "The true religion with God is Islam" (S. 3:17). *Salaam** (Peace).

SUMMARY

The youngest of the world religions is Islam, which began in Arabia in the seventh Christian century. It stands in the Western Biblical tradition because it is monotheistic and it interacted with Judaism and Christianity during its origin and early development. Both these historical factors are seen in the founder, Muhammad ("highly praised"), born about C.E. 570 in the Arabian city of Mecca. The religion of most of the people, especially the desert Bedouin, was a fairly primitive polytheism, but there were monotheists among the Arabs. We do not know much about Muhammad's early life or religious development; tradition dates his call as the Prophet in the Islamic month of Ramadan in C.E. 610, when he was instructed in a vision to "recite" the words which, with many others, were later recorded in the Qur'an. Continuing to receive such messages which were to be "read aloud" (*quran*), he began to proclaim monotheism in the name of Allah, the Arabian name for the one God. Over several years he gained a few converts among his own family and friends, and then gradually won other converts by his preaching of repentance before the judgment and reward or punishment of Allah. Because of growing hostility and danger, he and his followers withdrew to the city of Medina, where he consolidated his group and organized the community into the brotherhood of believers. The year of the *hijra* ("migration") is 622, and the Islamic calendar counts time since then as A.H., *anno Hegirae* in Latin, or "year of the hegira.' Within eight years he had returned to Mecca in triumph, and when he died in 632 the conversion of the whole of Arabia was well under way.

Muhammad was and is the Prophet, the Messenger of God, who coined the word "Islam" for the voluntary "submission" of a believer to the one God Allah, and proclaimed the message of that faith which now embraces over 900,000,000 people in a broad belt of lands extending eastward from the Near East through Asia and into the Pacific area. A member of the faith is a Muslim, one who submits to God, and Muhammad is supremely but only the Prophet who proclaims God and the faith, a human being and in no sense himself a divine savior figure. For 400 years after him there were the caliphs or "successors" who ruled Islam as it expanded with amazing rapidity into the neighboring lands and parts of Europe. This growth was largely by military conquest, but not all conversions to Islam were by force, for Jews and Christians were generally allowed to practice their faith, and millions of new adherents voluntarily made their submission, to Allah as preached by Muhammad, and to the faith of Islam founded by him.

In addition to the supreme scripture from God as recited by Muhammad and preserved in the Qur'an, there is the Hadith or Tradition of what Muhammad himself did or said, which thus became the custom or *sunnah* of Islam. There are also four schools and corresponding books of *fiqh* (jurisprudence or law) which embody different interpretations of the basic system of religiously based social structure and law (Shariah) which guides the Islamic community.

There is no official list or statement of Islamic doctrines, but most Muslims would include the following in a set of basic Islamic tenets:

1. Allah is the one and only God, infinite, eternal, incomparable, undivided, spiritual, transcendent, Creator, Ruler, and Judge of all.
2. There are angel messengers of God, and human prophets (*nabi*) to warn mankind, of whom Muhammad is supreme as the "seal" or last. Holy books also are from God, the Qur'an for Islam, to warn all people.
3. They warn of the coming judgment by Allah of all persons and their reward or punishment, but those who submit, Muslims, will receive God's mercy.

The "Five Pillars" are the fundamental religious laws or practices which constitute the worship and ritual of Islam: (1) The Creed, "There is no God but Allah, and Muhammad is his prophet," becomes a profession of faith when preceded by "I bear witness that. . . ." (2) Prayer, both public and private, is the heart of Islamic piety. (3) It is a religious duty to give alms for the poorer brethren. (4) The liturgical month of Ramadan is a fast, with abstention from food and sex required during the daylight hours of each day. (5) All Muslims who can afford it should make a pilgrimage (*hajj*) to Mecca and perform the pilgrimage rites in the Great Mosque and at other holy sites, at least once in their lifetime.

Islamic ethical and social institutions are shaped by *Sunnah* and Shariah. They developed into a system of many external rules and regulations, enforced by public opinion of the Islamic community, and graded in five degrees from "obligatory" to "forbidden." There are two principal divisions within Islam: the large majority of Sunni Muslims, and the Shiite minority of about one fifth of the total. Following the same basic religious beliefs and worship, they differ in that the Shiah, "partisans" or "adherents" of Ali, consider him and his son Husayn and their descendants the true spiritual leaders of Islam, and they reject the *sunnah* as Islamic law.

The essence of Islam, its meaning and heart to the believers, is that through submission to God, Muslims (submitters) gain the peace and security of giving in to the one who is in control, who rules, and who judges all at the end. Allah is merciful *to those who submit*. They submit. Thus they are sure of Allah's mercy, and they trust in his will; this brings a sense of trust, relaxation, calmness, and peace.

NOTES

1. In references to the Qur'an, "S" designates "sura" or chapter and verse. All quotations from the Qur'an are taken from Arthur J. Arberry, trans., *The Koran Interpreted* (George Allen and Unwin Ltd., 1955; reprint, 2 vols. in 1, New York: The Macmillan Company, 1970). Used by permission of Macmillan Publishing Co. Inc., and George Allen and Unwin Ltd.
2. Chan, Wing-Tsit, et al., comps., *The Great Asian Religions* (New York: Macmillan, 1969).
3. *San Francisco Chronicle*, July 9, 1996, p. 5.
4. Ismail al Faruqi, ed., "Islam," *Historical Atlas of the Religions of the World* (New York: Macmillan, 1974). Professor Faruqi's succinct and authoritative chapter is the best single summary description of Islam that I know.
5. Martin Van Bruinessen, "Muslim Fundamentalism: Something to Be Understood or Explained Away?" *Islam and Christian-Muslim Relations* 6, no. 2 (1995), pp. 157–171.
6. Richard Bell, *Introduction to the Quran* (Edinburgh: Edinburgh University Press, 1953), pp. 42, 43.
7. Alfred Guillaume, *Islam* (Baltimore: Penguin Books, 1964), p. 92.
8. Arthur Jeffrey, ed., *Islam, Muhammad and His Religion* (New York: Liberal Arts Press, 1958), p. 195.
9. Faruqi, "Islam," p. 264.
10. Refer to Philip K. Hitti, *Islam: A Way of Life* (Chicago: Henry Regnery, 1971), p. 46.
11. W. Montgomery Watt, *Islamic Philosophy and Theology* (Edinburgh: Edinburgh University Press, 1962), pp. 85 ff.
12. Reynold A. Nicholson, *The Mystics of Islam*, Khayats Original Report #19 (Beirut: Khayats, 1966), p. 115.
13. John Alden Williams, ed., *Islam* (New York: Braziller, 1961), p. 168.
14. Tor Andrae, *Mohammad, The Man and His Faith*, trans. Theophil Menzel (New York: Barnes and Noble, n.d.), p. 67.
15. Guillaume, *Islam*, p. 134.

TOPICS AND QUESTIONS FOR STUDY

1. Why do we call Islam a "Biblical" religion? How do Muslims count their descent from Abraham? What does "Islam" mean, and why is it not "Mohammedanism"?
2. Why is Muhammad called "the Prophet"? Since he is not a divine savior, what did he do for Muslims? Why are Muslims supposed to love him?
3. Define the distinctive character of Islamic monotheism. What is the nature of Allah? Why must Muslims submit to Allah?
4. How do Islamic literature and law resemble Jewish law and literature? What is the place of the Qur'an in Islamic belief and practice?
5. Explain why predestination is a special problem in Islam.

6. How can we explain the peculiar force and importance of public opinion in ethics, and of consensus in doctrine?
7. What is the source of the emphasis on the mercy of God? Why is God's mercy important at the time of judgment?
8. Explain why Islam grew so fast. What were the problems of such growth? What is the religious and cultural basis of unity among Islamic nations today?
9. Discuss how the experiential core of Islam is suggested in its name, and how submission brings relaxation and peace (*salaam*).
10. How and why is the caliphate the focus of the division between Sunni and Shia?

USEFUL BOOKS

The Qur'an

A. J. Arberry, trans. *The Koran Interpreted.* 2 vols. 1955. Reprint (2 vols. in 1), New York: Macmillan, 1970.
N. J. Dawood, trans. and notes. *The Koran.* Hamondsworth, England: Penguin Books, Penguin Classics, 1958 et seq.

Muhammad

Armstrong, Karen. *Muhammad.* San Francisco: Harper, 1992.
Kahn, Muhammad Z. *Muhammad, Seal of the Prophets.* London: Routledge and Kegan Paul, 1980. An Asian approach.

General

Esposito, John L. *Islam and Politics.* Syracuse, N.Y.: Syracuse University Press, 1984.
Gibb, H. A. R. *Mohammedanism.* London: Oxford University Press, 1964.
Lippman, Thomas W. *Understanding Islam: An Introduction to the Muslim World.* New York: Meridian, 1995.
Martin, Richard C. *Islam: A Cultural Perspective.* Englewood Cliffs, N.J.: Prentice Hall, 1982.
Nasr, Seyyed H. *Traditional Islam in the Modern World.* New York: Kegan Paul, 1994.
Rahman, H. U. *A Chronology of Islamic History.* London: Mansell, 1989.
Schimmel, Annemarie. *Mystical Dimensions of Islam.* Chapel Hill: University of North Carolina Press, 1975.
Watt, W. Montgomery. *Islamic Philosophy and Theology.* Edinburgh: The University Press, 1962, 1985.

GLOSSARY

Abbasid (ab bas eed): caliphate at Baghdad from the eighth to thirteenth centuries, claiming descent from Abbas, uncle of Muhammad *abu:* father of, common prefix in names

Allah: God

anno Hegirae: (Latin) year of the *hijra* or hegira; abbreviated A.H.

caliph: (*khalifa*) successor to Muhammad as leader of Islam Companions: early believers in Muhammad's message, at Mecca

Companions: see "caliph"

darwish: dervish, member of a religious fraternity

Exiles: those who went with Muhammad to Medina

Fatihah (fah tih hah): "the Opening" of the Qur'an

fiqh (fikh): "understanding," the body of Islamic jurisprudence

hadith (huh deeth): oral report or tradition; The Hadith—the collected traditions of Muhammad

hajj (hahdj): pilgrimage to Mecca; *Hajj*—one who has performed the pilgrimage (*hajji* in Turkish)

Hanafite: one of four schools of *fiqh*

Hanbalite: one of four schools of *fiqh*

Helpers: those who became believers of Medina

hijra: pilgraimage or "flight" of Muhammad to Medina; hegira

ibadat: acts to be performed in religious ritual

Iblis (ib lease): Satan

ihram: white pilgrimage robe

ijma: consensus of the community of faith

ijtihad: personal interpretation of the faith

imam: leader in prayer, head of the community

Imam: Shiite spiritually qualified leader

Imamiyyah: school of Islamic law followed by Shiah

iman: faith or belief

isnad: chain of names transmitting a *hadith*

jihad: striving for the faith; holy war

jinn: spiritual creatures of the divine will and power

Kaaba: the cubic stone structure in the center of the Great Mosque at Mecca

kafir (kah fear): infidel, nonbeliever

Khadija: a widow who became Muhammad's first wife, at Mecca

Kharijites: "seceders," fanatical moralistic sect of early Islam

Koran: Anglicized form of Qur'an

Al-Lat: one of three pagan "daughters of Allah"

madhhab: a school of jurisprudence, in general, to one of which a Sunni Muslim will adhere; plural is *madhahib*

Mahdi (mah dee): the last Imam, yet to appear

Malikite: one of four schools of *fiqh*

Al-Manat: "fate"; one of three pagan "daughters of Allah"

matn: original utterance of a *hadith*

mihrab (mihh rob): wall niche in mosque indicating direction of Mecca

mimbar: pulpit in a mosque

muamalat: "dealings" or regulations for human relations

Muharram: a month of the Islamic year

nabi (nah bee): a prophet

qibla: direction of prayer, toward Mecca

Qur'an: the sacred scripture of Islam

Quraysh: Muhammad's tribe, Anglicized to "Koreish"

rahman: "most merciful," a divine attribute

Ramadan: month of the fast

sahih (sah hee): sound or right, applied to *hadith*

salaam: peace—a salutation or salute

salat (suh laat): ritual prayer, supreme Islamic act of worship

Shafite: one of four schools of *fiqh*

Shahadah: "witness," the Creed, first Pillar: "*la illaha illah Allah, Muhammad rasul Allah,*" "There is no God but Allah, and Muhammad is his Prophet"

Shariah: general name for Islamic law

Shiah (she ah): followers of Ali; the sect of Shiites

shirk: polytheism, association of partners with God

Sufi (sue fee): Muslim mystic

sunnah: custom, usage

Sunnah: theory and practice of orthodox majority of Islam

Sunni or Sunnite: orthodox Muslim, contrasted with Shiite

sura: one of the 114 chapters of the Qur'an

tawaf: circuit of the Kaaba

ulema: body of trained Islamic scholars of religion and law; *ulama* in Arabic

Umayyad (oo muh yahd): first dynasty of caliphs, 661–750

Al-Uzza: one of the three pagan "daughters of Allah"

PART FOUR

Concluding
Comparative Essay

Now I drop the impersonal "we" and speak for myself in this comparative and evaluative conclusion. At the same time I remove the phenomenological mask and reveal that I do find a transcendent reality reflected in these religious traditions. But that at once throws us into polemics, because much modern thought says that the sacred and the supernatural have disappeared ("God is dead") and that religion is outmoded ("the opiate of the people"). Many students of religion, for various reasons, share this secular point of view enough to hold that religious studies themselves must be at least agnostic about the question of the objective reality, truth, or existence of the content of religion beyond the human ideas or activities which point to the transcendent. Therefore my statements about the agreement and differences that I find among these religions are going to sound a bit like theses, propositions for debate. Supporting data for my conclusions are taken only from Chapters 3 through 9, the seven religions.

But, although I do believe the language of religion denotes some objective reality, I also hold that the transcendent or supernatural is not fully knowable, and hence there are differing views of the supernal reality and its significance for human life. People claim in these seven religions to have been in touch with the sacred, to have experienced it and found it real. But they differ in their views of the supernatural, in how they describe or talk about it, and in what significance they find in it—what they make of it for human life. There is, therefore, much disagreement over the specifics, the concrete and definable aspects of the divine or transcendent among these religions.

This chapter is divided into two major parts. The first focuses on the transcendent or supernatural realm and its relation to the empirical world. I will use my three fundamental categories (tenets, ritual, ethics and institutions) in turn for statements, first, of a way in which as religions, all these faiths are fundamentally alike. Then I will spell out the specific differences among them under these same headings.

The second division of the chapter stresses the differences in the concept of salvation between Eastern and Western religions in general. My thesis is that the model of salvation is applicable to all the religions, and that there is a consistent and definable difference between East and West in each of four major aspects of salvation. This concluding summary comparison is unavoidably generalized, brief, and compendious, so that I am forced to use complex terms and language in this chapter.

THE TRANSCENDENT OR SUPERNATURAL REALM

There is no need to define "transcendent" and "supernatural" at length, for they denote something outside the realm of the ordinary and mundane, which in its essence or being surpasses the visible and measurable phenomena of daily existence. (It should be obvious that "transcendent" is not being used here simply as an adjective, the opposite of "immanent," but as a substantive category by itself.) Although it is thus defined or understood by contrast with the limited, ordinary, customary, and natural, the transcendent has a content of its own, but the description of that content varies.

There Is Such a Thing as the Transcendent

This is, after all, the first question about religion: Is anything there? Is religion's frame of reference an objective reality? In its most familiar Western terms, the question is: Does God exist? No quibbles about details of meaning can obscure the issue, for everyone finds it a meaningful question, and there are only two possible answers. Agnosticism is either in current slang and psychological terms a cop-out, or in technical terms an attempt to transform the metaphysical question (Does God exist?) into an epistemological problem (the knowledge of God). On this crucial question all the religions described in this book agree: the divine, supernal, transcendent, or sacred is real; it does exist. The only possible exceptions are Hinayana Buddhism and Confucianism. But Hinayana repudiates only the theoretical question, while in practice it presupposes the reality of a transcendent realm where the Tathagata has gone, and Confucianism posits heaven while not defining it.

The Uniqueness of the Transcendent

About the details of the content or description of the Godhead, the supernatural, there is disagreement. But there is complete agreement among these religions that the reality, being, or nature of the supernal is unique, *sui generis*. It has a special ontological status such that it is in no way dependent on other being—it is not like, nor contingent on, nor limited by, anything else in its being or existence. The traditional Western version of this is conveyed by the word "aseity" (self-existence) of God, meaning originating from and having no other source than itself. Although uniqueness is applied to a single sacred person in Western monotheism, and the sacred as unique is an impersonal category or class in Eastern religions, they agree that the divine is uniquely self-existent.

This "otherness" is what gives the holy in Rudolph Otto's classic description its fundamental sacred and numinous quality, prior even to the moral as he pointed out. The Tao is beyond both being and nonbeing. Zen Buddhism reverses the status of ordinary being and that which to the uninitiated is nonbeing; this ontological reversal is a standing "in-joke" for Zen devotees and is seen in Zen art. Mahayan Buddhism resorts to paradox in its attempt to delineate the inexplicable, special ontological character of ultimate reality, while Hinduism makes Nirguna Brahman, as unique and absolute, indescribable. In all three Western theisms God as Creator is self-existent, prior to and distinct from all created existence. In sum, all these religious traditions affirm that the transcendent has its own unique and distinct ontological status.

The Ultimate Reality Relates to Ordinary Existence

The first two categories, as we have seen, showed agreement among all the religions and almost no difference in detail; those which follow agree in general but differ in many particulars. There are two aspects of this relation: to the world in general, and to people as part of the world.

THE OTHER WORLD IS SOMEHOW RELATED TO THIS WORLD

The unique ontological status of the supernatural does not preclude, but rather makes possible, its relation to the ordinary empirical world. By not being bound to any one thing, the supernatural in some way impinges on all things. The general formula for this relationship is expressed by the names we have already been using for it: the transcendent, supernal, sacred, supernatural. It is the *other* world, that by which ours knows itself, and without which this one is meaningless. This is a functional or operational quality of the supernatural, what it *does* as contrasted with what it *is*. The essential action, the most fundamental operation, of the supernal reality under whatever name, therefore, is simply to relate itself—or at least to be related to—the cosmos, which is ordinary, secular existence. But the exact nature of that relationship makes the great differences in detail which arise in this category.

In relation to the world as a whole, the two Biblical religions and Islam as essentially derivative from them find God to be the Creator and Ruler of the world, which is created by and separate from God, and depends on him for its existence, nature, and working. It is real, but created and separate. Hinduism makes the category of pure Being, existence itself, into the Absolute, so that ordinary existence is included in the All but is unreal or illusory. It is neither created nor separate from the Godhead, but it is in some sense inferior in comparison to the ontological reality of ultimate Being. Buddhism treats the world as simply the essentially unreal scene of the human spiritual struggle to find itself in the transcendent. The Chinese religions see Heaven or the Tao, transcendent powers, not simply as the cause of order but also the source of order for the terrestrial realm.

THE SUPERNATURAL OR TRANSCENDENT ORDER HAS A SPECIAL RELATIONSHIP TO HUMAN BEINGS

Humanity has a distinctive relationship with the supernal order in all the religions of our study; this is another area of significant general agreement and differences on specific points. The bare fact that there is a mutual relation asserted between the supernatural and humanity is of course profoundly significant, for it could have been otherwise. Human beings could have been left without any knowledge of or relation to the spiritual powers on their (human) part. They could have been either ignored or manipulated by the sacred. Indeed, that is what the cynic or unbeliever sometimes charges against the divine.

> As flies to wanton boys are we to the gods,
>
> They kill us for their sport.

> *King Lear, IV, 1*

This fact—that all the faiths we studied make that relation the heart of religion—confirms the description of religion given in the Introduction, as the relation between persons and the supreme reality or being. I do not think that it is necessary to document this essential and crucial aspect with specific evidence. It is both implicit and explicit in all our categories and all branches of the several religions here described.

But the problems and differences appear when we go on to characterize the specific moral nature of that relationship, the aspect which the transcendent reality manifests toward human beings. This I have previously characterized as the second question of religion: What is the nature of the gods, and are they good or bad to us? The shocking character of the question is evidence that in Western terms it is unthinkable God could be anything but good. Yet logically the question must be considered, because it makes a very great difference. If there is a God and he is evil, then we are all in trouble, even the evil among us, because evil is as evil does. If a good God can do good to the good, then an evil God can do evil to the evil, and if he can he will, being evil. In fact, however, these religions concur in finding the sacred realm ultimately good, benevolent, or beneficent toward humankind, and not evil. This fact does not preclude the existence of evil powers—demons and evil spirits of some form—in most religions. In India, for example, mythology is full of evil spirits whom the (good) gods vanquish, and there are both good and evil spirits in Chinese mythology. Traces of Zoroastrian good–evil dualism appear in all three Western faiths. But, in the major traditions with which we deal, the supernatural is fundamentally a power over humanity for good, in spite of or against all powers of evil.

For Jews, Christians, and Muslims, God's goodness is inherent in and inseparable from him, and he manifests this goodness in all his dealings with people, even in his wrath. As was explained in that chapter, in Hinduism the goodness of the gods is manifested only in the epics and myths; but the essentially benevolent character of the Brahman is implied in its being described as the best of creatures and as the goal of the *atman* in the Upanishads. The eternal realm, which is assumed even if it is not discussed in Hinayana Buddhism, is likewise taken to be actually good and supportive of humankind. So it was of Gautama Buddha in his struggle for enlightenment when he was assailed by the evil tempter Mara; but the universe rejoiced in his enlightenment. Confucius made *jen*, the goodness of heaven, the other side of the moral order as its basis and guarantor. Although the Tao was described as ruthless, this was the ruthlessness of impartiality and not of malevolence, and, as the good way for humankind to follow, it is good toward people. Mahayana and Vajrayana Bodhisattvas manifest compassion toward all, and the cosmic Buddhas display goodness in their actions toward humanity. Zen *Satori* includes realization of the ultimate goodness of life. In effect, then, although there is some ambiguity and there are wide differences in the degree and the nature of goodness in the transcendent order or being of these faiths, it manifests itself (or is manifested) as on the side of good and not evil for people in the world.

Human Acknowledgment of the Supernal Reality in Worship

So many people have unlearned the immemorial gestures of human response to the transcendent, that worship and ritual are a lost art for billions of persons. Yet I suppose that in all ages those who have made more than a token gesture have been a minority. In any event, worship would seem to be a distinctive religious category, such that the primary meaning of the word—the paradigm case—is found in the context of religion. My thesis is simple: The religions say people can and should explicitly acknowledge and recognize the divine reality in appropriate words and ceremonies. Wherever people affirm a sacred power they also show their respect for, celebrate, and glorify that transcendent reality. In this, worship is the attitude, the frame of mind and turning of the heart, while ritual is the more or less stylized and habitual, external, and institutionalized form or expression, the gesture itself of words and actions. Thus observers completely unfamiliar with a ceremony they see will recognize it as religious from the bearing and demeanor of the worshippers, whose hopeful yearning toward the transcendent pervades the occasion.

Documentation for this general proposition is abundant and mostly unequivocal. The possible exceptions are some branches of Buddhism and philosophical Taoism. It is said that there was no worship in early Hinayana. The fact is that the Buddha's physical presence in the *sangha* made it unnecessary to make other gestures of relation to the transcendent, for in him it was among them. This fact accounts for the origin of the stupa in Hinayana Buddhism as a shrine enclosing a Buddha relic. He embodied their transcendent order, so after his death they enshrined a part of him. After that they gradually developed Buddha images, as art history has shown, and by then there was worship in the usual sense. Yet even without that there is ritual in branches of Buddhism which may omit the usual forms of worship. Buddhist customs, rules, practices of meditation are ritual in the sense of explicit, formalized gestures as a way of recognizing and even appropriating the supernal reality. Hence they fit our category here. By the same token Taoism like all mysticism, whose essence is to make the mystic one with the all, acknowledges and celebrates the ineffable truth and reality which it seeks. *Li* is central in Confucianism.

A concluding point of agreement in this area is that the religions concur in believing that such worship and ritual are significant and meaningful to the worshipper, the person who makes the gesture. It is good for humans to do this: In some way it helps them, there is value to it, there is a blessing in the very performance. The way in which it works, how or why worship comforts and fulfills the worshipper or ritual celebrant or meditating monk is variously described, yet is ultimately a mystery. But in all the traditions it differs from ordinary personal relations, which are "give and take" on some human basis of exchange even if the parties are unequal. Worship is from start to finish on sufferance of the supernal power; the worshipper is always and only a suppliant, the reward or blessing to him or her is completely and only by grace and gift of the god or power. Yet always worship and ritual enhance life in the very performance, in the gesture itself, by a mysterious efficacy apart from any specific or material transmission. The recent "discovery" by Westerners of Eastern meditation techniques and systems is but a new realization of this ancient truth.

The Transcendent Order as Context for Ordinary Life

In all these religious systems, the transcendent order provides the structures of meaning and value for both personal and social life. Or to start from the other, empirical side, the structures of both personal and social life are ordered in relation to transcendent or supernatural factors which provide their context, their frame of reference. There are two principal functions of the supernatural as it relates to personal and social life at the level of daily work and existence; religion provides both meaning and value for a culture. Meaning or significance is required for persons to divide up or sort out aspects of their experience in relation to their concerns and purposes. Thus, for example, one's automobile is usually significant only as transportation. But in 1977 newspapers told that a woman who died in Los Angeles specified that she was to be buried in her Ferrari, and she was; so the Ferrari had a new meaning or import. Values are the guidelines by which people arrange things in terms of how much and in what sense they are of worth. Now both meaning and value are contrasted with ordinary empirical facts or things, as a school of modern philosophic thought has emphasized. But that school of thought (logical empiricism) treated such terms and language as empty of meaning because they were not empirical, whereas the religions of our study say that their terms and structures of meaning put empirical things in their place. They do this precisely because they are not ordinary empirical facts but are derived from transcendent and eternal verities, based on a wider context, a supernal order, according to these religions.

Probably the most obvious example of this is Hindu society, where the castes or *varnas* which determine social status and much else are based on *karma* and are guides for life according to *dharma*. In Chinese religion, Confucianism flatly affirmed the value of the ordinary world and provided explicit structures for human social order which reflected the order of heaven, while Taoism guided people to discover the implicit order of the Tao and live accordingly in the lower or given world without need for explicit rules. Buddhism's pragmatic and empiricist concern with the world as the scene of individual striving toward salvation outweighs its metaphysics of the world as lacking permanent essence or being. In both major branches the laity are to live in, to treat or deal with, the ordinary world as an arena of both secular and spiritual battle and achievement. In Hinayana the *arhat* in the *sangha* is the true Buddhist and the layman is only half a holy man, yet laypersons should strive for advancement through self-discipline, sober habits, worthy associates, and ethical practices, as well as by acts of merit, and the social order should be guided by the truths and principles which the *sangha* practices and teaches. Mahayana has an ideal combined layman and Bodhisattva in Vimalakirti, who personifies and glorifies the spiritual power of the laity. In Japan the practice of Buddhism by all people will bring, they hold, personal and social well-being. The three monotheistic faiths can be most simply described under the rubric of "natural law" theories, for all of them find a divine structure of law, a God-given set of principles, eternal and universal, back of human systems of social order and personal values. The ordinary world of individual and social actions and institutions should be arranged and guided in accordance with eternal truths and principles which are God-given, transcendent, fixed, and certain. They are the basis of ethical precepts.

CONCLUDING CONTRAST: SALVATION EAST AND WEST

I have defined the essence of religion as the relationship between human beings and a transcendent or supernatural being, realm, or order. If that is so, then the distinctive religious categories are those which denote aspects of that relation, such as worship. The most distinctive, inclusive, and essential religious category under this model of religion, therefore, is salvation, broadly construed as deliverance of humanity out of spiritual estrangement from the supernatural, and restoration to the right relation between souls and the supernal reality. There are three aspects or moments of this process: first, that from which humanity must escape or be delivered, the soul-sickness of separation from the transcendent reality; second, the means by which the soul is healed of whatever keeps it apart from the supernatural being; third, the spiritual health (*salus*) and wholeness found in restoration of the sacred relationship. This model is applicable, *mutatis mutandis*, to all the religious systems we have described. It is necessary, however, to preface the three with the category of revelation, the method by which the knowledge of salvation is made available to those who are cut off by spiritual blindness from the supernal realm or reality.

Revelation East and West

In Eastern faiths the supreme or transcendent source of spiritual truth is impersonal and more or less abstract metaphysical being or reality, which is somehow knowable by human beings. It permits itself to be known, by *being* such that those who are able and willing to avail themselves of these intimations can detect its reality. At most it is a "to whom it may concern" memorandum from a supernal bureau or agency, not a direct communication from a divine person to a specific recipient as it is in Western terms. Hindu *rishis*, Buddhas, Confucian and Taoist sages by their own efforts pierce through the mists and hear, see, or grasp the eternal truth, apprehend the mystery, because it is always available and open to anyone who cares and strives. Like a kind of cosmic radio telescope, it sends out a constant tone—the music of the spheres, perhaps—to which anyone may tune in. Both the source and the recipient are impersonal: an abstract and general absolute on the one side and on the other anyone, the impersonal "one" of English, *man* of German, *on* of French. The recipient is an individual, but any individual—John or Jane Doe, not a specific person. In Western terms God, as personal and active will, reveals himself, speaks to specific persons, prophets; or in Christianity he addresses his own son. These speak the truth to the group, the collectivity which is formed around that revelation as a community of faith. A personal God explicitly and actively reveals himself to a definite individual as representative of a community of believers. The final contrast under this heading is that the Eastern message is abstract or theoretical, and is offered on a detached, unconcerned basis: "Take it or leave it, it's up to you." The Western God cares about his message, and his revelation calls for a decision of the will, active acceptance or rejection of him and his saving truth, entailing spiritual life or death.

Salvation *From* What? East and West

Eastern faith finds people in a spiritual condition which is essentially ignorance or darkness, primarily a negative, privative, intellectual or metaphysical state, although there may be specific moral symptoms which follow from it. The distinguishing mark is that it is a state of being or nature which is less than a person's true being or nature. That true state is a part of the ultimate and eternal reality or being which is implicitly theirs if they will only actualize it. Their error is in accepting, being contented with, their lesser condition of separation from the primal unity. Humanity before the God of Judaism, Christianity, and Islam suffers first of all from pride and rebellion in refusing to accept its creaturely status, to obey and serve God, under whose judgment it therefore stands. Estrangement or separation from God is a symptom of humanity's fallen state; the actual pathology is in the heart and will more than the mind and understanding. Creatures in a created world are meant to be happy and blessed, and their need is to be delivered from their self-defeating rebellion and concomitant spiritual lostness, by obedience and love to God. (The traditional word for this rebellion is "sin," but it suffers now from much dilution and distortion, so I have not used it.) Insofar as the Western religions follow Genesis, in all three humanity suffers from a collective guilt in a forensic or legal sense, which is based, according to the Bible, on an historical inheritance through a common spiritual ancestor. (In practice, only Christianity explicitly acknowledges this Biblical insight. There is no collective guilt in Judaism, and no doctrine of original sin in Islam; they claim the ancestor but disavow the guilt.) But this collective and historical aspect is absent in Eastern religions, because they are essentially ahistorical and have no decisive chronological event such as the Fall in the Bible. In Eastern religion there is at most a shared spiritual condition of the time cycles which are found in varied popular mythologies. Their personal, spiritual condition is essentially independent of time, history, and the group, being a personal ontological status of failure to actualize their potential, full spiritual essence or being.

Salvation How, *by* What Means? East and West

Eastern religionists save themselves, individually converting from illusory selfhood as separate entities to true selves as divine; Western religionists are saved by God to a blessed, true, redeemed creaturehood of and with, but always under, God. In Eastern faith human beings create themselves as their true selves, make themselves God, out of their old selves. Being essentially and truly God already, they have but to realize this Being at the true level. It is by themselves, from themselves, to their true Selves. The Buddha is the paradigmatic figure, for he did it by himself, with sheer determination, unconquerable will, preternatural intellect and understanding. Thus he conquered ignorance and desire, he grasped enlightenment, he attained Nirvana. As in Hinduism, with perhaps some difference in Confucianism and Taoism, the Buddhist believers can likewise, "sweltering at the task," do it themselves as Buddha did. And if there are, as I have shown, savior figures and doctrines of grace in Hinduism and Buddhism, still the primitive model of personal will is determinative of Eastern salvation. Yet there is no timetable, no assurance, no guarantee; the process is not automatic or mechanical, because there is a mystery as to how or when it is effected. All that is certain is that it is possible, and therefore one should try, strive, seek.

The differences are on the other side for Western faith. A personal act of will is necessary at some point; as in marriage, one must say, "I do." That is, there are elements of human striving; one must try, but salvation is effectuated only by God, with his help and grace. Finally, the believer does not earn redemption but receives it; salvation is given, not grasped or accomplished. The paradigmatic Western savior figure is Jesus Christ. The uncontrollable factors, the unseen elements, which in Eastern faith are an utterly inscrutable mystery, in Western religion are part of the invisible but enormous gesture of God; it is only by his good will and purpose that humanity is restored. In some way God ordered and decreed the punishment for humanity's failure, and therefore only he can bring people back to him. Therefore in all three, the cult concentrates on the saving work and purpose of God, whether for the chosen people, or the Christian believer, or the Muslim who submits. As part of a company of faith who wait upon the word and will of God, Western religionists believe and accept the promise, the gospel, the call, of the Savior God who saves them at the last.

Salvation *to* What? East and West

The Eastern believer escapes individually out of history and time into the timeless realm of Moksha or Nirvana; the Western believer is redeemed at the end of history and time, as part of the redeemed community in the Kingdom of God. This is one reason for the essentially individualistic piety of Eastern, and the essentially collective piety of Western, religions. Salvation for the Hindu or Buddhist, Confucianist or Taoist is attainment of their true status and condition of oneness with and in the ultimate Being, living in the indescribable blessedness of spiritual reality and wholeness. There is no more rebirth in the illusory world of time and space; that world is gone, for the believer is gone, like Buddha the Tathagata, "thus gone." Each self or soul unites or merges with the all-Soul. The *atman* realizes its true nature as *Atman* in the total Brahman-Atman, becomes the God that it always was. The Buddhist nonself reaches the ultimate nonworld of Nirvana there to be the true Buddha self. The true man of Tao unites with the Tao. The Confucian sage dwells with the ancestors in unending spring. There is no more separation, there are no more individual soul entities; pure resplendent Being is all-in-all. The discrete soul as a speck of pure being has been absorbed into the world soul; the illusion of separate existence has been overcome. Western salvation puts the redeemed soul as part of a redeemed humanity in a redeemed world. Creaturehood is no longer a curse but is blessed for all. The individual soul is still a discrete soul, but separation from God and other human beings is no longer estrangement and loneliness. Individual differences become the occasion not of strife but the ground of creativity and the basis of relationship and sharing in the blessed community under God. The soul fulfills its true function as that which relates to and is at home in God, and all souls sing praise to him.

In both Eastern and Western salvation, then, the eternal relationship between humanity and the supernal reality is actualized. That is religion as I have described it.

NAME INDEX

Names that are also included in the Glossary are shown by a parenthesis immediately following the name. There are two numbers, separated by a comma, in these parentheses. The first number is the page of the text on which the first significant use of the name appears. The second number is in bold face type and is the number of the page in the Glossary on which the term is glossed. A double set of parentheses and numbers indicates that the name appears in two different chapters and Glossaries.

Aaron, 245
Abraham, 244, 277, 357, 365, 385-386
Adibuddha, 120
Agni, (43, 43-44, 70, **92**)
Ahmad ibn Hanbal, 375
Akshobya, 120
Ali (Ali ibn Abi Talib), 360, 364
Allah, (355, 358, **397**)
Amida, (143, 152-153, **163**)
Amitabha, (109, 114, 120, 142, 147, **163**)
Amitayus, (120, **163**)
Amoghasiddhi, 120
Amos, 247, 254
Ananda, 104, 146
Antiochus Epiphanes, 272
Arjuna, 58-59
Al-Ashari, 379-381
Asoka, 104, 107-108
Avalokitesvara, (109, 119, 147, **163**)

Baal, (246, **288**)
Baba Nanak, 52
Abu Bakr, 360, 363
Bhagavan, (77, **93**)
Bhaishajyagura, (119, **163**)
Black Elk, 22-25
Brahma, (67, **93**)
Buddha, Gautama, 99-104, 117, 136, 149, 405, 406, 409

Calvin, John, 315-316
Chang Tao Ling, 217, 227

Chou, Duke of, 170-171, 175, 188
Chuang Tzu, (215, **237**)
Chu Hsi, 183, 190, (**208**)
Confucius, 174-180, 405
Constantine, 305

Dalai Lama, 110, 156-157
David, 246, 262
Devadatta, 104
Duke of Chou. *See* Chou, Duke of
Durga, (68, **93**)

Elijah, 247, 259
Esther, 272
Ezekiel, 254, 265
Ezra, 249

Fatima, 364

Ganesha, (70, **93**)
Garuda, (69, **93**)
Ghandi (Mahatma), 52-53, 88
Al-Ghazzali, 381-382

Hagar, 357, 385, 386
Abu Hanifah, 374
Hosea, 254
Hsi Wang Mu, 228
Husayn, 364

SUBJECT INDEX

Terms that are also included in the Glossary are shown by a parenthesis immediately following the term. There are two numbers, separated by a comma, in these parentheses. The first number is the page of the text on which the first significant use of the term appears. The second number is in bold face type and is the number of the page in the Glossary on which the term is glossed. A double set of parentheses and numbers indicates that the term appears in two different chapters and Glossaries.

Abbasid, (364, 364-365, **396**)
Abhidhamma Pitaka, (112, **162**)
abu, (358, **397**)
Acts of the Apostles, 302
advaita, (65, 65-66, **92**)
Affirmation doctrine, 323-324
African American religion, 25-31
Afterlife, death and, 18
agamas, (57, **92**)
aggiornamento, 319
Agnosticism, 402
Ahmadiyya, 390
alayavijnana, (134, **162**)
Allah, (355, **397**)
Alms, 385
American Christianity, divisions of, 318-319
American Indian religions. *See* Native
   American religions
American Judaism, divisions of, 276-277
American religions
   African American, 25-31
   Native American, 20-25
Amida, 152-153
amir al-muminin, 364
Amitayur-dhyana, 114-115, 143, 150
Analects, (173, 177, 178, 185, 193, 198, 201, 203, **208**)
ananda, (62, **92**)
anatta, (126, 130, **163**)
Ancestor worship, 194-195
Angels, 378
anicca, (130, **163**)
anno Hegirae, (356, **397**)

Apocrypha, (**351**)
Apocrypha, 272
Apologists, 321, 325, 326
Apostles, 301-302
Apostles' Creed, 327
Apostolic Age, 301-302
Apostolic Fathers, 303-304, 320-321, 325-326
Aranyakas, (55, **93**)
arhat, (105, 108-109, **165**), 407
Arian Christians, 307
Ark, 265, 267, 270
Art. *See* Cave art; Fertility rites and figures
artha, (86, 87, **93**)
Artha-Shastra, 59
Articles of Faith, of Maimonides, 263
Aryans, 42-43
Asceticism, Christian, 309
Aseity of God, 403
ashramas, (83, 85-86, **93**)
asuras, (44, **93**)
Atharva Veda, (55, **93**)
Atman, (52, 64-65, 74, 76, **95**), 138, 405, 410
atonement, (**351**)
Aum, (56, **93**)
avatar, (58, 68, 69, **93**)
avidya, (72, **93**)
Avignon Captivity, 311
avodah sheh bah-lev, 264
Awakening of Faith, The, 113

Baptism, 335-336
Bardo Thodol (Book of the Dead), 110